MORE FROM TH

REVIEWERS . . .

Power Tools provides readers with a solid foundation in the use of the tools and techniques that are a must for successful management of people and organizations in the 21st century. . . . It not only introduces the tools and techniques, but also takes the reader step by step to find out exactly what it would take to make these great ideas work.

DR. NASIR BUTROUS, Australian Catholic University

This text is an excellent road map through the maze of information available today in the market. The easy-to-understand insights would increase the implementation success rates for most organizations currently experiencing change.

SUSAN HARWOOD, PhD., Director, Human and Organizational Development, Motorola Systems and Space Technology Group

Power Tools is a valuable resource book, and should be read by every manager, aspiring manager, management student and management consultant.

ALICK KAY, University of South Australia

This is a very timely and informative book for managers who want to know the most current thought in managing organizations. The information is well organized and is at the manager's finger-tips.

DR. LAU CHUNG MING, The Chinese University of Hong Kong

DEDICATION

To Allyson
Friend, Lover, Partner

POWER
TOOLS

A LEADER'S GUIDE TO THE LATEST MANAGEMENT THINKING

John Nirenberg

PRENTICE HALL

Singapore   New York   London   Toronto   Sydney   Tokyo

First published 1997 by
Prentice Hall
Simon & Schuster (Asia) Pte Ltd
317 Alexandra Road
#04-01 IKEA Building
Singapore 159965

Simon & Schuster (Asia) Pte Ltd
A division of Simon & Schuster International Group

Printed in Singapore

1 2 3 4 5   01 00 99 98 97

ISBN 0-13-745845-2

Library of Congress Cataloging-in-Publication Data

Nirenberg, John.
   Power tools: a leader's guide to the latest
management thinking/
 John Nirenberg.
       p.   cm.
   Includes bibliographical references and index.
   ISBN 0-13-745845-2 (pbk.)
   1. Management.   I. Title.
 HD31.N533   1997
   658--dc21   96-30054
                                                    CIP

Prentice Hall International (UK) Limited, *London*
Prentice Hall of Australia Pty. Limited, *Sydney*
Prentice Hall Canada Inc., *Toronto*
Prentice Hall Hispanoamericana, *S.A., Mexico*
Prentice Hall of India Private Limited, *New Delhi*
Prentice Hall of Japan, Inc., *Tokyo*
Editora Prentice Hall do Brasil, Ltda., *Rio de Janeiro*
Prentice Hall, Inc., *Upper Saddle River, New Jersey*

CONTENTS

Sooner or later, if human society is to evolve – indeed, if it is to survive – we must match our lives to our new knowledge.

– **MARILYN FERGUSON**

PREFACE

This book is the culmination of a comprehensive search through the massive management literature to help you grasp its essence. *Power Tools* cogently synthesizes about 50,000 citations, 5,000 abstracts, 1,000 articles, and 400 books. It reports what really works for managing people and why so many seemingly good ideas fail.

Let's face it, there is definitely an info-glut of management prescriptions for organizational and personal success. Now you can avoid sinking into the organizational chaos created by an endless fad frenzy that sweeps through the business press. You can also avoid committing management malpractice with its demoralizing effects on interpersonal work relationships.

Most importantly, *Power Tools* summarizes the salient points of over 100 of the most frequently cited, or used, tools and techniques relevant to your organization's effectiveness in managing people. It shows you how to make these insights work for you. This book will enable you to keep abreast of the latest concepts and understand how you can personally cut through the buzzword blizzard to the essential truths about managing people.

If you think through the lessons discussed here, and act on your new knowledge, when you finish reading *Power Tools* you will be able to instantly utilize what works and avoid what does not. You can immediately put yourself, your organization, and those you manage on a healthy footing for success into the twenty-first century.

You *do* make a difference.

TODAY'S MOST PRESSING QUESTIONS

In addition to understanding the current thinking about management you will get answers to the following questions:

Productivity

- Why do organizations that embrace productivity improvement frequently fail?
- Why has reengineering failed in up to 80% of the companies that have tried it?
- What is the basis for continuous productivity gains?
- How can your organization unleash the intelligence, energy, and creative potential of each workpartner?

Organizational Learning

- Given all the talk, why has not anyone ever seen a fully functioning learning organization?
- What can you do to start a real learning process in your company?

Teamwork

- Today teams are all the rage but why are they failing fast, puttering out after the initial excitement fades?
- What does it take to develop teams that work and last?

Morale

- While thinking you are applying the latest wisdom and preparing for the global marketplace are you killing your future by allowing excessive stress to demotivate your colleagues and your staff?
- How can your organization create a committed, imaginative and productive work force?

Finally, have you had enough "flavor-of-the-month" thinking about managing people? Are you ready to find out how to make management ideas really work for you?

THE READER

Power Tools: A Leader's Guide to the Latest Management Thinking is for everyone wanting to understand the essentials of today's often confusing, sometimes conflicting, and always overwhelming flood of tools and techniques gushing from the business press. More importantly, this book is for the manager who wants to understand the underlying principles that lead to success and the practices that lead to failure. Students of management, as well as experienced managers committed to personal development, will find this an invaluable reference and immediately useful.

THE BOOK

Power Tools: A Leader's Guide to the Latest Management Thinking is divided into three parts. Part I is an overview of what it all means. In a few short chapters, the reader will learn about the current breakdown in our organizations, and why managers, unaware of the nature of the breakdown, desperately rush to each new tool and technique for a quick fix. Most frequently those managers are ultimately disappointed. You cannot blame them of course, we live in a nanosecond world, so each promised quick fix is embraced with the fervor of a miracle cure for the chronic organizational pain we suffer. Yet, being well-informed about the reasons for our behavior will enable us to choose the appropriate tools at the right time.

Part I also distills the common wisdom and wishful thinking of the major management tools and techniques into several basic principles to increase your chances of success while also informing you of why these same techniques may fail.

Part II delves deeply into the "Big 7" tools and techniques.

Part III presents an annotated compendium of over 100 additional tools and techniques in use today.

BACKGROUND RESEARCH

I have reviewed over 50,000 entries in various business and social science data bases for the management tools and techniques considered "most important" based either on their frequency in the literature or their relevance to contemporary management. In addition, this book project included reading abstracts, articles and books to distill the principles and lessons revealed here.

My general purposes were to:

1. include concepts that would stand on their merits and could be useful to others

2. determine when each concept works and when it does not

3. provide a simple, clear explanation of the underlying principles leading to success or failure in applying these concepts

4. examine several of the most popular tools, and concepts in depth for you to quickly assess their appropriateness for your organization before entering into huge financial commitments with consultants and major change programs

5. give you a framework to determine the appropriateness of these or any other management tools or concepts for you and your organization.

There are several inescapable findings you should be aware of that may change your attitude about following the fads bandwagon:

1. Each tool or technique was originally a custom-made solution for a specific organizational or individual problem. This insight led to several indisputable conclusions: (a) they were not copycat solutions, (b) they were the product of sound problem-solving environments, (c) the individuals and teams involved had the confidence and the courage to explore new methods of doing things and new ways of being with one another, (d) the inventors of these tools and techniques were committed to do what was necessary to make them work, and they were patient and willing to improvise and innovate.

2. Every tool, and technique reported here can be used effectively or ineffectively. There is nothing inherent in the tool that guarantees success or failure. Success depends on the appropriateness of the tool or technique to the circumstances and the "right" application.

3. Before using these or other tools and techniques, it is vital to remember that the use of any intervention involves other people and inevitably stimulates unintended consequences. These are social tools and other people are, by definition, involved, whether directly in the planning and application stages, or not. This has tremendous consequences on the probability of success of any managerial effort and the effectiveness of the tools and techniques mentioned here.

4. By the same token, there is not always a causal relationship between using these tools, and any specific outcome. Some have used

these tools when appropriate and applied them well, but failed. Others have used them appropriately and poorly applied them and succeeded. Still others have inappropriately used them and applied them poorly only to find in doing so their effort spurred a catalytic reaction that moved the organization into new, more appropriate, behaviors.

5. The point that deserves repeating here is that in virtually no case was it simply the use of a tool that led to failure. Hence, "Don't blame the hammer, when you smash your thumb." This may be a rude awakening to a manager who salvages his or her ego by blaming the inadequacy of the tool or technique. But remember, it is the manager, not the tool, that is responsible for the results of its application.

PART I: MAKING SENSE
Chapter One: Introduction: Setting the Context

This chapter alerts the reader to several paradoxes. On the one hand the insights are important and applicable to creating successful organizations. On the other hand the underlying organizational system acts as an immune system repelling many great ideas. Chapter One also suggests how to best use this book and what to look for in applying the insights reported later.

Chapter Two: The Breakdown and the Need for Help

Management is in disarray for many reasons. Much has occurred over the last several years to destabilize the management process. Issues, problems, and concerns, previously handled simply as a matter of policy or ignored altogether as not the responsibility of the organization are now so complex and volatile that managers following the conventional wisdom are incapable of dealing with them. Chapter Two identifies the contingencies, workplace issues, and concerns that have simply overwhelmed most managers.

In addition, a summary of symptoms is included in Chapter Two to help you determine if you, or your organization, suffer from the chaos of the times.

Chapter Three: Common Wisdom

By reviewing the massive business literature, some conclusions can be drawn about what works and what does not. This chapter derives the common wisdom and basic principles for lasting success for virtually all the techniques and tools. Here, we discover what we should have known all along: management is not rocket science . . . it is much harder. You will come to realize that while we have always thought of management as "soft stuff," hardly worthy of academic training, mastering it may take a lifetime.

Management is not an act, it is a process. Likewise, some people are not suited for management because they do not, cannot, or will not see that managing is an honor and a privilege. It is about building highly functional relationships. The human as well as financial costs of "not getting it" are simply too great for organizations to pay. Managerial malpractice is acutely unacceptable in business today. (Specific managerial malpractices will be discussed in Chapter Five and employee malpractices in Chapter Six.)

Chapter Four: Common Wishful Thinking

There are good reasons why otherwise sound tools and techniques become failed fads. There is a breathless anticipation of the results we will attain by simply unwrapping the new tool and putting it to use. Like a child playing with a hammer, all of a sudden, to many managers acquiring the tool, every concern, and issue becomes a nail.

Inevitably, new tools fail their users because of some common mistakes, the most obvious is using them inappropriately. In addition, toxic and inhospitable environments provide the wrong setting for almost any tool or technique detailed in this book. Applying tools in a manner inconsistent with the original intention is a prescription for failure.

In seeking success, managers hunger for the quickest, easiest, and most popular technique around – especially if they have been validated by the business press, big consulting companies, or best-selling book status. This chapter explores the "adoption addiction" phenomenon and offers an explanation for why we get drawn into the rabid pursuit of an instant panacea. In addition, this chapter offers suggestions for beating the quick fix addiction.

Chapter Five: Managerial Malpractices

This chapter discusses the importance of a manager's responsibility to others. Here, management is conceived as a sacred act – responsible not only for sound financial husbandry but for the well-being of those subject to a manager's decisions. The managerial role is clearly evolving into one with greater social responsibility than ever intended, ironically, because of the demise of paternalism. If the company is not taking care of its employees and if employees are not loyal out of a sense of duty, the manager's responsibilities for building a sound workplace environment and acting in a supportive way becomes much more important in order to attract and retain the best workers. Building solid relationships is not just the right thing to do but the necessary thing to do in the information age – especially since managers must harvest, not simply demand, the knowledge and talent of their workpartners.

It is the leader who assumes the role of facilitating the collective achievement of the group. From this perspective you do not use tools and techniques as many hoops through which guinea pig "subordinates" must jump. A leader uses tools as part of the larger duty to execute, in the most conscious way possible, actions necessary for the furtherance of organizational *and* employee success.

All too many managers are grasping at straws, failing to grasp tools and techniques to improve the numbers and their personal record of success with only slight consideration of the tool's intended use or secondary effects – the impact of the tools on their workpartners or the work environment. To some of these managers, workers are puppets and treated to every capricious turnabout in policy, whimsical change of strategy, and productivity improvement program. Secondary effects tell a different story. Workers respond to being "done to" and their responses unleash all manner of positive and negative outcomes which then have to be dealt with.

A catalog of managerial malpractices is presented in this chapter simply to show why so many tools and techniques get misused, fall from favor, or become passing fads. This chapter is not for managers weak of heart.

Chapter Six: Employee Malpractices

There is a symmetry in human affairs akin to the physical law that states "For every action, there is an equal and opposite reaction." As managers stumble into malpractice, so too, do employees.

Their methods are as varied and potentially as destructive of the common good, as the managerial malpractices. Organizations are not monolithic money-making machines. Employees make it happen. But if they are personally uninvolved, resist cooperating, have an attitude that helping others or doing different tasks "is not my job" they too bring down the enterprise.

Building an effective organization that is capable of justice and fairness to all and that rewards each person for their effort requires both the commitment and support of management and labor alike. Thus, here we look at employee malpractices and show that along with managerial malpractices they comprise both sides of the same coin – a self-defeating process inevitably harmful to the individual as well as the organization. This chapter is not for workers weak of heart.

Chapter Seven: Rescinding Hammurabi's Curse

Over 4,000 years ago Hammurabi the great Babylonian king first codified law in simple, easy to understand terms. It was Hammurabi who first separated management and labor and this division of responsibility has plagued us ever since. Today, it should be obvious, each of us needs to accept responsibility and be held accountable for the success or failure of our organizations. We must realize that we are all in the same boat. Thus, we must rescind the curse and heal the divisions that have created an adversarial management versus labor or labor versus management mentality. These battles sap massive quantities of energy from our organizations – energy we can no longer afford to squander.

Chapter Eight: Understand the System Before You Fix It

The fact that we find ourselves pursuing so many solutions to the same vexing problems and issues should be the first clue that perhaps a look at a systemic solution is necessary. Here we will look at the organization as a system and see how its inherent characteristics may be contributing factors to the problems and issues we face. You will understand how to identify and deal with systemic constraints and avoid having your next great idea getting shot down without a fair hearing.

Chapter Nine: A New Model for the Times

There is an alternative to the conventional wisdom that promises a new form of organization and a new approach to management. Chapter Nine will re-introduce readers to an integrative perspective on the use of management tools which also provides a new conceptualization of management and organization more suited to contemporary needs. It is called workplace community which is derived from an old idea but applied in a new and imaginative way.

Chapter Ten: Applying of the Wisdom in a Global Context

Because cultures differ, there is a suspicion that principles based upon the research conducted in one place is inappropriate to other places. That is sometimes true. The principles reported here, however, though entirely derived from American-based research, seem, almost surprisingly, quite compatible with cultures as varied as China, India, and Malaysia. On close examination we see that the principles are virtually universal. This chapter will discuss the application of the underlying principles to organizations outside of the United States. In fact we will find that the underlying principles discussed here are really just the latest iteration of ancient wisdom.

Chapter Eleven: Where do We Go from Here: An Agenda for Monday Morning

We always have a choice: to apply what we know or to continue to drift with the conventional wisdom and business as usual. And, of course, business as usual means business in trouble. Here is the moment of truth. This chapter encourages you to make an assessment of your willingness to practice the wisdom underlying these concepts and your organization's compatibility with the ideas that lead to success. Here you will discover what it will take for you and your organization to fruitfully utilize any of the people management techniques detailed later. Save yourself a lot of time and money by not using these techniques if you or your organization are not equipped to utilize them properly. Spend your time wisely. Attend only those workshops for ideas that stand a real chance for success in your organization. Engage consultants' help only when you know their advice can be properly utilized in your environment. Then, fully utilize the concepts most appropriate for you and your organization.

PART II: THE BIG SEVEN

Part II is a major compilation of the wisdom and wishful thinking regarding seven of the most important contemporary management tools, and techniques. Included are:

Chapter Twelve: Self-managing Work Teams

Self-managing and cross-functional work teams are becoming a commonplace solution for dealing with the complexity of modern times. The knowledge explosion has made it important to include representatives from multiple disciplines to address individual issues. This chapter explores the wisdom and wishful thinking of creating teams.

Chapter Thirteen: Systems Thinking the Learning Organization

The learning organization has captivated the attention of organizational thinkers, and managers alike. Given the complexity of the times and the ever changing competitive landscape, it is apparent that organizations, much like people, need solid learning skills. This chapter discusses the concept of the learning organization and what is necessary to make this tool succeed. One of the first tools to develop in creating a learning organization is systems thinking. The basics of systems thinking will be outlined.

Chapter Fourteen: Quality

The pursuit of excellence and, later, quality has been one of the most obvious but indescribable tasks facing managers. This chapter describes the challenge and outlines the quality concepts promoted by the three most visible quality gurus: Deming, Crosby, and Juran.

Chapter Fifteen: Reengineering

Reengineering is one of the most popular, if misunderstood, management concepts today. It has been called everything from a brilliant solution to the problem of reorganizing to a disaster foisted on the workplace by incompetent managers. This chapter will explore the wisdom and wishful thinking of this management tool.

Chapter Sixteen: Toward Authentic Communication

Perhaps the single most powerful unifying component of all the tools and techniques is the requirement for open and honest communications. The principle of fearless communication is one of the most difficult to establish and hardest to maintain. This chapter looks at three concepts to help each person broaden their tolerance for differences and to honor the need – indeed the necessity – for building an environment that fosters open and honest communication. They are Workout, 360-degree Evaluation and Diversity.

Chapter Seventeen: Japanese Management

In recent years, the Japanese management model has been the most powerful countervailing force to the American management model. This chapter looks at many of the components of Japanese management. In addition, it compares the underlying assumptions driving both the American and Japanese management models. Interestingly, while the two cultures are quite different we see a great example of how different means are used to achieve similar objectives. This is a principle first discussed in Chapter Ten.

Chapter Eighteen: New Paradigm Business

This last chapter in Part II is the most ambitious. It attempts a survey of many emerging concepts indicative of an entirely new way of doing business. Traditionalists may find many of these ideas far-fetched or too unrealistic. That may be so when viewed from the perspective of the industrial era paradigm. But this set of concepts requires an understanding of how the world of organizations has been and continues to be influenced by new technologies, new values, and a new understanding of the role of work in our lives. It shall prove a challenging as well as informative chapter, indeed.

PART III: AN ANNOTATED COMPENDIUM OF MORE THAN 100 TOOLS AND TECHNIQUES

The majority of entries include research citations to help you explore them further in depth.

* Monetary values in this book are given in US$.

If there is technological advance without social advance, there is almost automatically, an increase in human misery.

– **Michael Harrington**

ACKNOWLEDGEMENTS

Thanks again to Richard Ogle who provided superb meta-editorial advice and clarity, and to Allyson, of course, who encouraged me throughout. Thanks also to the many clients of the Center for Workplace Community who gave great feedback on our briefing, *The Latest Management Thinking*, which led to this book.

But none of this would have been possible without support from the anonymous reviewers and the commitment from Lam Wai Ling, managing editor of Prentice Hall, Singapore, who saw the potential of the manuscript.

Chapter One

INTRODUCTION: SETTING THE CONTEXT

HOW MANY TIMES have you gone to a seminar or workshop, spent a day or two or three and got really excited about the possibilities but returned to work only to find it remains the same old workplace? Did you ever get fired up but found your new enthusiasm squashed? Did you ever wonder why organizations worry so much about having motivated employees but stifle their energy?

I am a teacher and consultant. One of the things I enjoy most is conducting a workshop about community building in the workplace. After three days the energy level and sense of being connected to people who were literally total strangers just moments before, is truly moving. At the end of the workshop participants are energized. They can see a future for their organizations that, for most people, is unimaginable. They see an organization where fearless communication, decency to one another, making and keeping commitments, redesigning processes so everyone gets heard and taken care of, is the norm! It is very exciting.

Sometimes, during an in-house workshop, where all the participants are from the same organization and are glad to meet new colleagues or to learn about workpartners at a deeper level, a sense of sharing an important purpose in life emerges. A new opportunity to see each other afresh has been created. At the end of the workshop, the energy and connection is there. It is palpable. And thrilling.

The tragedy is that frequently that energy is lost. A few weeks pass and it's business as usual again. I cannot avoid feeling the pain of helping to raise so many people's expectations only to hear of their being crushed. I first thought I could simply improve the workshop, create even better materials; I appealed to participants to commit themselves to higher levels of service to their organizations. I would follow up, check-in with them after a time to see how things were going and nudge them a bit if needed. Still, same thing. Business as usual.

One day at a professional meeting I ran into a participant from one of my workshops. "It didn't work," he said. "We just didn't have the time and, well, it just got lost in the shuffle."

"That's too bad," I said, rather lamely. Then I thought to myself, this is like riding a merry-go-round grasping for the brass ring! Each workshop, seminar, new tool, and technique seems to suffer the same fate. Even when you get the ring you are still stuck on the same old merry-go-round. We need to get off! Then I added. "You know, we have to stop grasping at new tools and techniques just because we think the "old" ones haven't worked."

"Well," he said, "I'm not sure. Something's got to give. Maybe we just haven't discovered what it will take to make a lasting difference." His next workshop was on the promise of reengineering.

After that encounter I decided to look at the latest management thinking. The stuff of best-sellers. Reengineering, total quality, Japanese management, the new paradigm. I set as my purpose an attempt to get to the bottom of this paradox: so many people spending their lives wanting to be great leaders and managers; wanting to make valuable contributions; and wanting to motivate colleagues yet failing so consistently. I had to find out what exactly it would take to make these great ideas work. How could managers know up-front whether their organizations, and they, personally, were ready to use the new tools and techniques to their best advantage? How could the insights and wisdom available from so many practitioners, scholars, and organizations be put to good use instead of wasted?

The result is this book.

INSIGHT TO ACTION

I discovered myself flush with new insights but at a loss to convert those new insights into action. I took another look at the techniques and tools, and how they were used, and discovered that it was not the tools or techniques that were wrong; after all, they all worked. But they needed to be used properly and organizations had to be receptive to dealing with the ramifications of their use.

While much was to be learned, and at times the findings looked terribly simple, another troublesome paradox emerged. Many of the tools work only if the right conditions are present such as open communications, high integrity, and frequent opportunities to discuss issues between "bosses" and "subordinates" as partners. Yet, if the conditions are right, specific tools often become unnecessary; under the right conditions, organizations invent what they need to meet their unique circumstances in accordance with their requirements at the time. Thus, when General Electric (GE) was ready, it invented "workout," "360-degree evaluations" and "boundarylessness" via "cross-functional teams." They may have actually reinvented these concepts but to them, as a response to the specific set of circumstances they faced, they had the right environment to explore these new possibilities. They came up with these tools, among others reported here, and creatively solved their problems.

There was another hard but equally important lesson to learn: if the tools all worked (and they did, or they would not be all over the management literature), then why are they failing in so many organizations? Why were so many well-intentioned managers, like the fellow who had taken my workshop, learning so much and able to apply so little? Well, there are two answers to that. First, the organization is either inhospitable – like barren land to fertile seeds. Or, second, the manager does not have the skill to apply the technique properly. But, rather than admit you are wrong or that the organization simply was not suited to applying the new tools, we blame the tool or technique and move on to the next one.

Fads are made by people. Pet Rocks did not make themselves, or hoola hoops, or Nehru jackets, mini-skirts, CB radios or Pac Man or any of the myriad fancies we follow. We make them. In the management literature, the tools work. The hoola hoop works; it is great fun and still sells. Nehru jackets make sense for some people. Mini-skirts are back, total quality management (TQM) is great, reengineering can save millions of dollars, and new paradigm management is a recognition of important values, and a way of being, that many people find essential in the workplace. If these ideas become fads, they do so because of their excessive uninformed popularity; fads are made by managers zealously advocating the latest tool or a single tool when a whole workbench of tools is required. And fads are made because after the masses follow the "trend" only to be disappointed with their organization's or own personal failure, interest subsides and a new panacea is sought.

MORE PARADOXICAL TENSION

My study resulted in yet more paradoxical tension. On the one hand I want to share my knowledge of the tools and techniques and the underlying reasons for their success and why they fail. Anyone spending a career in business will find the summary an essential and indispensable reference of important tools and techniques. This knowledge alone will entice many readers to study these insights with the hope of finding the brass ring. There are indeed many possibilities for improving yourself, your workplaces and increasing efficiency and productivity. Parts II and III of this book look at the techniques themselves. But, in discovering the underlying wisdom and wishful thinking regarding the use of the tools, I also discovered that an organizational immune system is at work to repel new thinking and behavior. Thus, it was necessary to critique organizations and managers who inappropriately apply or misuse the tools; those who, perhaps unwittingly, become part of the immune system.

The substance of Part I is a look at the many ways organizations and managers fail in using the tools as well as the common wisdom they display when using the tools properly. The tension arises in revealing great new tools yet knowing there are real systemic reasons why they may only be partially successful – if at all.

Of course, until you face "The Moment of Truth" and decide if your organization can appropriately use the tools, you really will not know whether these tools and techniques will work for you. In that regard, you are invited to conduct an organizational diagnostic and self-appraisal in Chapter Eleven. In doing so you will know immediately if you and/or your organization is up to the challenge posed by using the tools. This diagnostic opportunity will save you much time, money, and disappointment, if done candidly, before embarking on the use of these tools and techniques. This is partly because the tools are inadvertently proposed for general use without regard to underlying conditions. This is no fault of the toolmakers, however. They simply have assumed that all organizations are like theirs: receptive to experimentation, use mindful trial and error, and are willing to do what it takes to solve problems they face. Thus, tools are presumed to work because they worked in the exemplar organization. We now know better.

While proponents of the tools in the management literature are guilty of an enormous underestimation of what is required to fully utilize their tools and techniques, they are typically sincere and not charlatans. We all sometimes fall into this wishful thinking as well. Heck, if General Electric used it, why can't we? In fact we often demand to see the evidence that others have used a tool successfully before we will try it, then stumble into the dangerous trap of not asking ourselves if we are as prepared as the exemplars were before embarking on the process. (See Figure 1.1.)

All of the tools will work in many organizations. They will be effective to varying degrees of success. Most of them offer an opportunity for very positive things to happen – even if the tool is not fully operationalized. Some tools, however, require a very high level of readiness to use at all. For example, if you intend to become a "learning organization" or change the organizational culture in another way, you must first examine the current values, norms, and individual capabilities within the organization. You cannot mandate learning. A learning organization is an environment which must be created but it also requires individuals who are learners, structures that encourage thoughtful trial and

Figure 1.1   The Purpose of *Power Tools:* Aligning Leadership, the Tools, and the Organization

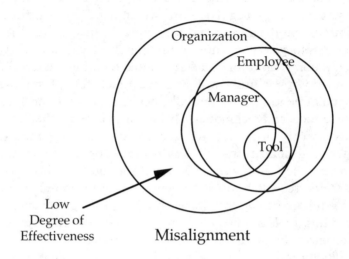

Low
Degree of
Effectiveness   **Misalignment**

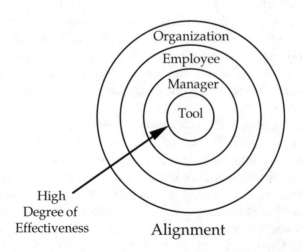

High
Degree of
Effectiveness   **Alignment**

error, a tolerance for ambiguity, and risk, etc. Thus, the proponents of a tool may be wildly underestimating the conditions required for its success and not lay out the required foundation for its best use.

Having said that, however, tools can be used to varying degrees of success and if conditions are not perfect, that should not discourage you. But at least you know up-front what to expect and you will have a realistic sense of what is possible in your own environment.

I would certainly encourage you to study art even if you are not da Vinci or Picasso. I would also recommend that you be patient. Developing a talent in this field requires as much effort as in others. Avoid the "make it so" mentality. Hats off to the crew of the Enterprise but your work with these tools will not be quick, easy, and flawless. Organizational change is messy, takes time, and has many unpredictable twists and turns. You can be prepared and this book will help you.

The wisdom shows that certain qualities are inherent in the organizations where the tools and techniques succeed. Authentic communication, positive relationships, and high integrity are vital qualities but there is little discussion in the literature around nurturing these qualities first – before the tools are used. They are often considered soft and "touchy-feely." Their dismissal in this way is direct testimony to just how important they are. Too often they are willfully ignored in organizations, it is "too time consuming," "too hard to measure," "too hard to practice," etc. These are warning bells that the organization would be wise not to ignore. If you hear them do not undertake a major use of the tools and techniques discussed later.

MORE WARNING BELLS

A recent survey by Yankelovich Partners should also set off warning bells regarding your organization's ability to fully benefit from your new knowledge.

In a survey for Kepner-Tregoe management consultants Yankelovich Partners found:

- "Workers don't like their companies . . . There is a real alienated work force."

- Sixty percent of workers say they are not rewarded or recognized for good job performance, while 63 percent believe poor job performance receives immediate attention.

- Sixty-three percent of workers say their supervisors do not know what motivates them to do their best.

- Empowerment is a joke in many companies. Workers still feel their input is not valued. Thirty-three percent said their employees *never* valued their ideas (emphasis added).

- Forty-one percent of workers feel their team assignments are unrealistic or unfair though 80 percent of their managers disagree.

(Reported in: Kerri Smith, "Study on Worker Attitudes Is Bad News for Business", *Rocky Mountain News*, November 5, 1995.)

With this kind of organizational climate, careful preparation before using the tools and techniques mentioned here would be wise.

Remember, not all tools are relevant to every organization. The reference section defines and gives you an immediate understanding of the purpose of the tool. You can judge instantly if it is appropriate for further study and application in your organization.

A review of the wisdom begs the questions: do we have the will and the character to commit to one another? Do we have the interest in learning the skills? The desire to make organizations work for everyone?

Other tough questions get asked about our work role that were once unacceptable or unnecessary: what is the kind of relationship we expect to have with the organization? What is an appropriate effort to make for the good of the organization? And, can we depend on the organization to consider us in the decision-making process?

Most of the techniques presuppose a participative mindset. When the tools and techniques are applied in hospitable environments their chance of success is greater than when applied in a resistant or closed environment where their effect will be only marginal at best and negative at worst.

APOLLO 13: THE INCREDIBLE SUCCESS OF A FAILED MISSION

You may remember the flight of Apollo 13 or seen the movie starring Tom Hanks as Commander Lovell. On April 11, 1970, Apollo 13 blasted off in what was considered another routine flight to the moon. No big deal. But then it happened: a breakdown in flight.

In watching the film version of the story unfold, several remarkable things occurred to make a rescue possible and successful. And, they all have a bearing on creating the proper environment for the successful use of the tools and techniques reported here. More importantly, they speak to real leadership and the incredible possibilities when people, faced with a challenge and unobstructed by their environments in their pursuit of a solution, can tap their full potential.

The first was the reliance each crew member had on the work of their colleagues. In this life or death situation when you might imagine widespread second guessing, and fear and panic breeding distrust, the crew of Apollo as well as the staff in mission control, implicitly trusted one another's abilities and accepted nothing short of positive and resourceful thinking. Everyone remained riveted on their goal as long as there was life aboard Apollo.

Second, everyone in mission control was expected to, and did, contribute every ounce of their expertise and imagination.

Third, each person communicated exactly what they knew, what they thought, and what they believed. There was no fear – except for the well-being of the crew on the verge of death in space.

Fourth, never having faced these circumstances before and not having contingency plans for this particular catastrophe, they immediately began creating options – each person leading or supporting – in relation to their skills and expertise.

Fifth, the successful action required three parts: (a) developing a unique solution that met all requirements of the problem; (b) communicating that solution which was akin to giving instructions for surgery over the telephone; and (c) following those instructions and participating in their modification in real time with virtually no room for error.

Sixth, and finally, when all was done that could be done to

remedy the on-board malfunction, there was still the problem of using the lunar module to accomplish an Earth landing which it was not designed to do. Here the crew had to manually maneuver the craft so that its entry into the atmosphere was angled perfectly. If they came in too wide, they would literally bounce off the atmosphere into outer space and die of starvation; too narrow and they would burn instantly like a bug in an electric zapper. Of course, they made it.

The lessons about human courage and cooperation are clear. What is not so clear, perhaps, is the importance of the management environment in mission control and on-board the spacecraft which made their efforts possible, which allowed for an expeditious and successful solution and for the perfect execution of the rescue flight plan.

If you create this kind of environment in your workplace all of these tools and techniques will serve you well. If you create that environment you will also be able to fashion appropriate tools and techniques on your own; certainly you will have the confidence to pick and choose and modify what you learn here to suit your needs.

THE DIAGNOSTIC

Once you take the diagnostic quiz at the end of Chapter Eleven and have considered the environment's readiness for these and other tools and find there are deficiencies in your organization, what should you do?

Leaders find that if they are personally ready and motivated, then beginning a conversation and dialogue with others about the future and using new techniques to get there, is an appropriate first step. The complete three step process is first, to communicate your intention, and to informally survey those you work with. Then, move into a directed conversation with potential allies and like-minded individuals who may join with you as early adopters of new techniques. Finally, with step three, engage in a deeper level of discussion – a dialogue. The three steps help set the stage for readiness. From awareness to understanding to commitment.

How to Use this Book

The ultimate purpose of this book is to keep you intelligently informed about new management thinking and to help you determine your personal and organizational readiness to apply what you learn. Further, the wisdom can be distilled to a rock-bottom declaration that it is all about authentic communications, strong positive relationships, and a character of high integrity. But see Chapter Three for a full discussion of the wisdom of these techniques and tools.

The book is divided into three parts and serves three related purposes. Part I is an introduction to the underlying truths revealed in a study of current management tools and techniques. You will learn the wisdom that leaders espouse, and model, to make these tools work for them. Part I is also a critique of why the tools may also lead to partial success or even complete failure. The focus shifts to the responsibilities of managers and organizations to use the tools properly. Part I also helps you diagnose your personal and organizational readiness to use the wisdom and the power of contemporary management tools.

Part II is a look at the most prominent tools at work today. The seven clusters of techniques and ideas that are discussed can help you and your organization succeed. Here you will explore the wisdom and wishful thinking for each one. You will know what it takes to make them work and what to avoid that leads to failure.

Part III is an annotated compendium of more than 100 tools and techniques that all managers should be aware of. It will serve as a ready reference and enjoyable browsing. It will keep you up-to-date and conversant in all of the latest management thinking. It includes many references for further study if you wish to explore the tools and techniques in depth.

While this book gives you an overview of more than 100 tools and techniques, it alone is not enough to provide you with all you need to know in order to use these tools. Rather, it will help you identify which ones may be useful for your specific needs. Then you can conduct additional study and locate appropriate assistance.

Part I

MAKING SENSE OF MANAGEMENT TOOLS AND TECHNIQUES

What distinguishes a fad or gimmick from earnest experimentation? The acid test isn't whether efforts to implement a new idea are initially successful. The bedrock issue is commitment and follow-up, whether or not the initial attempt is a success or a failure. Our tendency, however, is to try things out capriciously. When a new idea fails, we give up instead of investigating the causes of failure and addressing them systematically. Under the simplistic and misapplied principle that 'experimentation is good for organizations, many otherwise thoughtful executives become management gimmick junkies.'

– **RICHARD TANNER PASCALE,**
Managing on the Edge,
New York: Touchstone, 1991, p. 21.

Chapter Two

THE BREAKDOWN AND THE NEED FOR HELP

IT IS A cliché to talk about the need to be competitive and the chaos that has struck industry. In fact the *Industry Week* business book of the year for 1992 was *Leadership and the New Science* which provided lessons from the "new sciences" of quantum physics, and chaos theory, for managers wanting to make sense of a system seemingly out of control.

The "restructurings" and massive layoffs accompanying a continuous nationwide downsizing effort have wreaked havoc on our organizations and on the lives of individuals affected by the "restructuring" of their self-esteem, income, and lifestyle.

This upheaval has been attended by organizational contingencies and workplace issues that motivate managers to search for, and be willing to use, virtually any new tool that promises immediate relief.

THE MAJOR ISSUE: AN INADEQUATE SYSTEM FOR THE TIMES

At least 75% of all people in the US, and most of the industrial world from Singapore to Sweden, enjoy a reasonably comfortable material standard of living.

While technology continues apace, our lives get reconfigured with each new technological breakthrough and innovation. Rarely has humankind invented suitable social or managerial mechanisms to enable people to adapt to the contingencies of a high speed, high stress, high-tech life. With each new generation, biologically identical to the one before, our physiological capacity for dealing with the demands of a technological onslaught, remains virtually unchanged. Clearly there is a need for new social technologies with which humanity can fashion an intentional society; a society reflective of its aspirations and capable of dealing with the contingencies created by a pressing need to adapt. The way we manage and organize our collective endeavors needs to be rethought and redesigned. Traditional forms and methods are no longer adequate to deal with contemporary demands.

Managers, ever in search of excellence, are attempting to find new techniques to deal with twentieth century business breakdowns. Many are trying to reduce the societal stress that manifests itself at work when the demands for higher levels of performance in a high risk environment outstrip people's ability to cope. Managers seek to find ways of adapting bureaucracy to contemporary needs. The relentless pursuit of new social interventions – management tools and techniques to enable the organization to meet new demands – has resulted in the pursuit of a seemingly endless number of fads and fashions each promising a simple, elegant solution that can be easily applied. The promise of reducing the number and severity of problems while helping managers become more effective in harnessing human resources, is the sales hook for each new technique.

Yet, you will see that these management tools and techniques all "work." And, just as all carpentry tools "work" we will find that it is not the tool that is to blame when it is misapplied or the results are less than hoped for, it is the user of the tool who is usually responsible. When techniques are applied without exploring their underlying values and assumptions they result in less than optimal performance. It is like using a screwdriver to do the work of a hammer. You might still be able to pound a nail but it is much less effective, much slower, and the risk of personal injury or messing up the task increases.

When a technique does not achieve the desired outcome, or is used casually, we need to resist the temptation to blame the technique while failing to see its inappropriate fit or our unrealistic expectations or our inadequate knowledge of its proper use.

In a similar vein, when the underlying conditions and dysfunctions of an organization suggest that the system itself is inadequate to meet the challenges it faces, trying to utilize a technique to improve it is delusional at best and dangerous at worst. The underlying organizational inadequacies must be dealt with first. Adding more horses to a stagecoach with three wheels will not get you to Abilene!

Our energy source has evolved from animal to steam to nuclear power and cumbersome adding machines have evolved into super computers, but we in organizations are still structured according to the principles of the bureaucratic model – even though it separates the tasks of thinking and doing and was designed to command and control a pre-industrial, uneducated workforce. Much like the three wheeled stagecoach adding more organizational horsepower to an inadequate form will not increase performance. And adding more horses to a perfect stagecoach will not get you to the moon!

Today, grafting contemporary solutions on to an archaic system is an invitation to failure.

ORGANIZATIONAL CONTINGENCIES

Managers are grappling with ten serious organizational contingencies. To do so they seek out new tools. Most managers do not prepare for these contingencies until they must face them. And business schools are not adequately preparing students to deal with them either. When managers do deal with these contingencies they often feel, like the stagecoach driver, that demanding solutions that fit the requirements of conventional organizations may simply be wrong-headed.

The contingencies are:

1. Pressure for efficiencies. There is constant pressure for efficiencies (productivity improvement) cost reductions, streamlined processes, and the careful husbanding of all materials, labor, and time. That is the clarion call. For most managers, helpful tools and

techniques that claim quick results are too appealing to ignore. Not having a grasp of the underlying principles of the techniques leaves managers in a constant state of having to try virtually everything. Managers fear losing an opportunity – or worse – fear "falling behind the competition" and, perhaps, even losing their jobs.

2. Complexity and specialization. Complexity and specialization leaves most managers vulnerable. This is due to frequent breakdowns in coordination, information processing capacity, and interpersonal relationships that we put under enormous pressure to work flawlessly. Because of increased complexity and specialization, managers frequently rush to use new tools based on fear or faith alone; faith in the experts or your fear of not knowing how to make sense of what is happening soon enough.

3. Management knowledge explosion. It is impossible to keep up, with or without the information super highway. Maybe it is impossible to keep up because of it. In any case there is simply an info-glut of gigantic proportions. (According to one expert, a single edition of *The Sunday New York Times* has more information in it than a person living in Shakespearean England was likely to receive in a lifetime.) Managers need a way of navigating through the new knowledge to synthesize and apply appropriate intellectual resources. New management tools and techniques promise a short cut. But in their rush to get your attention purveyors of new tools sometimes promise more than they deliver.

4. Speed. The advent of speed as a competitive advantage in reducing cycle time and responding to customers has made many managers desperate for innovative short cuts. Any new technique that promises a way to reduce cycle time or to make efforts more efficient is embraced on face value alone.

5. Technology. New technology has had an incalculable impact on organizations necessitating new thinking and techniques to deal with its consequences. Thus, managers turn to gurus and new specialists for quick technological fixes to their problems. Embracing technological change is part of the cultural catechism. Even when the new technology complicates life, it is assumed it is for the better. Often the promised advantages of a new technology simply become tomorrow's necessary evil. This incessant escalation of the adoption of new technologies follows the inevitable two-step cycle. First, the new technology offers a competitive advantage, then it becomes a necessity.

6. A new work force. Besides the demographic changes that include an aging and increasingly diverse work force, an ethic of continuous learning is changing the psychological profile of the

workplace. Now workers demand and are expected to take more responsibility and to more clearly add value to the products and services created by their organization. Labor is no longer simply processing material but becoming a more dynamic element in the production of services and things.

Tools that promise better utilization of the work force and process simplification are too tempting to ignore.

7. A changing society. Though political winds shift with each election there are some durable themes that influence the nature of organizations: for example, an apparent continuing evolution of the democratic ethos accompanied by a refinement of individuals' rights and responsibilities, particularly as they are interpreted in the workplace. This phenomenon is most visible at the public policy level with efforts to safeguard the rights of minorities, women, the disabled, veterans, and others. A shifting sense of entitlement, at least among many professionals, is placing a burden on many employers who, interested in meeting the expectations of desirable prospective and valued employees, respond by expanding human resource programs.

8. The demand for innovation. The demand for managerial innovation stimulates a search for new techniques. Whether related to product development, or new strategies of work design the press for innovation is commonplace and overwhelming. It is typically driven by the need to create a "competitive advantage" and to cut costs. But, it is also about developing interpersonal systems and behaviors that motivate individual and group performance. The success of books such as *The One Minute Manager* attest to the need for managers to utilize tools that promise quick results.

9. Pressure for continual personal effectiveness. No one is exempt from the pressure to do more with less or to improve each quarter or every year. With every evaluation exercise, with every salary review there is an underlying pressure to show improvement. You must be better than last year, better than your colleague, and promise that next year you will be better still.

10. Time. Too often we neglect issues thinking that to take the time to focus on them is wasteful. We fail to realize that issues will fester and worsen only to become much more troublesome and costly in the future. Tools that promise to dispense with difficult challenges quickly are quite attractive to managers too sensitive about "time being money;" too committed to the idea that the thing they are paid to do is work, and work is about task and process related only to developing and producing a product or service. Time spent in dealing with the workplace environment or cultural contingencies is always last even

when it is shown to have such a dramatic impact on creating the product or service.

CONTEMPORARY WORKPLACE ISSUES

In addition to the contingencies mentioned above there are at least ten workplace issues that are of concern to every employee today. These issues probably generate more interest in discovering new ways of handling workplace situations than the contingencies just mentioned since they are virtually always on people's minds. These issues raise important questions.

1. Wages and benefits. Maintaining a fair, competitive, and cost-of-living-sensitive wage is an issue as real wages have declined over the last generation and employment security is now a thing of the past. In addition, determining what organizations should provide to their employees as well as wages is now part of the national agenda as health care and retirement funding receive Congressional attention. How will the benefits be determined and distributed: retirement, health care, day care, elder care, education support, housing allowances, bicycle subsidies for commuters, cafeteria discounts, on-premises dry cleaning, etc. The gap between the highest salary levels and the lowest is widening, and employees are increasingly feeling left out as executives take home bigger paychecks as reward for current record profits while labor generally has been intimidated into "givebacks" to temporarily secure their continued employment.

2. Employment instability. If there is a new contract between employer and employee, how can it clearly articulate the mutual responsibilities in a way that can also foster mutual commitment? How will it convey, at least in the short run, an assessment of the likely duration of the relationship? The new contract sounds deceptively lopsided to most employees whose security is reduced even while they must continuously increase their contribution.

3. "Boss/Subordinate" relationship. How will a working relationship be established and what will be its characteristics? Obedience or independence of thought? Trust or suspicion? Domination and submissiveness or peer partnerships? What are the new rules regarding boss subordinate relationships in an era of teams and networks?

4. Peer relations and performance reviews. Similarly, how will colleagues develop a working relationship? Will they see each other's work as their own? Or, will rivalries and competitiveness undermine

their effectiveness? How will people be evaluated and rewarded in teams and flattened hierarchies?

5. Personal development/family-work-spirit balance. A Gallup survey revealed that many people are working more and enjoying it less. Three out of four people in the survey said that if there is a conflict between work, home or friends, it is family members and friends who lose. (Thomas L. Brown, "Are You Living in 'Quiet Desperation?'", *Industry Week*, March 16, 1992, p. 17.)

Will people have time for family and personal growth? Or, will overtime and overwork characterize their work lives until they quit to go somewhere else or retire? In its effort to streamline, organizations are coercing people to put in far more than forty hours of work a week. How long can this remain justified in the name of "global competition?" How can organizations attract the best people when they are prevented from having a whole life? How long will it be acceptable to ask so many to work so long when unemployment and underemployment has reached tremendous levels?

6. Professional development. Will there be support for professional growth? Or, will mediocrity be demanded? Will employees be supported in learning new skills? Will training and support for individuals be forthcoming in an era of rapid employee turnover and frequent dismissals? Or will technology be introduced to replace people? Will the investment in technology continue to be regarded as a more cost effective way of achieving performance improvements than in increasing human skill? It is universal practice to include a maintenance and replacement budget for machinery but rarely a learning and development budget for employees.

7. Organizational and personal harassment. Will people learn how to communicate and to "be" with one another as they work together? Or, will hostility grow due to increased pressures and competitiveness in an insecure environment, so that detachment characterizes all relationships as everyone looks out for themselves? Sexual harassment, intimidation in its many forms and "one-upmanship" are still common. How will they be addressed? Will people simply remain human "resources" and be denied their full expression in the workplace? Will human needs simply be sacrificed for the attainment of organizational objectives?

8. Stress/overwork. How much will be demanded of each person? Will overwork be recognized as an acceptable organizationally induced reality? Or will individuals be blamed, labeled weak, and unable to keep up? Or, will the organization attempt to distribute work more equitably, understanding that humans have limitations?

9. Unclear sense of purpose/meaning/contribution. Will work remain something done solely for the benefit of others – distant, uninvolved stockholders? Will work just remain a means to a paycheck? Will your purpose and meaning in the workplace remain obscure? Will the vision of the enterprise always be opaque? Or, will people once again be motivated to create something important, share in something enduring, be proud to participate in a worthwhile effort? Work toward a desired future?

10. Workplace violence. Will we continue to allow the deterioration of social conditions in our workplaces, so that violence there becomes an ever-increasing indicator of societal breakdown? Will workplace violence become a means to achieve personal relief from an abusive situation? Are we creating workplaces and workplace relationships that are so imbalanced and abusive that violence becomes the chosen response for an ever larger number of people?

These contingencies and issues clearly generate the interest in new people management tools, techniques, and concepts. If you are not sure which of these issues and contingencies are relevant to your organization, the following symptoms are indicators that your organization may be experiencing trouble.

SYMPTOMS OF TROUBLE I

Your search for techniques is likely to begin when your organization experiences any of the following symptoms:

- High turnover/absenteeism/grievances or silent on-the-job withdrawal among workpartners.
- Increasing difficulty in hiring top notch employees.
- Weak morale, organizational culture, or an inadequate communications climate.
- Continuous stress with no end in sight.
- Frequent cycles of hirings and layoffs.
- Reorganizations that do not solve problems.
- A sense that people are unwilling to cooperate with others and do not care as much as they once did about their work or the organization.
- Creating and implementing new strategic plans take longer than necessary and are resisted.

- Declining or non-existent commitment and loyalty between employer and employee.
- Little recovery from a painful layoff or merger.
- Inefficient work flow processes.
- People no longer feel their work has meaning.
- Fear of speaking the truth.
- Confusion exists about the present and future purposes of the organization.
- The legitimacy of the current system is being questioned as more and more people believe the organization only serves a few people.
- People are no longer feeling useful, recognized, or fairly compensated, or that they are doing worthwhile work.
- There is never enough time to address these and other people issues.
- Management wants to get on with it, "just do it!" Get the work out anyway it can.

SYMPTOMS OF TROUBLE II

Your organization may be on the way to failure if you personally experience the following symptoms:

- You never know what to expect from the organization.
- The environment is very political.
- You are not part of the decision-making process.
- You are never asked your opinion.
- You get little or no feedback (positive or critical).
- Your speaking honestly is impossible.
- Your performance is never good enough; the emphasis is always on what you do not know or are not good at.
- You seem to experience continuously high levels of negative stress.
- You experience barriers between people because of a power imbalance.
- You find it impossible to keep up with all that you need to know.
- Your business competitors appear to be in a threatening position.

- You experience perpetual job and financial insecurity.
- Your corporate culture seems to be unraveling; you find it hard to know the organization's mission and values.
- You have been reengineered, downsized, or TQM'ed and it has not made a positive difference.

With the massive assault on the once stable workplace environment resulting in an unexpectedly chaotic world for managers, it is not surprising that managers were driven to perpetrate serious malpractices. The contingencies and issues that arose in the workplace required personal leadership and vision. No longer is a manager merely a coordinator and supervisor. No longer is being a bureaucrat in a rigid hierarchy sufficient to deal with the new realities. Successful managers are required to take initiative. Unfortunately, as the next chapter shows, many have failed miserably; so, too, have organizations locked-in to archaic structures, and inappropriate assumptions about management.

THE SEARCH FOR TOOLS

The modern search for techniques began with Robert Owen in early nineteenth century Scotland and continues actively today. With the writings of the late Konosuke Matsushita, the founder of Matsushita Electronics, a multinational, multi-billion dollar consumer electronics company based in Japan, we continue the search not only for techniques but for "a business ethos, a management ethic" – the subtitle of his book *Not For Bread Alone*.

But exactly what are we looking for? Techniques, and tools provide myriad nostrums from the basic (suggestion boxes) to the arcane (technology S-curves). The literature ever in pursuit of a quick fix offers apparently simple programs that promise instant results: Japanese management, self-directed work teams, reengineering, total quality management. You name it. No one can dispute the possibilities inherent in these ideas but in the rush to adopt these programs, as if they can be applied like medication, and one after another, confusion sets in, then disillusionment, then employee resistance, then total cynicism. Got a cough? Get a cough syrup. Think your personnel costs are too high? Reengineer. Our very idea about techniques – that they are easy, quick and effective without requiring much thought and without requiring much effort must be re-assessed. We must first realize that just as you cannot expect to compete in a marathon by training the night before, creating lasting solutions to vexing problems will take time, energy, and commitment.

When these tools and techniques sweep through organizations like fire through sawdust there is a good chance that the techniques are misapplied, insufficiently understood, and are being mandated by frustrated managers impatient with their "subordinates'" progress.

The use of these tools may also be a sign that while valuable in their own way, they are not really understood and used as intended. The tools and techniques replace real problem-solving efforts and a shared inquiry into the nature of workplace issues and concerns. To invite a discussion, a shared inquiry, might make us look inadequate. Our managerial mythology tells us to find and apply solutions single-handedly. We rarely confess an inadequacy much less routinely seek out help from those we manage. That very inhibition is the source of a great many failures. This denial is the gateway to our mental models about our personal role, our expectation of others, our willingness to be inclusive or not, our attitude about learning, and our ability to communicate meaningfully and responsibly with those we manage. All of these aspects of our style ultimately play themselves out in our implementation of the tools and techniques of management. They lay the foundation for success or failure.

The human habit of looking for the quick and easy way, the added allure of self-managed simplicity in a complex world, and managerial insecurity underlie the unprecedented managerial interest in quick fixes.

– MICHAEL E. McGILL,
American Business and the Quick Fix,
New York: Henry Holt, 1988.

Chapter Three

COMMON WISDOM

THERE IS A definite structure that underlies almost all of the management tools and techniques listed in Part III. The common wisdom shared among the vast majority of techniques includes:

• Fearless communication. In virtually every case, a manager must not only be clear and honest in communicating with those he or she manages but must encourage everyone else to communicate fearlessly – truthfully and directly – with him or her. This is the single most important aspect of each and every tool and technique. How could it be otherwise?

It is more than this as well. It is establishing a relationship among colleagues, wherever they are in the chain of command, that lets them know they can speak freely, can be open, can trust that their communication will never be used against them, and that their confidences will not be violated. There is no more important task for a manager to achieve than to be known as a person of high integrity who will listen and understand.

It is also more than mere interpersonal communication. The communications environment needs to be psychologically safe, supportive, and imaginative. People should feel comfortable enough to express themselves to each of their workpartners. This allows the environment to benefit from serendipity and spontaneity. It is the ultimate learning climate.

• Information shared freely. It should not be surprising that where there is fearless communication, information is shared freely. All techniques depend upon honesty and require fully informed individuals to participate in achieving organizational objectives. Everyone is entitled and must have access to whatever information they perceive is helpful to do their job, understand the organization, and prepare for the future.

• Disclosure of feelings and thoughts. Communicating about business issues is often thought to require the separation of your intuition and feelings from the task at hand. Many of the tools and techniques mentioned in this book integrate all modes of expression and consider intuition and feelings not only acceptable but required in the course of free and full communication.

• Authentic feedback. Feedback has become so stereotyped that the act of giving positive or negative feedback clearly seems to be an elaborate charade, a formulaic expression of the so-called Oreo approach. Give positive feedback, then negative and close on a positive note. Communicating has been one of the most troublesome aspects of life at work and we have come to suppress what we really think and to second-guess everyone in an intricate dance of caution and distancing behavior. Authentic feedback means to express yourself directly to people regarding the impact of their actions and their specific behavior. Preferably it is a natural part of the relationship and occurs as close to the act as possible. And, it is not just about negative events or behavior.

• Trust. Trust is knowing that others will accept you for who you are, that people will communicate with you face to face. That people will keep their agreements or tell you directly why they will not. It is knowing that you will be considered when decisions are made in your absence. It is being trustworthy; conveying to others, as you would expect from them, that you will keep confidences and will not abuse the information you have about others or the company. It is being direct with others and expecting them to be direct with you.

• Respect. Respect is understanding that others are trying to do their best and believe you are too. It is appreciating the contributions each person is making to the success of the organization and that each is aware of their own. Differences are honored. This includes the obvious demographic categories but also differences in capabilities, talents, and work.

• Inclusivity. Everyone is considered "in." The distinctions between management, and labor are mostly a matter of technicality. The organization needs everyone and each is expected to contribute fully and is recognized for meeting their responsibilities. Success is for everyone to achieve.

• Patience/persistence. All of the tools take time to prepare for, utilize, and evaluate. None of them will work without patience and persistence. Mere exposure to an idea via a seminar or a consultant's training is doomed to failure even before it begins. The mindset of easy, quickly applied learning leads to failure every time. Patience and persistence like commitment to anything else opens the way for the imagination to work on the realities uncovered during the attempt to utilize new concepts. Typically new contingencies and constraints are discovered during the application of new techniques. These are natural and take patience to deal with. The tools work when enough time and energy are devoted to seeing them applied fully; and, settling for nothing short of success.

• Mindfulness about your work and relationships. No technique can work without self-reflection and analysis. Being self-aware and open to looking at yourself and others in the process of utilizing a tool or technique is important to understand why it is, or is not, working. Being careful about attending to relationships and fully holding up your own end of the task at hand is a beginning. Reaching out to work with others for group success requires a higher level of mindfulness.

• Commitment to principles/values/vision is strong. Perhaps all of the tools and techniques are anchored in a clear picture of the purpose and direction toward which the organization is moving. Call it an awareness of principles, and values, and a strong vision. In all cases of successfully using the tools the objective is clear. There is a benchmark against which each person can measure their achievement and standard of performance.

• Encourages commitment, participation, innovation, service to peers. There exists an established standard of performance for excellence that is fully communicated and easily understood. This helps to reduce or eliminate arbitrariness and the influences of a self-centered ego. Empowerment and participation are built into many of the tools and techniques.

• Resourcefulness. Because of all of the above, people are expansive in their approach to their work. Being resourceful opens people to possibilities that remain invisible to most. In an open environment, a psychologically safe environment, people begin to access new parts of themselves and their relationships in imaginative and creative ways. The personal impulse to explore and to integrate new knowledge and experience into your work creates eventualities that are impossible to anticipate or develop in other ways. This is truly what personal learning is about and can only occur when the above conditions are met. It is resourcefulness combined with communications that makes the tools and techniques mentioned, work.

SUMMARY OF THE WISDOM OF MODERN MANAGEMENT TOOLS AND TECHNIQUES

Historically, successful management practices have utilized participative values. The practice of management has been on an inexorable march to a more egalitarian system from its origins in basic command and control systems. As we move into the twenty-first century, the successful management of people is about being open – seeing more, hearing more, understanding more, in order to meet the needs of customers and employees. This inherently requires the inclusion, participation, and communication of everyone. It is about creating a seamless partnership between customer, employee, and purpose. It is about intelligence – about pushing back your limitations and being open to new possibilities for creating a better more enjoyable more satisfying world. Most of all, perhaps, the act of management is about building strong relationships.

The organization is a social system. The techniques used to mobilize the creative talent and energy of employees makes contemporary business success possible. More and more organizations reach out to larger numbers of constituencies and stakeholders to invite them into a mutually rewarding relationship. Employees in enlightened organizations are truly becoming partners viewed as making an investment as important as that made by financial investors. Through a positive contribution of personal energy and commitment to success, each employee makes the organization possible. The innovation and creativity of the workforce, when unleashed, can do remarkable things. We see this every day in the products and services that fill the marketplace. And the techniques and tools discussed in this book all represent an enormous amount of positive and creative thinking.

Management is about joy and efficacy and purpose. It is about becoming more of who you are as an individual as well as for becoming more effective in the use of organizational resources.

Generative thinking, passion, values, quality, leadership, self-discipline, being ready and willing to change, rethinking old ways of doing things, being honest and trustworthy, communicating fully, being adaptable, resourceful and open to new experiences, confronting your fears, being compassionate and forgiving while being demanding of going the extra mile, coaching, listening actively and being responsive to customer, employee and boss are all aspirations of the effective person's contribution to organizational success.

Continuous improvement, change, customer satisfaction, and innovation all require continuous learning. And for constant learning to take place individuals need resources, time, respect, and the right to fail in pursuit of new expertise.

Learning-driven supportive, and committed interpersonal relationships are key. It is a way of being, a recognition of the importance of process. It is about proportion, perspective, balance, and sharing the common experience of life as well as of work.

For most organizations there is only one source of competitive advantage: brain power, motive power, and affinity for your work and one another. Surprisingly, few organizations realize this.

Success for organizations as much as for people is a matter of character. The character of an organization is expressed through its policies and behavior. It is especially so in regard to the management of people, the vast majority of whom deserve and expect to be treated with respect. Organizations do not seem to be getting it, however, as workplace environments are deteriorating under relentless pressure for profits and performance.

Success in using the tools is about the quality of relationships and integrity and commitment and the inclusion of others in developing a common work-view. It is about being considerate and reasonable with one another and taking responsibility for yourself, too. It is about clarity and focus and alignment. It is about caring for one another, the process, and the product.

It should be abundantly clear at this point that the act of management is an interpersonal skill. It is a skill that is desperately left wanting in most organizations because technical expertise has been confused with the ability to manage. It has been one of the worst and most frequent mistakes an organization makes. And it is because of this that most managers are ill-equipped to deal appropriately with the tools and techniques mentioned in the popular management literature. They are simply not prepared or inclined to utilize the tools properly or create an atmosphere which fosters their successful application.

The persistent emphasis on technical skills and the financial bottom line, results in not knowing (or caring) about how you work with people and appointing individuals inept in interpersonal skills. This frequent occurrence springs from a chain of command in which the only prerequisite for success is pleasing your boss – not relating well to your colleagues or "subordinates." This "kiss up, kick down" phenomena is one of many managerial malpractices (others will be discussed in Chapter Five). But those malpractices are often hidden from your boss because he only requires technical results and is treated with obsequious and deferential behavior.

The wisdom of management is not found in the functioning of a static chain of command or a bureaucracy burdened by red tape. It is the tireless belief in the possible, the persistent broadening of the arena in which more and more people can participate in sharing their concerns and influencing their destiny. It is in the flexibility and innovation of the person fully engaged in accomplishing their tasks by pursuing their dreams. It is a beautiful process to watch unfold when an organization with limited imagination and a depressing fearfulness gives way to enlightenment, inclusion, and commitment to building humane, productive work environments. It is an incredible process in which people are stimulated to contribute their best, enjoy a satisfying work experience, and create organizations from which products and services emerge that enrich our lives.

There is a natural, palpable flow of human energy when the tools and processes are used effectively and people in organizations share the challenge and responsibility to reach their goals. It is about individual responsibility and effective teamwork.

Each of the tools and techniques grew out of a specific company's experience. They recognized they had a problem, were willing to do something about it, and committed themselves to doing so even at the expense of the conventional wisdom – the way they have always done things before. Sacred cows were challenged, roadblocks to change removed and a new ethic instituted, when necessary.

Successful use of these tools includes a search for second order effects – the impact of an action and how it will be dealt with. It is, in short, an effort to anticipate what will happen once action is taken; to determine who will be affected, and to anticipate and deal with the personal as well as systemic responses. Thus, remaining flexible and being prepared to improvise is important.

Successful companies look for ideas everywhere but they innovate and customize and fashion each application to their own needs, experiences, and inclinations. They had the courage to go forward and cut their own path through the fad forest. They were not afraid to change their diet and increase their exercise to get in shape rather than hope for a diet pill to do the trick.

Figure 3.1 defines the seven basic leverage points for the tools and techniques. Each leverage point is defined and a logo helps identify it. This will prove useful as a quick reference in Part III when additional tools and techniques are defined and you wish to quickly identify their primary use.

In addition the following pages identify some examples of tools and techniques which are best applied to each of the leverage points.

Figure 3.1 The Seven Leverage Points for the Tools and Techniques

Intrapersonal

Tools identified in Part III with this icon will be useful

primarily as an intrapersonal intervention. The intrapersonal leverage point is the focus of self-development efforts pursued either by yourself or through guided interventions with others. The purpose is to enlarge your understanding of yourself and your capacity for a managerial role. It is also a way of getting in touch with your strengths and weaknesses in order to more fully understand your role in interpersonal relationships. Examples include: The Seven Habits, dream analysis, fire walking for confidence, meditation, empowerment.

Interpersonal

This icon identifies interpersonal interventions in

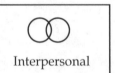

Part III. Broadly speaking, the interpersonal leverage point includes all behavior involving yourself and others. Of relevance to the workplace besides peer level relationships there are, of course, relationships with "superiors," "subordinates," and strangers. Examples include: servant leadership, outward bound, listening skills, managerial grid.

Figure 3.1 (*Continued*)

Group/Team

This leverage point focuses solely on the interpersonal

behaviors and functioning of an intact team or work group. This icon identifies tools most useful as a group or team intervention in Part III. Examples include: team building, quality of worklife, diversity.

Intergroup

This leverage point examines the relationships between

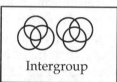

groups or departments. This icon will identify intergroup tools and techniques in Part III. Examples include: cross-functional teams, networking, matrix management.

System/Workflow

This focuses more on the process-technological aspects

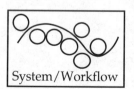

of work design and specifically how work is coordinated. This icon identifies a systems level leverage point for tools and techniques identified in Part III. Examples include: reengineering, rightsizing, downsizing, total quality, virtual organization, quality.

Figure 3.1 (*Continued*)

Organizational

This leverage point includes all aspects of the organiza-

tional environment from culture, and climate to system's change. This icon identifies organization-wide interventions in Part III. Examples include: Japanese management, Theory Z, reinventing the corporation, the learning organization.

Inter-organizational

This arena involves the activities of multiple organiza-

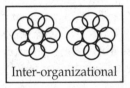

tions that are in relationship with one another in any of a variety of ways from allies to competitors to businesses that are customers or suppliers of one another. This icon identifies these interventions in Part III. Examples include: strategic alliances, outsourcing, just-in-time inventory.

PROPER USE OF TOOLS, TECHNIQUES, AND CONCEPTS

There are many distinct tools and techniques defined in Part III. Each one is most effective in distinctly different arenas. There are seven different kinds of interventions.

The companies that properly use the tools explored here demonstrate their understanding of the Ladder of Organizational Behavior. Figure 3.2 shows that for tools to work, especially those that have systems ramifications such as cultural change efforts, an organization must begin with a thorough examination of its existing culture, values, and norms to assess its compatibility with the proper use of the tool.

Any attempt to force new behaviors and techniques through a managerial edict will most likely lead to failure and the employees will dismiss the tools as fads. Real change takes place first and foremost when the tools and objectives of their use are consistent with the underlying belief structure of the organization. If there is an incompatibility either another tool needs to be selected, or the program abandoned.

If there is a willingness to explore a new belief structure and the organization exhibits a readiness for change and feels the need to do so, then the process can begin by identifying the culture, values, and attitudes that prevail and what specifically needs to change to establish a climate for success.

Norms and managerial practices are a reflection of the personalities in the organization and the practices that have been rewarded. If the required change is altering expectations about what is appropriate behavior, individuals will need to learn (or emphasize) new skills or be replaced. In this way new behavior will complement the new values.

Finally, work systems are aligned with the new values and norms and the techniques of day-to-day management can be utilized successfully. As you can see, much needs to be done before tools and techniques can be adopted.

Figure 3.2 The Ladder of Organizational Behavior

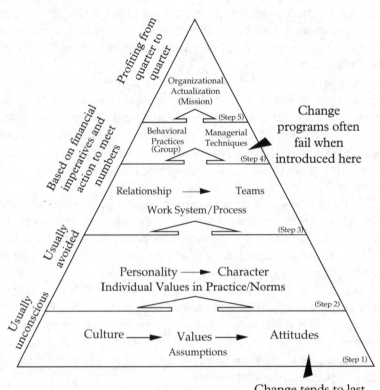

Getting Ready for Change

There are several personal qualities that have been found instrumental in managing people. These have been discussed earlier:

- Fearless communication
- Readily available information
- Self-disclosure
- Accurate/honest feedback
- Trust
- Respect/peer behavior
- Inclusivity
- Resourcefulness
- Patience

In addition, in order for these tools and techniques to be used successfully, there are situational requirements that must be considered.

Each manager must:

1. Determine the felt need and the readiness of the organization to change.

2. Gain absolute commitment in time and money. The organization must understand it will need the full support of top management. New practices, technologies, and forms of relationships take a great deal of effort to install before they return expected results.

3. Be sure everyone understands and is willing to live up to their new expectations. Set specific goals with workpartners, be prepared to learn, practice, and evaluate the new values and behaviors.

4. Hold everyone responsible for a share of the task.

The Three Most Important Qualities of Organizations Successfully Using the Management Tools: Communication, Communication, Communication

It is no exaggeration to say that we do not really know our closest work associates. Sure, we know descriptors: demographic characteristics, some past experiences, moods, and the many superficial aspects of their lives that we see at work. For the vast number of us our arms-length relationships makes our inability to work with one another in ambiguous or difficult times the Achilles heel of the workplace.

The apparent "getting along" and camaraderie often masks a lack of our real ability to relate to one another at a deep level. This difficulty frequently surfaces in damaging conflict and always at inopportune moments. Relationships that simply remain courteous and polite, for example, depending on the norms of friendliness can become a problem when times get tough and expectations and responsibilities create demands on the relationships that cannot be met. Then, the real distance between people surfaces to make communicating about the issues quite painful.

The point is not about creating intimacy per se, we have lives outside the workplace that provide that for us. The issue is whether or not people learn how to communicate with one another about aspects of relationships that have an immediate bearing on your responsibilities at work – whether that be positive or negative – and whether or not that kind of communicating can be done in a manner that does not escalate out of control.

Put another way, there seems to be a need to communicate with honesty, authenticity and putting forth your full capability – your full self in service to the self, the group, and the organization. Fearing self-exposure or upsetting prevailing norms or not being accepted or not being respected by the group or becoming vulnerable in any of a myriad ways to the social pressures in the workplace inhibit people. It causes withdrawal, avoidance, lack of commitment, diminished sense of purpose, and a diminished sense of self.

Without understanding one another, therefore, we do not know and cannot experience what we, together, are capable of achieving.

How often have we got to the point where one person has had to leave an organization because of a "personality conflict" with another? Or because of a simple difficulty they have had yet cannot bring themselves to even talk about it? People seem to prefer upsetting their whole lives before they will sit down with another person to work out a difficult situation. The fear of personal retribution or your own vulnerability is apparently too great. Yet the workplace could build the right communications environment into policy and into practice. We find that the most crucial element for all of the tools to work successfully is the right communications environment. It needs to be in place first.

Communicating for understanding is, therefore, about frankness, disclosure, and acceptance of others. It is about being present with other people until agreement and understanding is reached. It is about creating a non-judgmental environment to allow for inquiry and discovery of who we are, as people, in addition to solving a problem or a conflict. It is about creating a joint understanding of how we will judge our behavior and what is important in working together.

The way of getting to this point is through a conversation, a dialogue, regarding who we are, what is important, and how to live our values at work. It is then an exploration of the pathways of workplace relationships and how, together, we can create the structures and processes which enable us to live our values and work together. Then we continue the practice of communicating at a fundamental level, as in dialogue, to clarify our understanding.

The dialogue may take many forms. There is a school of thought that follows guidelines suggested by David Bohm who popularized "dialogue" as a way of developing shared meaning. The principle task among dialogue groups is to search for and examine your underlying assumptions – mental models – that may be driving your belief system. In so doing the group shares in the exploration of driving assumptions and beliefs. They explore ideas with a sense of detachment so that they do not get defensive about their ideas.

For most managers it is more important to simply develop a communicative relationship in which he or she can be authentic and accept authenticity from others; all the while creating a safe environment in which to do so.

For this to be meaningful you must be willing to become comfortable with, self-disclose to, and be accepting of, others. We must be compassionate and allow differing points of view to surface so that they can be explored. We must resist the temptation to judge and change others – at least during the dialogue process – until we fully comprehend the others. Thus, an attitude of non-threatening inquiry and communicating for understanding are cornerstones of dialogue.

It is not about politeness. Polite conversation often finds us stopping short of inquiry. It usually prevents us from being "different" or urges us on to be politically correct instead of authentic.

Each person must share the responsibility for creating meaning and maintaining a safe space for the conversation to continue. Eventually in our conversation we will find coalescence around shared beliefs and ideas about where to take our new knowledge. At that point we might be prepared to make the shift to an advocacy position and begin the process of looking at the issues and architecture of the organization.

PREPARATION FOR DIALOGUE AND COMMUNICATING FOR UNDERSTANDING

Personal Readiness

In preparing for a formal conversation, or dialogue, it is important to adhere to certain pre-conditions. This will enable each individual in the work group to consider the ramifications and implications of employing a new tool or technique and allows for a full inquiry into the group's readiness for change.

• Understand the concept of mental models and be willing to look at yours. This requires people to look at the assumptions they make about one another and their role. Mental models are simply the pictures we have in our mind about the way things are and ought to be. Sometimes these lead to what appears to be insurmountable differences and unresolvable conflicts. Surfacing them and reconsidering their accuracy and utility often helps people understand their motives and express themselves. In the process they may find bridges and the will to overcome, or at least work with, differences.

• Be willing to practice self-disclosure. This is the only effective way of being sure people can understand you. Whether you are explicit or not about who you are people will draw their own conclusions. If you disclose more about yourself they will be more accurate in their conclusions.

• Be open to the acceptance of others. When people feel they are being heard and not being judged they develop the confidence to disclose more of themselves. All of this is for the sole purpose of establishing a safe, accepting environment in which people can communicate meaningfully.

• Be able to suspend your urge to judge one another. Acceptance does not mean you agree with another's point of view or values, it means that you acknowledge who they are; that it is OK for them to be them. Thus, it is important not to judge a person but to hear them out. That is not to say you do not have values you hold dear. It means that they can be expressed without making another person wrong. This is especially important in creating a supportive communications environment.

• Understand the rules of dialogue. Clearly these rules are established to set the stage for understanding one another.

• Initially, have a focused problem/outcome orientation. Later, as the working relationship is explored, it is important to focus on issues that facilitate or impede understanding and cooperation.

• Be willing to learn and participate in self-development opportunities. Self-understanding is extremely important to communicate clearly and congruently.

• Know what it will take to align with the mission. Examining your role in the process is important. It is important that parties to the process keep in mind that their purpose is to create joint success and a working relationship. Discourage the expression of personal idiosyncratic needs best handled off-site or in therapy.

• Have an understanding/acceptance of goals. Likewise, consent to the goals and an understanding of the ends toward which the organization is striving is essential to determine your best use of skills and talents. But in a communications environment it is also important to understand and accept the purpose of the conversation. Purpose gives direction to your effort.

During the dialogue process:

• Give each speaker your undivided attention
• Listen actively
• Speak when moved (also when it is additive, contributory)
• Try to be ego-detached
• Be accepting of others

- Trust in the process
- Speak in "I" statements that demonstrate ownership of your beliefs and feelings
- Know the difference between your own and the group's agenda and how your participation is in service to one or the other

Organizational Readiness

While individuals must be prepared to communicate at this level, the organization as a whole must also be prepared. The organization must:

- Ensure each person's psychological/emotional safety. There is nothing more important.

- Build in a structure for due process. When differences arise and one person feels wronged they must have an avenue for determining fairness and for insuring proper treatment – especially if it has personal consequences such as when disciplinary actions are taken.

- Have people prepared with mediation skills. The due process program can begin with the simple step of having immediate third-party peer involvement to mediate differences whenever they arise.

- Help each person find their voice. The more frequent opportunities to participate in meaningful relationships whether for decision making, data gathering, problem solving or simply in the course of fulfilling the tasks of a self-managing team, the individual develops a clear sense of who they are and what they need. They find their voice.

- Recognize the existence and necessity for interdependence. Complexity requires interdependence and leads to creating cross-functional teams. New incentives and rewards will need to reflect this.

- Create clear/shared goals/mission. The organization must establish a clear mission and goals in order for each member to focus on their responsibilities. Otherwise enormous amounts of time and energy will be squandered trying to second-guess one another, play politics, utilize bureaucratic channels, and otherwise find out what you need to do and why.

- Allocate time for building the capacity for these behaviors among each person. Finally and perhaps most importantly people need time to converse, to build the right climate, and to thoughtfully apply the tools and techniques in Part III. They do not manifest themselves either quickly or easily and expecting that they will somehow be magically applied is a serious mistake unworthy of any manager.

REMINDERS

Companies that successfully use contemporary management tools also practice the following advice:

• Do not institute a change program without consulting all levels of employees. Listen to representatives selected by employee groups before venturing forward.

• Do not assume you know what the outcome of your program will be. Pay attention to all communications during the entire process, look for signals – "bread crumbs", anything that might tell you which direction things are going.

• Do not bother with a new program if the most recent "old" program is faltering. Make peace with the workforce involved in any "old" change programs which have ended shabbily. Apologize. Set aside time and create space for this to happen. Make sure people know they are heard and understood.

• Do not lie or cover up, conceal or hold back what you know about what is coming up. Tell the truth, say it as you are aware of it.

• Do not expect to be believed that you are serious about the current program, if you have said it before about another program and did not mean it. Trust others to believe what you do, not what you say.

• Do not expect people to care about something when they do not understand what you are trying to do or why you are trying to do it. Explain yourself, your agenda, and your methods clearly and routinely. Let people know before they have to ask.

• Do not expect your workpartners to jump through hoops for you, especially if you set the hoops on fire. Make work and life as easy as possible. Jump through hoops for your workpartners never expecting that they will have to return the "favor."

• Do not function on autopilot. Pay attention to the sky and your instruments in good times and bad. Be conscious. Act conscientiously. Be alert. Be attuned. And, most importantly, BE.

Are you willing to use the power that you have in the service of what you say you believe?

– **AUDRE LORDE**

Chapter Four

COMMON WISHFUL THINKING

WISHFUL THINKING OCCURS in either the design, application, follow through or assessment of the tools. Tools can be used inappropriately, rushed, incompletely applied, inadequately instituted, or expected to be fully operative too quickly.

Some people so thoroughly embrace a particular tool or technique – even becoming obsessed with it as not merely one of many management tools but THE tool to replace all others – that its use actually creates a productivity crisis and diverts attention from the broad spectrum of issues facing an organization. Sometimes managers develop a compulsive need to use a single technique. This obsession takes on the zeal of a religious conversion. When downsizing became the rage, companies did so in waves until productivity declined, stress overtook employees who remained, and morale fell to dangerously low levels. At the General Motors (GM) plant in Flint, Michigan, downsizing took so many people off the payroll that mandatory overtime sometimes resulted in 66-hour work weeks. The United Auto Workers (UAW) struck the plant demanding that people be hired back to reduce these unreasonable demands. They won. (Joan E. Rigdon, "Worn Out: Some Workers Gripe Bosses Are Ordering

47

Too Much Overtime", *The Wall Street Journal*, September 29, 1994, p. 1.)

Another mistake made by fad followers is the expectation that the experience of others can be replicated. The fad followers do not think through the fad but rush impatiently to adoption hoping that it will be a miracle cure for what ails their organization.

Not understanding the fundamental courage needed to take on a major change program can be a fatal mistake. Not thinking through the underlying problems that get in the way or which foster the persistence of the symptoms of breakdown can also be fatal.

> Champy (co-author of *Reengineering the Corporation*) says that the nature of real change is discontinuous and that the way an organization needs to operate in the future looks nothing like the way it operates now. Michael Beer, professor of business at Harvard University, argues that while people think of most of the programs companies introduce as fundamental, the programs basically glance off an organization. Most programs have limited impact, but do not penetrate the core issues in an organization. These programs are just different articulations of things that have to change, and he believes that the basic barriers are human ones. (Dawn Chipman, "The Cherry Pickers", *Across the Board*, June, 1994, p. 45.)

When techniques come and go so rapidly, each failing in its turn, there are usually some good reasons for disillusionment and cynicism. From management's perspective, when one fad's magic does not restore broken systems, impatience drives it to yet another one.

Some organizations would rather pay a Tom Peters $80,000 for a single appearance at an annual meeting to motivate the troops instead of paying a change agent an $80,000 annual salary to help the organization prepare for and adapt meaningful change.

And for labor, all these programs only amount to new hoops to jump through. Even when they enjoy the innovations and they are effective, such as when they participate actively in problem solving and doing good work, there is a distaste. They feel manipulated, even exploited as the benefits always seem portioned out to stockholders, and or top management. Over time, workers will pick and choose to participate and give their best just when it suits them. They resist jumping through hoops in an endlessly escalating level of managerial "fadaholism."

For any technique to be useful it must be aligned with the organization, its values, culture, and purpose.

The commitment needed to make the techniques work is just insufficient among those companies seeking a quick fix.

THE ROOTS OF FAILURE

Techniques and tools fail for many reasons:

- The lack of top management commitment and participation.
- Impatience.
- Misjudging the time necessary to make it work.
- Misjudging the financial costs involved.
- Misjudging the cost to existing relationships.
- Not being sufficiently skilled in the use of the tool.
- Being too demanding of early and extraordinary results.
- Not following up or following through.
- Committing self-sabotage to avoid real change.
- Ultimately finding the requirements for appropriately using the tools too scary or threatening.
- Being unwilling or unable to face up to the underlying conditions of the organization: its values, mental models, assumptions, norms and actual behaviors, policies and procedures that may conflict with the requirements of the change program or the use of management tools.
- Being unwilling or unable to deal effectively with human behavior – especially people's preparation, participation, and response to the technique/tool.
- Ignoring the "shadow side" of human behavior that emerges at work as well as in private life. Due to psychological illness, damaged individuals or simply the vagaries of the unpredictable mix of personalities and motives, destructive, defeatist behavior may surface and even threaten the larger sense of goodwill. Reining in these tendencies is an important step for long-term success in an environment that empowers individuals.

WHEN A TECHNIQUE BECOMES A FAD

There are several conditions that indicate the use of a tool or technique is undertaken because it seems to be the popular thing to do and not because it is the appropriate thing to do. Under the following conditions a technique attains fad status and is likely to fail:

- A single technique promises to easily solve a complex problem.
- A technique has popular approval and its use relieves the individual of personal problem-solving responsibility.
- A useful tool is deliberately (although perhaps subconsciously) misused in order to return to the status quo.
- The use of someone else's solution is an oblique way of focusing attention on a real issue without acknowledging the issue directly.
- It is just a tempting way to maintain status and power – adopting a technique shows that you are "on top of things."

WHY WE FALL FOR FADS
(The hoola hoops, pet rocks, and Nehru jackets of the management profession!)

There are compelling reasons why managers fall for the latest fads, some of the reasons are sensible and others are a reflection of their own inadequacies to judge the usefulness of the tools or sense the need to begin meaningful change efforts.

Even though a tool is popular because it promises new approaches and has succeeded for others it may be sensible to consider it for your organization. However, it still must pass the test of relevance; it must still fit with organizational contingencies.

Unfortunately, when tools become a fad it is because they are often applied without asking whether or not there is a useful fit with organizational needs (see Figure 4.1). Often they are used for the following inappropriate reasons:

- Everyone is doing it; it is new. The fad spreads, almost like a virus.
- It is over-promoted, over-promised and insufficiently understood.

Figure 4.1 You Know You are Caught in a Fad Frenzy When

(With Thanks to David Letterman)

10. You bought the latest management book (and have no intention of reading it).

9. You cannot remember the name of the last management book you read but you vaguely remember one chapter entitled "Exodus."

8. You request (or send a subordinate) to go to the latest management seminar about a concept you never heard of to deal with a problem you did not know you had.

7. You see the same people at that seminar that you saw at a seminar called "Leadership Secrets of Attila the Hun."

6. You thought you were up on the latest Japanese management techniques but at your last professional meeting you thought *kaizen* and *keiretsu* were forms of sushi.

5. You stumble across a file labeled "Vision, Mission and Values" but it is empty.

4. The cycle time for attending management seminars has fallen from three months to one month.

3. You and your boss' inner circle attends the Harvard Executive Program for two weeks at a cost of $15,000 but vetoes a one-day $99 seminar for your best assistant.

2. You know fad fever can be damaging when top management goes to a reengineering seminar, middle management goes to a career management seminar, and the front line goes to an organizing meeting sponsored by the Teamsters.

1. You use the same report for your last in-house management seminar to describe this new one!

- It looks promising, easy and sensible enough.

- It worked for someone else.

- It helps us keep up with the organizational Jones's.

- It might make us personally impressive or help us look more powerful.

- It looks easy and we do not realize what is required of ourselves, the organization, or others.

- It takes the pressure off of us to come up with our own solution customized for our culture, and organizational and personal needs.

Chapter Five

MANAGERIAL MALPRACTICES

TO BE A manager is an honor. Though often laden with profit-making responsibilities the role is also a service and, in many ways, because of its governance function, it is a sacred role. An individual embodies the will of the group, catalyzes disparate motives, and leads so all can succeed.

But in order to correctly deal with our new workplace environment, it is important to understand the inadequacies of those managers unprepared for the changes that have swept through American industry and why they have failed at using the tools and techniques that are so promising. In reviewing the literature about the failure of many managers (even those with the best intentions), it seems that there are some standard explanations. We call them management malpractices. It is because of the belief in the importance of the managerial role in the social system of the workplace that the following managerial malpractices are such heartbreakers. So much potential is lost. So much energy squandered. So many successes delayed.

You may detect a tinge of anger coursing through the following descriptions of these all too common malpractices. That is because of the great deal of pain these practices cause for so many people. Managers behaving in these ways are doing more damage than if they did nothing at all.

FIRST, AN ATTITUDE

This chapter focuses on a variety of ways incompetent managers are destroying the potential of millions of individuals.

First, we must start by understanding an attitude that permeates the thinking and behavior of many of the malpracticing managers. The attitude is of "superiority over" without "responsibility to" the "subordinate." Like governance, parenting, doctoring, and teaching, managers have a sacred responsibility to execute their duties without doing harm and in a way that enriches and enlivens those they touch.

While great pains were taken to cautiously assign powers to our political leaders with the inclusion in the US Constitution of many checks and balances, and separations of power, to guard against what was believed to be the inevitable corruption of those in office, we have totally ignored these principles as they apply to power holders (managers) in the workplace.

More importantly perhaps, the manager's job is no longer a simple one-person affair. Everything is in flux. New organizational forms are taking shape, new roles are being created and old ones are being redesigned. Managers need all the help they can get. Thus, it is understandable that managers ill-equipped to solve their problems independently seek out ready-made solutions. But it may be unforgivable when, by so doing, they are ignoring the potential of their own organizations and their work-partners – "colleagues and subordinates" – who are capable of great contributions. Clearly the thought of handling the managerial role, autonomously, is archaic and just an act of ego-gratification.

HAMMURABI'S CURSE

Frederick Taylor is considered the person who recommended separating management, the act of thinking, from labor, the act of doing. But it was Hammurabi, the King of Babylon, almost 4,000 years ago, who first established the principle that a manager was responsible for his or her workers.

Typically, a craftsman was held responsible for the work of his apprentices and as such each act of a laborer or apprentice was considered the act of the craftsman/contractor. According to the famous Code of Hammurabi, the first formal comprehensive law,

If a builder builds a house for a man and does not make its construction firm, and the house which he has built collapses and causes the death of the owner of the house, that builder shall be put to death. (Robert Francis Harper, *The Code of Hammurabi, King of Babylon*, Holmes Beach, Florida: Wm. W. Gaunt & Sons, Inc. (reprint), 1988, p. 81.)

To seal his laws, Hammurabi declared a curse: If a man does not pay attention to my words which I have written upon my monument; if he forget my curse and does not fear the curse of God; if he abolish the judgments which I have formulated, overrules my words, alters my statues, effaces my name written thereon . . . may the great God, the father of the gods, who has ordained my reign, take from him the glory of his sovereignty, may he break his scepter and curse his fate! (Percy Handcock, *The Code of Hammurabi, King of Babylon*, New York: The Macmillan Company, 1920, p. 43.)

And thus was born one of the first principles of management – separating the act of thinking from the act of doing. It was resurrected in the name of scientific management by Taylor at the turn of the twentieth century almost 4,000 years later.

This principle has been the basis for the separation of responsibilities and also a justification for the chain of command and the development of an adversarial relationship between what appeared to be mutually exclusive interests: management and labor. Management's interest was to assume full responsibility for the work and to make as much profit as possible through the maximum use of labor. Labor's interest was to collect the highest wage possible and ignore responsibility for the larger whole.

Believing this ancient formula still operable in a time of widespread education and the acceptance of your at-work responsibilities, many malpracticing managers fail because they demotivate and discard the potential of those they manage.

From Hammurabi to Taylor, the vast majority of the labor force was reduced to virtual wage-slavery disempowered from making decisions regarding their work and their lives in the workplace.

JEFFERSON'S NIGHTMARE

> Thomas Jefferson would probably find it sad, to say the least, that while democracy is breaking out in some of the unlikeliest places on Earth, Americans willingly subjugate themselves to unelected, virtually unaccountable bosses who tyrannize them daily. And, as Shorris has reminded us: In business, [people] do not arrive at totalitarian methods because they are evil, but because they wish to do the good in what seems to them the most efficient way, or because they wish merely to survive, or with no more evil intent than the desire to prosper. (Earl Shorris, *Scenes From Corporate Life*, New York: Penguin, 1984, p. 16.)

What is most amazing is the resiliency of many workers who still give their best under the most difficult conditions. Their ability to handle systemic problems is quite good, being resourceful they get around work flow obstacles and succeed in their endeavors in spite of a malpracticing manager. But what they cannot get around is the "boss" who can be malicious, bull-headed, unresponsive, ignorant, and fearful. While the organization often survives such managers, the waste of human talent is a dreadful commentary on the system. Surely such organizations suffer more than they know.

MANAGEMENT AS A FRINGE BENEFIT

In Jefferson's nightmare, attaining a management position is to acquire the most incredible fringe benefit of all – the ability to treat those you are managing as personal vassals to run errands, to be given assignments late Friday that are due on Monday, or to send some off to corporate Siberia for the pleasure of uprooting families to test their loyalty. Ah, the forced overtime; instilling the dread of job loss by invoking "the fear of foreign competition." Or, the corporate greenmail to relocate facilities to low-cost cities while extracting tax deferments, infrastructure paid for by the workers and low wages. Ah, the union givebacks to keep their members' jobs in a last ditch effort before plants are moved south or across the border.

These behaviors occur frequently enough. You would almost think it were normal, acceptable, behavior and not a form of organizational abuse. But the machinations of aspiring managers to do their own thing and see "subordinates" as mere instruments of their own will is often much worse. The first or second promotion frequently results in the creation of a "loose cannon" an individual who becomes unpredictable in the new role. Typically these individuals do not know how to use power, lack the confidence to express themselves, are inconsistent in what they require of others, are unclear about their ultimate purpose as managers, are uncomfortable with the relationship-building aspects of the job, and just can not seem to win the confidence of those they are now "responsible for" as they deploy their "human resources" in capricious or thoughtless ways.

The most vicious type of dysfunctional manager sees the appointment to the position as anointment: these managers perceive themselves as masters of a fiefdom. Direct reports become servants expected to follow through and carry out every conceivable whim thrust upon them. The truly frightening aspect of Jefferson's nightmare is that they are just modeling their own manager's behavior.

MANAGERIAL INCOMPETENCE BY IGNORANCE

Most managers have never formally learned how to manage people (to lead, coach, be with, support, encourage, inspire). Unless they received training in the armed services or through extracurricular activities in school or, perhaps, in self-financed training programs such as a Dale Carnegie leadership seminar, the people management aspects of collegiate business studies programs and on-the-job opportunities are simply too trivial to matter.

This is the frightening and demoralizing fact of worklife that is creating a tragedy of untold consequences for millions of people in the work force subject to the desperate trial and error methods used by most managers. The helter-skelter adoption of various strategies and techniques to lead and motivate, to communicate and inspire – in actuality, to cajole, control and intimidate others to perform for the good of the manager, the company and distant stockholders – have left professionals and union members fed up. The endless manipulative and disrespectful application of techniques that pass for sensible management has become a constant annoyance and source of stress for huge numbers of people. It is amazing that anyone responds at all to the call to give of themselves at work.

The constant process of reorganizing and instituting and reinstating short-lived "motivational" or "quality" or "efficiency" or "customer first" campaigns no longer fools anyone. Most managers using this helter-skelter approach only demonstrate their ignorance and whether or not they fail miserably their followers will be suspect of them and any "program" they try to implement.

Clearly managers are desperate to get results – economic results to justify their existence – but like a person in a darkened workshop it seems too many managers are convinced that any tool they grab will do.

It is a sure sign of managerial incompetence when one new technique is introduced before the last has been fully digested.

Managers frequently find themselves hostage to role models that are no longer appropriate. With all the MBAs out there, it is a national disgrace that their credibility is based solely on analytical skills and not on their ability to manage people. Of course it is not just a problem of inadequately trained MBAs, there is simply no required people-training for individuals who become managers. Thus, the act of management becomes a drawn out exercise in trial and error learning. As such, managers frequently have no idea about their responsibilities regarding the relationship between themselves and others. It is startling that in an ostensibly democratic country, managers, bosses, and owners feel entitled, because of a position or financial resources, to dominate those who hold a "lesser" position. "Subordinates" are virtual slaves. Many managers think nothing of the privilege they have as managers. Instead, they feel that managing is their "right" and, in fact, that they are "superior."

A manager living in the context of management as their "right" will, of course, eventually destroy their credibility. As this practice becomes widespread it destroys the credibility of the entire system. How long will it be before the many who have been subject to the capriciousness, arbitrariness and ineptness of incompetent "bosses" cry "enough!"

THE CONVENTIONAL WISDOM IS INDEED VERY CONVENTIONAL BUT NOT VERY WISE

The conventional wisdom tells us that the organizational system is fine. The structures are sound and the policies are sensible, just as they are; and, in order to institute any new change in the system it must first be shown that the new idea: (1) is more profitable (or cheaper) than an existing practice; (2) save time, and be instantaneously applied with near magical consequences; and (3) not diminish the standing or power of yourself or your bosses.

The criteria for selecting new tools and techniques includes: "We want a proven track record. Have other organizations done this? Show me it works!" This mindless modeling of mediocrity and the disdain for thoughtfulness and attention to the process of learning is part of the way of doing business today. Unfortunately, this behavior leads to a massive waste of money and time as managers rush from one idea to another to put Band-Aids on symptoms and ignore the true complexity of problems.

Accepting this practice, in fact "toughing it out," believing unquestioningly in the biases of those in power, being thoughtlessly loyal as a way of perpetuating the status quo – all premised on the idea that the most persistent, hardest working, most committed manager will rise to the top – perpetuates the conventional wisdom.

Ultimately this is a young person's game. It is full of the myths and hopes that focus your socialization before the disillusionment, the betrayal, and the hopelessness of it all is ultimately revealed. By mid-life when reality sets in and the years of duplicity, compromise, contradiction, burying feelings and the knowledge of what is really going on have taken their toll on your soul, you eventually withdraws from playing games in which everyone loses.

It is the rare person who survives the fabricated competitiveness and endures such extended periods of alienation from the self. Sacrificing the present for the promise of a grand future requires part of their humanity; a Faustian bargain indeed.

The saddest part of subscribing blindly to the conventional wisdom is that while we are ready to innovate and improve our "stuff" – the products and services we offer – we loathe anyone who would dare tamper with the system itself. Strange how we protect and defend a system that so painfully fails us. Why are we so reluctant to improve our relationships with one another, while so eager to build quality stuff?

RAW PERSONAL POWER
(The bottom line is just the excuse)

It is easy to understand an individual's lack of skill to practice sound people management. But, for some managers there is a deliberate, gratuitously malicious disregard of solid management principles simply because these do not reflect their personal preferences and inclinations. In few professional realms can an individual's prerogative be so arrogantly exercised.

An accountant cannot choose to disregard the GAAP (generally accepted accounting principles) no matter how personally objectionable the principles may be. Engineers cannot ignore the appropriate mixture of materials comprising concrete and expect to escape professional and legal sanctions. A lawyer cannot disregard court procedure when conducting a case. Yet anyone holding the position of manager can virtually do as they please in terms of the treatment of "subordinates." If a manager believes it is "motivational" to threaten the workforce with dismissal, so be it.

Managerial behavior was once acceptably paternalistic. Today that is no longer the case. Each person basically looks out for himself/herself. Loyalty is no longer expected either by the worker or the manager. The role you play at work is an unrestrained expression of your character. In a land of rapidly disappearing standards, that display takes on a patina of fear and uncertainty. Frequently, behavior manifests itself as mean-spirited, self-centered, egotistic, and narcissistic. All because alienated individuals are driven to tend to their own needs.

The accumulated knowledge and insights regarding "good people management" remains a matter of arbitrary application. We have experienced an erosion of what would once have been described as good etiquette or manners or "common sense." So, interpersonal relationships in the workplace have become muddled. Because of this, two movements have been trying to formulate a set of rights and responsibilities as well as a civil way of being for our times. They are the community building movement and the communitarian movement.

Regardless of these efforts, adherence is still a matter of personal choice. And that choice will be a reflection of your personality and character rather than what has been proven effective. Indeed, because we are increasingly subject to a system that unashamedly espouses the profit motive as the basis for all action, each decision is justified simply because it is the most profitable. Thus, the system itself encourages managers to disregard sound interpersonal behaviors. Even actions which we know to be more acceptable in terms of human values, more effective over the long run in building solid relationships and collective cooperation, are discouraged unless they can be proven to show short-term financial results.

The literature is replete with research support for the value of creativity and participation, of ownership and empowerment. The literature is also abundantly clear about the requirements for our collective satisfaction and survival. Resistance to practicing our knowledge is not due to the intellectual difficulty in understanding the concepts. It is due to the exercise of personal prerogatives, the expression of individual personality and the personal responses crafted (intentionally or otherwise) by individuals who do not practice valuing the collective and who choose to blame the constraints imposed by the system itself to substantiate this behavior.

For example, time pressure alone discourages, if not denies, many managers the means with which to practice what they know to be good interpersonal relations. This is so appalling to some people that the greatest pain suffered on the job is the knowledge that they are not living their values; they are caught up in a system which feels beyond their control. They live a demanding way of life requiring a sacrifice of part of their humanity just to "put food on the table."

Behaviors align with insights, prescriptions and ideology to enhance or maintain personal power. Even the organization's financial bottom line alone is not enough. As the CEO of Caterpillar said during a union busting effort, "How much is it worth to run your own company?" implying that the union was interfering with his ability to run the company. Apparently it is worth everything to some people. His efforts to consolidate power and reduce the role of the union cost the company untold opportunities and demoralized a workforce intimidated by persistent threats to replace them with non-union members. (Quoted in Robert L. Rose, "Labor Strife Threatens Caterpillar's Booming Business", *The Wall Street Journal*, June 10, 1994 p. B4.)

Sometimes even the bottom line does not count, when your personal power is at stake. Under criticism from investors for Reebok's market slippage against rival Nike, CEO Paul Fireman simply said, in a manner befitting Marie Antoinette, "If they're not happy, they should sell their shares." (Susan Pulliam, and Joseph Pereira, "Reebok CEO Fireman Faces Criticism by Institutional Holders", *The Wall Street Journal*, September 14, 1995, p. C1.)

Is it any wonder middle managers and those trying to direct a coherent effort for the good of the organization are starved for the latest fad – desperate for some technique or tool that will neutralize such egotism, a personal power pathology and "spiricide" – the deliberate destruction of the collective spirit?

> Hard times are sending some bosses back to the Stone Age. Beware of yo-yo empowerment, cost-cutting mania, and the new McCarthyism . . . At many organizations, the retreat from power sharing, open internal communications, and general humane-ness has been massive enough to thoroughly worry the experts . . . A few symptoms of management regression are (1) The brass grab back whatever clout they had begun to share . . . Yo-yo empower-ment doesn't just tick people off, it undermines them as well, poisoning the wellsprings of self-confidence and initiative. (2) The so-called leaders of the company begin to believe that cost-cutting is a corporate strategy . . . As one veteran manager put it: "You can't save your way out of trouble; you've got to sell your way out." (3) Top management imposes a sort of corporate McCarthyism, actively suppressing any criticism or dissent . . . People clam up for fear of losing their jobs. (4) Rambo comes back into fashion. Ask the president of one of the country's ten biggest headhunting firms what kind of chief executive will be sought after in the Nineties, and, after a moment of thought he replies, "The tough-ass CEO." (Walter Kiechel, III, "When Management Regresses", *Fortune*, March 9, 1992, p. 157.)

All of this is due to the lack of accountability to those you manage. As long as there are no checks and balances in the relationship there will be an abuse of power.

Left to their own devices, the untrained managers – the ambitious majority of ladder-climbers – seek advice much like desperate dieters who imagine that svelte figure being just an easy, effortless, quick-fix diet away. The management literature wreaks with bromides promising career enhancing power, methods for winning, profiting, beating the competition; tips on how to survive by clawing your way to the top.

> In any two-person relationship, the person who has the least power will hurt more and we don't appreciate the extent of the hurt. This is because the typical boss just has no idea what a powerful effect he has on the emotional health of his employees . . . I hope that five years from now we'll talk about employee abuse and neglect in the same way we've learned over the last ten years to talk about the abuse and neglect of children and women. (Mardy Grothe, co-author of *Problem Bosses: Who They Are and How to Deal With Them*, quoted in Walter Kiechel, III, "Dealing With the Problem Boss", *Fortune*, August 12, 1991, p. 98.)

One case dramatically demonstrates both the difficulty in challenging the status quo and the myth that managers always respond to scientific evidence that productivity improves with power sharing. A 1992 *Fortune* article reported that "The Gaines pet food plant in Topeka Kansas, just celebrated 20 years of self-management. For two decades under three owners . . . Topeka has always been placed first when its labor productivity was compared with that of other pet food plants within its company." Why have the other plants not followed the twenty years of evidence that the self-managed plant was most productive? It seems it is management refusing to compromise. It seems the need to crush change, even when it is demonstrably best for profits, is due to management's attachment to the powers and perks of office. It is the rare manager who can turn away from the seductive trappings of power for which they have vied throughout their professional careers. Without a change in the structures of the workplace, the redesign of internal relationships, and the reformulation of assumptions about your appropriate role in the workplace, real reform and power sharing will likely remain an elusive goal. And we know that it is power sharing and collaborative effort that make the tools and techniques work.

TRIAL AND ERROR MANAGEMENT LEADS TO A FAD FRENZY

A few pseudo-management tools and techniques – the exercises and variations on important concepts that become trivialized (e.g., dialogue, a vitally important technique, has taken on parlor game status), amounting to no more than vitamins to an AIDS patient. The cruellest form of hope foisted upon contemporary workers and middle managers alike is the notion that these tools, in their simplicity – fads according to the current critique – will actually make a difference in their working lives.

Trial and error management embraces each new concept with a fervor unknown outside cult circles. Even the most inglorious examples of the tools enter the bestiary of management techniques with only the slightest critical examination. A sure indication of nascent fad fever is hearing the refrain, "What's new?" at professional gatherings. These events result in groundless incantations of current buzzwords rather than real understanding and implementation with intentionality.

There is a desperate search for answers/stability/predictability among managers who have not realized that much of the malaise of organizational life is due to systemic issues. Lack of attention to the system is the reason managers experience so many and varied symptoms driving them in an apparent search for panaceas. Even managers who are capable, sincere and willing to treat breakdowns simply have not become aware that the locus of most problems is in the system itself.

MBA/DOA

For every profession and trade except business, it seems, a paper qualification is not enough. In those professions experience counts. Counselors have mandatory internships, doctors have residency, lawyers often clerk for judges or spend time in moot court, teachers do student teaching and serve under a master teacher, while earning tenure, and architects have a fifth year internship. However, many MBAs expect to receive the keys to the castle upon arrival on the job. Arrogance and the expectation of a quick path to the top have been frequent complaints about the MBA graduate.

It makes little sense to value qualifications for their own sake and then to allow that sole distinction to outweigh virtually all experience. While it may be one way of determining the most prepared candidate for a job, it does not make sense that the qualification should be the primary and sole evidence of worth. This is a major mistake when assessing either the preparation or the effectiveness of an individual to manage others. MBA programs today require only an infinitesimal number of courses on the management of people and virtually no practice.

To assert the supremacy of educational qualifications rather than hands-on knowledge, experience and expertise may be a useful way to make some choices, but it does not make sense to assume it renders a manager's actions infallible.

The Bully

A case comes to mind of the CEO wanting to make a quick, powerful first impression. A family brewery turned to an outside individual to become its CEO. His first two acts almost caused a revolution. After the company had devoted a long time instituting teams, he unilaterally declared that there was "no time for that anymore." Attention first had to be placed on "improving the profitability picture" as if teamwork and profitability are unrelated! Second, to get new ideas he believed it was necessary to "churn up the organization." His plan was to fire the "bottom ten percent" of performers each year even if the entire workforce was exceptional. It was this particularly nasty and misguided effort that the brewery owners refused to agree with. "After all, we have been like a family for generations." While his second act was reversed, the CEO remains at the helm, and the efforts of the organization development department to build self-managing, high-performing teams was obliterated overnight.

Not long after that adjustment the CEO was successful in disbanding the entire organization development (OD) department because it was no longer justified in light of the streamlining policy – "to do only those activities directly related to brewing and selling beer." This act generated doubts in the workplace spawning questions like, "when is the accounting department going to be laid off?" Here we have a combination of bullying behavior and managerial incompetence by ignorance. These actions represent a failure to understand the role and value of the OD department. Disbanding the OD department without discussion, sent a message that the new CEO planned to "motivate" his staff through fear. These events created a massive morale problem and the psychological withdrawal of hundreds of people from the workplace.

In the conventional organization the chain of command is, of course, more than the pattern of oversight or a metaphor, it is also a description of the ironclad linkages that preclude independent action. Yet according to the myths you can act independently, beat your competition (personal or organizational) and exercise your own power as you please.

The roller coaster ride of management "innovation" and "change" is hazardous to employees' mental and physical health. Employees and organizational support structures are so often toyed with that you wonder how anyone can put up with such capricious treatment for as long as the American workforce has. Perhaps it should not be surprising that workplace violence has become a rising category of crime.

So many people seem stressed out and on the brink of a major trauma it is up to management to take the lead in pulling back. As one sage said, "sometimes what you don't do is more important than what you do." As a manager, needing to prove your worth and wanting to build a record of achievement, it is always tempting to wield power but the situation may actually call for doing nothing.

NOBLESSE OBLIGE IS NOT ENOUGH

To a layman, executive pay is astonishing, the perks incredulous, the rationale for the largess logic-defying but the really amazing differences between a CEO and the rest of us can be found in the style of living and working. The case of Bill Agee at Morrison Knudsen partially illustrates the extent to which CEOs have become latter day princes.

After a string of questionable performances as CEO, venture capitalist and failed corporate raider, Agee was appointed CEO of Morrison Knudsen. Before he was finally ousted on the eve of the company's impending bankruptcy, he had administered his fiefdom, located in Boise, Idaho, from his palatial estate in Pebble Beach, California, several hundred difficult-to-get-to miles away. Not only did he remove himself from the company, he required executives to commute to work with him. The company chipped in $28,000 to move him to Pebble Beach. You can only wonder how that distance and that expense was justified to the board of directors. Given that investors lost 47% of their money over the course of Agee's six-year reign, his contribution to the value and financial health of the company would not exactly wash. (Marc Levinson, "A High Roller Craps Out", *Newsweek*, February 20, 1995, p. 44.)

At least there was a time when the rich and powerful also accepted a duty to manage with decency. We called it paternalism and its ultimate effects may have been the same as those from tyrannical management, but at least the intent was decent. It appears that those days are clearly gone.

The books we devour by respected and admirable retired CEOs such as the Max DePrees (*Leadership Is An Art, Leadership Jazz*) and James Autrys (*Love and Profit*), are perhaps the cruellest of temptations. We desperately want the prince to be benevolent so that the system can go on, take care of us once again and, in the end, the pain is relieved. We seem to want this so much that we actually come to believe monarchy works! By the time the books reach the best-seller lists their tales no longer represent reality because there is a successor prince – CEO. We hurry to the next promise and reveal our frightened selves thinking that there is a way to transform essentially psychological sweatshops into loving, caring, shared experiences of meaningful work. We have been counting on the latest technique to alter the realities of the organization to reveal not the organization's fundamental pathologies but a social system rewarding to those who make it work. Such delusions.

CONSEQUENCES

The consequences of maintaining a system that breeds manager-ial incompetence are many and destructive. Besides the obvious impact of breeding a cynical work force fed up with "flavor of the month" managerial manipulations, the management literature is made virtually irrelevant and the tools become mere instruments of exploitation. Worse still, is the dehumanization of those subject to this system's dysfunction; ultimately the organization suffers. The major fallout from persistent incompetence is employees asking consciously or unconsciously – "Who cares?"

Who Cares About Quality?

Imagine, you are not involved in decisions, your tools are mediocre or out of date, you are asked to do more in the same amount of time, expected to work limitless overtime, do not feel safe enough to say what you think and have no job security. Why would you care about quality? Personal work ethic? A personal sense of responsibility? A fair day's effort for a fair day's wage?

If individuals are routinely treated as disposable, expendable, inferiors, it is not likely that they understand what quality is and certainly cannot or at least should not be expected to actually care about contributing their best for such treatment. Want quality? Give quality.

Who Cares About Profits?

Tell the fellow buried in the Mickey or Minnie mouse costume at Disney World to care about profits when, in 1992, Michael Eisner the CEO of Disney was rewarded with $203,000,000! That is a lot of money. It is the most any manager has ever been paid in the recorded history of the human race. That is $812,000 per day or $1,353 per minute based on a ten-hour workday. By way of contrast, say the Disney employee in the mouse costume makes $10 per hour. That is $20,000 per year, or $80 per day or 17 cents per minute. Minute for minute, the ratio of the CEO's pay to his would be 7,958 to 1.

Looked at another way, CEO to CEO, the United States pays the President, the Vice President, 14 Cabinet Members, 9 Supreme Court Justices, 100 Senators, 435 Members of the House of Representatives, 50 Governors, and 10 Mayors of our largest cities a grand total of $77,902,989. Add to that 223 full professors of business at $53,200 each per year for 10 years and the total is still only $195,966,589. There is still $7 million left over!

At the end of the fiscal year, September 30, 1995, the US Labor Department announced that wages, salaries and benefits rose 2.7%, "the tiniest increase on record, showing employment compensation was failing to keep up with inflation." (John D. McLain, "2.7% Pay Increase Smallest on Record", Associated Press, *Rocky Mountain News*, November 1, 1995.)

Even without profits, managerial excess has no limits. It is not uncommon for executives to make huge salaries and bonuses even when a company is in bankruptcy. One of the latest outrageous examples involves Bradlees Inc., a New England discount department store chain. *The Wall Street Journal*, October 13, 1995 reported that "The company is asking (the bankruptcy court) for approval of a plan to pay Mark A. Cohen, its chairman and chief executive officer, a bonus of at least $2 million over five years. The company is also seeking to pay Peter Thorner, its president, a bonus of at least $1 million through June, 1998, and to increase his salary." To people who work for a living this is incomprehensible.

The double standard represented with this kind of behavior not only sends a message of hypocrisy but establishes a virtually insurmountable gulf between the interests of management and labor. It invites labor's psychological withdrawal from any effort to save the organization, let alone make it prosper in new and imaginative ways.

Who Cares About Customers?

Here, too, organizations ultimately disappoint their customers because of questionable management practices. The clarion call to delight customers will fall on deaf ears until organizations begin to treat employees well and heed the advice of Hal Rosenbleuth, CEO of Rosenbleuth Travel, one of the largest travel related companies in the US. He says, "the customer comes second." This statement is also the title of his book about how treating employees well translates into their treating customers well; when employees are served so too are the customers.

Service organizations are especially concerned with customer treatment since they are exposed to so many opportunities to retain or discourage customers. Not only is it important to serve people well but word of mouth is vital in the creation of a reputation that encourages or discourages the organization's current and potential customers. To a large extent, an organization's reputation is dependent on their lowest level employees. Poorly treated employees, however, cannot justify proactive, thoughtful, committed service to the business or its customers.

Sometimes the treatment is so bad that despite the risk of losing a low-paying job, employees will strike. The teamsters actually struck Super Valu Stores' warehouse and distribution center in Denver over "dignity issues." One of the reasons was management's suspension of "someone without giving them facts prior to the suspension." (Associated Press, "Teamsters Strike Super Valu Warehouse Over Dignity Issue", *Rocky Mountain News*, October 17, 1995, p. 3c.)

So the call for employee service to delight customers when the employee is treated without respect will fall on deaf ears. And this is a managerial malpractice.

Who Cares About My Job?

The ultimate personal defeat at work is for anyone, manager or worker, to simply wonder, "why should I care about my job?" Most jobs today are really a means to an end – making your livelihood, not an end in themselves. Only a small proportion of the work force can see a link between what they are doing, personal meaningfulness and a larger societal purpose. Even in industries with an obvious connection to a larger purpose such as agriculture, construction, teaching, and health care, the sole operative model of management is still command and control, a separation of thinkers from doers.

One of the most ludicrous examples of the persistence of this inappropriate model is in education. Virtually the entire work force has a college degree and most states require masters degrees for permanent certification. Yet teachers are treated as a subversive, Marxist element incapable of participating in the decision-making process regarding the larger educational issues facing a school district. They and their union are also seen as the cause of the declining performance levels in the schools. To verify this treatment you only need to read the local press around teacher contract talks or follow the continuing assault on the National Education Association (NEA) and teachers in *Forbes* magazine. Educators are treated as labor in the classical sense. "The 2.1-million-member National Education Association – which some years ago passed the Teamsters to become the country's biggest union – is the worm in the American education apple. The public may be only dimly aware of it, but the union's growing power has exactly coincided with the dismal spectacle of rising spending on education producing deteriorating results." (Peter Brimelow, and Leslie Spencer, "The National Extortion Association?", *Forbes*, June 7, 1993, pp. 72–84.) This was followed in the February 13, 1995 issue of *Forbes* with the claim that: "Parent/taxpayer unhappiness with the public schools combined with the Republican victory are starting to cut the floor from under the National Education Association's left-leaning monopoly over American education." Suggesting that correlation is causation, as in the first piece, or calling names, as in the second piece, demonstrate the virulence of the *Forbes* campaign of disinformation and obfuscation undermine the teaching profession and solving the larger educational issues in the US.

At least in professions and careers that have an obvious link with a societal purpose you can derive a good measure of satisfaction from work. In other fields and occupations, where your personal satisfaction is more a fabrication than an inherent part of the role as, for example, when making more money than others becomes a primary measure of worth and purpose, the distinction between the organization and the individual, management and labor becomes an almost daily reminder of why people experience a growing alienation at work.

FINALLY: IT IS REALLY ABOUT CHARACTER

It is not taught in business schools and seemingly not taught at home anymore either, but the lack of character exemplified by the low integrity in organizational relationships ("Sorry, but this is a business decision, nothing personal. You're fired."), declining respect for others and a studied unwillingness to communicate authentically: ("If I tell people what I really think, they'll use it against me."), are the underlying reasons for the widespread demonstration of managerial malpractices. There is widespread disregard for, or blindness to, building reciprocal, balanced relationships.

David Ingvar's research with Position Emission Tomography (PET Scan) shows computer-generated pictures of the neo-cortex during different states of mind. Ingvar finds that the brain turns off when people cannot anticipate a positive future.

– **MICHAEL MACCOBY,**
Why Work: Motivating and Leading the New Generation,
New York: Touchstone, 1988, p. 52.

Chapter Six

EMPLOYEE MALPRACTICES

There is a symmetry in human affairs akin to the physical law that states "for every action, there is an equal and opposite reaction." As managers stumble into malpractice, so too, do employees. Their methods are as varied and potentially as destructive of the common good, as managerial malpractices.

The lesson for managers is twofold. First, they must be on the lookout for these malpractices in their organizations and assess the extent to which they will impact the effectiveness of the tools and techniques described here. Second, many of these behaviors are actually employer-inspired. They are learned on the job. Though we know there is evil in the world and that some people deliberately engage in the malpractices listed here, often they are a response to some real, or imagined, affront by the organization or your manager. A broken confidence, an unreasonable disciplinary action, an overtime demand that interferes with a long-standing commitment away from the job, being disempowered in determining how you will do your job. The number of ways that we can foster the employee malpractices are endless.

Before engaging any new management tool examine your current organizational practices to determine their impact on employee motivation, self-respect, feeling of worth, and purpose.

FIRST, AN ATTITUDE

This chapter focuses on a variety of ways incompetent employees retard, even interfere with the work of organizations.

First, we must start by understanding an attitude that permeates the thinking and behavior of many of the malpracticing employees. The attitude reflects a feeling of being trapped, being a victim, having to "make a living" but not really being responsible for the quality of life you experience. Just like managers, we believe that employees, too, have a sacred responsibility to execute their duties without doing harm. Certainly employees must "do their job" but they must also bring a presence of mind to their task to enable them to perform it well and to further the collective good.

HAMMURABI'S CURSE

When Hammurabi separated managerial responsibility from labor, thinking from doing, he set in motion a pattern of behavior, reinforced in the twentieth century by Frederick Taylor, that not only deprived employees of pride in their work but built in a justification for, in effect, delegating upward, passing along to your managers even trivial decisions. As Taylor claimed, management does the thinking and labor does the work. Labor's response to this has been to disengage their minds from their work. Initiative would only lead to reprimands. Individual action would only result in putting your job at risk for a marginal personal gain at best. So, initiative, creativity and innovation which is a natural part of a craftsman's work was totally sucked out of industrial work according to the precepts of Taylor's scientific management.

Hammurabi's curse is truly haunting those organizations that now find after the downsizings and reengineerings that everyone needs to be more responsible, more proactive, more willing to use their imagination in fulfilling their tasks. But abdicating responsibility, not pursuing opportunities, not thinking creatively and imaginatively will result unless the separation of management from labor is reversed and risk-taking and initiative are rewarded not punished.

MALPRACTICE OR SELF-DEFENSE?
(A bad attitude as mental health)

To many union leaders, the workingman should remain distinctly different from management in order to maintain their independence and achieve their goals (presumably trade union goals, fewer hours, more pay, better working conditions, etc.). It almost amounts to non-compliance with your responsibilities. This certainly supports Hammurabi's curse:

> To the eternal workingman management is substantially the same whether it is made up of profit seekers, idealists, technicians, or bureaucrats. The allegiance of the manager is to the task and the results. However noble his motives, he cannot help viewing the workers as a means to an end. He will always try to get the utmost out of them; and it matters not whether he does it for the sake of profit, for a holy cause, or for the sheer principle of efficiency. (Eric Hoffer, *The Ordeal of Change*, New York: Perennial, 1963, p. 64.)

To some, having a 'bad attitude' is a cause célèbre. What is a bad attitude? I'd say it's a general unwillingness to submit to the conditions of wage slavery. It's demonstrated most dramatically in a surly, uncooperative manner on the job, but must usually be more subtle. The worker with a bad attitude is always looking for ways to work less (procrastination, losing things), to surrender less time to the job (coming in late, leaving early, long breaks and lunches, lots of sick days), to further private pleasures and human interaction on the job (talking a lot, smoking dope), and by doing one's own creative work on the job.

A bad attitude is a fundamentally normal, human response to the utter absurdity of most modern work. It's a mystery to me why more people don't demonstrate a bad attitude – I suppose it's because they fear unemployment and/or lost income and have learned to smile and hide their true feelings. Of course I've done that too, and all too often. You can't get a job in the first place without smiling and lying through your teeth!

Sometimes people don't demonstrate bad attitudes because they actually enjoy their work. Why people enjoy work is harder to explain, but I postulate three basic reasons: (1) the work is a convergence of avocational interests and paying work (this is extremely rare); (2) the work, though boring and/or frustrating, is preferable to the individual's life with family or friends, or lack thereof; and (3) going to work saves one from finding and creating meaning, of deciding what's worth doing (this is obviously not an explicit motivation, but I think it is a subterranean spur). In the latter two cases, the job serves as a safe haven from the vacuum of meaninglessness in which society would otherwise leave the individual. Providing economic security reinforces this feeling.

To seek positive reinforcement for one's wage labor only validates a system whose very premise is the degradation of creative human activity – the exchange of skills, affection and loyalty for money. (Chris Carlsson, *Bad Attitude: The Processed World Anthology*, New York: Verso, 1990, pp. 94 and 114.)

Jefferson's Nightmare

Thomas Jefferson would probably find it sad, to say the least, that while Americans willingly subjugate themselves to un-elected, virtually unaccountable and often abusive bosses, they have lost the pride in their work and self-respect to demand their rightful place in the decision-making process at work

Though the vast majority of people still put in a fair day's work for a fair day's pay their reluctance to take a more meaningful role in the organization's success and to appreciate their impact on the whole, leaves them so much less than what they could become.

Work as a Fringe Benefit

The long struggle between capital and labor often breaking out in violence when their interests collided has only demonstrated their mutual ignorance about the very system providing wealth and life to all. But employees have been traditionally hired at the lowest possible pay to do the easiest possible work that they find all personal meaning has been removed from their daily work. Work has been so fragmented and reduced of skill for so many that people have responded in a perfectly natural way, by in effect asking, "So what?"

If workers seem to be nonchalant or take their job as a necessary evil or see it as a fringe benefit to enjoy while they can, it might be because of employee malpractice and it might be related to their treatment at work or how their work is designed and rewarded. And of course, it can be an inherent characteristic of some employees who are incapable of taking responsibility, building self-respect, and honestly earning their wage.

EMPLOYEE INCOMPETENCE BY IGNORANCE

In an age of increasing complexity requiring committed customer service and high quality products and services, some employees seem unwilling to learn how to improve their performance. Mediocrity results and the whole enterprise is jeopardized because of the lack of personal concern. This malpractice seeps into every part of the organization when it is allowed to exist anywhere.

Incompetence by ignorance is also apparent when employees demonstrate how uninformed they are about the very business world they work in and when they are unaware of how a business works. Management would do well to teach employees how a business works and the link between your personal performance and the bottom line.

There is no excuse for an organization to accept incompetence and mediocrity because of your ignorance of how you and your work fit into the larger picture. You must be kept informed.

RAW PERSONAL POWER

Any social arena sets the stage for interpersonal posturing, competitiveness, the expression of dominant or submissive behavior, showing signs of sexual interest, displays of ego assertion and defense, expressing your personality in its creative, spiritual, emotional fullness and other human qualities. In the workplace so focused on the acquisition of money and power, it is no surprise that the struggle to display your own or resist other's power becomes a major workplace drama. This is accentuated since there is such a definite hierarchical categorization of each person's assigned power. So the behind-the-scenes competition for informal power can be quite intense.

Personal power, influence and leadership can also be advanced through utilizing the rumor mill and grapevine. All of these efforts represent employee malpractice and absorb a considerable amount of time and organizational resources.

De-emphasizing formal power differences, privileges and secrecy defuse many of the effects of power struggles and the acquisition and the use of raw personal power by employees.

Using raw personal power or in other ways just focusing on self-oriented behaviors (SOBs) without the slightest concern for the good of the whole demonstrates this employee malpractice.

SENIORITY AS COMPETENCE

One employee malpractice that defies the competitive environment is insisting on seniority as a way of determining raises, promotions, job security and some rewards. Seniority has its obvious utility, especially in a volatile employment market when it reduces coercion, age discrimination, and blackmail of employees. It also diminishes the abuse of evaluation systems when competence and performance are roughly comparable and such systems foist the supremacy of artificial or marginal differences as a way of controlling and intimidating a work force.

Employee malpractice occurs when incompetent individuals or the "retired-on-the-job" use seniority as an excuse to ignore their responsibilities or to exercise distasteful qualities such as constantly speaking ill of others, always resisting change and not keeping your skills up-to-date.

THE BULLY

The bully uses his or her personal influence or force of character to spread ill will, to lower performance standards of workpartners, to resist any request for cooperation with management, to demand unreasonable treatment, play the victim, use the organization's telephones and cars and supplies for personal use, be destructive of things and spirit and complain at every opportunity about what is wrong with others, the products, and the company.

The bully is also a complainer, a victim, and a bad-mouther. This kind of malpractice needs to be addressed immediately or it affects the morale of the workplace like a fast spreading cancer.

PASSIVITY

Many people do not care and cannot be motivated about the

work world. To them it is simply an unfortunate way of spending time before the weekend. Others knowing their work or particular assignments are wrong simply shut-up and go along.

Here we are talking about two different kinds of passivity. One, a malpractice by design and the other a malpractice by fear or apathy. Both are dangerous. The first deprives the workplace of your full potential and the second may actually contribute to the sabotaging of the organization.

The first may leave the lights on in an unused room or not notice the tools left all over a worksite as the crew returns to the plant or can see a form has missing data but does not care; does not consciously notice.

The second knows sugar water has replaced apple juice in an infant food product, or the gas tank of a recreational vehicle is prone to explosion on slight impact, or a blood donor is HIV positive and either is too lazy to say anything or is told by a supervisor to look the other way.

Failing to act, failing to anticipate the effects of your actions or inactions, being passive, has its consequences whether intended or otherwise and thus, becomes an employee malpractice.

In both cases individuals lack a personal vision, they neither see where they or the organization is going and do not seem to care. In the second case there are dangerous consequences but the employee in either case is diminished by not being fully human. The rationalization for this behavior is often feeling powerless or trapped or kept an outsider without formal organizational influence. But being the victim, having no personal vision, unable to see your life in its larger frame of reference is truly to make yourself a victim settling for a job and not experiencing a sense of purpose.

CONSEQUENCES

Employee malpractices have the same kinds of results that management malpractices have. Everyone is hurt by them and the organization just limps along.

When these malpractices prevail they begin a negatively reinforcing cycle of managerial behavior – behavior that itself may have precipitated the employee malpractices in the first place. Workers are seen as lazy and untrustworthy, needing a lot of supervision, not being able to take part meaningfully in organizational decisions, and so forth.

The worst consequence for managers, however, is that they are contagious. If these malpractices survive they influence others and destroy a favorable work environment. Their survival also undermines management's credibility since management is depended on to take the responsibility to deal with these behaviors. They poison the efforts of the real contributors. If the environment is too polluted with these individuals the best performers will move elsewhere.

FINALLY: IT IS REALLY ABOUT CHARACTER

Ultimately, we are responsible for ourselves, the choices we make and the relationships in our lives. How we choose to be whether self-reliant and strong, whether a cooperative member of a workplace doing worthwhile things, whether a passive victim of the times falling out of control from one circumstance to another, who we are is causal. That is, our character is our energy source. Our character tells us how we will act on what is acceptable or not acceptable.

It is how we express who we are that makes our life have meaning and organizations are as legitimate a venue as any in which to take responsibility for living our lives fully. Not to do so is to willingly be less than who we are and who we can become. It is to hand over our destiny to someone else.

We are what we think.
All that we are arises with our thoughts.
With our thoughts we make the world.
Speak or act with a pure mind and happiness
will follow you as your shadow,
Unshakable.

– THE DHAMMAPADA,
The Sayings of the Buddha,
London: Wildwood House, 1976.

Chapter Seven

RESCINDING HAMMURABI'S CURSE

WE HAVE SEEN that between Hammurabi and Taylor the separation of management from labor and the distinctions between owners and employees have become so embedded that most people believe the separation is in fact a reflection of the natural order of things. We know better. But we have a difficult time imagining a different future and at some level are hesitant to alter the familiar, the status quo, to try something new albeit more consistent with our inner longings and spiritual well-being.

Paraphrasing the *Declaration of Independence* we can see just why Hammurabi has endured: Prudence, indeed, will dictate that Corporations long established should not be changed for light and transient causes; and accordingly all experience has shown, that mankind is more disposed to suffer, while evils are sufferable, than to right themselves by abolishing the forms to which they are accustomed. However, the *Declaration* goes on to call us to our 'right and our duty' when it says: "But when a long train of abuses and usurpations, pursuing invariably the same Object, evinces a design to reduce them under absolute Despotism, it is their right, it is their duty, to throw off such Management, and to provide new Rules for their future security."

While there is a great deal of evidence suggesting that people are seriously questioning the legitimacy of a system that increasingly serves fewer and fewer people, the pain level has not yet reached, though it is fast approaching, a critical mass. Toto (the dog in the *Wizard of Oz*) is about to pull the curtain on the frail, powerless wizards who are tightly holding on to the reigns of power and privilege belching fear in their incantations of "global competition," "market forces," and "getting government off our backs" warning the masses to obey or all their jobs will disappear.

WE ARE ALL IN THE SAME BOAT

Times are changing for everyone. While labor is feeling the brunt of it, management, too, is experiencing a drastic change in the way it conducts itself. William Bridges tells the story of how a tanker captain experienced what amounted to a radical change in the operation of his ship – one that was successfully executed and affected each member of the crew:

> I'm a captain of a large ocean going tanker. My job has changed dramatically because of the way we use and share information. For example, I used to be the first person on the ship to get the weather reports. That was because I was the only person on board with a computer. Also, at any given minute I could tell what our fuel consumption was and sometimes knew before the ship's engineer that we had an oil leak. All of this because of my computer.
>
> It's not that way anymore. Everyone aboard the ship now has access to all the information I have through their own networked computers. Before, I gave all the orders. Now, I make recommendations. Each crew member knows what they have to do. They don't wait for orders anymore. Based on the information they have they simply do what needs to be done.
>
> I was afraid of this at first; I didn't feel as needed as before. But, you know, it's a lot less stress and the crew's more satisfied with their jobs.

This illustrates the technological influences that have dramatically changed our workplaces, our role expectations, and our personal responsibilities. It signifies a potentially epochal shift away from Hammurabi's and Taylor's notion of the separation of management and labor toward a cooperative, collegial, shared experience of achieving organizational objectives. But we must still choose to make this shift. Otherwise we will be continuing a struggle designed for dominance or submission that character-ized the old way of doing things. If we make that choice our or-ganizations will remain hobbled by the internecine war between management and labor that should now clearly know better regarding what is needed to compete in the volatile world marketplace. What this means is that the fundamental relation-ships in the workplace must be clarified. We are all in the same boat. We will sink or sail together.

THE DNA OF ORGANIZATIONS: FUNDAMENTAL RELATIONSHIPS

The nature of our work is no longer defined by one person, car-ried out by another and supervised by yet a third. Today some people are experimenting with a way of relating to one another that is not simply based on dominance and submission. Today that is no longer acceptable. In fact, it is the very thing that limits creativity, decision-making and quick, innovative action. So from the typical hierarchy of relationships such as parent-child, hus-band-wife, ruler-subject, owner-slave, boss-worker, we are rapidly reformulating the relational mix to include safeguards and reci-procity to reduce and eliminate abuse and unilateral action. In the workplace this means relationships are becoming more and more collegial among and between all levels. Employees are not just called associates and workpartners but are demanding to be treated as such. This is not to deny the existence of all hierarchy but it is to change the nature of the hierarchy. Power becomes muted, senior people are accountable to those they influence as well as to those who select them. Positions of responsibility are earned through competence and are accountable to the whole not merely those above. The senior role is earned based on behaviors that lead to the fulfillment of objectives all can see and identify with, and not merely the unilateral exercise of personal preference or benevolence.

The organizational DNA consists of the relationship between a boss (b), a subordinate (s), and a colleague (c). The conven-tional representation of this relationship is illustrated in Figure 7.1.

Figure 7.1 The Organizational DNA: The Basic Building Block of Conventional Organizations

The barrier between a "boss" and a "subordinate" (B&S/B&C) is always present no matter how good the relationship, because the boss is held responsible for the subordinate. This breeds an undercurrent of fear. For the subordinate the fear is due to the boss' control of assignments, evaluations, pay increases, etc. and for the boss there is a reciprocal fear of letting go of control. Thus, the relationship is sub-optimized by the very nature of the conventional principles of organization when "superiors" take responsibility for "subordinates"; subordinates learn to relinquish responsibility when they are required to submit. (And the roots of their inevitable dysfunction are sewn.)

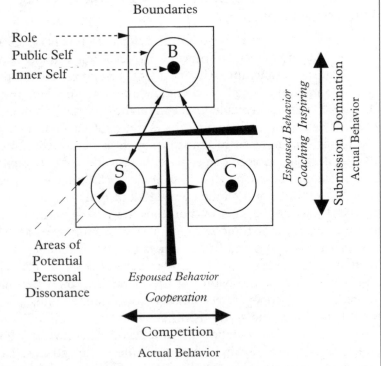

While colleagues (S&C) must cooperate to fully utilize their talents only individual rewards and promotions are available. Thus there is competition between them. Even when colleagues are well-intentioned, those who are ambitious and seek managerial careers, must out-perform the others. Thus, there is always an element of suspicion that colleagues may do something to succeed at another's expense by withholding information or engaging in self-serving political behavior. The conventional organization sub-optimizes its human resources by its very underlying design principles.

Figure 7.2 is a representation of how organizations can over-come traditional role barriers to create peer relationships.

Organizations can function differently if they restructure the nature of their relationships. For some organizations this is tantamount to genetic engineering but as we will see in Parts II and III, the latest management tools and techniques presuppose a shift in the role of management and the nature of organizations. The talk about a "new paradigm" is directly related to a new understanding of the possibilities inherent in new approaches to organizing the workplace and attending to the work. This will be explored further in Chapter Seventeen.

THE IMPORTANCE OF UNDERSTANDING MENTAL MODELS

Behavior that achieves the mission of the organization springs from a set of values and beliefs about how the world works and what constitutes acceptable relationships between people in the workplace. Without understanding what mental models of values, attitudes and beliefs drive the actions of individuals and groups within the organization it is impossible to impact behavior effectively and accurately align managerial techniques and practices.

A mental model is a view of the world. It is based on your underlying beliefs, values, and perceptions. When world views are shared by a culture they constitute a societally, self-reinforcing paradigm perpetuated through the socialization process. This is also true for organizations.

Mental models do change as conditions change. As incremental changes accumulate over time they eventually stimulate a reconsideration of beliefs and motivate adaptive responses by individuals, whole organizations and societies. A new world view emerges and individual mental models come to reflect each person's new perception of the world. This leads to changes in behavior. For example, when the legitimacy of monarchies was questioned individuals could consider democracies and republics.

Since mental models influence and drive behavior and are either in harmony with, or in conflict with, other people's in the workplace, it is important to understand the mental models we

Figure 7.2 Building Peer Relationships

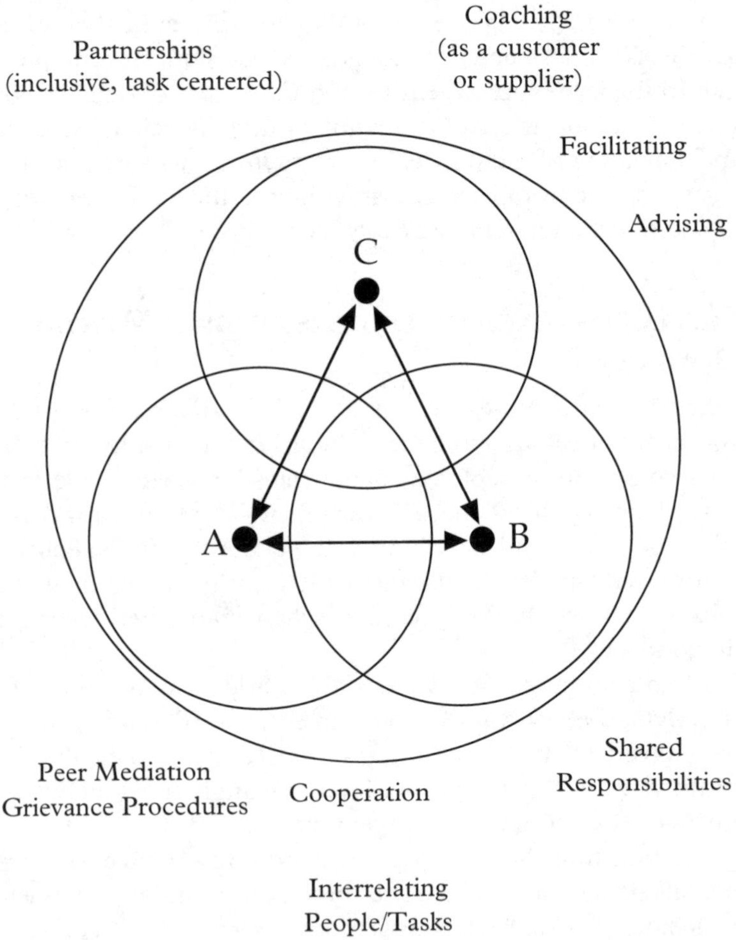

Coaching
(as a customer
or supplier)

Partnerships
(inclusive, task centered)

Facilitating

Advising

C

A → ← B

Peer Mediation
Grievance Procedures

Cooperation

Shared
Responsibilities

Interrelating
People/Tasks

The object here is to break through traditional role barriers (see Figure 7.1) and the separation between individuals based on rank in order to include all relevant individuals in decision making and problem solving. In doing so, issues become that which all people attempt to resolve rather than perceived as the sole responsibility of the "boss." The nature of relationships changes from a dominance/submissive role to a collegial partnership. This is only possible when the skills, knowledge and contributions each is capable of making tend toward equality. This can happen in most knowledge work.

hold and how they influence our interpersonal relationships and the success of our organizations.

VIBES: MENTAL MODELS AT WORK

The VIBES construct (value initiated behaviors) illustrates the thought process you undertake to confirm original beliefs and world view. Unless circumstances change dramatically or we are very open-minded and in the pursuit of learning, our world view is likely to remain untouched. The process begins with current beliefs and values which lead to judgments and attitudes and result in a set of behaviors expressive of original beliefs ultimately reconfirming our original beliefs.

In the first example (see Figure 7.3 VIBES I), a manager believes people are lazy and do not want to work. Thus, he or she must carefully supervise "subordinates" to be sure they are working according to instructions. Because the manager acts from a position of mistrust he or she behaves strictly and delegates little. "Subordinates" respond to this treatment in a rebellious or passive-aggressive manner, sabotaging or slowing down work processes. When this happens, they are treated more severely confirming the manager's original beliefs. This process recycles through a manager's behavioral repertoire. VIBES II and III provide additional examples of this process.

The importance of this insight cannot be overstated. Your values and beliefs direct a course of action. Each of us carries filters imbedded in our perceptual equipment that seeks to confirm our beliefs. Only when there is sufficient dissonance that we cannot rationalize will we change the belief or modify our behavior.

One of the most powerful examples of the durability of mental models, even to the point of engaging in self-defeating behavior, was reported by Richard Pascale in his 1991 book, *Managing on the Edge.*

A STORY

The following story dramatically illustrates the power of different mental models and how they act as powerful causal influences on the construction of personal reality and behavior.

Figure 7.3 Mental Models at Work

This is an illustration of the thought process you undertake to confirm original beliefs and world view. Unless our world view is challenged it is likely to remain intact.

VIBES I:
(Value Initiated Behaviors)

A Manager's Perspective

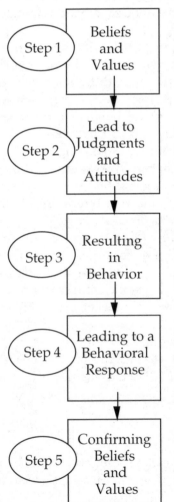

Step 1	Beliefs and Values	As a manager I believe that subordinates are basically lazy and dislike work.
Step 2	Lead to Judgments and Attitudes	I assume, therefore, that to get the most out of subordinates, I must watch over their every move.
Step 3	Resulting in Behavior	I behave in a strict manner, delegating little responsibility and demanding that everything be cleared through me first.
Step 4	Leading to a Behavioral Response	My subordinates react to this parent-like stance by acting like rebellious teenagers. I have to lean on them all the time or they will never do what I tell them.
Step 5	Confirming Beliefs and Values	Consequently, my original belief is confirmed; subordinates are basically lazy and dislike work.

Figure 7.3 (*Continued*)

VIBES II:
(Value Initiated Behaviors)

A Subordinate's Perspective

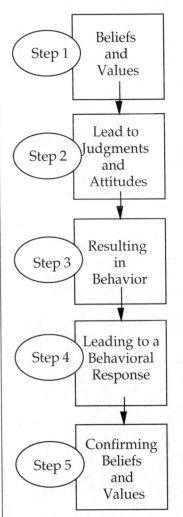

Step 1 — Beliefs and Values

I do not believe I am worthy (capable). (Often this is unconscious.)

Step 2 — Lead to Judgments and Attitudes

I assume, therefore, that the feedback I get supports this belief. Thus, when I hear positive feedback, i.e., "your last report was great," I think that the other reports must have been awful.

Step 3 — Resulting in Behavior

I behave like a victim. I do not take responsibility or initiative because I am afraid I will demonstrate my unworthiness. I will seek approval first for everything I do.

Step 4 — Leading to a Behavioral Response

My boss, then, does not see me as responsible and I must be closely supervised and told what to do.

Step 5 — Confirming Beliefs and Values

Consequently, my original belief is confirmed; I am unworthy. But I do not want to be unworthy which creates tension (cognitive dissonance). I either resolve this by changing beliefs (I am worthy) or behavior (I proceed to demonstrate incompetence).

Figure 7.3 (*Continued*)

VIBES III:
(Value Initiated Behaviors)

An Owner/CEO Perspective

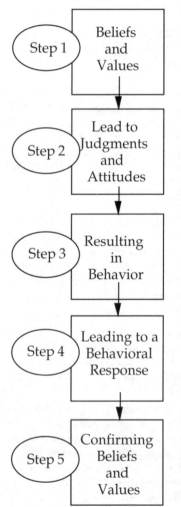

Step 1 — Beliefs and Values	I own the company and feel privileged.
Step 2 — Lead to Judgments and Attitudes	Because I am the owner and I travel so much for the company I am entitled to a private plane; which, by the way, allows me to use my private pilot's license.
Step 3 — Resulting in Behavior	The company plane is more important than employees having computer workstations because my needs are most important.
Step 4 — Leading to a Behavioral Response	Employees gripe about not having computer workstations yet the company owns a plane (they devalue the importance of their work thinking the owner devalues the importance of their work by not giving them the tools to do their jobs effectively).
Step 5 — Confirming Beliefs and Values	I own the company. I decide how to spend its money. (The complainers can work somewhere else if they do not like it here.)

In its venture with Toyota in Fremont, California, General Motors placed sixteen of its high-potential managers within the Japanese-run entity to watch and learn firsthand how the Japanese manufacture automobiles. The results in Fremont have been astounding. In 1980–81, absenteeism was in excess of 20%, and it ranked among the worst plants in the GM system for quality. Under Japanese management, grievances are down to thirty or forty per year, and absenteeism is less than 3%. Compared to other GM plants on quality, it scored 140 out of a possible 145 points. Fremont's productivity is three times the best GM rate (at its most modern and highly automated factories); defect rates and capital costs are one third GM's best plants.

To the GM managers on the scene, "the secret" is not hard to grasp: the Japanese do it primarily with people. Rehiring the union members, most of whom had worked at the plant prior to the venture, they inherited the worst UAW local in the GM family. Through an intensive training effort and allowing workers at Fremont to set their own work standards, rotate jobs, and exercise major control over the assembly line design, they transformed the workers' mindset from an adversarial to a cooperative tone.

Even with this extraordinary achievement proven with record numbers, an elaborate social system blinds management from exploiting opportunity within its grasp. Despite the fact that the GM managers on the scene were submitting detailed, and increasingly empathetic, reports on Toyota's "low tech/high motivation" formula, GM doggedly invested in technology ($60 billion over the period 1982–85 – enough to buy both Honda and Nissan). Why? Because the traditional rules of GM emphasize engineered solutions, not human or motivational solutions (except for a few cosmetic efforts at team building).

In the face of an experiment so successful (occurring within a former GM facility with a former GM work force), you might expect GM to study it with keen interest. Instead, we discover a pattern of conduct that almost suggests covert sabotage.

States Michael Naylor, director of strategic planning: "One of the activities I must invest in is countering the current disinformation campaign against Fremont. The basis of this attack rests on the assertion that . . . 'Fremont is a failure,' or 'they hand-picked their employees, which is not the real world,' or 'it was a start-up situation, which is not true to life.' These are defenses that GM has erected against the learning that ought to occur."

General Motors imposes tight restrictions on its employees' access to Fremont. This made it almost impossible for interested managers to study and comprehend what makes Fremont successful. Little attention is directed to the most important ingredient – Fremont's managerial philosophy and its approach to people.

A General Motors intern, who had taken part in a tour of GM executives through the Fremont facility, provides this powerful anecdote:

> From the front of the line, the voice of the guide droned on, discussing the quality of the materials-handling system, robotics, innovative painting, etc. But I had lost interest. I was fascinated by the work force. I kept comparing them with my familiar world in the assembly plants in Flint, Michigan. I wondered what they had done to these people to make them care like this.
>
> Then we were in the middle of the body shop watching a group of four men in an assembly operation. Several of the visiting GM managers had lagged behind the rest of the tour group to watch these men work.
>
> "Have you ever seen anything like it?" marveled one. "Look at 'em go!"
>
> "How do they train them to work like this? It's unreal."
>
> "They train each other. Isn't that what they told us?"
>
> "Yeah, but check that equipment. It's so primitive."
>
> We were about to move on and catch up with the rest of the group, but one of the visiting plant managers hesitated and scoffed, "It's probably an act. There's no way in hell those guys could keep up this pace all day. They probably pick up speed every time a tour comes through their area."
>
> They pretended to move on but eased behind an obstruction and made their way back to peer cautiously out at the men. I stayed with them. In front of us, the workers, unaware they were being observed, continued to move quickly and efficiently at their job.
>
> One manager turned to the other. "You know, I couldn't do that job with less than six men in my plant."
>
> "You gotta give these Japanese credit," the other said. "How could they get those suckers to design their own work processes?

And with no experience?"

They continued to watch in silence for another few minutes. The men before them never let up their pace. Finally, the visiting plant manager could stand it no longer. He clapped his hands and stepped out from behind his hiding place. "Bravo!" he yelled at the workers. "You guys are something else! If only I could have people like you!"

The workers turned and smiled at the men as they left, but I lingered behind to hear their reaction. One of them turned and said to the others: "It's too bad, isn't it, they don't realize that they already have people like us."

(Edited From Pascale, Richard Tanner, *Managing on the Edge*, New York: Touchstone, 1991, p. 72.) Used with permission.

Don't put people in boxes.
Give them responsibility.
Not goddamn rules!

– **MICHAEL CONWAY, PRESIDENT,**
America West Airlines.

Chapter Eight

UNDERSTAND THE SYSTEM BEFORE YOU FIX IT

THE ATTEMPT TO manage, to take charge, set direction and lead is almost too tempting for ordinary managers to resist. In fact managers are rewarded for acting, and are looked at oddly if they spend too much time thinking. The use of techniques is often a random attempt to apply what is "in" in order to look normal, keep the troops on their toes and treat the most pressing signs of trouble.

It is important to understand that organizations are systems and that each organization is at the nexus of forces which shape it. Identifying these forces helps you design and/or select appropriate tools to respond to concerns, challenges, and change.

Managerial efforts frequently result in frustration and the deeper underlying principles of success remain elusive because the prerequisites for successful use of the tools are unknown and there is a lack of awareness of second order (or side) effects.

O-THIS! INFLUENCES ON ORGANIZATIONS: MASTERING THE FORCES OF CHANGE

The forces that influence organizational dynamics are easily visualized with the O-This model represented in Figure 8.1. We see that the organization is at a confluence point and will be re-shaped as it responds to these forces.

The organization and its employees are embedded in a culture and an historical context. Major influences from the larger society – especially socializing influences – will determine the behavioral context, the set of assumptions and expectations that people bring regarding their experience of the workplace. This influence shapes the work ethic. In a country with an historical trend for expanding rights and entitlements there will be a strong influence on the organization for fairness. The nature of the economy is also part of this influence. Thus, in a country like the United States, we find a market economy wherein private property rights and laissez-faire beliefs prevail.

Contemporary society influences the type of organization through its laws, public policy initiatives, norms, values, and mores. And, as we have seen, the cultural assumptions about what constitutes proper relationships in the workplace influence the role you play on the job, how you communicate and what expectations you hold of others. The nature and quality of our interpersonal relationships are the most fundamental building blocks of our organizations.

The individual is the most important determinant of the type of organization. In the larger society you can exercise choice, free will, and participate imaginatively in decision-making. The individual, to the extent that he or she is educated and allowed to utilize his or her capabilities, can greatly influence the organization's structures, rules, and processes used to reach its objectives. The type of organization also depends upon the extent to which individuals are engaged in their workplace and the operative governance processes.

Recent changes in computer and telecommunications technology have reshaped organizations of every kind. Computers have freed individuals and decoupled people from human supervision. The result has been either a gravitation toward a freer more responsive, customer-centered and flexible organization or toward a more tightly controlled "rule by the

**Figure 8.1 The Changing Organization —
Organization ≥ Technological, Historical/Cultural,
Individual and Societal Forces**

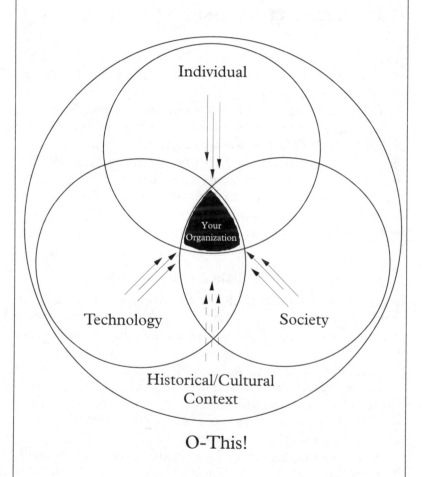

Individual

Your
Organization

Technology   Society

Historical/Cultural
Context

O-This!

numbers" organization. Looking at the various forces and how they shape your organization will help you determine where problems originate and what tools will be useful in solving them.

The Changing Organization
Organization ≥ Technological, Historical/Cultural, Individual and Societal Forces

Generally speaking, this model helps managers look at specific contemporary forces at play within the organization; forces that beg for a response. An organization's response has typically been limited to the boundaries of the conventional wisdom that clearly represents a mindset becoming less capable of dealing with new realities. The mindset of the industrial era is becoming more inadequate to deal with the postindustrial era each day. But evidence arrives in increments and until a critical mass of evidence accumulates, usually typified by a breakdown of some sort, individuals in organizations have no motivation to reconsider the conventional wisdom.

Four General Systems of Management

Organizations respond to the forces swirling around them in typically one of four ways. Identifying the particular system characterizing an organization will help managers make a proper fit between the techniques and tools and their current needs.

A managerial system develops from the prevailing assumptions and values of the times but specifically from those in control of the organization. Over thirty years ago four general management systems were identified within the industrial era ethos – all within the same paradigm.

System One. It is called Exploitative/Authoritative which is characteristic of the efficiency expert mentality. Under this thinking, the owners and their managers can figure out the best way to handle virtually any contingency and labor is perceived to be hired hands who put in their time and obey their bosses. In its pure form people are treated as virtual machines. Sweat shops, mines, and assembly lines come to mind.

System Two. Benevolent/Authoritative is a slight variation on System One. In fact, you can draw gradations along a continuum where the four systems have evolved from an authoritarian extreme on the left-hand side toward a more participative form on the right-hand side. System Two recognizes that people at work form, by their very presence, a social system that influences their performance; people are capable of thought and free will. This system utilizes social science research that demonstrates a modified, benevolent paternalism might result in greater productivity than a strictly authoritarian System One.

System Three. Consultative is the first managerial system that recognizes the value of employee contributions and suggests that open communication may be useful to tap employee knowledge. The employee point of view is considered worth listening to, particularly when circumstances are unpredictable or when there are various possible interpretations of the efficiency expert's recommendations. Where individual prerogatives and personal choice may enhance performance, System Three encourages the revelation of those insights. This system became popular when social science discovered that individual involvement leads to higher productivity through enhanced interest in, and commitment to, your work. The jobs that come to mind here are typically white collar such as research, marketing and sales. Some blue collar possibilities exist as well. An example is craft work.

System Four. Participative represents substantial employee involvement in their work. You can easily imagine assemblers, quality engineers, packaging designers and customer representatives getting together to solve product quality issues. You can also visualize a group of corporate buyers discussing strategies and suppliers or analyzing the best way to approach materials acquisition for a new product. This system is based on a team or collaborative effort. Quality circles come to mind as does the total quality movement where employees in work groups actively make decisions about, and take responsibility for, their work.

The conventional wisdom has cited Systems One through Four as representing different paradigms. The management literature is replete with contrasting organizational scenarios claiming the transformation of organizations from a System One mentality to a System Four mentality. The recent popularity of self-managing teams is an example of an attempt to move organizations toward the participative style of System Four.

One very popular theory of managerial archetypes suggests that there are basically two underlying philosophical tendencies among managers that guides their ultimate behavior toward either System One or System Four. The first is a limited view of mankind that believes people are lazy, do not want to work and do not want responsibility. This is called Theory X. The other view sees mankind as wanting to take responsibility, being capable of self-direction and able to make a contribution in the workplace. This is called Theory Y. Theory X managers are most comfortable in a System One environment and tend toward autocratic behavior, while Theory Y managers feel most comfortable in a System Four environment. See Figure 8.2 for a summary of the authoritarian versus participative management archetypes represented by Theory X and Theory Y.

THE ORGANIZATIONAL IMMUNE SYSTEM

Each organizational system creates a style, a comfort zone, a way of being that defies the intrusion of new ideas. It rejects transplants. This is familiarly called "the not invented here syndrome." No matter what the possibilities, the innovation or the proven utility of an idea, it will die, if it does not conform to the system.

All organizations, no matter how noble will reject ideas that are incompatible with the prevailing environment. In this regard organizations can be said to manifest an organizational immune system. Thus, it is important that if change is to be introduced it first deals with the dimensions of the organization's culture, values and attitudes in order to establish a reasonable foundation for success.

We can see, however, from Figures 8.3 and 8.4 how typical hierachies set the stage for conflict and the rejection of change.

Individuals practice behaviors consistent with the culture and values of the organization. In a sense it is an alignment of the VIBES with the culture. Then relationships, individual and team norms, and work processes can be designed to reflect the underlying values and create a new pattern of norms that will be receptive to the new requirements of a change program. Once

Figure 8.2 The Authoritarian versus Participative Management Archetypes

Theory X

Management is responsible for organizing the elements of productive enterprise – money, materials, equipment, people – in the interest of economic ends.

With respect to people, this is a process of directing their efforts, motivating them, controlling their actions, modifying their behavior to fit the needs of the organization.

Without this active intervention by management, people would be passive – even resistant – to organizational needs. They must therefore be persuaded, rewarded, punished, controlled – their activities must be directed. This is management's task.

The average man is by nature indolent – he works as little as possible.

He lacks ambition, dislikes responsibility, prefers to be led.

He is inherently self-centered, indifferent to organizational needs.

He is by nature resistant to change.

He is gullible, not very bright, the ready dupe of the charlatan and the demagogue.

Theory Y

Management is responsible for organizing the elements of productive enterprise – money, materials, equipment, people – in the interests of economic ends.

People are not by nature passive or resistant to organizational needs. They have become so as a result of experience in organizations.

The motivation, the potential for development, the capacity for assuming responsibility, the readiness to direct behavior toward organizational goals are all present in people. Management does not put them there. It is a responsibility of management to make it possible for people to recognize and develop these human characteristics for themselves.

The essential task of management is to arrange organizational conditions and methods of operation so that people can achieve their own goals best by directing their own efforts toward organizational objectives.

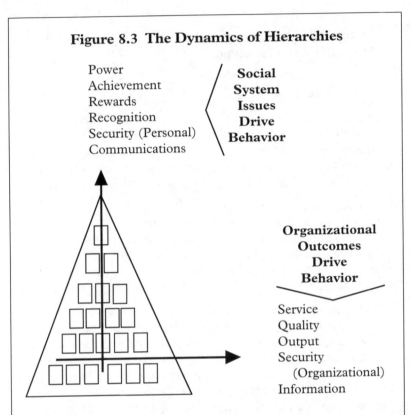

Figure 8.3 The Dynamics of Hierarchies

Power
Achievement
Rewards
Recognition
Security (Personal)
Communications

**Social
System
Issues
Drive
Behavior**

**Organizational
Outcomes
Drive
Behavior**

Service
Quality
Output
Security
    (Organizational)
Information

There are competing interests in organizations which explains why so many tools and techniques die before they even have a chance. There is a work flow that focuses on getting the product or service delivered to the customer. Reengineering, cross-functional teams, aspects of Japanese management, and many other techniques focus on this activity. Workers at this level can focus clearly on the processes and value added at each step.

On the other hand, the organizational superstructure is a support and staff function whose lingua franca is power, political maneuvering and protecting your turf. The goals are markedly different than at the operative levels of the organization as finance, strategy and marketing dominate their interest. Thus, the larger the organization's hierarchy the greater the arc of conflict and the more frequent will be the breakdowns facing the organization. Though both activities are necessary, the imbalance in power between the operatives and the superstructure frequently results in breakdowns and waste. The tools and techniques do not stand a chance if the interests are so divergent that effectiveness itself, does not matter.

Figure 8.4 Why Good Ideas Fail: Arc of Conflict

The more levels:

the stronger the status quo
the greater the conflict
the longer it takes to reach a shared understanding
the greater the distortion in communication
the more intense the need (and desire) for control
the more alienated people become
the harder it is to meet output goals
the harder it is to be creative
the more specialized the work
the more complex the workflow process
the slower the response time
the more obscure the goals
the more frequently destructive political behavior occurs

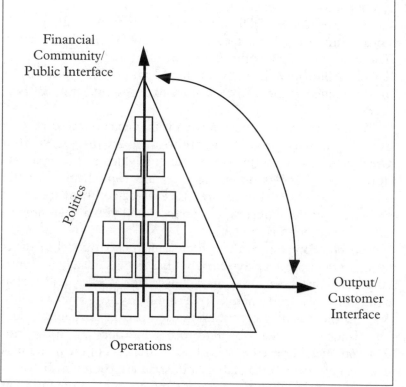

there is an alignment between each of the steps in the ladder of organizational behavior (see Figure 3.2), and the management system is identified and a felt need for change exists, the probability of successfully using change techniques increases.

Today the challenge remains to move management from a position of fear and a limited behavioral repertoire to a position of confidence and the ability to act from "an instantaneous apprehension of the totality" as R.G.H. Siu says in *The Master Manager*. A Theory X individual can only act from his or her fear and limitations and is unable to imagine others not behaving from those same fears. The Theory X person is also unable to imagine the value of other people having different talents and abilities. It is the most limited world and inappropriate for today's managerial challenges. The increased sensitivity to issues of cultural diversity and gender issues in the workplace demonstrates the difficulty of acknowledging the legitimacy of managerial styles other than the dominant model that controls most large organizations. This is, in part, symptomatic of the rigidity accompanying a Theory X orientation.

The prevalence of Theory X types in conventional organizations is, in part, a happenstance of the era of their ascendancy. The new era demands the skills, openness and flexibility of the Theory Y individual in a new context. That person appears to be in ascendance as the transformation to a postindustrial era proceeds.

What many writers have missed is that each of these systems even though dramatically dichotomized into a System One/System Four continuum, is still embedded in the organizational form that has dominated western capitalism since the dawn of the industrial revolution. Likewise, all of them are firmly embedded in the industrial era mindset and virtually all organizations represent this model.

System Four represents a more enlightened model of management than previous Systems, but has not adequately responded to the way society, the marketplace, the worker, and global competitiveness has changed. Certainly, System Four is more open to the potential contribution each person can make to the organization's problem-solving process and does try to tap into that potential, but even System Four is still part of the manipulative, management versus labor, industrial era paradigm. Though it attempts to get the most from the members in an organization and is more flexible in meeting the contingencies of the market-place it still does not fully meet the needs of the individuals in the organization or create a balanced reciprocal relationship between management and labor. The basis for relationships in Systems One through Four remains essentially utilitarian and exclusionary. There is an imbalance in power resulting in a dominant-submissive relationship; and no matter how apparently kind a manager is, a wedge of fear and suspicion lies between the "subordinate" and the "boss." The "subordinate" fears the "boss" use of power and the "boss" is afraid to let go of control. Many managers instinctively know this and have been at a loss regarding innovations to correct the disequilibrium between what the organization is demanding of the individual and what it is willing to return to the individual.

WHY HAS MANAGEMENT THEORY NOT BEEN INFLUENTIAL IN CHANGING MANAGEMENT PRACTICE?

The short answer is, theorists have not addressed the systemic shift. Most conventional management theorists become apologists for the conventional organization and purveyors of manipulative techniques. They claim to be just reporting what is; that is not their job to suggest what ought to be. But, by ignoring the larger issues of governance and accountability and the symptoms of the system's breakdown, management writers have missed the real story. The system is breaking beyond repair. The tools and techniques, though appearing to promise a quick fix, require a fundamental rethinking of the conventional wisdom. They require that everyone get in and bale since we are all on the same sinking ship.

Each year the business press tries yet again to find the words to convince the power wielders to be a bit more thoughtful, to seek a bit more enlightenment. In spite of the thousands of books that have demonstrated the wisdom of inclusive, participative, communicative, thoughtful, humane management, it is still practiced only by a small portion of managers and organizations – and only at their convenience.

Despite the many studies and all the empirical research about the need for managers to become more cognizant of their human as well as economic responsibilities, little has changed. It is as if the nature of business and business people is simply not amenable to such exhortations. Thus, regulation over the years has tried and, with more success than anyone would care to admit, has established an increasingly more caring baseline for acceptable behavior. The environment, minorities, and consumers have all had to be protected from this beast we call business. Leveling the playing field has been hard work. Yet, the big players are succeeding in returning to a free-for-all as their interests have captured the regulatory machinery in Washington and are speedily turning back the clock.

Clearly knowing better and doing better are very different animals. There are good reasons for the failure of knowledge to make an impact on the day-to-day management of people. First of all, the proof of their findings, as indisputable as it may be, cannot by itself change values or behavior. Traditional researchers start with an acceptance of the system they study. Thus, they do not question the system or its underlying values and assumptions which ultimately dictate the form of organizational structure and the consequent impact on behavior, governance, and accountability.

FINANCIAL HUSBANDRY AS THE SOLE VALUE IN MANAGEMENT

Since the person who owns or manages money is also a risk taker, and the one ultimately responsible for making the investment profitable, it follows that concern for financial gain is all that matters. Yet ordinary people know it is not. You may argue that indeed the risk to investors is real and quite substantial. True. But from the point of view of the personal and/or societal impact, however, the financial risk takers may not have the most to lose.

Investors, as the silent partners in organizations choosing to live by the market's roulette wheel, in effect place financial bets in a transient and disconnected fashion while employees wonder how long it will be before those investors lose interest or demand an impossible return for the use of their money and move on to bet elsewhere.

You choose to take the risk when the chances of gain are thought to be favorable. It is recognized that loss is possible;

indeed that possibility is always present. In most cases investors who do lose, are not destroyed. When they do lose, however, their personal lives remain basically the same. That is not the case for employees whose very livelihood is threatened with the loss of income. If equivalent employment is unavailable the ill effects of organizational failure can lead to financial ruin and personal trauma for every employee. The society, too, loses in a variety of ways from the loss of taxable income, spending power, the additional welfare demands and psychological disruptions to families and individuals due to idleness and purposelessness. Yet success brings financial gains and perhaps additional security to the investors while the employee can only hope that his or her job will remain intact.

We have seen that outstanding performance and consistent contributions do not substantially reduce your continued risk as an employee. So, the system secures capital and enlarges it while leaving labor without so much as a guaranteed retirement plan or a secure job.

The employees should be more active partners determining the methods and strategies of the organization. If you invest you believe. When you buy Microsoft stock you do so to follow a technology that has an obvious future and a technology that has a commanding influence in the market. As an investor you are betting on the ideas and imagination of each employee as well as the company's managerial and technological competence. But a company is more than a technology, it is the result of the people who make it happen. In Microsoft's case almost 20% of its employees are millionaires because they have been included in the reward process as well as having invested in their own company stock. They were as much risk takers as other investors. Most companies, however, cannot come close to giving this level of recognition to the people who make their success happen.

This brings us to Nirenberg's Law: Where the bottom line is only a financial indicator, and in the absence of law or regulation to the contrary, the dollar is always the sole measure of value ($>Non-regulated Social Values). The dollar is prepotent.

As Harry Boyte reminds us, the "conscience of the commonwealth, no matter how serious and creative, is no antidote to the lure of affluence, the momentum of technology, or the dynamic of the marketplace." (*Community Is Possible*, New

York: Harper & Row, 1984, p. 187.) This is especially so when the conventional wisdom is a wisdom of materialism.

As one of my graduate level business students said, "It's not about what is right or wrong, it's about what's best for the business. Make the most money and minimize risk. If it's not illegal don't worry about it and if the fine is less than the return for breaking a law, do it."

The second reason for the indifferent acceptance of research is that the research itself is no guarantee that applying its lesson will lead to success. Management research is like a photograph; the photo is not the object and never captures it fully. There are hidden aspects and whoever points the camera composes the field of vision. It is usually too narrow to generalize broadly. And, there are still too many invisible subtleties regarding the organizational personality and its unique combination of culture, personal will, individual intentions and people's ability to follow through on truths.

The third reason for the failure of management theory to influence organizational behavior is that it follows practice. Hence, changing organizations can be said to be influencing the empiricists instead of vice versa; and the imaginative futurists or visionaries are discounted as impractical because they point to the possible, to what organizations can become, instead of merely reinforcing what organizations have been. Management theory has been an articulation of the past. It is derived from historical data on what companies have done. Management theory must also include a look at what is possible.

The fourth reason is that organizations do not know what to do with new insights. They are usually not inclined to utilize management research regarding social or interpersonal issues. They are seen as either irrelevant or a luxury, a secondary priority to "getting the work out" as if getting the work out has nothing to do with societal interests or interpersonal behavior.

The fifth reason management theory fails to achieve widespread adoption in practice is that the prevailing mental model is simply too strong an influence to be challenged short of a restructuring – a massive endeavor. As Gall has said, in a not entirely tongue-in-cheek assessment, "Big systems either work on their own or they don't. If they don't, you can't make them." (John Gall, *Systemantics: How Systems Work and Especially How*

They Fail, New York: Pocket, 1978, p. 78.) Argyris, of Harvard adds, "The impact of the formal structure influences leadership behavior toward being more 'autocratic' even when there exists informal norms emphasizing a more egalitarian climate and when the leaders consciously try to be more 'democratic'." (Chris Argyris, *Personality and Organization*, New York: Harper & Row, 1957, p. 70.)

A sixth, and perhaps the most important reason, is that a management idea's legitimacy is based solely on the extent to which it directly contributes to productivity or profits. All issues ultimately are reduced to this. There is no other purpose for being. But from an individual's point of view there may not be any legitimacy to the productivity or profit motive if they are manipulated, treated with disrespect or otherwise believe they are in an exploitative relationship with the organization.

Management theory has not conceptualized organizations or a manager's responsibility in running organizations as building a good society. Governance, in terms of the management of people, has not been considered an important issue.

Attending to social governance issues has become necessary for at least four reasons: (1) There is a divergence of values between the owners/managers and everyone else in organizations. (2) People have virtually no choice. They must be wage earners and are thus placed in a relationship to the organization and its managers that has, inescapable, unavoidable, similarities to the relationship of an individual to the state. Your role, by virtue of the lack of choice as an employee takes on the appearance of servitude – especially when you have to be subordinated to the power of a governing body that disallows your earned civil rights. (3) The disequilibrium between similarly trained people has led many to challenge the legitimacy of the system itself. Few inherent distinctions exist between the preparation or qualifications of one person over another to justify disparities in treatment. (4) The existence of unrelenting abuse due to the imbalance of power and the disregard of individual rights in all industries and organizations of all sizes is causing an increasing number of people to question the legitimacy of the "system."

Not only is the system being questioned because of the abuse it showers on its members who have little or no recourse but the very ends it serves are being challenged. Comfort and convenience – the driving forces of the industrial era – showed great strides in improving the standard of living. The need for continuing material gain is becoming harder and harder to visualize. For the people asked to sacrifice for the system – no longer able to procure benefits for themselves – the accumulation of wealth for others while experiencing a declining sense of well-being, makes no sense.

None of these issues are currently being addressed in any meaningful way by the management establishment or academe. In part this is due to the misguided claim that management research is "value-free" in the scientific tradition. This mythological claim defies reason. But, to question the legitimacy of the system or the research establishment supportive of the system, is itself an act of treason.

DIFFERENT GAMES/DIFFERENT RULES

Business schools are inhabited by scholars seeking scientific answers to their questions. Applying science as it is known in the physical world has been their objective. They set a hypothesis, create constructs to identify and measure the variables under examination, collect data, use rigorous mathematical calculations, and proclaim probabilities – conclusions that often pass as "the truth." Finding a "truth" in this same way in business was an admirable but totally misguided objective. Finding "a truth" has doggedly eluded business researchers delving into the human affairs of management. In the realm of business, social variables are simply not uniform as is usually the case in the natural world.

Managers want proof that strategies, techniques and processes will work before adopting them. There is a façade of rationality and certainty in almost all business endeavors. Thus, it is not unusual for managers to want proof that any new technique or tool works. As we have seen, all tools work. Applying a tool successfully is a matter of personal ability and will; and this is hard for managers, who depend on "scientific findings," to grasp. But as the ladder of organizational behavior and the above distinction between social research and naturalistic research shows, certainty is not guaranteed but created in accordance with your ability and commitment. In fact, "truth" in the social sciences is often a matter of choice; simply a matter of what we believe.

Thus, while a single exception would invalidate a natural or physical "law" and replication of experimental conditions is seen as a basic requirement to verify almost anything among physical scientists, in social science that is almost never the case. In social science, correlations, probabilities and tendencies are the strongest conclusions that can be achieved. However, managers do not like them – even when they are found to reach "the .01 level of confidence" (the statistical equivalent of certainty). There are simply too many good exceptions to the rule.

So, while the natural world has, at least from the atomic level, fairly consistent properties, such conditions are virtually impossible to find in business and other social science arenas. Even after scholars reduce their hypotheses and variables to an apparently manageable few, whatever conclusions they draw are severely limited.

In the social realm, however, unlike in the scientific realm, one case proves what is possible. And, since humankind is capable of choice, of applying intelligence, of change and of volition – intentional action to meet expressed and unconscious needs and wants – creation of the possible is the goal. Agreement is the key. Your experience need not be universal to be valid. Your choices need not be replicated by all others. Your experience and choices need only satisfy the desires of a particular person or group. Arriving at agreement is a political not a scientific process. The beauty of this truth is that a single example proves the possible and it becomes the inspiration for others. Rather than requiring consistent and perpetual replication and uniformity, social experiments can be, and indeed must be, personalized. Managers and organizations that realize this and begin the process of creating their own solutions and approaches to their own problems and apply the tools described here in terms that make sense for them are successful. These managers and organizations customize and innovate as their needs require. It is because of innovation and customization that there are so many promising possibilities for the future. To do this we must awake from Jefferson's nightmare and dispel Hammurabi's curse!

Chapter Nine

A New Model for the Times: Emerging Wisdom

A Vision of the Future

THE NEW MENTAL model melds the efforts of management and labor, recognizing that all parties to a change effort, to new strategic directions, to interpersonal commitments, will take an appropriate role in determining the course of action. In doing this many of the pitfalls associated with management tools and the reasons for their becoming passing fads are eliminated. After all when collaboration occurs the way is cleared for sensible involvement. Mutual commitment to a course of action is then understood by all parties to be in their best interests.

That is not to say that every event, each decision, all actions will always be personally acceptable but the environment asks individuals to keep the collective interests in mind and to remember that while you may not get what you want this time, you will at other times. In either event the organization's success is in everyone's best interest. The horizon of commitment must extend beyond the present moment and you must be prepared to participate and give and take. You must understand that rights come with responsibilities. You must realize that everyone is needed to insure the organization's success.

When an understanding of an organization as the nexus of a large interested group of stakeholders can be conceptualized as a community the implications are profound.

THE ORGANIZATION AS POLITY

A polity is an organized society. Indeed, to this day, the legitimacy of any governing body is based on the extent to which it is representative of the will of the governed. Over the course of history humankind has had a variety of governing bodies.

The nation-state, until recently, has been the most familiar determinant of our quality of life as a society. We have seen, however, that government's role is declining while the role of the corporation in general and all workplaces, in particular, are becoming the arbiters of our quality of life and our standard of living. Next to our own families, it is within the workplace that issues most dear to us originate.

It may not seem more than "making a living" when we go to work each morning but our relationship to the workplace is consuming more hours and mental energy than any other relationship in our lives, including our families. The workplace has clearly become the center of our lives whether it is because of the social relations we develop with colleagues in fulfilling our responsibilities, the financial lifeline it establishes for us, or because of its influence on our self-concept and our identity as a productive member of the larger culture.

The hours we put in are not detached from other aspects of life. They are integral. We cannot compartmentalize the workplace experience even if we do not take work home with us. Work is integral to who we are and the life we lead. As such, the workplace is becoming the new polity simply because it influences us deeply. It is because of this that the next great awakening regarding the role we play in determining our affairs will focus on the relationship we have to our workplace.

While this is obvious to a growing number of people, this is no small consciousness raising exercise. We have become so accustomed to going to work and submitting to the will of others, following orders, being obedient, that seeing the workplace as a polity or community is difficult. To do so requires our attentiveness and participation in workplace governance and for many people this comes as a shock, an unwanted demand, and an unwelcome responsibility.

Most non-union and middle management workers have been quite content to ignore the larger issues of our organizational lives. We trusted in the powers that be and we did not fully grasp the importance of our role in the organization's success. Therefore, we limited our responsibility to trading our time and our effort for a paycheck.

This is a luxury we can no longer afford since the very survival of our workplace is so important to us. Paternalism is dead and because it is dead no one is looking after us anymore. Unions do not seem to be taking up the cause. Loyalty to country, state and town has vaporized and their efforts to build community have been passed on to volunteer groups and enlightened corporations. If we do not look after our interests no one else will. It is that simple.

In order to fulfill our new responsibilities to ourselves we need a seat at the table where decisions are made. We need to develop a real partnership with each person in the organization. We need to be considered and act as citizens of the workplace. And we need to jointly determine how best to secure our common futures. Again, to many people this seems obvious and to others either an unnecessary or bothersome chore for which they have no inclination. This is, of course, until it is too late. Until their jobs are threatened or lost. Then it IS too late. Involvement at that time will be a desperate act to hold on to the past and not a solid overture to fully participate in creating a bright future.

The problem with management tools and techniques is their inherent one-sidedness. We call it management but by any name it is still a set of methodologies used by managers to make and implement decisions regarding all organizational citizens for the benefit of owners and top executives. Management tools and techniques fail for the same reasons that undemocratic governments fail – they do not derive their legitimacy or their power from the governed. As the new definition of management and organization (mentioned later) gets widespread acceptance, legitimacy will be restored and collaborative, accountable systems will prevent the kind of abuses and failures managers are now experiencing. With collaboration and accountability to the new workplace citizenry, these tools and techniques will be used effectively, as intended.

A CHALLENGE TO CORPORATE LEGITIMACY

While the tools and techniques of management thinking have been created to help organizations improve themselves and better serve their stakeholders, there is a growing concern, at a fundamental level, that all is not well with the current system. Many people are seriously questioning the legitimacy of the corporate world, particularly its treatment of employees and consumers. (The new paradigm of business discussed at length in Part II will delve into the specifics of this challenge.) But the challenge is still made with the intention of improving the system and, therefore, most changes really do not reflect a new paradigm at all. Most of the new paradigm is about developing an environmental consciousness and acting "socially responsible." They simply seek greater corporate sensitivity to the larger public.

But a growing number of people, including many present and former corporate employees, are questioning the system itself. And for one good reason. Corporations have clearly grown beyond the control of the state. They are superseding the state in terms of their effect on the quality of life on the planet and it is their power that is transforming our very notion of appropriate forms of societal influence and governance. It is not only what they do to the environment and local cultures and economies wherever they go, however, that is sufficient reason to be concerned. What is not so readily understood is how corporations represent a totalitarian governance structure for the overwhelming number of people who must work for a living. And in this regard they exercise a much larger influence over our lives than we would like to admit. And, it is a larger influence over our lives than we would like to accept.

Human systems of governance evolved from families to tribes, then villages, towns, city-states, nations and nation-states. Now we are entering a new era of corporatism which means that large global corporations are superseding nations as the loci of our well-being. To work for any organization today is to be beholden to them; unless, of course, we have the option of not working. The organization provides our livelihood through wages. In complying with unquestioned obedience to continue in its employ we lose control, we remain without influence over our worklives and are ultimately deprived of our right to life, liberty and the pursuit of happiness. Though there are many employers, one corporation today is much like another. There is simply no real choice. One place may be more benevolent than another but in all cases we surrender ourselves to the wishes of managers and owners in return for a paycheck upon which our ability to survive is determined. For some, questioning the validity of this form of influence, is a shocking reminder of the dark ages when people traded their freedom for protection by lords and knights. And as in the dark ages the deal is spurious; labor today is sacrificed for profits much like the serfs lost their protection and were sacrificed in territorial and religious wars.

Though organizations have such widespread influence over our lives, employees have virtually no say in the governance or future direction of the organization. Why? Because we have been conditioned to believe that corporations are the instruments of "investors" and employees are merely hired hands.

FROM PAIN TO CHANGE

There is a pervasive though amorphous pain and anger seeping throughout the worker culture. For the most part it seems government, immigrants, ethnic, and racial minorities are the targets. But as syndicated columnist Barbara Ehrenreich said:

> The root cause of the anger is economic insecurity. That's the no brain analysis. Once you get past the silly stuff, you see that ours is no longer a political culture in which you can criticize employers, much less 'big business.' We have a political culture in which the happy myth is that employers are philanthropists because they've given you a job – not that you give them labor power and don't get paid enough for it, but that they have given you a job.
>
> So there is no way you can say, "My life is miserable and it's because of corporation X or the store down the street." You say, "I don't have enough money to support my family on $25,000 a

year. What about this 15 to 20 percent that's going to the government, to a bunch of immigrants and welfare clients?" The great success of the right is to make the working class grovel with this constant feeling of scarcity. (Barbara Ehrenreich in "Just Calm Down: Dry Wit and Trenchant Wisdom from Barbara Ehrenreich", *Utne Reader*, May–June 1995, p. 71.)

And it is fear and a scarcity mental model that immobilizes us from considering the real causes of our malaise – an analysis that would bring us to question our way of life. While "progress" motivated earlier generations especially in their pursuit of comfort and convenience, the economic treadmill we have found ourselves upon is returning an almost indistinguishable increment that leaves people wondering if it is really worth the effort at all. Not everyone feels that way, of course. To members of the group who are committed to and see meaning in their lives, and measure their worth according to their service to the corporation, it is very serious. The president of Frito-Lays says "I wake up every morning thinking, 'I haven't sold one bag of Fritos yet.' " (Robert Frank, "Frito-Lay Devours Snack-Food Business", *The Wall Street Journal*, October 27, 1995, p. B1.) But more and more people are asking themselves "What is it all about?" and "Why am I giving myself to a corporation when its impact on my life and the world is so awful?"

"Progress" seemed to make sense. Indoor plumbing, washing machines, TVs, electric lights, etc., did seem to improve the standard of living. Interstate highways, jet travel, and polio vaccines made a difference. In today's world, however, the constant stress to squeeze more and more out of each day to add the next dollar to the bottom line is not clearly linked to our standard of living and certainly not to our quality of life.

Today, our real purchasing power is less than in 1975. When we look around us we see a ton of "stuff" but find ourselves on a spending treadmill that matches our work treadmill. Arguably neither is changing the quality of our lives. And we feel somewhat abused by the astronomically rich telling us to work hard, put in endless overtime because if we do not, corporate officers try to motivate us by telling us we do not deserve, and will not get, what they have. Put simply, the "global competition" bogeyman will get us.

And just what is the system getting us? Well, remember

Michael Eisner's 1992 compensation and benefits totaling $203 million? The system believes this makes sense but resists raising the minimum wage because that may cause inflation! The poverty line for an individual in 1992 was set at $7,143. That equals $3.57 an hour. At that rate Michael Eisner's one year financial take would support 14,209 people at double the poverty line. Put another way, Eisner's take for 1992 was almost equal to the gross national product of Grenada, the small Caribbean nation the United States invaded in the early 1980s.

On October 26, 1995, at a garment district rally in New York City for the American Federation of Labor and the Congress Industrial Organizations (AFL-CIO) at which Secretary of Labor Robert Reich spoke, Juanita Grillo "emerged from one clothing shop, saying she had just been replaced in her $6-an-hour job by a worker willing to [do her job] for $4.50 an hour. 'It's disgusting,' she said, shaking her head." (Asra Q. Nomani, "AFL-CIO Sweeney Kicks Off Tenure in Rally After Rousing Speech by Reich", *The Wall Street Journal*, October 27, 1995, p. 2.)

So, a real paradigm shift requires more than a fine tuning of the system. It requires a reconceptualization much like American founders reconceptualized their role in governing their own affairs. It requires a formal deliberate rethinking of the role of the corporation in our lives, as early Americans rethought the legitimacy of a monarchy and created the first nation based on a constitution with an elected head of state. They proclaimed for all the world to hear that the individual has a right to determine his own affairs and be represented, or participate directly, in the governance of the state. Likewise, the time has come for us to re-examine workers' role in the governance of the workplace but are used by people stuck in the old way of thinking. Most of the techniques presuppose a new mindset more amenable to the postindustrial paradigm and a democratic ethos in the workplace. When applied in a hospitable environment their chance of success is greater than when applied to a conventional environment where their contributions will be only marginal at best.

TOWARD A NEW PARADIGM?

"As 'the Earth goes around the sun' became the somewhat inadequate summary of the Copernican revolution, so 'consciousness as causal reality' is that of the 'second Copernican revolution.'" (Willis Harman, *Global Mind Change*, New York: Warner, 1990, p. 14.) This recognition of consciousness as a causal reality is inclusive of the unconscious; the point is that the human mind creates its own reality. Along with this understanding is the acceptance of the notion of volition – giving direction to our energies. If we create ideas important to ourselves, believe in our own efficacy and decide to follow a path to realize that which we desire, we stand a chance to create a fulfilling reality. This new thinking has profound implications for the way we are in the world. Our state of being is thus a creative act and we can make our collective world reflect our aspirations. And though there will inevitably be conflicts and disagreements among people, the new role of management is to facilitate the design of an acceptable common future.

Willis Harman, former professor at Stanford University and now President of the Institute of Noetic Sciences, has said regarding the onset of the French, American and Russian Revolutions, that:

> . . . there have rather consistently been certain advance indications that appeared one to three decades before the major change became apparent. These lead indicators included:
>
> • Alienation, purposelessness, lowered sense of community
>
> • Increased rate of mental disorders, violent crime, social disruptions, use of police to control behavior
>
> • Increased public acceptance of hedonistic behavior (particularly sexual), of symbols of degradation, of lax public morality
>
> • Heightened interest in non-institutionalized religious activities (e.g., cults, revivals, secret practices)
>
> • Signs of anxiety about the future, economic inflation (in some cases)

(Willis Harman, *An Incomplete Guide to the Future*, New York: Norton, 1979, p. 117.)

These indicators are intensifying now, but the rough contour of a new paradigm may afford the culture a way of transforming itself peacefully and with intention.

The new paradigm for business entails rescinding Hammurabi's curse and dismantling the unidirectional chain of command to replace it with a multidimensional nexus of relationships.

Greed alone is not a sustainable substitute for the urge to develop, to progress, to seek comfort and convenience, to extinguish the misery and hardship of a preindustrial society. To just have more of everything is also an artificial purpose when convenience, comfort and economic security have been achieved.

For the first time in the postindustrial revolution the vast majority of us have reached a plateau where the call for more does not seem necessary and in ecological terms is downright dangerous.

Deprivation is now more frequently a matter of perception than a physical or economic phenomenon. It is now for us a matter of will not the lack of means to create a satisfying and respectable place for everyone in our economy.

In terms of our workplaces, they too are able to demonstrate our aspirations and best practices but all too often remain sites of despair. There is an alternative. As the new paradigm continues to gain credibility and people freely imagine and design new workplaces, a transformation seems ever more likely.

A comparison of the industrial era paradigm with a postindustrial era paradigm is illustrated in Figure 9.1. (See also Chapter Seventeen for a more complete discussion of the shift.)

NEW AMERICAN WORKPLACE

A new paradigm would result in the transformation of work-roles, not just a system repair. Toward that end The Office of the American Workplace and the Association for Quality and Participation recommend twelve management strategies for creating successful organizations. Together they constitute partial elements of Paradigm 2, the postindustrial model:

- Worker empowerment
- Work teams
- Employee centered workplace policies
- Continuous innovation/improvement
- Customer and worker-driven quality

Figure 9.1 Archetypal Organizational Paradigms

Paradigm 1 Industrial Era Model We/Them	Paradigm 2 Postindustrial Model Us
Incremental responses to environment as determined by dominant coalition.	Choice: the community consciously, intentionally chooses its future and creates the necessary processes to attain it.
Strategy is decided by a few at the top and dictated to entire entity; serial short-term synthetic visions of a public relations nature.	Commitment to a vision jointly created forms the basis of a long-term strategy.
Responsibility in job holder according to either job description or results of delegated tasks.	Responsibility in each member according to tasks continuously determined in workflow process.
Accountability to your boss' sole criteria of performance; colleagues secondary.	Accountability to colleagues and others dependent on your performance.
Exclusivity; entire status and reward structure based on limiting access to benefits and decision-making centers.	Inclusivity; each member is a citizen of the workplace community and entitled to participate in the management of the community on an equal basis.
Decisions made by the few closest to the top without necessarily consulting with others.	Representative or direct participation in all decision making.
Gain sharing for management; pain sharing for everyone else.	Gain/pain sharing by everyone.
No individual rights beyond employment contract and those legally mandated.	Extensive individual rights with individual responsibilities as members of a workplace community.
People as means to others' ends; a necessary evil; a cost to the system.	People as ends in themselves; a valuable asset; increases the economic value and the quality of worklife of the community.
Financial criteria the only valid measures of the organization.	Multiple organizational outcomes validated; financial health an assumed requirement but social responsibilities of being part of a larger community acknowledged and individual satisfaction of each member a legitimate goal.

- Tools for competitiveness
    statistical process control
    benchmarking
- Flexible production processes
- New worker skills
    business
    financial
    negotiating
    creative problem solving
    self-motivation
- Worker management cooperation
- Innovative compensation plans
    skill attainment
    performance rewards
    quality and teamwork measures
- External partnerships
    strategic alliances
- High involvement leadership

("Improve Ability to Compete, at New American Workplace Conference", *AQP Report*, October/November 1994, p. 16.)

A New Paradigm Means a New Definition of Organization

One profound implication of the new paradigm is a new definition of management and leadership. It would stimulate the metamorphosis of organizations into communities because we would no longer be passive components in a bureaucratic world. We would become active members in dynamic, intentional workplaces.

In turn, the very idea of an organization will be reconceptualized as inclusive of all who are part of it, and eventually will include all its stakeholders in a meaningful role in the determination of the organization's future.

Ultimately, we cannot think of total quality in the products we produce or the services we provide without thinking of the total quality of our worklives and the relationships that are the fundamental building blocks of the workplace and marketplace. Many more people besides the "investors" and managers have an important stake in the success of the organization and will demand a larger role to play in its governance.

A NEW PARADIGM MEANS A NEW DEFINITION OF MANAGEMENT

Management and leadership used to be defined as "working with and through people for organizational objectives." Now, leading edge organizations define management as "the act of relationship building in order to achieve mutual objectives for mutual gain." Max DePree, CEO of Herman Miller furniture makers, said, in terms of his managers and leaders building a covenantal relationship with employees:

> A covenantal relationship rests on shared commitment to ideas, to issues, to values, to goals, and to management processes. Words such as love, warmth, and personal chemistry are certainly pertinent. Covenantal relationships are open to influence. They fill deep needs and they enable work to have meaning and to be fulfilling. Covenantal relationships reflect unity and grace and poise. They are an expression of the sacred nature of relationships. (Max DePree, *Leadership is An Art*, New York: Doubleday, 1989, p. 51.)

AN END TO EMPLOYEE AS PEASANT . . . THE BEGINNING OF EMPLOYEE AS CONSTITUENT

Workers want – indeed need – the organization to succeed. And management demonstrates its unwillingness to invite labor into the process of making it happen and sharing in the rewards. Most managers are not consulting labor and are not accountable to labor.

Massive numbers of like-minded people are demanding that organizational governance and social responsibility, the renewal of a sense of community, and the formation of a vision of a satisfying future be placed high on the organizational agenda.

Our ability to control our organizational lives needs to be perceived as real and our willingness to intentionally and consciously create our common future must be stimulated and supported as the next century arrives and unfolds. We need to do this as surely as the founding fathers and the post-revolutionary citizens of the original thirteen states needed to focus their attention on nation-building. And, although society is an evolving system, today the signs are present that unless we take some deliberate action to adjust course, very destructive forces may propel us into a position where our choice in the matter is removed. Events are already eliciting a reflexive, reactive stance instead of a proactive stance.

SYSTEM FIVE

In order to align organizations to accommodate our new knowledge and the emergent postindustrial Paradigm 2, we must penetrate the self-imposed invisible wall at the edge of System Four and create System Five. Like the first time you tried something physically risky, or any significant personal challenge, many people will find moving into System Five a frightful experience – especially if they believe that the four systems of management truly constitute the entire realm of what is possible. But once the step is taken, no matter how tentative, you will find the fears quickly dispelled; you may even become exhilarated and sense amazing new possibilities not unlike when you fall in love albeit perhaps without the romantic overtones.

System Five is the organizational representation of the new requirements of the postindustrial paradigm. This also becomes a self-reinforcing process when the societal paradigm shift facilitates the organizational changes required for the full development of System Five.

System Five builds community. This is the first step in transcending the organizational imperative and the industrial era paradigm. Though you could point to the progress in moving from System One to System Four, the fact remains that the individual is not in control of his or her own destiny. Though it appears to be a more humane system, System Four is still a bifurcation between the owners and managers on the one hand, and, on the other, the employee who will always remain dependent, "subordinate", and controlled.

The shift through the paradigmatic membrane at the limit of System Four into System Five necessitates a conceptual leap to develop a new mental construct. All employees will become organizational members and play a role in creating meaning for themselves in the workplace and for the organization as a whole. Eventually, written codes such as a constitution or by-laws will form the basis for a new social contract and will be developed by each organization. The worldwide democracy movement is the leading edge of this aspect of the transformation of our organizations.

COMMUNITY: NEW APPLICATIONS FOR AN ANCIENT IDEA

The workplace as a community is not just another metaphor for organizations. This is a fundamental shift in the nature of what an organization is, who it serves and how it is governed.

Community is caring. Caring about your work, your colleagues, the standing of the organization in the marketplace and its success. It is also about knowing the organization will consider you in each of its decisions and that you have a stake in the outcome of those decisions. All will gain and suffer accordingly. It is experiencing a sense of belonging and wanting to contribute. It is about taking your responsibilities seriously and making an effort to improve your ability to contribute and participate. It is about thinking and being fully present in your experience of the organization.

And it is a context, an environment, wherein participants sense that they belong, are an integral part of the organization – as if a citizen of the workplace – with both a right to be there, and a desire to be there and with a felt need to contribute.

7Ps

In building community in the workplace there are seven key factors to attend to that are easily remembered as the 7Ps.

1. The enterprise is committed to making a product or providing a service that is financially rewarded in the marketplace. Thus, the organization can survive. The organization is **profitable**.

2. There is a shared consciousness that **productivity**, innovation, customer satisfaction and other business functions of the organization must be fulfilled. Everyone clearly sees the link between their behavior and the functioning of the organization.

3. The organization operates in a way that encourages the personal development of each member. Training programs, frequent feedback and fearless communication between workpartners is valued and practiced.

4. The organization, as a nexus of social behavior, creates a sense of place as if the organization is a neighborhood or small town. There is a felt connection among workpartners as they share in the experience of the organization.

5. Everyone in the organization is encouraged to share a sense of purpose; to know and appreciate the contributions they make to the organization, others make to them and the contributions the organization makes to society.

6. There is a real **p**artnership in the process of accomplishing the goals of the organization which overcomes the arbitrary divisions that separate management and labor, department from department and person from person. A sense of partnership is inherent and the feeling of inclusion in the organization is the norm. These, in part, are conveyed with equitable rewards and perhaps an opportunity for real financial ownership.

7. Finally, there is also a felt **p**sychological ownership of the organization's outcomes that result, in part, from personal commitment. This is due to a strong sense of place and purpose but also because each person shares in the financial results of the organization. Each person is a part of a pain- and gain-sharing program based on the organization's performance in the marketplace. They have a stake in the organization beyond simply keeping their jobs.

These principles contribute to the creation of workplace community and they are embedded in the management literature as creating the conditions under which people-management tools and techniques work best.

Chapter Ten

APPLYING THE WISDOM IN A GLOBAL CONTEXT

HAVING COME THIS far you might wonder: does effective managerial behavior vary according to specific cultural contingencies? You might ask, "How does this apply to me in Singapore or Malaysia or China or England or India or Australia or Kenya or Russia or France?"

I believe the wisdom and wishful thinking reported here applies in all commercial, governmental, and non-profit organizational settings. My personal experience as an employee in a Japanese organization, a predominantly Malay organization, a Singaporean organization and an Australian organization have led me to this conclusion. I would not say, however, that the wisdom would be applied in the same way in each of these settings. Rather, each organization demonstrated its unique way of applying the wisdom; while the particular means varied somewhat, the ends were remarkably the same.

I was particularly struck with each organization's pursuit of excellence; each wanted to be effective, to be noted for its achievements. Each leader, though to varying degrees, strove to epitomize success by setting an example for others and by striving to make the entire organization more efficient by focusing each person's consciousness on their contribution to the work to be done. In addition, each colleague seemed determined to fit in and to become mindful of the purposes of the organization. In return, each wanted to feel they were a part of something important, that they served a purpose beyond themselves and they were recognized for their role in the organization's success.

Still, we must ask for more evidence. Is there a basis for the belief that the principles reported here are relevant to other cultures? How would the wisdom be applied in Asia, for example? Of course, the application of the wisdom will succeed when it reflects the realities of the organizational culture in which it is being applied. That is as true within a nation's borders as it is in diverse national settings.

There are two influences at work within organizations everywhere that promise to influence the spread of the wisdom reported here. First, these insights are universally compatible; and, second, the insights have been found effective in furthering the organizational imperative.

UNIVERSALITY: THE PRIMARY FORCE FOR ADOPTION

Upon close examination, we discover something rather extraordinary about the research. It validates ancient truths. We find that the underlying principles themselves are virtually as old as the written word, and that ancient civilizations codified these concepts eons ago.

> It is written in the book of instruction by Ptah-Hotep, an Egyptian Pharaoh, to his offspring, as early as 2700 BC, that: If thou art a leader commanding the affairs of the multitude, seek out for thyself every beneficial deed . . . . Truth is great, and its effectiveness is lasting . . . . If thou art one to whom petition is made, be calm as thou listenest to what the petitioner has to say. Do not rebuff him before he has said that for which he came . . . . (John A. Wilson, *The Culture of Ancient Egypt*, Chicago: University of Chicago Press, 1951, p. 84.)

In another manuscript of instruction from ancient Egypt, it is written, "Proclaim thy business without concealment . . . . One ought to say plainly what one knoweth and what one knoweth not" (adapted from A. Erman, *The Literature of the Ancient Egyptians*, trans. Alward M. Blackman, New York: E.P. Dutton and Co., 1927, p. 55).

Sun Tzu, writing in *The Art of War* around 500 BC offers words of wisdom as valid in the West today as in his homeland, ancient China: "If wise, a commander is able to recognize changing circumstances . . . . If sincere, his men will have no doubt of the certainty of rewards and punishments. If humane, he loves mankind, sympathizes with others and appreciates their industry and toil. If courageous, he gains victory . . . ." (Sun Tzu, *The Art of War*, trans., Samuel B. Griffith, New York: Oxford University Press, 1971, p. 65.)

In India, in the fourth century BC, Vishnugupta wrote Arthasastra, an inquiry into the act of leadership. Regarding the qualifications of a state officer, he wrote, the candidate for high office should be:

> . . . well trained in arts, possessed of foresight, wise, of strong memory, bold, eloquent, skillful, intelligent, possessed of enthusiasm, dignity and endurance, pure in character, affable, firm in loyal devotion, endowed with excellent conduct, strength, health and bravery, free from procrastination and fickle mindedness, affectionate and free from such qualities as excite hatred and enmity – these are the qualifications of a ministerial officer. (Vishnugupta, Arthasastra; trans. S. Shamasastry, Mysore, India: Sri Raghuveer Printing, 1956, p. 14.)

Islam, too has spoken for capable leadership. "The best leaders are those who love the people and are in turn loved by them . . . The rulers should defend and honor the property, the life and dignity of all their subjects irrespective of class or creed." (Syed Al Atas Hussain, *Siapa Yang Salah*, Singapore: Pustaka Nasional, 1973.)

Clearly the wisdom of modern management is the latest link in a long chain of insights first identified by the ancients and refined by each generation thereafter. They indeed are universal and timeless.

Today in modern Singapore we see a deliberate effort to reinvigorate the practice of ancient wisdom through the recent attempt to strengthen Confucian ethics in the schools. Perhaps more than any other single effort to identify and instill a set of ethical practices among the next generation of managers, Singapore is blending the ancient wisdom with contemporary managerial skills.

> There is a remarkable similarity between Confucian thought and modern humanistic philosophy. It is a belief system focused on the full realization of the human being. The cultivation of the self as a centre of relationships represents a continuous development, a total commitment and a holistic approach. It is in this sense, a process of education for the creation of an open-minded character which can relate meaningfully to an ever enlarging network of human relationships . . . This exploration requires communication. Therefore, communication is also a crucial concept in the Confucian ethical tradition, which is sometimes characterized as a philosophy of mutuality . . . In Confucian thought, then, relationships are not based on the one-dimensional imposition of ideas and power upon others but on the concepts of mutuality and reciprocity . . . To be qualified to influence others, the leadership must cultivate itself . . . (Tu Wei-Ming, *Confucian Ethics Today: The Singapore Challenge*, Singapore: Federal Publications, 1984, pp. 6–10.)

The principle of equifinality applies here. That is, while the results may be the same, the manner in which they are achieved may vary according to local sensitivities.

In their book *Managing in a Plural Society* (Singapore: Longman, 1990), Hamzah-Sendut, John Madsen, and Gregory Thong made the point that a manager must be open-minded, polite, show respect, and operate with the manners of local custom. And those qualities are means to an end. The responsibilities of management remain the same: to conserve resources, make a profit, provide a quality service or product, and to be efficient in the conduct of your business. In a sense the rest takes care of itself after establishing this foundation. Business is business.

Thus, many of what are becoming universal requirements for running competitive world-class organizations are really culture free – even though it also means individual behavior may need to change to accommodate new workplace demands. And as Singapore moves from a low wage manufacturing center to a high wage knowledge and service economy, for example, it relies on the ability of its people to make the transition – to, in effect, change aspects of their culture to align with the purposes of business.

Ballard and Kleiner believe necessary factors in a cultural understanding should include "ways of thinking; leadership and management style; employee motivation; body language; attitudes toward: humility, honesty, individualism, loyalty and power; communications styles and skills; and, expectation of treatment." Perhaps the most interesting aspect of their research was validating the difficulty of studying culture in the first place. Their inquiry focused on the requirements of managing a multi-cultural work force within the United States testifying to the existence of sizable variances and sub-cultures imbedded within a national culture. ("Understanding and Managing Foreign-Born and Minority Employees", *Leadership and Organization Development Journal*, Vol. 9, No. 4, pp. 22–24.)

Recent psychographic research demonstrates the existence of a panoply of lifestyles with a virtual endless array of significantly different and legitimate values and sub-cultures. Michael J. Weiss, for one, differentiated forty significantly different neighborhood types! (*The Clustering of America*, New York: Perennial Library, 1988.) Some organizations in California, USA, that employ a large work force representing the entire spectrum of skills from wage-labor to salaried micro-chip designers, report a virtual United Nations of races, religions, and cultures present in the workplace. Hewlett Packard reports its employees speak over seventy languages. This is indeed a universal phenomenon yet the wisdom, with modification to specific organizational circumstances, can be applied everywhere.

CONVERGING CULTURES: THE SECOND FORCE FOR ADOPTION

Negandhi's ("Management in the Third World", *Asia Pacific Journal of Management*, September 1983, pp. 15–29) often quoted convergence theory postulated a growing similarity in cultural and organizational aspects as nations similarly adopt industrial/postindustrial paradigms of economic and industrial organization.

Managers cannot resist fulfilling their fundamental purpose regardless of where they practice: live out the organizational imperative. This imperative requires the constant striving for efficiency and effectiveness while carefully husbanding resources. It imposes an extra-cultural business logic wherever organizations are located. Thus, while national differences exist, the tools and techniques reported here will be applied, in some fashion, everywhere; for, it is through using these tools that the organizational imperative is fulfilled.

With cultural convergence accelerated by the organizational imperative it seems that the ultimate arbiter of what practices are tolerated, encouraged or extinguished, is the "bottom line." Cultures are adapting to the requirements of technology and efficiency. And certainly many examples have demonstrated that where there is mutual gain, cultures have changed, "development" has taken place.

Global competition seems like a new force in contemporary affairs but business has thrived in a multinational environment since the Phoenicians established trade routes to the limits of the then known Indo-European world and the Chinese consolidated virtually all of East Asia.

CULTURE'S LAST STAND

In an era of global competition and computerization, organizational systems take on very similar characteristics in spite of the culture of origin. Once a nation begins the process of industrialization and attempts to follow in the footsteps of the now post-industrializing nations of the West and Japan, systems and cultures begin to converge. Though there are impressive differences between nations of the post-industrializing world, the behaviors of individuals and the structures they create to express their economic, political and cultural aspirations become very much alike.

In part, the organizational imperative has been responsible for this. The requirements of efficiency and competitiveness do constrain your choices. The collapse of communism in the Eastern block is the most dramatic recent example of how, in spite of ideology and the sheer force of those in power, the existence of competitive economic activities requires a compatible system of interpersonal behavior coupled with rational processes to facilitate the achievement of organizational goals.

Less dramatic but nevertheless widespread and equally significant, evidence exists that individuals seek and believe they require democratic forms of management to fully achieve organizational potential. In a leadership module presented by this author as part of a series of management development seminars over a ten-year period throughout Southeast Asia (Malaysia, Singapore, Indonesia), participants were asked questions regarding effective and ineffective leadership behaviors and the consequences of that behavior on subordinate attitudes and behavior.

Though the questions were designed to stimulate seminar discussion about the leadership role and to understand effectiveness within the local context, in every case participants believed that leaders should behave in a more open and participative fashion in order to inspire confidence and motivate employees. The participants believed that organizational effectiveness improves with participative leader behavior. Modern managers in organizations conscious of the competitive global situation are tending toward agreement on some of the fundamental methods for achieving high performing work groups. And broadly speaking that indicates an evolution toward democratic and participative systems. The tools and techniques described in this book are typical of the efforts made to increase participation, individual contributions and the creative input necessary to survive and prosper in the competitive marketplace.

Organizations evolve as technology, the demands of society, and the individual behavior of managers interact for the purpose of enabling organizations to become better competitors in the global marketplace and for the society to develop the quality of life desired of its people.

The requirements of management are the same in all cultures but cultural influences coupled with personality factors determine how a particular manager will fulfill his or her role and what behavior will be expected of the manager. Certainly, the cultural influences will determine how the tools and techniques will be used. But the ends will reflect the common wisdom.

The ruler must be righteous to enable the subject to become obedient. If the ruler is not righteous, the minister can offer criticism. If the ruler is dogmatic and authoritarian, the subject can revolt and choose a better one. *The Book of Mencius* considers revolution to be the right of the people.

– TU WEI-MING,
Confucian Ethics Today:
The Singapore Challenge,
Singapore: Federal Publications, 1984.

Chapter Eleven

WHERE DO WE
GO FROM HERE: AN
AGENDA FOR
MONDAY MORNING

BEFORE EMBARKING ON using any new tool or technique (or change program) consider:

- How/When it works
- Pros and cons
- What works
- What to avoid
- Results to expect
- Commitment needed to make it work
- Cost (money and time)
- Pitfalls to watch for
- When to skip it

Knowing now what makes these ideas work and why they sometimes fail there are basically three areas to assess before undertaking any major change effort or using any of the tools and techniques defined in Parts II and III.

CONDUCT A SELF-EXAMINATION

- Do you know if your values, skills, and interests meet the challenge to use the tool effectively?
- Do you know what you need to know and where to find out more to effectively introduce and champion the process throughout its use?
- Are you willing to learn and to change as circumstances warrant?

CONDUCT AN ORGANIZATIONAL AUDIT

- Is your boss and are your colleagues ready to consider new ideas?
- Do your colleagues and the organization have an interest in learning new techniques and exploring new possibilities?
- Is the culture of the organization supportive of change and inquiry?

CONDUCT A REVIEW OF THE PROBLEM AS A CATALYST TO YOUR ACTION

- Has the problem been adequately defined?
- Is everyone able and willing to do what is necessary to take responsibility for the outcome of the effort?
- Is the program geared to enable each person to assume a role in solving the problem?
- Is everyone represented in determining the desired outcomes?
- Can they personally commit to action from the position of being a volunteer?
- Are there incentives to change and is not changing dealt with fairly?

BUILDING COMMUNITY

Given the enormous energy and time that is spent dealing with management issues, individuals seem motivated to figure out a way of making the workplace effective for them. There are many things that you can do now without formal approval or a budget or yet another technique to "catch on." You might consider:

- Affirming one another
- Taking breaks together and talking about improving relationships between colleagues
- Creating a theme and program for your own pursuit of goals in terms of social, avocational, or career interests
- Using the bulletin board for notices to share common interests, affirmations, complaints, suggestions, and creative ideas
- Building real friendships at work through social clubs, teams, ride sharing, lunches . . .
- Redesigning your physical workspace to be more expressive of yourself and others
- Initiating informal gatherings/meetings/support groups/interest groups . . .
- Seeking out and implementing new skill training
- Sponsoring lunch-time speakers or activities for personal growth
- Urging a resolution of those things that bug people wherever you find them
- Starting a circular of events and interesting resources for the special interest groups
- Becoming a mediator to those in conflict
- Being a mentor to a "junior" person
- Sponsoring a think-in/be-in/do-in on a persistent work relevant problem
- Identifying abusive behaviors, policies and procedures then getting like-minded individuals to commit themselves to challenging the systemic or personal roots of the abuse and changing conditions that encourage abuse
- Speaking your mind tactfully and fearlessly on work issues and calling on others to do the same
- Developing cross-group activities such as sporting events involving everyone from different departments
- Reinforcing the idea that everyone is working for the organization; breaking down barriers between departments and specialists and spreading the idea of community
- Finding new ways of serving the community

- Establishing in-house volunteers for social/community problems where employees help other employees

You can make a difference. The tools and techniques listed in Parts II and III of this book can help but the key ingredient is your energy, your enthusiasm, and your commitment.

THE MOMENT OF TRUTH: AN ORGANIZATIONAL ASSESSMENT

Now is the time to see where you and your organization stand. So here is your "Moment of Truth."

Directions:
Think of your current job and organization. Circle the number you believe best represents the most accurate answer: 1 = Never to 10 = Always

(1) I can speak truthfully (without self-censorship) to anyone in the organization

    1   2   3   4   5   6   7   8   9   10

(2) I feel included in decisions affecting me

    1   2   3   4   5   6   7   8   9   10

(3) People in my workplace trust that new programs will be given an adequate trial

    1   2   3   4   5   6   7   8   9   10

(4) I am always involved in the planning process when it affects my work

    1   2   3   4   5   6   7   8   9   10

(5) People in my organization tell me when my work is not up to expectations

    1   2   3   4   5   6   7   8   9   10

(6) People at all levels in my organization have respect for each other

    1   2   3   4   5   6   7   8   9   10

(7) It is my experience that people in my organization involved in new programs put forth their best effort to make them work

    1   2   3   4   5   6   7   8   9   10

(8) People in my organization demonstrate personal resourcefulness

    1   2   3   4   5   6   7   8   9   10

(9) People in my organization are conscientious

    1   2   3   4   5   6   7   8   9   10

(10) People in my organization build strong interpersonal relationships

    1   2   3   4   5   6   7   8   9   10

(11) I can accurately describe the vision of my organization

    1   2   3   4   5   6   7   8   9   10

(12) My organization encourages new ways of thinking

    1   2   3   4   5   6   7   8   9   10

(13) In any change program in my organization, it is expected that all policies, procedures, programs, levels and personnel are open to scrutiny

    1   2   3   4   5   6   7   8   9   10

(14) People in my organization are committed to self-development

1   2   3   4   5   6   7   8   9   10

(15) People in my organization believe they make a constructive contribution

1   2   3   4   5   6   7   8   9   10

(16) People in my organization believe that their contributions are recognized

1   2   3   4   5   6   7   8   9   10

(17) The organization publicly takes responsibility for past mistakes before embarking on any new change program

1   2   3   4   5   6   7   8   9   10

(18) People in my organization develop and implement innovative ideas

1   2   3   4   5   6   7   8   9   10

(19) My organization provides ongoing communications training

1   2   3   4   5   6   7   8   9   10

(20) People in my organization hold informal discussions about improving our workplace

1   2   3   4   5   6   7   8   9   10

(21) People in my organization hold formal discussions about improving our workplace

1   2   3   4   5   6   7   8   9   10

(22) My organization provides time for exploring new work methods

1 2 3 4 5 6 7 8 9 10

(23) My organization provides time for thinking and planning

1 2 3 4 5 6 7 8 9 10

(24) I have a real sense of belonging in my organization

1 2 3 4 5 6 7 8 9 10

(25) My organization takes time to show its appreciation for my work

1 2 3 4 5 6 7 8 9 10

(26) I have a clear sense of what I am expected to do

1 2 3 4 5 6 7 8 9 10

(27) In my organization personal initiative is appreciated

1 2 3 4 5 6 7 8 9 10

(28) People in my organization are good listeners

1 2 3 4 5 6 7 8 9 10

(29) My work motivates me

1 2 3 4 5 6 7 8 9 10

(30) I really enjoy working with people in my organization

1 2 3 4 5 6 7 8 9 10

(31) I do not hesitate to tell people in my organization how I feel about my work

    1   2   3   4   5   6   7   8   9   10

(32) When people are angry about decisions at work they can discuss them with the appropriate people

    1   2   3   4   5   6   7   8   9   10

(33) I am proud of the organization I work for

    1   2   3   4   5   6   7   8   9   10

(34) Conflict is handled straightforwardly in my organization

    1   2   3   4   5   6   7   8   9   10

(35) People in the organization do not complain about internal politics

    1   2   3   4   5   6   7   8   9   10

(36) People in my organization volunteer to help their colleagues

    1   2   3   4   5   6   7   8   9   10

(37) My organization celebrates achievements

    1   2   3   4   5   6   7   8   9   10

(38) My organization is willing to change policies and procedures when appropriate

    1   2   3   4   5   6   7   8   9   10

(39) (You choose a statement you feel is important that was not addressed here. Write it below the numbers and circle your answer.)

    1   2   3   4   5   6   7   8   9   10

(40) (Choose another statement you feel is important that was not addressed here. Write it below the numbers and circle your answer.)

1   2   3   4   5   6   7   8   9   10

LOOKING BACK AT THE MOMENT OF TRUTH

Management is essentially a process to align human effort and resources with organizational goals. In order to succeed, each person in the organization must be able to communicate. That is the only way understanding and alignment can be achieved. It is the only way problems can be uncovered and resolved. It is the only way commitments can be made. And, it is the only way to coordinate and focus activity.

An ability to create an environment that fosters truth-telling, motivation to achieve the organization's objectives, and a desire to acquire and apply knowledge toward reaching the vision of the organization enhances human potential and organizational survival. It is that simple.

In looking over your responses to the forty questions you will immediately know if your organization has met the challenge of building a constructive, focused, and high performing environment. If it has not; that is, if the scores represent a mean of less than seven, it is unlikely that any new management tool will fully succeed. Thus, with scores below seven an organization must first take care of the fundamentals before it can confidently implement any new management program. Tabulate your results on Table 11.1.

Table 11.1

Record your answers below and compute your average.

1. _____   11. _____   21. _____   31. _____

2. _____   12. _____   22. _____   32. _____

3. _____   13. _____   23. _____   33. _____

4. _____   14. _____   24. _____   34. _____

5. _____   15. _____   25. _____   35. _____

6. _____   16. _____   26. _____   36. _____

7. _____   17. _____   27. _____   37. _____

8. _____   18. _____   28. _____   38. _____

9. _____   19. _____   29. _____   39. _____

10. _____   20. _____   30. _____   40. _____

Total Points _____
Divide by 40 = _____

(or 38 if you did not complete items 39–40)

Part II

THE BIG SEVEN TOOLS AND TECHNIQUES

With the great problems now facing human society, it seems increasingly important to find simple non-sectarian ways to work with ourselves and to share our understanding with others.

– CHOGYAM TRUNGPA, *SHAMBHALA*,
Sacred Path of The Warrior,
New York: Bantam, 1984.

THE BIG SEVEN TOOLS AND TECHNIQUES

- Self-managing Work Teams
  (also Cross-functional Teams)

- Quality
  (also Excellence)

- Reengineering

- System Thinking
  (also The Learning Organization)

- Japanese Management
  (More than 21 Individual Aspects)

- Toward Authentic Communication
  (Workout; 360-degree Evaluations;
  Diversity)

- The New Paradigm
  (Twelve Tools and Perspectives)

To create a winning team, you must temporarily set aside the fascination with game science and take a hard look at what's true for you.

What are your beliefs? This is a critical question. I would say your long-run success depends on the answer. Your beliefs are what make things happen. Beliefs come true. Inadequate beliefs are setups for inadequate performance. And the belief of the coach – the leader – become self-fulfilling.

– DON SHULA,
Coach of the Miami Dolphins,
the only coach in the National
Football League with an unbeaten
season and the coach holding the
record for lifetime wins in the NFL.
Everyone's A Coach.

Chapter Twelve

SELF-MANAGING WORK TEAMS

The old self-management was taking care of yourself while you followed the leader. The new self-management is acting toward the business at hand as if you had an ownership stake in it.

> – William Bridges, "The End of the Job",
> *Fortune,* September 19, 1994, p. 68.

What It is

SELF-MANAGING TEAMS are one of the most powerful new developments in work design. They are empowered groups of people able to set objectives, solve their own problems, make their own decisions, and respond to necessary demands in their environment as they see fit. Often cross-functional by nature, a self-managing team takes upon itself duties normally reserved for supervisors and foremen. Thus, they have been crucial in reducing the number of layers in the hierarchy and speeding up the responsiveness of the organization. Typically they are involved in scheduling, personnel selection, training and evaluation of team members, conflict resolution, and distributing rewards to their members.

Today, three years after the plant introduced work teams, 44-year-old Garcia seems more like one of its managers – rejecting products that don't meet quality standards and sending home excess workers if machines shut down. PepsiCo Inc.'s Frito-Lay unit, like a growing number of U.S. manufacturers, is slashing the number of middle managers while counting on teams of hourly workers such as Garcia to take charge of the daily decisions that can dramatically boost quality and reduce costs. Such worker empowerment can yield dramatic results. At the Lubbock plant the number of managers has dropped from 38 to 13 since 1990. The hourly work force, meanwhile, has grown by over 20%, to about 220. And despite less supervision, the plant has logged double digit cost cuts and seen its quality jump into the top six of Frito's 48 U.S. factories, from the bottom 20, since adopting teams. (Wendy Zellner, "Team Player: No More 'same-ol-same-ol'", *Business Week*, October 17, 1994, p. 95.)

"Reports from the field credit this work design innovation with many positive benefits, including higher productivity, better attendance, less turnover, and improvements in both product quality and the quality of working life for employees." (Frank Shipper, Charles C. Manz, "Employee Self-Management Without Formally Designated Teams: An Alternative Road to Empowerment", *Organizational Dynamics*, Winter 1992, p. 48.)

Becoming self-directed requires an understanding of the process: "Stages in its development include start-up, confusion, leader centeredness, tightly formed work teams and finally self-directed work teams." (Jack D. Orsburn, Linda Moran, Ed Musselwhite, and John H. Zenger, *Self-Directed Work Teams: The New American Challenge*, Burr Ridge, Illinois: Irwin Professional Books, 1990.)

The following stepping stones are important to achieve successful self-managing teams: (1) Realize that self-directed work teams are developed over a period of time. They should not be expected to be fully functional upon creation. (2) Awareness training should take place long before installation and should focus on establishing a shared understanding of what to expect, a shared identity, and the role each person will play. (3) Remember that each team is unique and should be provided customized training and attention to specific team related issues as needed. (4) Know that not everyone will welcome the empowerment effort and be ready to deal with that. (5) Create a policy that everyone must come to believe, and this must be true, that no one will suffer for improvements in productivity due to team effort. (Based on: Bob Hughes, "25 Stepping Stones for Self-directed Work Teams", *Training*, December 1991.)

Wisdom

"It would be difficult to find a single organization that has achieved significant, sustained improvement in productivity and quality without a parallel increase in the level of employee involvement in managing the enterprise." For Catalytica Associates, a chemical products manufacturer, self-managing teams are responsible for producing a segment of finished work. Their structure is flat which encourages most decision making in the business units themselves. (James A. Cusumano, "The Winning Team", *Chemical Marketing Reporter*, April 11, 1994, p. SR 11.)

According to Jack Orsburn, self-directed work teams improve quality, cost, scheduling, and decision making. (Nancy A. Hitchcock, "Can Self-Managed Teams Boost Your Bottom Line?", *Modern Materials Handling*, February 1993, p. 57.)

Be prepared. Each member of the team needs specific interpersonal skills, especially communications skills. Shared responsibility for the outcome is a must as is discretion over your specific area of work. Self-management ultimately means that each person will internalize the role and responsibilities of former supervisors and foremen. In doing so each person needs access to information and the skills needed to analyze, interpret, and use it.

Work teams should meet frequently, include time to get to know one another personally, take time to analyze past efforts and think about future tasks. The benefits of a self-managed work team include: (1) reduced absenteeism; (2) increased productivity; (3) increased employee satisfaction; (4) a multi-skilled work force; (5) increased flexibility in work practices; and (6) decreased need for managers. (Mahmoud Salem, Harold Lazarus, and Joseph Cullen, "Developing Self-Managing Teams: Structure and Performance", *Journal of Management Development*, Vol. II, No. 3, 1992, p. 24.)

If you are moving toward self-managed teams using a supervisor-leader model: There are several ways for supervisors to inspire and instill team responsibility. Some guidelines are: (1) The supervisor must be respected and trusted. (2) Team members should be aware that they are accountable to the team. (3) The team should be given as much freedom and authority as possible. (4) Managers should remember that building a dependable team takes time. (5) Team members should be kept busy and challenged in order to build a sense of shared responsibility. (6) The supervisors should stress accountability daily and praise team members when deserved. (7) The team should be allowed to form its own mission statements and set its own goals. (8) Supervisors should let team members discuss each other's job descriptions and, if necessary, adjust them. (9) The team should keep the big picture in mind. (10) Supervision of the team should be minimal. (11) It should be stressed that mistakes do happen. (Joseph D. O'Brian, "Making Work Teams Accountable", *Supervisory Management*, April 1993, p. 1.)

If work teams are to be successful, the following linking skills need to be in place: (1) active listening; (2) communication; (3) problem-solving and counseling; (4) team development; (5) work allocation; (6) team relationships; (7) delegation; (8) quality standards; (9) objective setting; (10) interface management; and (11) participative decision-making. (Charles Margerison and Dick McCann, *Journal of European Industrial Training*, Vol. 16, No. 2, 1992, p. i.)

Productivity is an on-going process when individuals are motivated and working on a conceptual or information-rich assignment. The creative mind, the incubator of thought, is always at work and when the conditions are right the focus on productive outcomes is not only possible but probable. This is blocked when individuals or the organization distract contributors by reducing their concerns to day-to-day politics, careerism and organizational survival. The damage is incalculable when human systems are so upset by the pettiness of the workplace that creative impulses are stifled.

According to Wolf Schmitt of Rubbermaid, self-managing teams are the keys to innovation and responsibility:

Construct a series of teams that replicate the management structure of the parent, like leaves on a plant. Give each team responsibility for creating, improving, and marketing a series of products. When a new [product] line springs up, put together a new team to handle it. And when a line runs out its lifespan, disband the team . . . According to Schmitt, "A plant will lose a piece of itself, but that doesn't kill it. Instead, the energy goes into another part of the plant." (Marshell Loeb, "How to Grow A New Product Every Day", *Fortune*, November 14, 1994, p. 269.) This gives teams a feeling of ownership and entrepreneurship, and allows the company to get into and out of businesses in a hurry.

The informal, non-bureaucratic, low-overhead style that characterized W.L. Gore & Associates at its founding has stuck – even though the firm now has over 5,000 employees and is rapidly approaching $1 billion in sales. Lines of communication are direct – person-to-person – with no intermediary. There is no fixed or assigned authority. There are sponsors, not bosses. Natural leadership is defined by sponsorship. Objectives are set by those who must 'make them happen.' Tasks and functions are organized through committee. This is the basis of what they call the lattice organization. (Frank Shipper, Charles C. Manz, "Employee Self-Management Without Formally Designated Teams: An Alternative Road to Empowerment", *Organizational Dynamics, Winter* 1992, pp. 50–54.)

Inside the Baltimore cardboard-box plant in Chesapeake Packaging Co., a subsidiary of Chesapeake Corp., based in Richmond, VA, are eight separate 'companies' created by plant manager Bob Argabright. The companies correspond to the departments of any similar plant. Unlike departments, those companies choose their own leaders, do their own hiring, and determine their own work processes. They take responsibility for budgets, production, and quality levels. They deal with their own customers, internal and external. The Baltimore plant was losing money when Argabright took it over, in 1988. It turned a small profit in 1989, doubled that profit in 1990 and again in 1991, and saw profits rise 60% last year (1992), all while sales remained flat. (John Case, "A Company of Businesspeople", *Inc.*, April 1993, p. 79.)

Wishful Thinking

A survey of 200 people who experienced self-managed work teams found that among those that failed or faltered, five themes emerged: (1) employee mistrust of management's motives; (2) a lack of clarity of what is expected; (3) resistance; (4) management's lack of participative skills; and (5) lack of top management commitment. These obstacles are intertwined. If managers lack participative skills, employee trust tends to decline. If people do not know what is expected, they tend to resist. If managers are not inclined toward participation, they will lack commitment. (Darcy Hitchcock, "Overcoming the Top Ten Team Stoppers", Journal for Quality and Participation, December 1992, p. 42.)

The time it takes to make decisions often seems excessive when a team grapples with the issues. Some think it needlessly complicates the decision-making process. Failure is also due to insufficient training, management's veto of team decisions, out-of-sync compensation and reward systems, lack of praise and continued support.

> Companies generally make six common mistakes when developing and training teams: (1) confusing 'getting to know one another' with skill building; (2) offering sensitivity training instead of behavioral skills training; (3) confusing the acquisition of knowledge with the acquisition of skills; (4) trying to get training done fast or cheap; (5) doing the wrong things at the wrong time; and (6) purchasing ineffective training programs that look or sound good but do not produce behavioral changes. (William C. Byham, "Lessons From the Little League", *Across the Board*, March 1992, p. 52.)

"Some individuals never get comfortable with the skills needed in a team environment such as open communication, self-correction, conflict management, and problem solving." This is partly due to the continuing emphasis on individual performance and rewards. (Gail B. Combs, "Take Steps to Solve Dilemma of Team Misfits", *HR Magazine*, May 1994, p. 128.)

One of the most difficult roadblocks may be cultural. "Americans raised to function as individuals, to respect and accept authority, and to expect increased wages based on seniority, do not easily adjust to the team concept and can hinder a team's effectiveness" (Shari Caudron, "Teamwork Takes Work", Personnel Journal, February 1994, p. 41).

Commitment Needed to Make It Work

In addition to the time spent on task, self-managing teams

require a great deal of coaching, skill building refresher courses and time to process issues that arise in the course of their work. Initially this will disturb managers and employees alike because of the seemingly endless waste of time and the morass of issues that can emerge. However, with coaching and facilitation skills, the manager can help the teams through this difficult stage and see that they get the proper footing for self-development. Later, as the start-up difficulties are reduced time will be saved in several ways: first because new routines will become more efficient and second, by continuously working with one another team members will come to learn process short cuts and understand each other's talents and limitations and how to best utilize them given the responsibilities they share.

Management support is critical. "In a study of 4,500 teams in more than 500 organizations, Wilson Learning Corp. determined that organizations' existing infrastructure, policies, and procedures often pose significant threat to work teams' success." (Erica Gordon Sorohan, "Managing Teams", *Training and Development*, April 1994, p. 14.) Thus, the environment must be prepared to accept the new emphasis on teams and training in interpersonal and group management skills must be provided to overcome inevitable conflicts and bottlenecks. Remember, the organization can choose its employees and seek out those who can function in this kind of environment but policies and structures must also be consistent with the objective of having teams. Where employees are not immediately ready, training can go a long way in overcoming both your inability to work in a self-managing environment and your anxiety of doing so.

Exemplars

Industry Week's 1993 awards for best plants recognized Johnson & Johnson Medical, Inc., and Unisys Government Systems, two among a total of 25 plants, all of whom: put a major emphasis on employee empowerment, the use of work teams, and continuous improvement programs. In addition, 96% of the award recipients rely heavily on TQM, just-in-time/continuous-flow manufacturing, supplier partnerships, customer satisfaction programs, employee cross-training, use of cross-functional teams, inventory reduction strategies, and efforts to ensure delivery dependability. Most of the finalists have launched self-directed work teams in a major way. (John H. Sheridan, "How Do You Stack Up?", *Industry Week*, February 21, 1994, p. 53.)

Others (An Infinitesimal Sampling)

Displaymasters • Cablec Utility Cable, Yonkers, New York • Gates Rubber (Siloam Springs, AZ) has empowered self-directed work teams resulting in reduced lead times, improved quality, and reduced work-in-process by 300% • GTE Telephone Operations-West Area • Motorola Satellite Communications Division • W.L. Gore & Associates

CROSS-FUNCTIONAL TEAMS
(One method of establishing boundarylessness)

Eighty-six percent of 500 companies in a *Training* magazine survey reported using cross-functional teams.

– *Training*, May 1994.

What It is

"According to Jack Welch, the boundaryless organization is where the barriers of hierarchy, function, and geography dissolve, and cross-functional teams are empowered to act quickly and in partnership with customers and suppliers." ("Alfred Sloan, Move Over", *Chief Executive*, July/August 1993, p. 36.)

Cross-functional teams are teams composed of individuals from different departments or from within a department that represents a variety of functional specialties. They are usually brought together due to a problem that is interdepartmental or interdisciplinary and often as a task force to solve product development issues or to address unique customer needs. Self-managing teams are frequently cross-functional by design.

Two of the most popular uses of cross-functional teams are for fast customer response and fast product innovation because they bring together individuals from all relevant organizational functions to focus on specific issues.

One of the first successes of the cross-functional teams at Thermos was the electric grill. It proved exceptionally motivating without the need for an entirely new compensation system. As one team member and director of R&D said, "Our reward is that the team owns the project from beginning to end, and that gives us a sense of pride. The real reward is a new product that gets up and flies." (Brian Dumaine, "Payoff From The New Management", *Fortune*, December 13, 1993, p. 103.)

Wisdom

> *Training's* 1992 'Industry Report' found that 8 out of 10 US organizations with 100 or more employees have assigned people to some working group identified as a team. In the largest organizations, those with 10,000 or more people, the figure is closer to 90% . . . In the survey, 45% of all employees who are members of any team belong to a permanent work team. Thirty percent are assigned to temporary project teams and 18% are members of long-term cross-functional teams. However, only 6 out of 10 respondents say that work teams have improved management's morale, and one out of 10 say that workers or managers have become disillusioned with the team concept. While the presence or absence of cross-functioning self-managing teams does not explain disenchantment in most companies, it does have an across-the-board effect on other attitudes. [Companies] with self-directed teams were significantly more likely than those without to report that teams have increased profits, improved customer service, and boosted morale of both employees and managers. (Jack Gordon, "Work Teams: How Far Have They Come?", *Training*, October 1992, p. 59.)

Cross-functional teams foster creativity, shorten decision-making time, increase the sensitivity to other's constraints, prove effective even at a distance through groupware and teleconferencing, and focus on adding value to specific interdependent goals.

> For Honeywell, Commercial Flight Systems, it is important to link people horizontally by process rather than function. People whose disciplines range from production to crafting to procurement to inspection are actually seated in places that are adjacent to one another . . . The objective of co-location is to wipe out the old 'this is my department – that is your department' mentality. Members of these teams see themselves working for the team not the department they ostensibly come from. (Tracy E. Benson, "A Braver New World?", *Industry Week*, August 3, 1992, p. 48.)

Team members must be able to think and speak fearlessly and to engage in disputes over ideas, strategies and methods with the purpose of discovering the best and most suitable approaches to meeting their needs. Learning to disagree without anger or resentment is the norm.

"To improve teamwork, four conditions should be present: (1) shared targets, (2) quality relationships, (3) a sense of pulling together, (4) balanced leadership." These factors work best when imbedded in a sense of organizational direction and purpose. (Kenneth Stott, and Allan Walker, "Ruining or Developing Teamwork – Take Your Choice", *Practicing Manager*, October 1992, pp. 25–27.)

Imagine project teams that attract people because of the specific skills needed to achieve the team's goal and draw them from anywhere in the company. Imagine further that these teams will have a rotating leadership function determining leaders according to the problems being faced at the moment. Then imagine a collection of teams transcending companies – even countries that form a suprateam of representatives from participating companies and all of this to accomplish a single project. With the achievement of the objective the teams disband. They reform as needed when new tasks arise. This is how partnerships in a joint venture are beginning to operate. Each project sponsor handled the facilitation and logistics when the tasks at hand involve them. When project sponsorship changes, facilitation and logistics is handled by a new team at a new location. This is roughly the way Motorola's Satellite Communications Division handled its Iridium Project. It is also the way that international cooperation has been conducted around various treaties linking telecommunications, postal, and transportation systems.

The key? No impermeable boundaries to limit the achievement of the project.

In order to improve its technological process, the Chemicals Division of J.M. Huber Corp. integrated its technology, marketing, and manufacturing functions by establishing cross-functional teams that work directly with external customers . . . The division follows such basic principles as: (1) flat organization, (2) technology ownership, (3) reward, (4) joint research programs and partnerships, and (5) entrepreneurship. Their primary focus seems to be innovation and customer response. (Satish K. Wason, and Sushil K. Bhalla, "Managing the Technological Process", *Quality Progress*, January 1994, p. 81.)

Perhaps for shear imagery, Eastman Chemical deserves the prize. The organization chart is now called the pizza chart because it looks like a pizza with pepperoni on it. Each pepperoni typically represents a cross-functional team responsible for managing a business, a geographic area, a function or a core competence in a specific technology or area. (John A. Byrne, "Congratulations. You're Moving to A New Pepperoni", *Business Week*, December 20, 1993, p. 80.)

Chubb LifeAmerica uses cross-functional teams to provide regional marketing support, product development and information systems. "The benefits of such teams include increased productivity, the shifting of staff to support growth, improved customer service, increased employee morale, increased flexibility, and the creation of a learning organization." (Martin Leshner, and Anne Browne, "Increasing Efficiency Through Cross Training", *Best's Review*, December 1993, p. 39.) In order to achieve the goals of cross-functional teams individuals must be ready to think in terms of team performance, not just personal performance; the old rules about the way "it's supposed to be" need to be revised or discarded altogether.

"Cross-functional teams can greatly facilitate the successful implementation of projects when they identify superordinate goals, provide accessibility to its stakeholders, have physical proximity to one another and operating rules and understandings." Cross-functional cooperation is also a significant predictor of both task achievement and high morale. (Mary Beth Pinto, Jeffrey K. Pinto and John E. Prescott, "Antecedents and Consequences of Project Team Cross-Functional Cooperation", *Management Science*, October 1993, p. 1281.)

In health care cross-functional teams are especially useful in providing what the Lutheran Hospital calls a seamless continuum of patient care. From first contact to last, all services focus on patient care in a way that resembles a movie instead of a series of snapshots.

"Concerns to be addressed if team usage is to be beneficial to the firm include: (1) member communication; (2) member authority; (3) team authority; (4) intra-team decision making; and (5) inter-team authority responsibility relationship." (John W. Henke, A. Richard Krachenberg, Thomas F. Lyons, "Cross-Functional Teams: Good Concept, Poor Implementation", *Journal of Product Innovation Management*, June 1993, p. 216.)

Successful teams always have two things in common – they are committed to a shared purpose and specific performance goals . . . Appropriate characteristics for successful change teams include: (1) Teams should be the right size. (2) Teams should have adequate levels of complementary skills. (3) Teams should have a truly meaningful overall goal. (4) Teams should have specific goals. (5) Teams should have a clear working approach. (6) Teams should have a sense of mutual accountability. (Jon R. Katzenbach and Douglas K. Smith, "The Rules for Managing Cross-Functional Reengineering Teams", *Planning Review*, March/April 1993, p. 12.)

(Whirlpool) took a one-time restructuring charge in order to refocus its refrigeration factories. It began to tackle the task through cross-functional teams operating on a number of levels. The structure goes right down to the plant floor, where union and management work, hand in hand, to manage plant activity. The employees get extensively involved in all activities in the plant, and everyone shares in the gains made in manufacturing. (Robin P. Bergstrom, "Where Nothing Constant Remains Unchanged", *Production*, February 1993, p. 46.)

"What we value most is boundarylessness. It's the ability to work up and down the hierarchy, across functions and geographies, and with suppliers and customers. We have gotten rid of the Not Invented Here syndrome. We'll go anywhere for an idea." (Jack Welch, "A Master Class in Radical Change", *Fortune*, December 13, 1993, p. 83.)

Another element of its start-up culture that Silicon Graphics is determined to preserve is the attitude that organizational boundaries should never prevent someone from offering an idea or a helping hand. The company has a cadre of 'chief engineers' without product responsibility whose job is to make sure that those developing new products are using the hottest, latest technology. (Steven E. Prokesch, "Mastering Chaos at the High-Tech Frontier: An Interview with Ed McCracken", *Harvard Business Review*, November/December 1993, p. 143.)

Cross-functional teams helped the Aid Association of Lutherans, which operates a big insurance business, increase productivity by 20% and a reduction in case processing time by as much as 75%. This was accomplished in part by reducing the number of levels in the hierarchy and redistributing decision making to the lowest levels. In order to be most effective of course, a company will need to cross-train its work force enabling individuals to understand the other functions of a cross-functional team as well as to take over in situations where staff shortages require back-up. (John Hoerr, "Work Teams Can Rev Up Paper-Pushers, Too", *Business Week*, November 28, 1988, p. 64.)

Cross-training, if not cross-functional teams, is a boon to retail giant, Target. It discovered that it had so narrowly defined each employee's role that it had plenty of hours to fill while employees complained of too few hours! By simply cross-training Target expanded opportunities for employees and, thus, solved both problems.

Teamwork also encourages people to get more involved and to participate in decision making more frequently. As an added incentive employees who are cross-trained are frequently able to increase their pay as the value added by their new skills increases productivity.

"Now, after three years of hard work, Peterson, 49, has taken a bureaucratic culture organized by function – marketing, manufacturing, engineering – and replaced it with flexible, interdisciplinary teams." (Brian Dumaine, "Payoff From The New Management", *Fortune*, December 13, 1993, p. 103.)

Leadership usually rotates on a team according to the expertise in demand at any moment. In this regard cross-functional teams are staffed by peers with enough responsibility and the will to do well that leadership is a reflection of problem-solving needs and group responsibilities rather than the need to control, direct or supervise. When there is a deadlock an external figure can always be brought in to sort it out.

"General Foods found that its best chances for approaching levels of peak performance are by establishing interfunctional business-work teams." (Marc Bassin, "Teamwork at General Foods: New And Improved", *Personnel Journal*, May 1988, p. 62.)

Part of a cross-functional team's success is due to shared ownership of specific outcomes, involvement, and responsibility. In a cross-functional team, each member regardless of specialty contributes to all aspects of the task. So an engineer on a product development team would also play a role in helping develop a marketing strategy for the product.

Teams are the most effective vehicle to stimulate member participation and involvement. Their benefits include: more sharing and integration of individual skills and resources; untapping and use of unknown member resources; more stimulation, energy and endurance by members working jointly than is usual when individuals work alone; more emotional support among team members; better performance, in terms of quality and quantity, more wins, more innovation; more ideas for use in problem solving; more commitment and ownership by members around the team's goals; more sustained effort directed at team's goals; more team member satisfaction, higher motivation and more fun; the sense of being a winner, greater confidence and the ability to achieve more. (*Ibid.*, p. 64.)

Teams should have goals; defined roles; an understanding of how they will be facilitated and coordinated; time to learn appropriate skills and examine interpersonal processes; and celebrations, rewards and recognition.

What you may not know is that Shuttle by United was designed entirely by a cross-functional team of employees from all levels of the company. Never before in the history of our airline has such a concerted effort been made to ensure that a product was designed and implemented by the people who work closest with our customers every day. (CEO, United Airlines, Gerald Greenwald, "New Voices", *Hemispheres*, November 1994, p. 11.)

In the heydays of People Express or America West airlines, cross-functional training was obvious because ground staff could be seen doing everything from reservations to baggage handling to check-in and, not infrequently, acting as flight attendants on flights far and wide. It worked. The camaraderie made both airlines palpably customer-oriented and resulted in cult-like followings and enormous appreciation from flyers who picked up the spirit.

To add to the effectiveness of cross-functional teams some companies use incentive pay to encourage employees to learn additional skills and be able to use them as occasions arise. So cross-functionality and multi-skilling often work together to enhance the productive capacity of teams.

In return for extraordinary freedom and trust, workers are expected to take the initiative, use their heads, and get the job done. To help them use their noggins Chaparral Steel makes sure at least 85% of its 950 employees are enrolled in courses, cross-training in such varied disciplines as electronics, metallurgy and credit history. (Brian Dumaine, "Unleash Workers and Cut Costs", *Fortune*, May 18, 1992, p. 88.)

Wishful Thinking

It is too easy to call a group a team. When the popularity of the concept grows as fast as the team concept you can only expect that it will be misapplied. No doubt we will learn to call groups teams regardless of how well they meet the criteria, just as we changed the term administration to management, and manager to leader.

> There is still room for authoritarian, individualistic approaches. According to Edward E. Lawler of the Center for Effective Organizations: . . . more traditional approaches to management – authoritative, non-participative, non-team approaches – are more likely to succeed when the organization competes primarily on a low-cost strategy and when direct labor costs account for the great bulk of the total cost of the organization's products or services. (Ron Zemke, "Rethinking the Rush To Team Up", *Training*, November 1993, p. 55.) Translated, this means if you run a sweat shop or back office operation you still have a little time left to behave in the old-fashioned way before changing technology and shifting customer needs catch up with you.

Some cross-functional teams are really a matrix structure where members have two bosses; one is the traditional functional boss and the other is the team or project leader. That structure which is not self-managing results in the same drawbacks as a matrix system: answering to two bosses, being evaluated by two bosses, having to meet the objectives of two bosses that are often at cross purposes.

Conflicts of interest among team members might arise due to a matrix-like structure where individuals never really fully develop a team identity and remain loyal to your functional department. Under these circumstances differential power impedes the bonding process that depends on a sense of team egalitarianism.

> The most common problems in conducting new product develop-
> ment with cross-functional teams is the overuse of teams coupled
> with an absence of the help the teams needs to develop into high
> performance units . . . (They need) strong management commit-
> ment, adequate resources, support for taking risks and a means to
> communicate. (Paul O'Connor, "Managing Product Teams", *R &
> D*, July 1993, p. 67.)

Initial team formation may upset managers not wanting to alter
their role. It will also upset many employees who prefer not to get
involved at work.

Obstacles to teams include the lack of skill and not
understanding your role or the operating principles of the other
functions; personal competition and an inability to let go of the
need to "own" the outcome as an individual (ego-centeredness);
lack of support from other units and former managers; lack of
organizational commitment and continuity; inappropriate
compensation/reward systems that do not encourage teamwork;
and lack of career significance if an individual's exposure or
experience on a team does not contribute to their résumé.

Commitment Needed to Make It Work

Cross-functional teams can only succeed when multi-functional
departments commit themselves to the process and lower
traditional barriers such as competitiveness, one-upmanship, and
rivalries.

Exemplars

General Foods Worldwide Coffee and International • GE •
Honeywell, Commercial Flight Systems • Motorola Satellite
Communications Division • Multiplex Co. • Shenandoah Life •
Precision Technology Corp.• Edy's Grand Ice Cream • Rolls-
Royce Motor Cars • Whirlpool • AAL

All work is empty save when there is love.

- **KAHLIL GIBRAN,** *THE PROPHET,*
New York: Alfred A Knopf, 1970.

When we fail to grasp the systemic source of problems, we are left to 'push on' symptoms rather than eliminate underlying causes.

- **PETER SENGE,**
The Fifth Discipline,
New York: Doubleday Currency, 1990.

Chapter Thirteen

SYSTEMS THINKING

A system cannot understand itself. Understanding comes from outside.

– Tim Stevens,
"Dr. Deming: 'Management Today Does
Not Know What Its Job Is' ",
Industry Week, January 17, 1994, p. 21.

What It is

"SYSTEMS THINKING IS a discipline for seeing wholes. It is a framework for seeing interrelationships rather than things, for seeing patterns of change rather than static 'snapshots.'" (Peter Senge, *The Fifth Discipline: The Art and Practice of the Learning Organization*, New York: Doubleday Currency, 1990, p. 68.)

Systems thinking is the recognition that all activity takes place within an arena of action and that for every activity within that arena there are multiple causes and effects which are themselves often undetectable and unpredictable. In more common terms it is the recognition of a connection between and among all things. To think in a systems fashion is to identify, explore, and understand, the connections between things. In organizational terms, the organization is the whole system and the functions and/or work processes represent sub-systems.

169

Wisdom

Understanding dynamic complexity is essential since a system is a representation of active interrelationships. Every influence is both a cause and effect; there is frequently a delay between action and outcomes which may vary from seconds to years. There are almost always unintended consequences or side effects that may not be visible for some time and their links to an original action may remain undetectable. Feedback is important and inevitable and can be positively or negatively reinforcing. Change takes place as feedback leads to action.

Systems seek homeostasis, which is balance, and human systems often do so implicitly due to adherence to a shared norm or expectation. Action is taken when what exists is less than or more than what is deemed desirable. A thermostat instigates action to keep a room at a steady temperature. A drive for the status quo is also representative of this drive for homeostasis as people attempt to maintain the status quo when it is threatened by change.

An understanding of systems thinking allows for influence upon the system to be leveraged. Leverage in a system is an action that will have a disproportionate influence on the system's fundamental or symptomatic problems.

Balancing forces (sometimes thought of as resistance to change) always seem to accompany forces for change (either positive or negative) – and reinforce behavior.

Intension influences action which influences desired outcome. Feedback informs us of the condition of the pattern and suggests to us what next step to take. However, our actions influence the process and thus influence the feedback we receive which in turn influences next steps and so on. (See the explanation of reinforcing and balancing loops in Figure 13.1.)

As a system, it is impossible to assign direct responsibility to an event or a person since each element in the dynamic has influence. Thus, everyone shares responsibility for the whole system.

Used with process maps, systems thinking offers the ability to see the entire workflow and its major influences. The beauty of the technique is that in illustrating the flow and impact of decisions and components of the workflow process with the feedback loops and balancing forces at work, the flow chart is

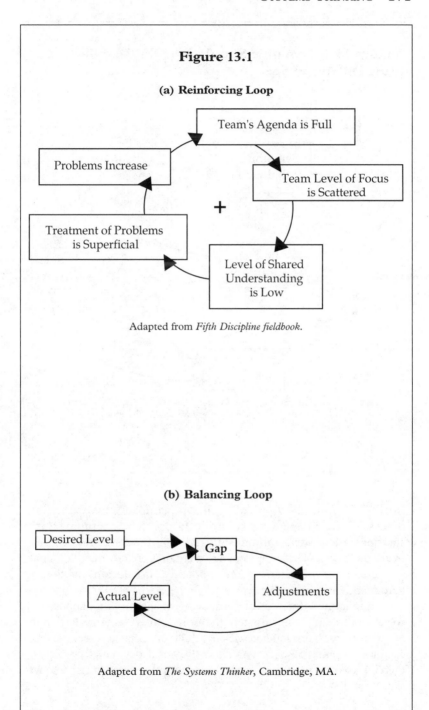

Figure 13.1

(a) Reinforcing Loop

Adapted from *Fifth Discipline fieldbook*.

(b) Balancing Loop

Adapted from *The Systems Thinker*, Cambridge, MA.

Figure 13.2 Dynamic Simulation "Shifting the Burden" Archetype

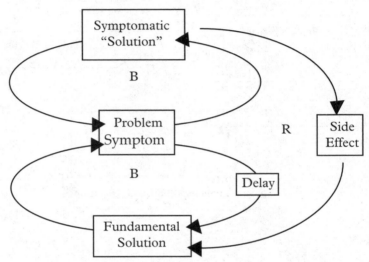

Adapted from Peter Senge, "The Leader's New Work: Building Learning Organizations," *Sloan Management Review*, Fall 1990, p. 7.

In this "Shifting the Burden" archetype template, two balancing processes (B) compete for control of a problem symptom. Both solutions affect the symptom, but only the fundamental solution treats the cause. The symptomatic "solution" creates the additional side effect (R) of deferring the fundamental solution, making it harder and harder to achieve.

Shifting the burden creates a short-term solution that appears to solve a problem. Unfortunately the symptoms re-emerge later and often to worse consequences. Senge tells of a classic case: "Using corporate human resource staff to solve local personnel problems, thereby keeping managers from developing their own interpersonal skills."

Figure 13.3

Systems thinking requires a grasp of four levels of awareness

First level: Events
Second Level: Patterns of Behavior
Third: Systemic Structure
Fourth: Mental Models

To work through the levels answer:

- The problem is . . . identify an issue
- Tell a story about the issue . . . describe what happened
- Then ask, "how did we through our internal thinking, our processes, our practices, and our procedures create the circumstances [good or bad] that we face now?"

Source: Michael Goodman, and Rick Karash, "Exploring Your Own Story" in Peter M. Senge, Charlotte Roberts, Richard B. Ross, Bryan J. Smith, Art Kleiner, *The Fifth Discipline Fieldbook*, New York: Doubleday Currency, 1994, p. 103.

able to disassociate (or highlight) the effect of ego, power, and individual choices that normally influence the system.

It helps to put what we can know about a system in perspective – particularly by seeing the dynamics at work when modeled.

Wishful Thinking

Systems thinking, in being a holistic technique that requires the active involvement of managers across disciplines, also demands very specific training in its principles especially in understanding the archetypes and their variations. In this regard it asks for a disciplined and an especially time-consuming commitment to apply the technique to problems which involve many, or most, of the sub-systems of the organization. Worthy as this is, it is a daunting task for many action-oriented managers who retreat from such apparently intellectual exercises without a clear promise of the results to be gained.

You might ask, however, what is the alternative? Organizations are systems. But the pressures of the conventional management apparatus to reward individuals, create competition between sub-systems, and to avoid cooperative cross-functional planning and problem-solving activity that requires disciplined thinking and shared responsibility, is a disincentive for applying the principles and fully utilizing this technique.

All influences (and their degree of influence) are very difficult to assess and there is pressure to evaluate/judge prematurely and to seek out and to assign blame or personal responsibility.

Identifying differences between symptomatic issues and real/fundamental issues is often difficult. There may also be an unconscious denial to face the fundamentals. Resistance is also a common occurrence because of the apparent enormity and the frequently highly sensitive nature of the fundamentals – particularly when there is a lot at stake either personally (power/money) or psychologically (self-concept, world view, values).

". . . you cannot gain a systems understanding unless you can take part in changing it. Otherwise, you will continually see the system sabotage your well intentioned efforts." (Charlotte Roberts, and Jennifer Kemeny, "What You Can Expect . . . As You Practice Systems Thinking", in Peter M. Senge, Charlotte Roberts, Richard B. Ross, Bryan J. Smith, Art Kleiner, *The Fifth Discipline Fieldbook*, New York: Doubleday Currency, 1994, p. 94.)

Exemplars

Few actual business applications have been reported in the literature and the major books about systems thinking say little of the causal effect of the conventional organizational system itself. In effect, systems thinking accepts the nature of organizations as a given within which leverage is sought to produce the desired long-term business results but seems not to realize the larger system itself is deliberately designed for short-term results.

Commitment Needed to Make It Work

As with many techniques, time is required as is the commitment of top management to allow the process to unfold. In this, as with many other techniques, dealing with the operative mental models of the system's participants is an essential component although often ignored because of the depth of interaction required to truly utilize the knowledge. It can be a lengthy process with uncertain, hard-to-control outcomes.

Perhaps most of all, managers must be willing to engage in a discussion of their values, beliefs and attitudes and be able to examine the impact of those beliefs on their actions. While important to do, this can be a very unsettling experience to say the least.

> Learning is a treasure that accompanies its owner everywhere.
>
> **– Chinese Proverb**

It seems to me that anything that can be taught to another is relatively inconsequential, and has little or no significant influence on behavior . . .

I realize increasingly that I am only interested in learnings which significantly influence behavior . . .

I have come to feel that the only learning which significantly influences behavior is self-discovered, self-appropriated learning. Such self-discovered learning, truth that has been personally appropriated and assimilated in experience, cannot be directly communicated to another.

– **CARL ROGERS,**
On Becoming A Person,
New York: Houghton Muffin, 1961.

THE LEARNING ORGANIZATION

A consummately adaptive enterprise with workers freed to think for themselves, to identify problems and opportunities, and to go after them.

> – Dumaine, Brian;
> "What the Leaders of Tomorrow See",
> *Fortune*, July 3, 1989, p. 48.

What It is

A learning organization is an adaptive enterprise that acquires and applies new knowledge. It encourages and supports employees' efforts to develop their individual capacities and share knowledge with one another. It is ultimately a cooperative, creative, and innovative workplace.

> A learning organization is defined as an organization skilled at creating, acquiring and transferring knowledge, and at modifying its behavior to reflect new knowledge and insights. (David A. Garvin, "Building A Learning Organization", *Business Credit*, January 1994, p. 19.)

According to Peter Senge in *The Fifth Discipline*, there are five components to a learning organization: systems thinking, personal mastery, an understanding of mental models, building a shared vision, and team learning.

"Workers teach themselves how to analyze and solve problems. It is the job of the manager to encourage experimentation, to have workers find better ways to do things." (Brian Dumaine, "What the Leaders of Tomorrow See", *Fortune*, July 3, 1989, p. 48.)

Wisdom

> Organizational learning requires examining and working with the entire system. By focusing on 12 key factors that influence an organization's ability to learn and change, the task may become more manageable. Those 12 factors are: (1) strategy/vision; (2) executive practices; (3) managerial practices; (4) climate; (5) organization/job structure,; (6) information flow; (7) individual

and team practices; (8) work processes; (9) performance goals/feedback; (10) training/education; (11) individual/team development; and (12) rewards/recognition. (*Training*, June 1994, p. 41.)

When an organization detects and corrects errors in order to carry out present objectives, that is single loop learning. No real change. When an organization also modifies its underlying norms, policies and objectives – questions its very nature – it is double loop learning. Double loop learning is having the ability and the willingness to look at and question the underlying assumptions about your organization and yourself in light of feedback.

Seven innovations that work for learning organizations are: (1) learning's contribution to competitiveness; (2) improved learning rates; (3) adoption of stretch goals; (4) safefailing; (5) systems for enhancing and sharing learning; (6) stimulation of core process knowledge; and (7) new status of knowledge workers. (Aleda V. Roth, and Ann S. Marucheck, "Innovations That Work For Learning Organizations", *Planning Review*, May/June 1994, p. 33.)

Distinctive policies and practices are responsible for learning organizations' success: (1) systematic problem solving; (2) experimentation with new approaches; (3) learning from their own experience and past history; (4) learning from the experiences and best practices of others; and (5) transferring knowledge quickly and efficiently throughout the organization. (David A. Garvin, "Building A Learning Organization", *Harvard Business Review* July/August 1993, p. 37.)

A learning organization must be grounded in 3 foundations: (1) a culture based on transcendent human values of love, wonder, humility, and compassion; (2) a set of practices for generative conversation and coordinated action; and (3) a capacity to see and work with the flow of life as a system. (Fred Kofman, Peter M. Senge, "Communities of Commitment: The Heart of Learning Organizations", *Organizational Dynamics*, Autumn 1993, p. 5.)

Ford's Vic Leo has suggested a three stage architecture of engagement: (1) finding those predisposed to this work; (2) core community-building activities; and (3) practical experimentation and testing.

The organization must establish: (1) a learning culture; (2) continuous experimentation; (3) network intimacy; (4) accurate information systems; (5) reward systems that recognize and reinforce learning; (6) human resource practices that select people for their ability to learn; and (7) a leader's mandate for unlearning and learning. (Michael E. McGill, and John W. Jr. Slocum, "Unlearning the Organization", *Organizational Dynamics*, Autumn 1993, p. 67.)

A learning organization is an organization that encourages and expects collective thinking from all its members . . . by: (1) adapting a willingness to identify and challenge the paradigms existing in the organization; (2) valuing output and the skills necessary to yield that output; (3) rewarding the thinking and not just the doing; (4) eliciting input and buy-in to the vision, values and performance expectations from employees at all levels within the organization; (5) making performance expectations explicit and providing opportunities for growth; (6) accepting and encouraging mistakes; and (7) performing a fault analysis prior to implementation. (Lauren Jones, "We Need to Reexpand Our Organizational Brains", *Journal for Quality and Participation*, June 1993, p. 28.)

Personal qualities are needed to work well in a learning organization: ability to learn, probably having higher education experience, ability to work without supervision, a problem solving ability, good interpersonal skills. (M. J. Barrow, and H. M. Laughlin, "Toward A Learning Organization 1: The Rationale", *Industrial and Commercial Training*, Vol. 24, Issue 1, 1992, p. 3.)

Executives at Jossey Bass Publishers act as teachers, designers and stewards. Leadership is widely shared and human resource functions are enfolded in line positions. Work teams formulate and implement strategy and change has been institutionalized in a "holonomic shamrock" organizational structure. (Craig C. Lundberg, "Creating and Managing A Vanguard Organization: Design and Human Resource Lessons from Jossey Bass", *Human Resource Management*, Spring 1992, p. 89.)

Harnessing different ways of knowing: multiple realities evaluation, conflict, unbounded systems thinking. (Richard H. Franke, "The Unbounded Mind: Breaking The Chains of Traditional Business Thinking", *Executive*, August 1993, p. 96.)

> Motorola reports: We used to hire people because they could manipulate parts, they could put things together with their hands . . . Now we really need the whole worker. You have to have somebody to do simple programming, read, write commands, interpret information on terminals, and do preventive maintenance. (Norm Alster, "What Flexible Workers Can Do", *Fortune*, February 13, 1989, p. 63.)

"Management is a thing of the past. We are in a time that spells the end of corporations except for those that turn into confederations of intrapreneurs." (Norman Macrae in Jane Ferguson, "Economists Tout Intrapreneurship", *San Francisco Business Journal*, August 9, 1982, p. 10.)

> Eight specific factors influence an organization's capacity for learning. These are: (1) The extent to which an elite group or single point of view dominates decision making. (2) The extent to which employees are encouraged to challenge the status quo. (3)The induction and socialization of newcomers. (4) The extent to which external data on performance, quality, consumer satisfaction, and competitiveness are cultivated or suppressed. (5) The equity of the reward system and distribution of status and privilege. (6) The degree of empowerment of employees at all levels. (7) The historical legacy and folklore, and (8) the integrity of contention management processes – particularly with respect to surfacing hard truths and confronting reality. (Richard Tanner Pascale, *Managing on the Edge*, New York: Touchstone, 1991, p. 236.)

Wishful Thinking

There are barriers and limitations preventing organizations from becoming learning enterprises. Peter Senge outlines several organizational learning disabilities which inhibit the organization's capacity for learning. They are:

1. Believing that "I am my position." This limits your consciousness and motivation to a specific job description by seeing yourself merely as a particular profession or set of skills. Thus, individuals do not see the organization's performance as their responsibility and become disassociated from it.

2. "The enemy is out there." For any mistake there is a convenient villain who can be blamed. This prevents inquiry, openness and dialogue – and particularly systems thinking.

3. "The illusion of taking charge." Doing something and asserting responsibility to solve problems (address issues/events) demonstrates our competence and position.

4. "The fixation on events." Because every event is believed to have a cause and since we have a position and are supposed to know what is happening, we must take responsibility to determine the explanation of events. It results in very short-term, particularistic decisions and a very limited understanding of the whole. Life is seen as a series of events rather than an unfolding of a process.

5. By focusing on events we are blind to processes. The boiled frog syndrome demonstrates the long-term impact of apparently superficial short-term occurrences. Because incremental changes are not perceived as important their accumulation goes unnoticed until it is effectively too late. The boiled frog syndrome is a dramatic demonstration of this. It was first popularized by Gregory Bateson. If a frog is placed in a pot of water at room temperature and the temperature is gradually raised to boiling point, the frog will boil to death because of its inability to detect the danger. Thus, we, too, face a similar fate if we neglect the long-term implications of current conditions as innocuous as they may appear in the present.

6. "The delusion of learning from experience . . . We learn best from experience but we never directly experience the consequences of many of our most important decisions . . . and the analysis of the most important problems in a company, the complex issues that cross functional lines, becomes a perilous or nonexistent exercise." In short, it is possible that twenty years of experience is one year repeated twenty times.

7. "The myth of the management team." Because of norms and pressures and the idea of keeping up appearances, hard decisions and dissenting voices are not heard. Too often they are lost in the need to maintain a "united front," or to "pull together," or to go along with the prevailing wisdom" and to "be professional". Thus, the so-called team discussion is merely an exercise in group think.

Fragmentation, competition and reactiveness (single loop learning) are barriers to thinking and acting like a learning organization.

Commitment Needed to Make It Work

Confronting these collective learning disabilities is vital. Developing a safe environment where fearless communication is possible and a questioning attitude are not only possible but essential to uncover weaknesses in current positions and to unlock the group's potential.

Exemplars

Ford • Royal Dutch Shell

Chapter Fourteen

QUALITY

Quality is a journey not a destination.
Quality is Job One

– The slogan that spearheaded a revolution at Ford
resulting in the historic success of the Taurus.

What It is

TO MANY PEOPLE quality is the emphasis on the creation
and attainment of performance targets reflective of an
increasingly high standard. Quality goals signify the continuous
search for improvement as well as a standard of performance.
Quality is sometimes thought of as a means of continuously
improving processes in order to narrow variation, eliminate
defects, and spur constant innovation.

Sometimes quality is defined as attention to work processes
in order to optimize information and materials handling in a way
that provides a customer with the kind of experience they have
come to expect. Quality may also be defined as exceeding a
customer's expectations. Developing a quality program usually
includes: (1) a commitment to satisfying the customer;
(2) routine employee involvement in determining best practices
and performance standards often through benchmarking or self-
development; (3) a daily search for incremental improvements;

(4) free and open communication in the pursuit of improvement; and (5) a focus on work processes, not individuals per se in creating improvements (and overcoming faults).

Some organizations have set very high targets and simply will not accept less. Motorola was one of the first to espouse the objective of reaching Six Sigma Quality where reaching 99.9997% perfection is an initial goal.

According to Mary Walton, author of the *Deming Management Method* the transformation to a quality-centered company is a five-stage process: (1) decide to adopt; (2) incubate through getting others on board and setting up a quality planning council that includes management and labor; (3) write a vision and mission statement and a set of values that will guide the effort; (4) planning and promotion; (5) education; and (6) continuous improvement.

For three other quality gurus, quality means something different. For Crosby quality is conformance to requirements. For Juran it is fitness for use, having quality specifications to begin with. For Taguchi it means minimizing the losses a product imparts on society from the time it is shipped (see Figure 14.1).

Wisdom

Andersen Consulting says companies should use quality consciousness to improve the entire workflow process, not just a few sub-processes. Motorola suggests employment security among those asked to redesign their processes. According to Teleport, a strong focus is required to make quality efforts succeed.

". . . when complex change is divided into 5 stages – awareness, evaluation, initiation, implementation, and adoption – the process becomes easier to manage." (Kelly Scott Petrock, "A Blueprint for More Productive Teamwork", *Manufacturing Systems*, February 1994, p. 28.)

Northern Telecom includes a customer report card on their efforts in their quality improvement program. The customer decides what is important to them and develops a report card on that. (Bob Stoffels, "Quality Roundtable: Weeding Out the Myths", *America's Network*, 1994, pp. 6–8.)

Wishful Thinking

"Surveys show that up to 2/3 of US managers think TQM has failed in their companies" (Rahul Jacob, "TQM: More Than A Dying Fad?", *Fortune*, October 18, 1993, p. 66.) There seems to be an overemphasis on process improvement without measuring output improvements.

> The challenge for Xerox and other US companies is to move beyond quality and find ways to leverage the inherent competitive advantage: the American worker and the American work culture. Companies should take five steps to keep growing and improving and to be more productive: (1) eliminate the bureaucracy; (2) leverage diversity; (3) build 'communities of practice' – small, self-managing entrepreneurial units; (4) build a learning organization; and (5) enhance the use of information technology. (Paul A. Allaire, [Former CEO Xerox Corp.], "The New Productivity", *Executive Excellence*, January 1993, p. 3.)

> Joseph M. Juran, one of the foremost leaders of the quality movement said: he has not been very enthusiastic about the progress of the American quality movement. The biggest single reason that quality movements fail is the lack of real participation by senior managers . . . Juran said that he sees nothing wrong with the banners and slogans that go along with many quality initiatives; it does bother him when 90% of the quality initiative is package and 10% is substance. (Jack Gordon, "An Interview With Joseph M. Juran", *Training*, May 1994, p.35.)

> Ten reasons for total quality failure: (1) Disguising cost control as total quality. (2) Measuring too many of the wrong things. (3) Lack of support from the top. (4) Too much too soon. (5) Too little, too late. (6) Dual structures. (7) Focus on activities versus results. (8) Can't get out of phase one. (9) No one gets rewarded for quality and customer satisfaction. (10) Total quality considered a fad. (Mark Graham Brown, "Why Does Total Quality Fail in Two out of Three Tries?", *Journal for Quality and Participation*, March 1993, p. 80.)

"TQM is in danger of becoming yet another expensive, unproductive fad because efforts are focusing on processes instead of results." (Ken Myers, and Ron Ashkenas, "Results-Driven Quality . . . Now!", *Management Review*, March 1993, p. 40.)

"The assumption, 'if we fix all the performers, we fix quality' is absolutely nonsense. It doesn't pass the common sense test, because no performer can be any better than the processes he or she must work with." (Gary Rummler, "Managing The White Space", *Training & Development*, August 1992, p. 27.)

Commitment Needed to Make It Work

As usual, the CEO must be committed and clear objectives are required.

Quality is a frame of mind as much as it is attention to detail and the workflow process. In that regard, it is constantly educating each employee on customer demands, new ways of meeting those wants and in broadening their perspective of their responsibilities and skills. Continuous learning and expanding creative abilities is required.

Exemplars

Martin Marietta Energy Group • Donnelly, Corp. • Ensoniq Corp. (a small electronic instrument manufacturer) • AlliedSignal Corp. (Sent all 86,000 employees to a four-day course on total quality. They plan to do it again!) • Florida Power and Light • Hospital Corporation of America • Globe Metallurgical of Beverly, Ohio

Figure 14.1 Views of the Major Quality Gurus

Philip. B. Crosby	W. Edwards Deming	Joseph M. Juran
Quality is conformance to requirements.	Quality is continuous improvement through reduced variation.	Quality is fitness for use.
The Four Absolutes of Quality Management: (1) The definition of quality is conformance to requirements (2) The system of quality is prevention (3) The performance standard is zero defects (4) The measurement of quality is the price of non-conformance	The Seven Deadly Diseases: (1) Lack of consistency of purpose (2) Emphasizing short-term profits and immediate dividends (3) Evaluation of performance, merit rating or annual review (4) Mobility of top management (5) Running a company only on visible figures (6) Excessive medical costs (7) Excessive costs of warranty fueled by lawyers on contingency fees	The Quality Trilogy: (1) Quality improvement (2) Quality planning (3) Quality control
Fourteen-Step Quality Improvement Plan: (1) Management commitment is defined, created and exhibited (2) Quality improvement team is formed (3) Measurement to determine areas of improvement (4) Cost of quality measures are developed as a stimulus (5) Quality awareness is created in everyone (6) Corrective action is taken on problems previously identified (7) Zero defects planning (8) Employee education of all employees in the company (9) Zero defects day is held to let all employees know there has been a change (10) Goal setting for individuals and groups (11) Error cause removal by employees sharing with management (12) Recognition for those who participated (13) Quality councils to communicate regularly (14) Do it all over again to emphasize quality improvement never ends	The Fourteen Points: (1) Create constancy of purpose for improvement of product and service (2) Adopt the new philosophy (3) Cease dependence on mass inspection (4) End the practice of awarding business on price tag alone (5) Improve constantly and forever the system of production and service (6) Institute training on the job (7) Institute leadership (8) Drive out fear (9) Breakdown barriers between staff areas (10) Eliminate slogans exhortations, and targets for the workforce (11) a. Eliminate numerical quotas for the workforce b. Eliminate numerical goals for people in management (12) Remove barriers to pride of workmanship (13) Encourage education and self-improvement for everyone (14) Take action to accomplish the transformation	Ten-Step Quality Improvement Process: (1) Build awareness for the need and opportunity for improvement (2) Set goals for improvement (3) Organize to reach the goals (4) Provide training throughout the organization (5) Carry out projects to solve problems (6) Report progress (7) Give recognition (8) Communicate results (9) Keep score (10) Maintain momentum by making annual improvement part of the regular systems and processes of the company Source: (Steve Gibbons, "Three Paths, One Journey", *Journal for Quality and Participation*, October/November 1994, p. 36. Reprinted with permission from the *Journal for Quality and Participation*. © The Association for Quality and Participation, Cincinnati, OH.

EXCELLENCE

> The challenge for most people in organizations has almost nothing to do with competitors. It is about reaching a shared understanding of a standard worth reaching and then striving for it.

What It is

Excellence was a phenomenon sparked by the book *In Search of Excellence* in the early 1980s. It is all about focusing on the customer, sticking to core competencies, communicating, managing by walking around, being creative, decentralizing some functions, and getting people involved.

Peters and Waterman identified eight factors that contributed to excellence but only if the spirit underlying the factors was vigorously maintained. Having a customer orientation, for example, is not enough. A company must be vigilant in keeping customers satisfied and attempt to anticipate their needs. Even that is not enough. Employees must be rewarded for contributing to customer satisfaction and be encouraged and supported in independent decision making in how best they can personally contribute to this goal. Excellence then becomes responsiveness, integrity and service.

Wisdom

There are many formulas for creating excellent companies. Peters and Waterman originally proposed eight: (1) a bias toward action; (2) simple form, lean staff; (3) continuous contact with customers; (4) get people involved in productivity improvement; (5) operational autonomy; (6) focus on a key business value; (7) do what you know best; and (8) simultaneous loose/tight controls. (Thomas J. Peters and Robert H. Jr. Waterman, *In Search of Excellence: Lessons From America's Best Run Corporations*, New York: Harper & Row, 1982.)

> According to Peters and Waterman: The specific content of the dominant beliefs of the excellent companies is narrow in scope, including just a few basic values: (1) a belief in being the 'best'; (2) a belief in the importance of the details of execution, the nuts and bolts of doing the job well; (3) a belief in the importance of

people as individuals; (4) a belief in superior quality and service; (5) a belief that most members of the organization should be innovators, and its corollary, the willingness to support failure; (6) a belief in the importance of informality to enhance communication; and (7) explicit belief in and recognition of the importance of economic growth and profits. (Thomas J. Peters and Robert H. Jr. Waterman, "The Essential Traits: Hands-on, Value-driven", *San Francisco Examiner*, April 29, 1983.)

Ten years after *In Search of Excellence*, the search continues. Again, management writers are imploring organizations to heed what is already known and they reiterate the characteristics, qualities, and dimensions that create excellence. According to *Management Review*, "Successful companies (1) maintain close ties with their customers; (2) centralize policy, decentralize execution; (3) use integrative mechanisms (coordination); (4) invest in human capital (training, development and recognition); and (5) maintain an ongoing improvement/results orientation." (Douglas G. Shaw and Vincent C. Perro, "Beating the Odds: Five Reasons Why Companies Excel", *Management Review*, August 1992, p. 15.)

The following ten management guidelines apply in any setting and define the parameters of excellence: (1) Establish and maintain credibility. (2) Create an environment of respect and trust. (3) Sense and diagnose the work environment. (4) Communicate clearly. (5) Demonstrate common sense leadership. (6) Manage. (7) Inspire hard work, attention to detail and a commitment to quality. (8) Motivate. (9) Foster a client orientation. (10) Share a vision of growth, development and improvement. (Arthur H. Friedman, "Ten Commandments of Management", *Executive Excellence*, March 1992, p. 8.)

Wishful Thinking

"Anyone in charge of an organization with more than two people is running a clinic." The truth of this wry comment comes from the fact that while people want to cooperate, they also want to control their own destiny. And it is this universal desire to control our own destiny that creates conflicts of interests within organizations. (Abraham Zalesnik, "Real Work", *Harvard Business Review*, January/February 1989, p. 57.)

Structural changes, new processes and exhortation, the typical tools managers employ to motivate employees and to face the marketplace are not enough to sustain long periods of excellence. Cynicism in the workplace is rampant and justified. Declining real wages and increasing pressure to put in more uncompensated time are facts of life. What has become a requirement for any organization expecting superior effort is treating employees as owners.

Excellence requires the belief that it is others' satisfaction – employees, customer, society, investor – that need to be forefront in your thinking and acting. Processes and objectives must focus outward to the recipient of our action. What impact do we have? Are we engaging each employee and customer? Have we built a lasting relationship? Can we change together in sync? The demands for this orientation challenge people at two levels. First, can we know the essential qualities we are trying to establish? Can we even be in sync when so much changes so fast and is often subject to whimsy? Can a manager or an employee displace their own interests for long periods of time and function totally with an outward orientation? What of their own needs and desires as they are expressed in the workplace? What happened to the need to achieve or express your own power? The so-called dark side of excellence is the hidden or undisclosed motives and behaviors which are simply self-serving and egocentric which can not always be controlled, repressed, or neutralized. This side needs to be dealt with because it impacts our behavior and relationships. Excellence may require the finest character and people of the highest intentions, motives and skills. Can we develop these attributes in each employee? Can everyone be counted on to maintain their highest levels of performance at all times? Can we create methods to quickly deal with aberrations? Are we at least willing to accept the need to deal with the aberrations and do so with compassion and integrity?

Thus, it is vital to examine why our management techniques – our search for excellence – so often ends up empty-handed. It is time to look at the deeper issues of human behavior, needs and wants as well as the constraints imposed by the systems and structures we are embedded in to explain why the search for excellence so often results in less than optimum performance and fragmentary results.

Q: Tell the truth, wouldn't it be easier to write a book about the 100 worst companies?

A: Definitely. Not too many people have good things to say about the companies they work for. And Studs Terkel, who really has his nose to the ground on this, says things have gotten worse for working people (his bestseller *Working* was published in the 1970s). ("An Interview With Milton Moskowitz, Co-author of *The 100 Best Companies to Work for in America*, "What Makes A Great Company?" *Executive Edge*, September 1993, p. 1.)

Exemplars

Hewlett Packard • Levi Strauss

Reengineering – a bloodless term for corporate bloodletting on an unprecedented scale.

– JOHN A. BYRNE,
"The Pain of Downsizing",
Business Week, May 9, 1994, p. 61.

Chapter Fifteen

REENGINEERING

An important proximate cause of incivility is reengineering, by
now the Great Satan of corporate life.

> – Marilyn Moats Kennedy in: Julie Connelly,
> "Have We Become Mad Dogs In The Office?",
> *Fortune*, November 28, 1994, p. 197.

What It is

THE MOTHER OF all contemporary fads, "Reengineering
is the fundamental rethinking and radical redesign of
business processes to achieve dramatic improvements in critical
contemporary measures of performance, such as cost, quality,
service, and speed." (Michael Hammer, and James Champy,
Reengineering the Corporation: A Manifesto for Business Revolution,
New York: Harper Business, 1993, p. 31.)

Reengineering to many people is a euphemism for downsizing. Though frequently downsizing follows, reengineering is
about redesigning the organization around core processes rather
than functional and vertical hierarchies. The trend toward a flatter, horizontal, team-based process-centered design is clear.
Simply put, "managing across" is more important to get the work
out than "managing up and down." It is more efficient in designing the organization's inputs as they "flow" to the customer.

". . . some 41% of senior executives admit they are currently reengineering something at their corporations . . . the freedom to throw it all out and start fresh is tempting. Reengineering gives strategists permission to do just that. Michael Hammer defines reengineering as using the power of modern information technology to radically redesign business processes in order to achieve dramatic improvements in their performance." (Jill Vitiello, "Reengineering: It's Totally Radical", *Journal of Business Strategy*, November/December 1993, p. 44.)

Wisdom

Reengineering is ". . . a change process that circumvents organizational politics by bringing objective information from the bottom directly to the CEO by-passing any self-serving or out-of-touch management levels that may lie in between. The following steps detail the process of overcoming bureaucratic defenses: (1) Appoint an independent project leader. (2) Develop broad-based support. (3) Form the project team. (4) Train the project team. (5) Begin diagnosing the organization. (6) Calibrate initial findings. (7) Develop a straw-man organization. (8) Present the straw-man organization. (9) Develop a final organization and implementation plan. (10) Implement the plan. (Craig J. Cantoni, "Eliminating Bureaucracy – Roots and All", *Management Review*, December 1993, p. 30.) (See Figure 15.1.)

At American Modern Home Insurance, a reengineering effort established as its goal to determine ". . . the fewest possible levels of management with day-to-day operating decisions being made at the lowest possible level." (Robert Janson, "Thanks to Its

Figure 15.1

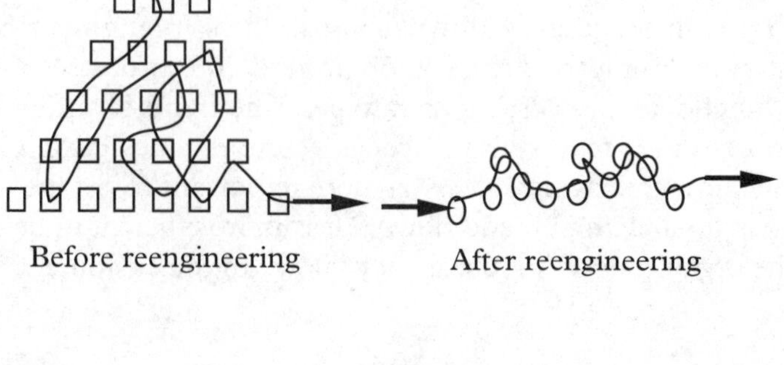

Before reengineering   After reengineering

Employees This Reengineering Effort Worked", *Journal for Quality and Participation*, December, 1993, p. 78.)

> The process to be redesigned must be broadly defined in terms of cost or customer value in order to improve performance across the entire business unit. The redesign must also penetrate to the company's core, fundamentally changing the six crucial depth levers of roles and responsibilities, measurement and incentives, organizational structure, information technology, shared values and skills. (Gene Hall, Jim Rosenthal and Judy Wade, "How to Make Reengineering Really Work", *Harvard Business Review*, November/December 1993, p. 119.)

> When companies decide to redesign their business processes at the customer interface, they are very likely to create the case manager role, which involves mediating between the customer and a complex organizational and information structure. The case manager provides a way to increase organizational efficiency, timeliness, and customer satisfaction. (Thomas H. Davenport and Nitin Nohria, "Case Management and the Integration of Labor", *Sloan Management Review*, Winter 1994, p. 11.)

One dramatic success story with reengineering is offered by AT&T Credit Communications Systems. Their effort involved 200 jobs and 600 people. "It virtually eliminated errors, improved response and overall customer service, and drove accountability, responsibility and decision making further down the organization." (Thomas C. Wajnert, "Redesign for Results", *Chief Executive*, May 1994, p. 44.)

> Another success was the redesign effort at Southern California Gas. They recommend a process that consists of five phases: (1) planning; (2) internal learning; (3) external learning; (4) redesigning the process; and (5) implementing changes. When an organization is getting started with its reengineering process there are seven guidelines that must be followed: (1) select a project manager; (2) organize the effort; (3) select project team members; (4) define the scope; (5) set project objectives and targets; (6) set role of consultants; and (7) establish continuous learning. (Charles Goldwasser, "Lessons Learned: The Initial Reengineering Project at Southern California Gas," *Planning Review*, May/June 1994, pp. 34–38, 46.)

The preeminent goal of reengineering at Pacific Bell is to increase value, not just to cut costs . . . (In determining the value added) Pacific Bell Pioneered the Process Value Estimation (PVE) methodology, an objective way of comparing the amount of value added by a given component process before and after reengineering efforts. (Thomas J. Housel, Arthur H. Bell, Valery Kanevsky, "Calculating the Values of Reengineering at Pacific Bell", *Planning Review*, January/February 1994, p. 40.)

The benefits from information technology deployment are marginal if only superimposed on existing organizational conditions. An information technology-enabled business transformation has five levels: (1) localized exploitation; (2) internal integration; (3) business process redesign; (4) business network redesign; and (5) business scope redefinition. (N. Venkatraman, "IT-enabled Business Transformation: From Automation to Business Scope Redefinition", *Sloan Management Review*, Winter 1994, p. 73.)

After the downsizings in a typical cut-the-fat program people find they are stuck with the same old problems but people are working harder and the bureaucracy is still there albeit a smaller one. As one person graphically put it, "we reached the end of the runway" and, no doubt, needed a new approach to find efficiencies and cost savings. The process-focused or horizontal organization is one such device.

When McKinsey & Co. advises clients they recommend that each core process has an "owner" to see that it functions well and a "champion" that oversees its continuing place in the organization's strategic plan.

"Hallmark . . . reengineered its new product process around US holidays . . . The Valentine's Day team, for example, would be a group of artists, writers, lithographers, merchandisers and others who work just on valentines." (Patricia A. Galagan, "Beyond Hierarchy: The Search for High Performance", *Training & Development*, August 1992, p. 21.)

General Telephone and Electronics (GTE) was able to reengineer its Telephone Operations unit to double revenues, cut costs in half, and to chop cycle and systems development times. All this, while chopping about 25,000 employees and still having higher levels of employee and customer satisfaction. (Joseph Cosco, "The Razor's Edge", *Journal of Business Strategy*, 1994.)

Wishful Thinking

James Champy, a co-author of *Reengineering the Corporation*, the book that established the concept as one of the most popular management tools of the 1990s reports that "'Reengineering is in trouble'. Despite notable successes at such companies as Bell Atlantic Corp. and Federal Express Corp., many reengineering efforts have fallen far short . . . 'I have also learned that half a revolution is not better than none. It may, in fact, be worse.'" ("Reengineering: What Happened?", *Business Week*, January 30, 1995, p. 16.)

Management guru Tom Peters fundamentally disagrees with some of the basic tenets of reengineering. The essence of reengineering, as he sees it, is first hooking functions together horizontally rather than vertically; and, second, reinventing the organization as you go horizontal in order to take 24 steps out of a 25-step process. What Peters dislikes about reengineering is that its root word is "engineering." He is fearful that an era of "neo-Taylorism" is approaching. That is, reengineering becomes the new "one best way" to organize horizontally, forever, as opposed to the old, one best way to organize vertically, forever. The reason that is wrong is because to set an organization's design in stone is absolutely antithetical to a marketplace where it is not known what will come next. (Thomas Kiely, "Unconventional Wisdom", *CIO*, December 15, 1993.)

"The most difficult aspect of a reengineering process is getting the senior managers to agree that they need to reengineer and then selecting the right processes." (Diane Filipowski, "Is Reengineering More Than A Fad?", *Personnel Journal*, December 1993, p. 48L.)

Sometimes costs and ambitions outstrip the benefits – especially if the project is too narrow and merely attempts to add an incremental improvement instead of an entire process overhaul.

"Despite their popularity, 4 out of 5 reengineering programs have been unsuccessful. There are several reasons why the majority of reengineering programs fail, including: (1) many programs lack senior executive sponsorship; and (2) few organizations follow a detailed reengineering methodology." (Raymond L. Manganelli, "It's Not A Silver Bullet", *Journal of Business Strategy*, November/December 1993, p. 45.)

Fortune magazine concurs: "... it is estimated that between 50 and 70% of reengineering efforts fail to achieve the goals set for them." (Thomas A. Stewart, "Reengineering: The Hot New Management Tool", *Fortune*, August 23, 1993, p. 40.)

"Common mistakes in planning and executing reengineering projects include: (1) unclear definitions; (2) unrealistic expectations; (3) inadequate resources; (4) taking too long; (5) lack of sponsorship; (6) wrong scope; (7) techno-centrism; (8) mysticism; and (9) lack of an effective methodology." (Mark M. Klein, "The Most Fatal Reengineering Mistakes", *Information Strategy: The Executive's Journal*, Summer 1994, p. 21.)

In addition, Hammer and Stanton cite being too timid in the redesign, not testing redesign in a "laboratory," placing some aspects of the business such as compensation and sacred cows off limits, ignoring concerns of people and mistaking functions with processes. (Michael Hammer, and Steven A. Stanton, *The Reengineering Revolution: A Handbook*, New York: Harper Business, 1995.)

> Reengineering has become synonymous with downsizing. No wonder, companies coincidentally downsize after they reengineer. "Initially, BellSouth Telecommunications' primary motivation for using reengineering after its merger was downsizing and the need to be aware that the market is changing, the work content is changing, and market demands. (But) reengineering is also about improving customer satisfaction, positioning the company for increased revenue, and saving money on non-labor costs." (Connie Brittain, "Reengineering Complements BellSouth's Major Business Strategies", *Industrial Engineering*, February 1994, p. 34.)

> While it appears to be on the leading edge, reengineering is really a repackaged product that does more harm than good . . . Evolutionary change stimulates morale and imagination, creating conditions for rewarding organizational learning and for inspiring employees to discover innovative ways to deal with adversity and competitive challenges . . . As currently practiced, reengineering assumes that a company's own people cannot be trusted to fix whatever ails their organization. (Paul A. Strassman, "The Hocus Pocus of Reengineering", *Across the Board*, June 1994, p. 35.)

> Most failures to realize the potential return on process-improvement investment arise from committing one or more of the

'7 deadly sins'. These sins are: (1) Process improvement is not tied to the strategic issues the business faces. (2) The process-improvement effort does not involve the right people. (3) The process improvement teams are not given a clear, appropriate charter. (4) The top management team thinks if it is not doing away with the existing organization, it is not making significant improvements. (5) Process designers do not consider how the changes will affect the people. (6) The organization focuses more on redesign than implementation. (7) Teams fail to leave behind measurement system and other parts of the infrastructure necessary for continuous process improvement. (Frank Popoff, and Alan P. Brache, "The Seven Deadly Sins of Process Improvement", *Chief Executive*, June 1994, p. 22.)

Adweek reports a study of fifty of the Fortune 1,000 companies that reported being in a reengineering process but "were merely making incremental, operational improvements as opposed to changing their fundamental ways of doing business." ("Mythical Reengineering" *Adweek*, May 2, 1994, p. 18.)

"Business process reengineering will not provide a long-term shield against the forces of global competition or a permanent foundation for maintaining the standard of living in the US," said Henry F. Duignan of Ross Operating Valve Company. The problem with most current theories for reinvigorating US manufacturing, including reengineering, is their emphasis on wealth maintenance through greater productivity, which gets translated by corporate management as laying off workers, rather than creating new wealth-enhancing strategies and new higher paying manufacturing jobs. (John H. Sheridan, "Reengineering Isn't Enough", *Industry Week*, January 17, 1994, p. 61.)

Reengineering is the supernova of our old approaches to organizational change, the last gasp of efforts that have consistently failed. What is reengineering but another attempt, usually by people at the top, to impose new structures over old – to take one set of rigid rules and guidelines and impose them on the rest of the organization? . . . Reengineering doesn't change what needs to be changed most: the way people at all levels relate to the enterprise. We need to be asking: Has the organization's capacity to change increased and improved? (Margaret Wheatley, quoted in Tom Peters, "A Paean to Self-Organization", *Forbes ASAP*, September 1994, p. 154.)

Perhaps most damaging but to be expected, "CEOs still primarily evaluate their companies on profits and stock performance according to a survey performed about reengineering by Booz Allen & Hamilton." (Ronald Henkoff, "CEOs Still Don't Walk the Talk", *Fortune*, April 18, 1994, p. 14.)

> Critics, including some prominent executives, believe massive downsizing has become a fad, a bone to throw Wall Street when investors begin baying for cost cuts . . . Fear is almost palpable in the corridors of the reengineered workplace, where loyalty takes a backseat to survival and personal advancement. (John A. Byrne, "The Pain of Downsizing", *Business Week*, May 9, 1994, p. 61.)

> "When they started talking about another round of downsizing, people were a little more anxious because they feel they're already stretched thin. Now we'll have to learn to work smarter and completely change the way we do things," says Nancy P. Karen of the reengineering effort she is going through. "Working smarter also means working harder – much harder." She once directly supervised 26 people, instead of the 79 [she supervises now], and she used to work more normal hours as well. No longer. Karen now puts in 50 to 60 hours a week, from 8 a.m. to 7 p.m. every weekday at NYNEX' White Plains Office. (*Ibid.*, p. 67.)

In order for downsizings through reengineering to work the company must find effective ways to deal with the new workload and configuration of processes before the layoffs.

When top managers have golden parachutes through change and employees remain uncertain whether they will receive any monetary severance, the environment of a reengineering program becomes laden with fear, resentment and low morale not to mention the thoughts of conscious (or unconscious) sabotage.

Finally, the fear of the future for middle managers at mid-life can be extraordinary and lead to obsessive concern for self and not the work that still needs to get done.

Commitment Needed to Make It Work

> It is important to understand the intellectual commitment as well as the time and financial commitment required to make any change effort a success. In thinking of the reengineering process in a larger context, it is really the prelude to radical change. At

any business, the revolutionary process starts with an analysis of the business environment and the recognition that radical change is the organization's best response to the challenge it faces. The first stage is turbulent, marked by conflict, denial, and resistance. Next, leaders and employees begin to create a shared vision of what their company should become and turn their attention outward to customers and competitors. In the final phase, the company creates systems for compensation and appraisal that enforce the new values and help reshape corporate culture. (Stratford Sherman, "A Master Class in Radical Change", *Fortune*, December 13, 1993, p. 82.)

Exemplars

American Modern Home Insurance Group • Ford • Mutual Life • GTE • AT&T • Blue Cross of Washington and Alaska • Bell Atlantic • Union Carbide • Wal-Mart • IBM Credit • Pacific Bell • Mutual Benefit Life • Chevron Chemical • Hills Pet Food • AlliedSignal • The Travelers • BellSouth • Hale Municipal Hospital • Ryder System

Business reengineering means putting aside much of the received wisdom of two hundred years of industrial management. It means forgetting how work was done in the age of the mass market and deciding how it can be down now. In business reengineering, old job titles and old organizational arrangement – departments, divisions, groups, and so on – cease to matter. They are artifacts of another age. What matters in reengineering is how we want to organize work today, given the demands of today's markets and the power of today's technologies.

– **MICHAEL HAMMER AND JAMES CHAMPY,**
Reengineering the Corporation.

Chapter Sixteen

TOWARD AUTHENTIC COMMUNICATION

"We've got to take out the boss element," Welch says. By his lights, 21st century managers will forgo their old powers – to plan organize, implement and measure – for new duties: counseling groups, providing resources for them, helping them think for themselves. "We're going to win on our ideas," he says, "not by whips and chains."

– Thomas A. Stewart,
"GE Keeps Those Ideas Coming",
Fortune, August 12, 1991, p. 41.

IT IS HARD to overestimate the importance of communication. Not in the sense of quantity, we are buried in messages and data, but in the sense of relating to one another in the workplace authentically, respectfully, and without fear. Toward this end, many of the techniques strive to establish a psychologically safe environment in which to discuss the needs and problems at hand. Yet, real communication between people, as peers, still seems to be the exception rather than the rule.

The following techniques, workout and 360-degree evaluation, are attempts at eliciting honest, constructive, and frank communications between individuals in the work environment. The concept of diversity that is discussed after the techniques, is a formal attempt by organizations to understand, appreciate, and work with differences among people in the work force so they do not interfere with the contribution and potential of each person. All are efforts to achieve a communicative atmosphere for the purpose of helping the organization succeed.

WORKOUT

What It is

This is a method of making managers responsive to employees. It calls for a frank public discussion of issues characterized by managers answering employees' questions with direct answers, or a promise to get the answers, within a fixed period of time. General Electric popularized this program.

Workout has four goals: (1) Building trust. (2) Empowering employees. (3) Eliminating unnecessary work. (4) Creating a new paradigm which includes ideas such as boundarylessness, integrated diversity, searching out and improving upon 'best practices', and global leadership in their markets. (Noel M. Tichy, and Stratford Sherman, "Walking the Talk At GE", *Training and Development*, June 1993, p. 26.)

Wisdom

> In the culture we are building today, people are willing to take each other on. If they disagree, they go at it. They're still a little reluctant to deal with me on those terms, but they're pushing me more than they ever did before. And I'm learning not to stake out a position so quickly that it preempts them. (GE, CEO, Jack Welch in William Weiss, "A Master Class in Radical Change", *Fortune*, December 13, 1993, p. 88.)

Workout can foster an atmosphere like a New England town meeting. It has four major goals:

> Building trust; empowering employees; eliminating unnecessary work; and creating a participative paradigm

Figure 16.1   Three Stages to Building a Workout Program

Stage One:

The Event:
3-day off-site discussing problems (30–100 people, informal)
Bosses locked out of discussion until the final day
Any retribution by bosses would be career limiting
On the final day bosses make on-the-spot decisions and agree, say no, or ask for more information which may lead to a maximum of a one-month study

Move toward boundarylessness – removing the ceilings and walls (changing the language, e.g., subordinates to work-partners, human resources to member relations)
Cross-functional (self-managed) teams
Managers into leaders (coaching, facilitating, working toward participation)
Employee empowerment
Best practices/benchmarking/reengineering

Stage Two:

In-tact, cross-functional work teams do their own workout
Consultants replaced by own staff
Task oriented (specific) to common problems (general)
Raise the bar to optimize reengineering process

Stage Three:

Change Acceleration Program – managers now manage the process
Initiate, accelerate, maintain change
Constantly communicate
Constantly assess

Adapted from Noel M. Tichy, and Stratford Sherman, *Control Your Destiny or Someone Else Will*, New York: Harper Business, 1994.

Workout is a form of institutional conflict. Honda uses a similar technique. They encourage everyone to call for a *waigaya* session when necessary. During these sessions everyone is required to lay their cards on the table and speak directly about their problems. The Japanese have learned to disagree without being disagreeable. (Tracy Goss, Richard Pascale and Anthony Athos, "The Reinvention Roller Coaster: Risking the Present for a Powerful Future", *Harvard Business Review*, November/ December 1993, p. 107.)

Wishful Thinking

Workout does not account for the downside or "shadow" or the inability to deal with second order consequences – unanticipated reactions and rivalries that lead to the expression of hostilities and political behaviors that surround the process.

Workout is a way of communicating through confrontation and it takes a special event and a mandate from the CEO to make this form of inter-level communication workable. It is, in a sense, the battering ram to open those "my door is always open" doors of executives who consciously or otherwise discourage real communication. Alone, it will not change much except it will afford seasonal opportunities to vent some steam.

Commitment Needed to Make It Work

It took Jack Welch several years to make workout an acceptable part of the culture and not without applying considerable pressure from his office. Again, top management must be willing to stick with it until it is successfully grafted on to a culture that can, and will, resist it until it knows the change is inevitable.

Exemplars

GE • IBM called their equivalent program "probing" • Honda has a similar program and calls it a *waigaya* session

360-DEGREE EVALUATIONS

What It is

360-degree evaluation is using the input from subordinates, colleagues, customers, and bosses to create an overall picture of your performance. It is used for training and development purposes as well as for personal feedback. It is not supposed to be used for promotional or pay determinations.

Wisdom

> At GE: To create greater allegiance to a process, rather than to a boss, the company has begun to put in place so-called 360-degree appraisal routines in which peers and others above and below the employee evaluate the performance of an individual in a process. In some cases as many as 20 people are now involved in reviewing a single employee. (John A. Byrne, "The Horizontal Corporation", *Business Week*, December 20, 1993, p. 79.)

In order to make it work follow these five steps: (1) Establish program goals. (2) Decide who will be evaluated. (3) Determine whether a standard evaluation procedure can be used. (4) Decide how many evaluations will be collected. (5) Communicate the ground rules. And use it appropriately. (Marcie Shorr Hirsch, "360 Degrees of Evaluation", *Working Woman*, August 1994, p. 20.)

The popularity of this system is growing because of the widespread disillusionment with evaluations generally. Performance appraisals have come under attack for various reasons, most notably, that they are more of a control device than a learning tool, they are too infrequent, not comprehensive enough, inadequately conducted, lack follow-up, and require skills boss-evaluators simply do not have.

"The feedback – generally anonymous – includes such topics as the manager's ability to take charge, coach workers, delegate responsibility, manage conflict and communicate clearly." (Joann S. Lublin, "Turning The Tables: Underlings Evaluate Bosses", *The Wall Street Journal*, October 4, 1994, p. B1.)

> How do managers rate themselves? Only about a third produce self-assessments that generally match what co-workers concluded.

Another third – called 'high self-raters' – have an inflated view of their talents, says Ellen Van Velsor, a researcher at the Center for Creative Leadership. The remaining third rate themselves lower than co-workers do. An oversize ego, it turns out, is murder in a manager. Almost invariably, the high self-raters are judged the least effective by co-workers. (Brian O'Reilly, "360 Feedback Can Change Your Life", *Fortune*, October 17, 1994, p. 93.)

Wishful Thinking

"If management style can be criticized and torn apart after the fact, why can't it be systematically discussed and critiqued up front?" (Clinton O. Longenecker and Dennis A. Gioia, "Ten Myths of Managing Managers", *Sloan Management Review*, Fall, 1991, p. 81.)

"According to a 1992 Wyatt Company survey, only 12% of companies include subordinate contributions in their performance appraisals." (Catherine Romano, "Fear of Feedback", *Management Review*, December 1993, p. 38.) 360-degree evaluation requires a level of frankness and interpersonal skills that make the expression of deliberate negative political behaviors unlikely.

The new but now familiar techniques of corporate communication – focus groups, surveys, management-by-walking-around – can block organizational learning even as they help solve certain problems. These techniques promote defensive reasoning by encouraging employees to believe that their proper role is to criticize management while the proper role of management is to take action and to fix whatever is wrong. Worse yet, they discourage double-loop learning, which is the process of asking questions not only about objective facts but also about the reasons and motives behind those facts. Double-loop learning encourages people to examine their own behavior, take responsibility for their own action and inaction, and surface the kind of potentially threatening or embarrassing information that can produce real change. (Chris Argyris, "Good Communication That Blocks Learning", *Harvard Business Review*, July–August 1994, p. 77.)

When it is designed to provide information that you can use to become a better manager, scores from your handpicked pals or from randomly chosen associates typically turn out remarkably similar. But when used as the basis for formal performance evaluations, things change. Friends pump up your score, rivals become remarkably lukewarm, and that staff boob you keep reaming out cuts you dead. (Brian O'Reilly, "360 Feedback Can Change Your Life", *Fortune*, October 17, 1994, p. 93.)

The worst indictment? The process has been terminated when unfavorable upward appraisals have been received. Several bosses have been known to intimidate staff into favorable responses and others dismiss criticism as popularity contests. One manager at Citicorp said, "The people who work for you are not qualified to comment on your ability to lead or not to lead." He lost his job after a power struggle with his own boss. (Joann S. Lublin, "Turning The Tables: Underlings Evaluate Bosses", *The Wall Street Journal*, October 4, 1994, p. B1.)

Some do not believe that the feedback is not attached to pay and promotion decisions even when explicitly stated. One manager told his subordinates after a bad review that if the evaluations did not improve next time staff changes would be made.

Commitment Needed to Make It Work

Managers are selected because of their technical skills and often because of their political skills. They are not chosen to answer to their subordinates or because their social skills are finely tuned – especially not so in regard to their behavior with subordinates. The commitment required to make 360-degree evaluation work is more than most techniques since this directly exposes a manager to personal ridicule from colleagues and subordinates in a way that may leave them vulnerable. Thus, caution is the primary approach taken by managers and unless forced to do so these programs seem to die quickly. Indeed, the skills required to listen and act upon feedback are, in themselves, often too daunting for many people to meet. And yet these are exactly the skills organizations need most.

Exemplars

GE • Rosenbluth Travel • AT&T • Amoco Production • Mass Mutual Life Insurance • Deloitte & Touche • Raychem • Nestle's Perrier • General Motors • Pitney Bowes • Chase Bank

Control Your Destiny
or Someone Else Will.

– Book title about GE also representative of
their attitude toward the market
(Noel M. Tichy and Stratford Sherman,
Control Your Destiny or Someone Else Will,
New York: Harper Business, 1994).

DIVERSITY

America is a construction of mind, not of race or inherited class or ancestral territory. It is a creed born of immigration, of the jostling of scores of tribes that become American to the extent to which they can negotiate accommodations with one another . . . America is a collective act of the imagination whose making never ends, and once that sense of collectivity and mutual respect is broken, the possibilities of American-ness begin to unravel.

– Robert Hughes, "The Fraying of America",
Time, February 3, 1992, p. 44.

What It is

Diversity has come to mean "to accept varied personal characteristics in the labor force." Women, racial and ethnic minorities, the physically and mentally challenged, people over forty, people with divergent sexual preferences, people of all religious sects, and individuals with language differences should not be denied access to, nor fair treatment and promotions within, the workplace.

This is more than affirmative action. It is a pro-active position that recognizes the differences between people are real and, at the same time, can be assets of the organization. To fully utilize these differences an organization needs to combine intelligence and sensitivity. Diversity is about helping people bridge the gap that differences often create. It is not just about gender, race, ethnicity, age, or physical disability. It is about understanding and appreciating different ways of thinking and being.

"PG&E defines diversity as any difference in race, gender, age, language, physical characteristics, disability, sexual orientation, economic status, parental status, education, geographic origin, profession, lifestyle, religion, or position in the hierarchy of the organization." (Ronita B. Johnson and Julie O'Mara, "Shedding New Light on Diversity Training", *Training and Development*, May 1992, p. 52.)

To appreciate and value the customs, habits and beliefs of others. There are three components of diversity management: (1) Managing diversity focuses on the diverse quality of employees' worklife needs, such as child care, family leave, and flexible holiday schedules. (2) Valuing differences centers around interpersonal qualities, such as race, gender and language. (3) Equal employment opportunities-affirmative action (EEO/AA) directs attention to laws that guide recruitment and promotion. But, managing diversity looks at the needs of employees and not just the cultural diversity of employees. Managing diversity also requires putting policies and procedures in place that empower managers to meet the diverse needs of employees. (Lisa Jenner, "Diversity Management: What Does It Mean?", *HR Focus*, January 1994, p. 11.)

Dealing with diversity must be a way of life. Diversity issues require a constant effort to attend to their smooth integration of differences into the organizational mainstream.

Wisdom

Affirmative action was the deliberate attempt to recruit women and minorities to fill positions. The perception among many, especially white males, was that (rightly or wrongly) a quota existed and reverse discrimination was being practiced. Managing diversity is teaching everyone that differences can be valued, indeed harnessed for the good of each person as well as the organization. Living in a multi-cultural environment requires acceptance, appreciation and inclusion of others different from ourselves, at least in the mainstream of our organizations.

"Discussions of cultural differences and attempts to eliminate negative stereotypes are often beneficial to employees and may enhance their communication and morale." (Catherine Ellis and Jeffrey A. Sonnenfeld, "Diverse Approaches to Managing Diversity", *Human Resource Management*, Spring 1994, p. 79.)

Monsanto uses 'consulting pairs' to resolve misunderstandings before they become larger problems. The consulting pairs project is based on the perception that in a diverse work force many conflicts will grow out of differences in fundamental – and therefore unexpressed – assumptions and expectations about behavior . . . One of the main aspects of the program is called a 'join up', a facilitated discussion between any supervisor and employee(s) who are new to each other. Another important part of the program is issue resolution, whereby a consulting pair is assigned to help resolve a working-relationship problem. (Jennifer J. Laabs, "Employees Manage Conflict and Diversity", *Personnel Journal*, December 1993, p. 30.)

"According to a study reported in the *Academy of Management Journal*, racial and ethnic diversity enhances a work team's effectiveness." (Erica Gordon Sorohan, "Work Teams Demonstrate Diverse Advantages", *Training and Development*, October 1993, p. 9.)

Diversity training has a better chance of not provoking backlash if certain steps are taken. These include: (1) Get management support. (2) Involve employees in the design of the program. (3) Work from an inclusive definition of diversity. (4) Use qualified diversity training professionals. (5) Put an end to political correctness policing. (Michael Mobley and Tamara Payne, "Backlash! The Challenge to Diversity Training", *Security Management, September* 1993, p. 35.)

"Rapport-building is the central challenge of supervising the culturally diverse. By focusing on what people have in common professionally rather than on how they differ personally, supervisors can operate on a common wavelength with culturally diverse employees." (Philip M. Van Auken, "Supervising Culturally Diverse Employees", *Supervision*, August 1993, p. 11.)

Managing diversity is conceptually different than equal employment opportunity, which was primarily a battle against racism and prejudice. By valuing work force diversity, management seizes the benefits differences bring. The specific challenge facing corporate managers in the coming decade will be how to manage a slower-growing labor force comprised of more female, immigrant, minority, and older workers into a more skilled, productive and adaptive resource. (Dean Elmuti, "Managing Diversity in the Workplace: An Immense Challenge for Both Managers and Workers", *Industrial Management*, July/August 1993, p. 19.)

When using a group's own dynamics to show how diversity affects work interaction and performance, things to keep in mind include: (1) Allow group members to become comfortable with each other before showing them what they can learn from group interactions. (2) Be sensitive to individual comfort levels. (3) Avoid putting a trainee (or any person) in the position of having to explain to the group how all women, or all people of color, or all members of any other group, think or feel. (Steve DeValk, "Holding Up A Mirror to Diversity Issues", *Training and Development*, July 1993, p. 11.)

One of the most difficult areas to deal with is homosexuality, but "The key to unlocking the corporate closet is to end the cycle of silence, secrecy, and invisibility that many homosexuals and heterosexuals support, either knowingly or unknowingly. Just talking about the issues is a valuable first step." (Jay H. Lucas and Mark G. Kaplan, "Unlocking the Corporate Closet", *Training and Development*, January 1994, p. 34.)

Legal developments are expanding the rights of gays to be free of hostile work environments and to share fully in the US promise of equal employment opportunity . . .

It is important to differentiate gay and lesbian workplace issues. Recommendations to be followed to achieve a non-hostile workplace include: (1) Recognize sexual orientation as another element in work force diversity. (2) Provide equal compensation for equal work. (3) Apply the lessons but not the strictures of affirmative action. (4) Develop education and training programs early. (Charles R. Colbert III and John G. Wofford, "Sexual Orientation in the Workplace: Strategic Challenge", *Compensation and Benefits Management*, Summer 1993, p. 1.)

Work force diversity is a perfectly valid management need. The following 4 factors can serve as a guide to the effectiveness of a company's affirmative action policy: (1) whether an affirmative employment plan exists that can serve as a non-discriminatory rationale for the employment decision; (2) whether consideration of applicant's sex or minority status is justified by the existence of an obvious imbalance in the workplace mix; (3) whether the plan emphasizes that supervisors should consider a variety of practical factors (such as turnover rates or types of job openings) in addition to any statistical or numerical goals; and (4) whether the plan does not unnecessarily restrict or hinder the rights of white male applicants or create any barriers to their advancement . . . Any comments that can alter a person's chances of employment or promotion can be grounds for discrimination proceedings. (Timothy P. Walker, "Discrimination and The Law", Part 2, *Supervisory Management*, September 1992, p. 10.)

One of the most dramatic and important diversity training programs is conducted at United Parcel Service. Their community internship program takes managers off the job for a month and puts them through an experience that will sensitize them to people who live in different circumstances . . .

> Managers could find themselves serving meals to the homeless, helping rid an urban neighborhood of drugs, helping migrant farm workers build temporary houses and schools, or helping teachers manage a classroom of kids in a Head Start program. So far more than 800 managers have participated. (Bob Filipczak, "25 Years of Diversity at UPS", *Training*, August 1992, p. 42.)

"Research has established beyond any reasonable doubt that well managed heterogeneous groups are more productive than homogeneous ones. Managing diversity is about improving corporate performance." (Jack Gordon, "Rethinking Diversity", Training, January 1992, p. 23.)

> Levi Strauss & Co. spends $5,000,000 a year in a 'Valuing Diversity' Program to meet the needs of 56% of its 23,000 employees who are members of minority groups. They have a Diversity Council, which regularly meets with the corporate executive committee. (Alice Cuneo, "Diverse by Design: How Good Intentions Make Good Business", *Business Week*, 1992, p. 72.)

Training an entire work force can be a monumentally expensive proposition. Ronita B. Johnson and Julie O'Mara described how PG&E, the huge California utility, exposed each of its employees to a diversity training program by using 110 of its own employees. First, they were trained in an intensive six-day program that focused on the potential trainers' self-knowledge, leadership skills, subject matter understanding, and facilitation skills. One key to its success was the non-judgmental approach of the original program design. As one trainer put it:

> I let all employees who are participating in the training know upfront that the material and discussion may make them uncomfortable but that I'm not there to judge or change values and beliefs. I'm there to provide an opportunity to explore the thought processes that affect their behavior in the workplace. (Ronita B. Johnson and Julie O'Mara, "Shedding New Light on Diversity Training", *Training and Development*, May 1992, p. 50.)

PG&E believes that diversity trainers should possess four vital qualities: (1) self-knowledge; (2) leadership skills; (3) subject matter understanding and expertise; and (4) facilitation skills. Their train-the-trainer program consists of four phases: (1) questionnaire and in-depth interviewing; (2) an intensive six-day train-the-trainer workshop; (3) the facilitation of a four- or eight hour training session by the trainee; and (4) certification as a diversity trainer. PG&E believes that managing diversity improves its competitive advantage in recruiting and retaining employees, which improves productivity, quality, creativity, and morale. (*Ibid.*, p. 44.)

When employees are trained in how-to-conduct diversity training for their own companies certain benefits may be realized: (1) They already know the company, many of the people they will train, and the needs of the group better than an external training consultant. (2) They are available for pre-training activities and post-training activities and serve as a constant reminder of the commitment the company has made to support diversity training and interpersonal understanding. (3) Follow-up and continuing needs assessment and reinforcement can be provided seamlessly.

PG&E believes that managing diversity improves its competitive advantage in recruiting and retaining employees and that it increases productivity, quality, creativity, and morale. The company believes that managing diversity creates better customer service, improves its public image, and boosts consumer confidence and credibility . . . According to the company's view, managing diversity 'requires the creation of an open, supportive, and responsive organization in which differences are understood, encouraged, appreciated and managed.' (*Ibid.*, p. 51.)

Networks established for demographic sub-groups can help and hinder relations but generally they do alleviate some of the pain, insecurity and stress being part of a group that feels isolated, or having special needs. Mentoring programs also may help "outgroups" navigate the system and understand how to get ahead. Hughes Aircraft Co. is one of many that has an extensive program to address issues of diversity. Their program also has an outreach component to help minorities and women think about, prepare for and acquire technical skills to enable them to eventually work for the company or another similar company. Their "Youth Motivation Task Force" sends hundreds of company employees to local schools in the southern California region where it is located to encourage students to think about a technical career. (David Barclay, "Commitment From the Top Makes It Work", *IEEE Spectrum*, June 1992, p. 25.)

Stereotypes not only divide people, they create narrow and restrictive mindsets. It is not just about race or gender or age, stereotypes can apply to almost any imaginable category; occupational categories and the amount of money you have, for example, can lead to stereotyping. The engineer or programmer who is a nerd; the statistician or accountant who is a dull number-cruncher or the poor person who is seen as a loser, all suffer from gross generalizations and inaccurate descriptions based on the flimsiest of data.

Wishful Thinking

Women only hold 2% of big company board seats and the only woman CEO of a Fortune 500 company in 1992 shared the job with her husband. Only 18% of American workers earning $50,000–75,000 a year were women as of 1989. Only 12% above $75,000. ("The Spare Sex", *The Economist*, March 28, 1992, p. 17.)

> If women suspect they are undervalued at work, and see little hope of promotion, other ways of spending their time are bound to start looking more attractive . . . The leading reason women gave for [leaving work] was not marriage or motherhood, but dissatisfaction with their career prospects . . . At one Johnson & Johnson unit, departing female managers complained that they had felt isolated from their male colleagues. (*Ibid.*, p. 18.)

As important as diversity training is, only 18% of the HR executives in the 3rd annual Personnel 100 (largest companies based on revenues) said that diversity still remains a challenge! (Diane Filipowski, "HR Remains A Challenge", *Personnel Journal*, December 1993, p. 51.)

A Hay Group study listed fourteen business issues and asked human resource professionals in 1,405 US organizations to rank their priorities.

According to 58% of respondents, the most important business issue concerned improving quality. Controlling the cost of benefits ran a close second, with 55% listing it as one of their top priorities . . . only 12% considered work force diversity a top priority while 44% said that it was important. (Bob Filipczak, "What's Nice, What's Necessary", *Training*, January 1993, p. 76.)

A major challenge for all employees is to assimilate into the mainstream of corporate life. Women and minorities are often excluded from social activities or left out of informal communication networks. The result appears to be a sense of isolation, lower organizational commitment, and ultimately, a decision to seek employment in a more hospitable environment. (Benson Rosen and Kay Lovelace, "Fitting Square Pegs Into Round Holes", *HR Magazine*, January 1994, p. 86.)

In many corporations, a glass ceiling exists between middle management and top management. That glass ceiling still remains largely impenetrable for all minority groups and white females . . . To bring individuals through the glass ceiling, companies need to examine how their cultures work and they can do so by answering the following questions: (1) Is the corporate culture fertile ground for diversity? (2) Will top management become involved? (3) Are hiring and promotion criteria in step? (4) Has mentoring shattered the glass ceiling? (5) What is the true goal of the diversity program? (6) Do hiring criteria promote the desired outcomes? (7) How successful is the company at growing its own talent? (8) Has the company evaluated its recruitment assumption? (9) Do minority career paths have a dead end? (10) Will management be able to see the forest from the trees? (Andrew Harris, "Break the Glass Ceiling for Senior Executives", *HR Focus*, March, 1994, p. 1.)

At the Federal Aviation Administration men were coerced into running a gauntlet in which they were aggressively fondled by females . . . Louise Eberhardt, president of the firm that designed the program: "I think we need to explain that generally, what it was, is one minute of men experiencing what women in male-dominated organizations experience often, daily . . ." During another program at the FAA, "Black employees at sensitivity training sessions have been encouraged to go off by themselves, discuss their problems in a 'white, male-dominated society,' and then return to the main room and verbally assail some individual white male employees." (Daniel Seligman, "Thinking About the Gauntlet", *Fortune*, October 17, 1994, p. 214.)

"Diversity training can spark new ways of thinking and working. It can also cause confusion, disorder and hostility." (Victor C. Thomas, "The Downside of Diversity", *Training and Development*, January 1994, p. 60.)

There may be much anger and a feeling of victimization. This polarizes people and often sub-groups expect, even look for evidence that will support their fear that differences and abuses exist. Radical feminists, for example, have in their writings demonstrated an inability to trust the system and an unwillingness to assume an equal role or partnership with males at work. Rather, for them it is simply about a power struggle for control not equality. This is met with resistance and for many men, this behavior will preclude their willingness to partner – especially if they perceive themselves becoming disadvantaged by women's success. Even those male advocates for fairness will be put in a defensive position and will resist diversity efforts out of the belief that it is a win/lose struggle where they can only lose.

Ineffective diversity training can raise the expectations of women and minorities, increase the fear and resistance among white males, and harm an organization's diversity efforts . . . Sybil Evans, assistant editor of *Cultural Diversity at Work*, suggests that employers connect the training to specific business outcomes and results. Another key to the success of training is to implement strategies that support diversity as an overall business philosophy. (Shari Caudron, "Training Can Damage Diversity Efforts", *Personnel Journal*, April 1993, p. 50.)

Aversive racism is subtle and rampant. When it is uncovered it may lead to more deeply held feelings that result in racism. Aversive racists may be identified by the following characteristics: (1) They endorse fair and just treatment of all groups, at least in principle. (2) They unconsciously harbor negative feelings toward other races. (3) They experience anxiety and discomfort when forced into interracial interaction. (4) They will adhere strictly to established rules and codes of behavior during interracial interaction. (5) They express negative feelings in subtle ways that they can rationalize. (John Dovidio, "The Subtlety of Racism", *Training and Development*, April 1993, p. 57.)

Having the programs, doing the training, raising consciousness is no guarantee that attitudes or behavior will change. Ongoing attention to the issues, the tensions, conflicts and irritations that arise is vital. It is a matter of respecting everyone and treating everyone decently. Unfortunately, diversity is still more a demographic concept than a reflection of a socially integrated workplace reality.

"The biggest challenge facing diversity trainers today is how to handle backlash." Some explanations for backlash include: (1) Shifting demographics are placing different groups in proximity of one another and race and gender issues are frequently used for political purposes. (2) White males feel under attack since it is typically the white male establishment that maintains power in large organizations, particularly the *Fortune, Business Week* and *Forbes* lists of biggest companies. Thus, they believe they are unfairly stereotyped and assumed to be guilty of discriminatory biases by virtue of their self-interest and their position in the organizational hierarchy, if not actual behavior. At the same time it is white males who feel discriminated against in reverse when applying for promotions and find remedies for past biases call for filling jobs with minorities or women – sometimes less qualified than they. (3) The diversity training establishment itself consists of almost all women or minorities. (Michael Mobley and Tamara Payne, "Backlash: The Challenge to Diversity Training", *Security Management*, September 1993, p. 35.)

Diversity training is still seen as something white males need to take. Because insensitivity to others is not limited to the dominant males, training needs to encompass a broader attitude of general acceptance and inclusion in the purposes and functions of the organization. If done carelessly it sets up a contentious, divisive atmosphere. Yet, it is especially needed where sexual harassment or bias suits have been successfully launched.

"HUD memoranda have specified that certain off-hour activities (e.g., 'participate as active members of minority, feminist, or other cultural organizations') will be expected of anybody hoping to receive an 'outstanding' job evaluation." (Daniel Seligman, "Thinking About the Gauntlet", *Fortune*, October 17, 1994, p. 214.)

Commitment Needed to Make It Work

Acceptance of others is a permanent attitude and each company must be vigilant about maintaining an environment free of hate, discrimination, and prejudice. Time needs to be spent just introducing different people to one another and exposing everyone to the beliefs and habits of members of different groups. Just having an opportunity to share their experiences with one another is a prelude to understanding and definitely begins the process of reducing ignorance, fear and distance between people at work. Even this rather minimalist approach to the issue, however, needs an ongoing commitment and time needs to be made available regularly to make it happen.

Exemplars

McDonald's • The Olive Garden • Applebee's International • Lotus Development • Levi Strauss • Mobil • Prudential • United Parcel Service • Hughes Aircraft

Chapter Seventeen

JAPANESE MANAGEMENT

Every company, no matter how small, ought to have clear cut goals apart from the pursuit of profit, purposes that justify its existence among us.

– Konosuke Matsushita

What It is

The Japanese system of management is still the focus of much attention in the world because of its success in the global economy. Japanese management is a basket of techniques that countries have attempted to import for various, specific purposes. Overall, however, as a system, Japanese management is self-reinforcing and effective because of its synchronicity with Japanese culture.

The aspects of Japanese management which seem to be of most interest to Americans have been: quality circles which led to total quality management and the utilization of the Deming System; bottom-up decision making (the *ringi* system) which encourages suggestions, ideas and initiative from first line employees (especially relevant in customer intensive processes);

223

corporate strategic alliances; *keiretsu* (groups of companies) acting more as a conglomerate than an alliance; just-in-time inventory/delivery (JIT) which saves tremendous inventory and storage costs; the *kaizen* system which is attention to continuous improvement (related to the quality movement); flattening the hierarchy which allows for speedier innovation and decision-making; and, lean production which emphasizes in addition to JIT, a system of process engineering that continually reduces and streamlines inputs and processing.

One of the latest techniques recently imported to the US is the so-called 4S model which as a purported management strategy has supposedly revolutionized productivity at Wellex Corporation.

> Like the better known kaizen, 4S establishes a culture in which management and employees communicate openly toward a common goal – continuous improvement. However, 4S goes beyond kaizen. Rather than focusing on manufacturing processes it takes a grass roots approach helping each individual attain the highest level of personal effectiveness. In addition, 4S costs almost nothing to implement and is almost zen-like in its simplicity . . . In 4S, employees are asked to structure their work and personal lives around 4 basic steps: organization, orderliness, neatness and cleanliness. (Ingrid Abramovitch, "Beyond Kaizen", *Success*, February 1994, p. 85.) *Kaizen* means constant improvement. 4S is a holistic concept inclusive of personal improvement as well as organizational improvement.

Wisdom

Japanese management at Bridgestone and New United Motors Manufacturing, Inc. proved more successful than matched American-managed companies in a recent study, ". . . the key came in the higher expectations the Japanese managers held for their workers. High expectations engender delegation, participation, and a sense of trust, all reciprocated with high performance." (Thomas A. Mahoney, and John R. Deckop, "Y'gotta Believe: Lessons From Americans vs. Japanese-run US Factories", *Organizational Dynamics*, Spring 1993, p. 27.)

> Japanese companies operate as if all personnel are part of a small family business. This was supported by another study claiming

Japanese managers see a work team as an environment in which information is shared in pursuit of improved performance, while Americans used groups to share responsibilities and reduce risks. By using failure as a learning device, Japanese teams are able to tackle positive things rather than concern themselves with avoiding the negative. (Jeremiah J. Sullivan, "Japanese Management Philosophies: From the Vacuous to the Brilliant", *California Management Review*, Winter 1992, p. 66.)

Japanese plants in the US demonstrate a totally different attitude about the purpose of management. "The plant views career advancement as an opportunity to impact the basic work of the organization, rather than a chance to escape from that work into an office, and many policies serve to reinforce this orientation." (Thomas A. Mahoney, and John R. Deckop, "Y'gotta Believe: Lessons From Americans vs. Japanese-run US Factories", *Organizational Dynamics*, Spring 1993, p. 37.)

SPECIFIC DIFFERENTIATING ASPECTS

Understanding the mission and philosophy of the company (see Figure 17.1 Matsushita Electronics)

Lifetime employment (at least avoiding layoffs as long as possible and then only after seeking alternatives)

Employee loyalty and identification with the company

Just-in-time inventory system (*Kanban*)

Age-based seniority promotions

Company unions

Ten-year evaluations

On-the-job training (OJT)

Long-term planning

Acceptance of personal responsibility and commitment to the group (subordinate self-interest to the good of the company)

Quality circles

A teamwork orientation

Respect for individual as a part of the organization

Bottom-up decision making (*ringi* system)

Flat hierarchy

Job rotation throughout various functions

Lean production

Preserving the "Wa" (harmony)

Figure 17.1 Matsushita's Seven Principles

(1) National Service through Industry
   We will contribute to the progress and welfare of the community and nation.

(2) Fairness
   Without this spirit no one can win respect nor can be respected no matter how wise or capable they may be.

(3) Harmony
   We shall work together as a family in mutual trust and responsibility.

(4) Struggle for Betterment
   It shall be our policy to encourage trust and self-reliance that each may gain self-respect through his or her own endeavor and struggle hard for betterment.

(5) Courtesy and Humility
   We shall respect the rights of others. We shall be cordial and modest. We shall praise and encourage freely.

(6) Adjustment and Assimilation
   As the world moves forward we must keep in step.

(7) Gratitude
   We shall repay the kindness of our associates, our community, our nation, and our foreign friends with gratitude.

Keiretsu (groups of companies where decision making is often made by the parent for supplier companies)

Honest communication

Waigaya sessions: sessions called by an employee to speak frankly about any issue whatsoever (nothing is off limits)

Wishful Thinking

Karoshi – sudden death from overwork is a category of death in Japan that is not categorized anywhere else. The commitment expected of individuals may be too exacting. Also, the paternalism inherent in the Japanese management system no longer works in most of the industrialized world. There is no longer a reciprocal understanding that workers will be loyal and committed in return for being taken care of. The modern workplace is becoming increasingly cutthroat.

Cultural compatibility with any technique is a primary causal influence of its success. Transplanting Japanese techniques was always difficult because of this. Attention to Japanese methods has waned, however, because living in a heterogeneous culture, Americans create suitable innovations on a very pragmatic basis. Does it work? Some parts do. Some parts do not. Many techniques have been tried and many did not work in the US as designed by the Japanese, in large part, because of cultural differences.

Even in Japan there is criticism of the wisdom of using their management style in the United States: "Today, almost without exception, those companies are in the red. According to a survey conducted by the Ministry of International Trade and Industry, the local US and European subsidiaries of Japanese manufacturing industries are posting large deficits." ("What's Killing Japanese Business? 'Japanese-style Management'", *Tokyo Business Today*, July 1993, p. 24.) While it is an interesting self-critique the analysis suffers from the same flawed reasoning that propelled the American obsession with Japanese management techniques in the first place: a conception that a particular technique was the underlying basis for economic performance.

In a case of a (hidden) participant/observer at the Subaru-Isuzu Automotive facility at Lafayette, Indiana, it was found that while the structures were ostensibly designed for worker participation, management . . .

tightly controlled the topics that could be raised for consideration and decision making by consensus was simply a
mirage . . . Many things that had a direct effect on workers'
lives, such as overtime, line speed, and shift rotation were not up
for discussion. The willingness of American workers to feel obedience to the Japanese system is in doubt. Evidence of worker
resistance to Subaru-Isuzu Automotive (Indiana) from July,
1989 through January, 1990 emerged in various individual and
collective forms. Sabotage occurred when workers in one of the
trim and final teams discovered how to stop the assembly line
without management tracing their location. Collective resistance
also emerged in the form of (1) protest, direct confrontation with
management; (2) jokes; and (3) organized agitation at team and
department meetings . . . The data failed to support the contention that participation schemes increase worker control. The
assumption that decentralized authority structures increase
worker autonomy must be questioned. (Laurie Graham, "Inside
a Japanese Transplant: A Critical Perspective", *Work and
Occupations*, May 1993, p. 147.)

Self-discipline, peer pressure and team leaders all pushed the
individual to accept their "end of the bargain" and thus served to
maintain a high level of pressure on individual performance. This
feeling of duty to the mission, your job and your team eventually
was abused by management in creating ever increasing demands
upon the worker in order to have 60 seconds of every minute
focused on the achievement of the task at hand. In so doing it
became impossible for all to keep up and cracks in the commitment, camaraderie and compassion of leaders led to a divisiveness that ultimately pit workers against managers. (*Ibid.*)

Apparently the bloom is off the rose. But American practice
and understanding of participation has changed much since the
early days of adopting Japanese participation schemes. The new
model is about real empowerment and self-management while
the earlier notions of Japanese style participation were still
focused around submitting good ideas, passively, through quality
circles.

In a ringing indictment of Japanese management, Yoshimichi
Yamashita wrote that:

The next generation of Japanese managers must immediately
confront the consequences of their upbringing: (1) The typical

Japanese senior manager does not instinctively precede action with reason. (2) Typical Japanese managers cannot evaluate themselves critically. (3) The Japanese executive has trouble thinking strategically. (4) The Japanese manager has little grasp of creativity. (5) The Japanese manager does not speak the international language of management – English. (Yoshimuchi Yamashita, "Japanese Management: A Study of Stagnation", *Directors and Boards*, Fall 1992, p. 24.)

Commitment Needed to Make It Work

As with all techniques developed in other cultures or even different organizations, utilizing Japanese management techniques will be difficult unless the underlying cultural assumptions and practices are consistent with the technique. (See Figure 17.2 the Ladder of Organizational Behavior.)

Exemplars

Honda • Sony • Bridgestone • Matsushita

> To be sure, Japanese companies are extremely hierarchical organizations in which everyone is keenly aware of his or her place. But everyone is also made to feel an indispensable part of the community – a fact that many Japanese argue constitutes a crucial difference between American and Japanese industry.
>
> – **Robert C. Christopher**,
> *The Japanese Mind*,
> London: Pan, 1984.

Figure 17.2

Cultural contrasts that explain the difficulties in transferring the Japanese style of management to an American environment

American	Japanese
Verbal, explicit, low context communications	Non-verbal, high context, implicit communication
Success and failure are personal matters	Ego is subsumed for good of group. Success or failure is less ego-centered
The individual's identity is strongly ego-centered. Failure of the group is not your responsibility	Failure of group may bring personal shame
Commitment to desire and personal ambitions	Commitment to obligations
Emotions and uncontrolled passions run high. Dramatic, "big-picture" statements are common	Emotions controlled, simplicity, modesty, and refinement are esteemed
Individuality and taking care of self are highly regarded	Relationships to others and your role in the group are vital
Truth is impersonal, objective	Truth is the expression of personal integrity and what is necessary to maintain relationships
World is mastered, is a composite of parts. Dualism of man versus nature is evident	World is whole, independence is impossible
Moral dualism, right and wrong, winner and loser	Morality is relative, winner and loser share responsibility for winning and losing
Assertiveness and individuality are seen as necessary. Silence may mean disagreement	Conspicuous idiosyncrasies and dissension are avoided. Silence is agreement
Rights, privileges are entitlements (birthright)	Obligation, devotion to ancestors, country, family (birth debt)

Figure 17.2 (*Continued*)

American	Japanese
Pragmatism valued, anti-intellectual	Having a good mind is reinforced
Criticism is impersonal to improve performance	Criticism of your idea is criticism of yourself and it de-motivates
Doing preferred over thinking; having as a way of life	Being as a way of life; becoming as purpose
Majority rules	Consensus
You must work to live	Life is work and work is a matter of honor
Decision making depends on consequences to the individual	Decision making based on consequences to the group
Accomplishments must be personal, visible, measurable and continuous; needs explicit feedback	Individual has a place in group and is motivated to enhance the group, implicit feedback
Social life lacks permanence and depth, avoids personal commitments	Deep and lasting relationships are natural, makes personal commitments

The proper thing, to the Japanese way of thinking that I was taught at home, is to make use of the motivations you share with people to accomplish something that will be to the advantage of both.

– **Akio Morita**,
Made in Japan,
New York: Dutton, 1986, p. 12.

Figure 17.3 Honda Motor Corporation

Company Principle

"Maintaining an international viewpoint, we are dedicated
to supplying products of the highest efficiency yet at a
reasonable price for worldwide customer service."

Management Policy

Proceed always with ambition and youthfulness
Respect sound theory, develop fresh ideas, and make the
most effective use of time
Enjoy your work, and always brighten your working
atmosphere
Strive constantly for a harmonious flow of work
Be ever mindful of the value of research and endeavor

Operating Principles

Quality in all jobs
Learn, Think, Analyze, Evaluate, and Improve
Reliable Products
On time with Excellence and Consistency
Better Communication
Listen, Ask, and Speak Up

The problem is to find a form of association which will
defend and protect with the whole common force the
person and good of each associate and in which each,
while uniting himself with all, may still obey himself
alone and remain as free as before.

This is the fundamental problem.

– **ROUSSEAU**

Our deepest fear is not that we are inadequate.

Our deepest fear is that we are powerful beyond measure.

It is our light, not our darkness, that most frightens us.

We ask ourselves, who am I to be brilliant, gorgeous, talented and fabulous?

Actually, who are you not to be?

You are a child of God. Your playing small doesn't serve the world.

There's nothing enlightened about shrinking so that other people won't feel insecure around you.

We were born to make manifest the glory of God that is within us.

It's not just in some of us; it's in everyone.

And as we let our own light shine, we unconsciously give other people permission to do the same.

As we are liberated from our own fear, our presence automatically liberates others.

– **Marianne Williamson**,
A Return to Love,
Quoted in the *Utne Reader*, January/February 1996.

Chapter Eighteen

NEW PARADIGM BUSINESS

WHAT IS CALLED new paradigm business is a term that represents many beliefs and values about the way business should be run. Each stakeholder group may use the term to mean a validation of their interests. Employees talk of being empowered to act for themselves and for the larger purposes served by their organizations. Consumers talk about a quality revolution and attention to service as a new paradigm. Environmentalists talk about sustainability to mean using resources in a way that preserves or replenishes them. In short, the so-called new paradigm is a prismatic concept – depending on your point of view.

In almost all uses however, the concept shares a certain underlying perspective: inclusion of different stakeholders' interests in the organization's decision-making processes; socially responsible adherence to public policy as it relates to hiring, retention and promotion issues; environmental sensitivity in the use and recovery of resources; and, the respectful treatment of people in the workplace.

And, it is much more than that. It is about an ethos that includes the value of experience and building relationships in addition to materialism and status; it is about hope and a feeling of abundance rather than fear and a feeling of scarcity. (See Figure 9.1 for a comparison of the differences between the new and old paradigms.) Perhaps the most important distinction between the paradigms is one being a command and control, top-down, management versus labor mentality and the other representing a partnership mentality where management and labor cooperate for the benefit of their organization.

"New paradigm approaches require strategies to assist in power shaping and new communications patterns." (Elmer H. Burack, Marvin D. Burack, Diane M. Miller and Kathleen Morgan, "New Paradigm Approaches in Strategic Human Resource Management", *Group and Organization Management*, June 1994, p. 141.)

The new paradigm should be built on five principles: (1) The organization should be treated as a moral person with responsibilities toward individuals, and equal attention must be given to individuals' responsibilities toward the organization. (2) Such an organization must be viewed in the fullest sense as a community, in which each individual is accorded dignity and value. (3) An individual can contribute knowledge, skill, and creativity only when both a covenant and a contract exist between the members of the community. (4) Persons are treated as ends within themselves and as real assets. (5) In the structure of a business community, an individual can function creatively, providing peers with the full benefit of personal talent, knowledge and skill. (Michael Quigley, "Ethical Downsizing", *Executive Excellence*, March, 1992, p. 18.)

Change management specialists assert that fewer than one in five endeavors to implement major change initiatives, such as business process redesign in companies succeed. These successful initiatives require nothing short of a paradigm shift. Existing paradigms are frames of reference expressed through rules, policies, procedures, structures, values and beliefs. These frames of reference must be recognized, challenged and transformed. An effective technique for achieving paradigm breakthroughs is by establishing stretch goals – goals that seem impossible today and can only be achieved by challenging current assumptions about business and its processes. (Rocco W. Belmonte and Richard J. Murray, "Getting Ready for Strategic Change: Surviving Business Process Redesign", *Information Systems Management*, Summer, 1993, p. 23.)

In medicine, utilizing the mind-body connection enlists a patient's own attitudes and emotional resources to promote healing. In business enlisting the motivations and resourcefulness of each employee through empowerment and inclusion within the very concept of the organization is utilizing more of the available talent in the service of goal attainment.

The following sections describe several of the major components of what is becoming known as the new paradigm as it is applied to the management of people and resources. This includes new perspectives on the work force (Contingent Work Force), Social Responsibility, Sustainability, The New Science, and Spirituality in Business (the workplace). It then considers new tools such as Reinventing Organizations (Government and Business), Vision/Mission/Values, Transformational Leadership, Empowerment, Healthy Companies, and Workplace Community.

NEW PARADIGM BUSINESS: CONTINGENT WORK FORCE

The unemployment rate dramatically understates the pain, the distress, and the amount of unemployment out there.

– Lawrence Chimerine, advisor to DRI/McGraw-Hill,
quoted in, Christopher Farrell, "Numbers Do Lie.
Just Look at Unemployment", *Business Week*,
December 23, 1991, p. 26.

"Temporary-help employment grew 10 times faster than overall employment between 1984 and 1993, government figures show." (Julie Amparano Lopez, "Negotiating In Your Best Interests As a Contract Worker", *Wall Street Journal*, September 14, 1994.)

"But the number of Americans working part-time jobs out of 'economic necessity' rather than preference is the highest since the early 1980s – roughly 6.4 million last year out of 21 million part-timers, according to the Bureau of Labor Statistics." (Brian Tarcy, "Contingent Workers: Where's the Fit?", *Across The Board*, April 1994, p. 36.)

A temp fills an unforeseen absence such as a receptionist being sick or a data entry clerk not showing up one day. A contingent worker is more of a planned part-timer or temporary worker with a longer employment horizon (but usually less than a year) or for some period that may or may not be renewable.

"Welcome to the slow track . . . The thinning of middle management ranks nationwide has been profound. U.S. companies have eliminated nearly one of every four positions since 1980." (Joseph Weber, "Farewell Fast Track", *Business Week*, December 10, 1990, p. 192.)

What It is

> The US contingent work force comprising part-time workers, temporary employees, and independent contractors hired to work on specific projects in place of full time permanent workers, has become the fastest growing segment of the labor market . . . These 'virtual' employees and independent contractors now total some 35 million people – or one out of every four civilian workers. (Larry Reynolds, "Washington Confronts Part-Time America", *Management Review*, February 1994, p. 27.)

> Platts Marketing may be a prototype of the 21st century company. Not only do the firm's president and his 30 part-time employees work out of their homes, but all of Platts' employees are leased from a 3rd party – National Staff Network. By signing with National Staff Network, President Douglas Platts not only rid himself of payroll headaches, but he was also able to provide his people with benefits for the first time. (Debbie Galant, "Are Part-Time Workers Getting Their Due?", *Institutional Investor*, July, 1993, p. 45.)

While many jobs are part-time by nature and many people wish to work only a few hours a day such as students, parents of young children and retired persons, many people are taking part-time work or several part-time jobs because they cannot find full-time work. It is also a lot cheaper for employers to use part-timers instead of full-timers to save the benefits and administrative expense in carrying a larger payroll. For job seekers it is a "limboland" between a past full-time job and the next. It has advantages for both the hiring company and the job holder. They both get to benefit. The job holder gets to test out new environments, try new jobs, meet new people, gain new skills, and rotate out of boring jobs. The hiring company gets work accomplished, jobs filled and are not tied to these people.

"What we are witnessing is not just the playing out of an economic cycle but a sea change." (William Morin, CEO Drake, Beam, Morin quoted in: Louis S. Richman, "America's Tough New Job Market", *Fortune*, February 24, 1992, p. 52.)

Wisdom

The Organization Man of the 1950s and 1960s is being replaced by the migrant manager and freelance professional of the 1990s . . . With big corporations no longer rewarding loyalty and performance with lifetime guarantees of employment, individuals are transforming themselves into itinerant professionals who sell their human capital on the open market . . . They're assembling skills they can market in different industries, joining new networks of professional groups, and checking out key search firms before they're laid off. They're taking interim job assignments and entering the growing ranks of executive and professional temps. (Bruce Nussbaum, "I'm Worried About My Job", *Business Week*, October 7, 1991, p. 94.)

"Even companies looking for permanent executives increasingly insist on 'test-driving' prospective hires in interim assignments before making a commitment." (*Ibid.*)

A move to just-in-time hiring through employment services, leasing and temp agencies relieves organizations of the responsibility of long-term commitments to people. Organizations no longer need to have support programs for large pools of workers – especially where companies no longer desire to be responsible to manage a large work force. Most employers will say it is to meet the challenges of a fast changing marketplace but do not act in ways that value employees.

"Most employers pay a contract worker 20 to 40% more than they would a full-time staff member." But these figures are generally for management and technical staff and the figure includes benefits the individual must arrange for himself or herself. (Julie Amparano Lopez, "Negotiating In Your Best Interests As a Contract Worker", *Wall Street Journal*, September 14, 1994.)

Wishful Thinking

"For many employers hiring part time workers has been an easy way to cut benefits. However, smart companies are finding that partial benefits can produce full time loyalty." (Debbie Galant, "Are Part-Time Workers Getting Their Due?", *Institutional Investor*, July 1993, p. 45.)

"How do you build collaborative effort if everyone in a corporation is working for himself?" (Robert Kelly, author of *The Gold Collar Worker*, in *Business Week*, October 7, 1991, p. 95.)

"Contingent workers," "part-timers," "secondary employees," "flexible workers," "throwaway employees," "peripheral employees" or whatever they are called will simply be a drain on resources as they continually must attend to securing their next assignment. Commitment, loyalty, creative potential is all limited by their need to search for and attain a secure income stream. While some temp or interim managers might like short-term challenges and may succeed in earning a premium for their willingness to accept and commit to a short-term goal, their first few weeks or months are devoted to figuring out where they are and their last few weeks or months are devoted to figuring out where they are going. It might be appealing to some and they may even be grateful for having a challenge as well as a job at first. But, a lifestyle of this insecurity will no doubt be fit for only a small percentage of all those who find themselves contingent employees.

Part-time workers may bring down labor costs but their mix in the workplace causes morale problems for those who are full-timers. You can almost hear the refrain: "There but for the grace of God . . ." It does not take much imagination to wonder what the impact is on the motivation of the so-called permanent staff when they see similarly skilled employees making less, working right along with them and see that perhaps it is only a matter of time before they are asked to take a pay cut or suffer the same fate. Even among managers some have been fired to be hired back as consultants at a reduced salary.

"One of the greatest spurs to this just-in-time approach is, ironically, the US Congress. Its efforts to protect full-time employees – through restrictions on plant closings, for instance, and complex requirements for equality in benefit plans – have backfired by encouraging employers to hire temporaries instead." (Michael Barrier, "Temporary Assignment", *Nation's Business*, October 1989, p. 34.)

L.M. Consultants, a small engineering-consulting firm in Miami, laid off Mr. Burns two years ago. He says it brought him back a few days later as an independent contractor with a paltry $30,000 one-year contract – about half his salary. He received no benefits or perks. He felt 'lucky just to have a job.' . . . When the firm extended his contract last year for another year, he made several demands. The upshot: He commands about $80,000 a year and gets a quarterly bonus for meeting certain performance expectations. (Julie Amparano Lopez, "Negotiating In Your Best Interests As a Contract Worker", *The Wall Street Journal*, September 14, 1994.)

He was a lucky one. Others have gone back to work at half their salary with no raises in sight.

What can you expect from a temp or part-time or contingent worker when they are seen as disposable employees, and only filling holes? Respondents in one study of part-time workers commented that ". . . they were given insufficient autonomy to do their job correctly and not allowed to make valuable input into decisions that affected their work groups." (Daniel C. Feldman and Helen I. Doerpinghaus, "Missing Persons No Longer: Managing Part-Time Workers in the '90s", *Organizational Dynamics*, Winter 1993, p. 59.)

Temp workers have no motivation to see the company do well. What is their stake? Furthermore, "Employees with contractor co-workers reported less trust in their organization than did those in employee only work units." (Jone L. Pearce, "Toward An Organizational Behavior of Contract Laborers: Their Psychological Involvement and Effects on Employee Co-Workers", *Academy of Management Journal*, Vol. 36, No. 5, 1993, p. 1082.)

Says Jack Gordon, editor of *Training* magazine: "I don't know how you talk about flattening the pyramid and empowering workers simultaneously while talking about how half the work force is going to be contingent." Adds Kathleen Christensen, professor of environmental psychology at the City University of New York, "Some say that contingency work is the ultimate in empowerment, but it's a different thing to empower someone and make sure the supports are there. Contingent workers are really on their own; they feel like they're second-class citizens." (Brian Tarcy, "Contingent Workers: Where's the Fit?", *Across The Board*, April 1994, p. 38.)

The implications of a large pool of contingent workers that drive down labor costs and allow employers to eliminate conventional benefits is to diminish the standard of living and shift the burden of competitiveness to the lowest tier of the labor supply.

". . . even the most creative work design begs the question of how unready most organizations are to manage this work force of temps, part-timers, consultants, and contract workers effectively." (William Bridges, "The End of the Job", *Fortune*, September 19, 1994, p. 64.)

NEW PARADIGM BUSINESS: SOCIAL RESPONSIBILITY

Corporations behave according to their own unique systems of standards, rules, forms, and objectives. The most basic rule of corporate operation is that it must produce income and must show a profit over time. All other values are secondary. Human beings within the corporate structure are prevented from operating on their own standards and are seriously constrained in their ability to influence corporate behavior . . . Corporations, and the people within them, are not subject to moral behavior. They are following a system of logic that leads inexorably toward dominant behaviors.

– Jerry Mander, "The Myth of the Corporate Conscience", *Business and Society Review*, Spring, 1992, pp. 56–63.

What It is

Broadly speaking the social responsibility of business is to do no harm. There is much debate over this claim. The debate ranges from "Business' only responsibility is to make money" to "Business should be an exemplar of public service in addition to making a profit." In this context, exemplary behavior includes fair treatment of employees, maintaining a healthy workplace, having an environmentally benign impact, and abiding by the spirit as well as the letter of the law."

Human Rights: Toward an Employee Bill of Rights

Now

There is a basic basket of rights which define conditions of work, pay, work procedures, selection and dismissal of employees, minimum wages, hours of work, minimum breaks, safety and health conditions, family leave policies, affirmative action, etc. In governing conditions of work the laws of the nation in regard to the workplace are focused almost entirely on the contractual obligation between employer and employee as a purely economic exchange with only minimal concern for other relevant aspects of workplace relationships.

Some privacy rights are protected in some states, as well as some protections against unfair dismissal but they are spotty and shallow. In challenging an employer, over personal treatment or workplace relationships, the employee has few resources and the process favors the employer who, in many states, retains the right to hire and fire at will.

Mirroring the minimal obligations employers have to employees, the worker today has few responsibilities. This is also the consequence of the prevailing conception of a solely economic contract between employer and employee. Basically, showing up, obeying a boss, and conforming to a minimal performance standard will meet the average worker's obligations.

Tomorrow

In addition to the basic economic relationship, concern has arisen for safeguarding the following seventeen freedoms:

Freedom
- from discrimination in the hiring process
- of trust
- of speech
- of expression in all forms
- from intrusions
- of safety and health
- from stress
- from assignment/re-assignment without consultation
- in off hours
- from all forms of harassment
- of information

- from propaganda
- to participate
- in fringe benefits
- to access due process
- from abusive firing
- of affiliation

And, new workplace responsibilities will arise to complement these new rights. Each employee will have the responsibility to:

• participate in both individual and workgroup-based learning experiences to upgrade existing skills and to acquire new skills and competencies throughout their tenure with an organization

• seek to find new ways to contribute to the good of the enterprise

• perform at or above the requirements of their role as established at the time of membership

• assume your rightful share of the responsibility for achieving the community's financial and social objectives

• participate honestly in decision-making opportunities at the work group level and in other bodies that have a bearing on the quality of worklife environment, the quality of output and the economic performance of the company in the marketplace.

• express yourself authentically and ethically in all relationships

• seek out help when necessary and to be available to help others

• maintain allegiance to personal values

ON BALANCE: AN ORGANIZATIONAL BILL OF RIGHTS/RESPONSIBILITIES

Now

To judge from the conventional wisdom organizations have only one responsibility: to make money. When incorporated, an organization enjoys several important rights such as: limited liability for acts committed by it (and only to the extent of assets within its holdings), the right to hire and fire personnel, the right to demand compliance of labor, and the right to raise money through the issuance of stock. One key right, the envy of mortals, is the right to perpetual existence contingent upon financial viability. This is made possible through the transferability of ownership.

Tomorrow

Corporations were originally chartered to perform a social good supervised by the chartering government agency. Today, they are established mostly for private use and gain. The society's oversight capabilities have recently been diminished and will need to be restored as corporate behavior plays an increasingly important role in determining the quality of life and the standard of living for us all.

> In the aggregate, as Parenti has pointed out: By controlling society's capital and labor, corporate conglomerates are able to build and demolish whole communities, preempt vast acreages of land, plunder and pollute the natural environment, manipulate entire technologies, shape the development of whole regions, obliterate fragile ancient environments, map the lines of national and international trade and transportation, control media content, create new wants and markets, destroy old skills, values and tastes, and control the destinies of people throughout the world. The multinationals exercise a coercive power of a magnitude difficult to comprehend, impinging upon our lives in a multitude of ways, often without our knowing it. How then can anyone speak of the corporation as a 'private' organization, as if its decisions and actions had no effect on our collective destiny? (M. Parenti, *Power and the Powerless*, New York: St. Martins Press, 1978, pp. 179–80.)

An emerging philosophy claims that business serves a variety of stakeholders – anyone who has an interest in the survival and impact of that business. Moreover, this philosophy calls for business, especially big business, to assume an instrumental role in the execution of social policy such as creating healthy, non-discriminatory workplaces.

Further, organizations of all kinds are broadly seen as having responsibilities beyond making money or serving clients. These are seen as needing to manage their affairs according to high standards of ethical conduct, honor a social contract and include every one of its employee-members in decisions that affect them.

While the organization is self-determining and can rightfully require conformance to its mission from its members, wider stakeholder issues that have emerged in recent years will also need to be integrated into the organizational charter. The call for corporate social responsibility, environmental sensitivity, and workplace democracy, for example, may become a required responsibility for the organization to earn its right of self-determination and autonomy.

Recalibrating the roles of stakeholders will also require a redefinition of the boards of directors to include stakeholder representatives in addition to financial investors. Individual and corporate accountability for wrongdoing will also be needed.

Figure 18.1 A Quick Assessment: Workplace Rights For All Organizational Members

(On the line to the left of each "right" rank order the following in their importance to you. Check those that apply today in your organization. Below each statement, mark an X to indicate the degree of freedom you experience now in your organization and with a Y, mark the degree of freedom you believe all members should experience. The breadth of the gap gives you some idea of the importance the discrepancy has for you.) The rank will give you an idea of how strong a priority the item is for you.

— Freedom in the hiring process

 none   some   much   a lot   complete

— Freedom of trust

 none   some   much   a lot   complete

— Freedom of speech

 none   some   much   a lot   complete

— Freedom of expression in all forms

 none   some   much   a lot   complete

— Freedom from intrusions

 none   some   much   a lot   complete

— Freedom of safety and health

 none   some   much   a lot   complete

— Freedom from stress

 none   some   much   a lot   complete

— Freedom from assignment/re-assignment without consultation

 none   some   much   a lot   complete

— Freedom in off hours

 none   some   much   a lot   complete

Figure 18.1 (*Continued*)

— Freedom from sexual harassment and other forms of organizational harassment

    none   some   much   a lot   complete

— Freedom of information

    none   some   much   a lot   complete

— Freedom from propaganda

    none   some   much   a lot   complete

— Freedom to participate

    none   some   much   a lot   complete

— Freedom in fringe benefits and pay

    none   some   much   a lot   complete

— Freedom of due process

    none   some   much   a lot   complete

— Freedom from abusive firing or layoffs without consideration

    none   some   much   a lot   complete

— Freedom from discrimination

    none   some   much   a lot   complete

— Freedom of affiliation

    none   some   much   a lot   complete

Overall

    none   some   much   a lot   complete

In addition to the above compendium of freedoms must be added the concern for ethical behavior in dealings with all community stakeholders. This is implied in many of the freedoms but covers a broader range of activities. It would also be inclusive of non-employees such as dependents of employees, suppliers, customers or clients, and members of the neighborhood in which the organization is situated.

Examples are, producing safe products, disposing of waste in a form that presents no hazards to others, and aspiring to use the best practices including doing no harm to people or the environment in any way.

Which areas hold the highest priority for you to change? How might you become a constructive voice for change?

Wisdom

Organizations evolve as societies do. Those that are not open to change through democratic processes invite harsher methods as pent-up frustration and or injustice inspires more and more radical forms of involvement.

> In a few companies, breakdowns are designed to occur as part of the process of change. They are regarded as a desirable means of revealing previously ignored or concealed patterns of behavior that must be altered if quantum change is to take place . . . By extending participation to divergent stakeholders, conflicts are certain to erupt. By designing breakdowns and confronting possible conflicts early, stakeholders get a chance to identify and deal with their interests in a way that may prevent serious damage later. (Richard T. Pascale, "Intentional Breakdowns and Conflict by Design", *Planning Review*, May/June 1994, p. 12.)

The future can be envisioned and created.

> The future-state visioning process stresses the development of stakeholder understanding and commitment as it builds a solid principled base for action . . . The main steps in the process are: (1) Develop a list of stakeholders and try to view the future through their eyes. (2) Develop a broad description of the likely future environment. (3) Create a comprehensive future-state vision of what the organization could accomplish before considering the present state. (4) Contrast the future state with the present state.

(5) Express the values that will guide the organization as it seeks to achieve its vision. (6) Ensure that the future vision is expressed in terms of actionable concepts. (7) Develop the vision in a participative way involving the main stakeholders. (8) Avoid planning strategy or action until the new vision and values have been developed. (J.M. Stewart, "Future State Visioning at National Rubber Company", *Planning Review*, March/April 1994, p. 20.)

At Rubbermaid, Inc., it is believed that ethical and creative partnerships with consumers, customers, suppliers, communities, shareholders and associates will enable the company to improve the value it creates to delight its partners . . . Only through consistent ethical behavior can the trust which allows genuine business partnerships to form and to grow be established. There are three types of levels of trust: (1) mutual or contractual trust; (2) competence trust; and (3) goodwill trust. (Wolfgang R. Schmitt, "The Ethics of Partnerships", *Executive Excellence*, November 1993, p. 15.)

Wishful Thinking

Relying on personal enlightenment and the development and expression of individual wisdom amidst the most materialistic culture in the world may be delusional. The business system is under increasing pressure to squeeze every penny of possibilities out of every moment. Rewards, promotions, esteem, status, and personal well-being are all tied into the system which promotes the husbanding and constant expansion of financial resources – the only readily accepted measure of success in the business world.

To expect more than lip service or the most general attention to ethical behavior, fairness in the broadest sense of the word, or good works, aside from increasing earnings or decreasing costs, may simply be a contradictory, and some would say, a totally inappropriate expectation of a system now understood to have been designed to meet personal and not societal ends. It was not always this way. Corporations were established under charters from government to enjoy certain benefits in return for accomplishing a public purpose. They were designed as the first privatized public services. Today, however, regulation and public guidance are seen as burdensome and hampering their function – impediments to their rightful profit-making purposes.

Exemplars

Many of the Fortune 500 companies have formal ethics policies and guidelines for appropriate behavior. Some have ombudspersons and seek out comments regarding ethical practices and "good corporate citizenship." The best known examples, however, of companies that deliberately strive to achieve positive social purposes as corporate ends in themselves are Levi Strauss, and Smith and Hawken.

NEW PARADIGM BUSINESS: SUSTAINABILITY

> I think we can say in no uncertain terms that business is destroying the world. And while consumers and producers are becoming aware of their interrelated impact upon the earth, what also needs to be said is that business can restore the planet upon which we live.

> – Paul Hawken,
> "The Ecology of Commerce",
> *Inc.*, April 1992, p. 93.

What It is

By reducing the quantity or quality of resources faster than they can be renewed, depletion occurs.

> The phenomenon is often referred to as the consumption of the resources' principal or 'capital': the capital generates income that can be tapped for human consumption. A sustainable economy can therefore be defined as one that leaves the capital intact and undamaged so that future generations can enjoy undiminished income. (Thomas F. Homer-Dixon, Jeffrey H. Boutwell and George W. Rathjens, "Environmental Change and Violent Conflict", *Scientific American*, February 1993, p. 38.)

> The word 'sustainability' can be defined in terms of carrying capacity of the ecosystem, and described with input-output models of energy and resource consumption. Sustainability is an economic state where the demands placed on the environment by people and commerce can be met without reducing the capacity of the environment to provide for future generations. It can also be expressed

in the simple terms of an economic golden rule for the restorative economy: Leave the world better than you found it, take no more than you need, try not to harm life or the environment, make amends if you do. (Paul Hawken, *The Ecology of Commerce: A Declaration of Sustainability*, New York: Harper Business, 1994, p. 139.)

Wisdom

The Coalition for Environmentally Responsible Economies (CERES), a group of investor and environmental groups, proposed a corporate code of conduct that holds signatories to a pledge to protect the biosphere, restore the environment, and practice a sustainable use of natural resources among other things. Industry is indeed realizing its responsibility to the environment and finding that exercising that responsibility can actually be profitable.

> Best practices of environmental leadership include: (1) A mission statement and corporate values that promote environmental advocacy . . . such values include stewardship in regard to ecology, frugality and sufficiency in regard to resources, fairness and appropriateness in relation to society, and accountability, participation, proactivity and long termism in regard to process. (2) A framework for managing environmental initiatives. (3) Green process/product design. (4) Environmentally-focused stakeholder partnerships. (5) Internal and external education initiatives. (Kathleen Dechant and Barbara Altman, "Environmental Leadership: From Compliance to Competitive Advantage", *Academy of Management Executive*, 1994, Vol. 8, No. 3, p. 7.)

American companies are legally obliged to file details of 300 substances on the Toxic Release Inventory. One large chemical company, Monsanto, has deftly turned the obligation into an opportunity by setting a five-year plan to reduce its worldwide air emissions of toxic chemicals by 90% and presenting its progress in an environmental report. In July, the company proudly announced that it had achieved its goal . . . Dow Europe tabulates pollutants to air, water and soil from its individual plants and lists the extent to which they have been reduced or increased in recent years. Dow also lists 'unwanted events', including not just accidental spills but complaints and fines imposed . . . Union Carbide tracks performance against a 'reasonable care' program devised by the

American chemical industry. ("A Green Account", *The Economist*, September 4, 1993, p. 69.)

Wishful Thinking

The concept of sustainable development, however, calls for moving business decisions simultaneously toward a healthy environment and a healthy economy. Such a mindset requires a fundamental rethinking of traditional notions of disposability, risk, responsibility, and the right to pollute beginning at the top of the organization and moving right through it. (Kathleen Dechant and Barbara Altman, "Environmental Leadership: From Compliance to Competitive Advantage", *Academy of Management Executive*, 1994, Vol. 8, No. 3, p. 7.)

It may be impossible to develop a sustainable approach to economic management because of virtually uninhibited and uncontrolled reproduction. Population growth alone leads to threatening shortages of resources. Even arable land is diminished because of the simple need to house the expanding population which, of course, reduces its ability to feed itself. The continued skewed distribution of access to, and benefit from, resources is an added reason that inadequate husbandry may ultimately lead to societal conflict and destruction.

Commitment Needed to Make It Work

Sustainability requires a massive shift of mindset. Since the industrial era paradigm is so embedded in the fundamental structures of our world and expressive of a material-value system that includes the acceptance of waste, exploitation of the environment and a disposable, throw-away attitude toward your "things," it seems the voluntary commitment required to turn around this behavior will be nothing short of monumental.

Exemplars

Deja Shoe • Patagonia Inc. • Esprit • Procter & Gamble • AT&T • IBM • Apple Computer • Clorox • Rubbermaid • Moore Business Forms • Johnson & Johnson • Olin

NEW PARADIGM BUSINESS: THE NEW SCIENCE/CHAOS THEORY

> To some physicists chaos is a science of process rather than a state, of becoming rather than being.

> – James Gleick,
> *Chaos: Making A New Science,*
> New York: Viking, 1987, p. 5.

What It is

The new science is quantum physics and the study of sub-atomic phenomena. Many new discoveries regarding the nature of matter and energy and their relationship have overturned the Newtonian/Cartesian world. Recent attention has been focused on chaos theory and its application to human organizations and this inquiry is leading to a new definition of the person-to-person, person-to-event and person-to-organization relationships in human systems.

The science of chaos became a popular subject of fascination with the publication of James Gleick's book on the subject. (James Gleick, *Chaos: Making A New Science*, New York: Viking, 1987.)

"A system is defined as chaotic when it becomes impossible to know where it will be next . . . [But] the most chaotic of systems never goes beyond certain boundaries; it stays contained within a shape that we can recognize . . ." (Margaret J. Wheatley, *Leadership and the New Science*, San Francisco, CA: Berrett-Koehler, 1992, p. 21.)

"Chaos occurs when people move into such deep confusion that they let go of their conceptions of how to solve a problem. However, once people let go, they have the capacity to come up with bold solutions that integrate all of the information." (Joe Flower, "The Power of Chaos", *Healthcare Forum*, September/October 1993, p. 48.)

Wisdom

"Many companies are facing dramatic change. In this climate, the important new skill for leaders has become the ability to manage chaos while participating in the radical transformation of the way the company does business." (John Huey, "Managing In the Midst of Chaos", *Fortune*, April 5, 1993, p. 38.)

> If organizations are machines, control makes sense. If organizations are process structures, then seeking to impose control through permanent structure is suicide. If we believe that acting responsibly means exerting control by having our hands into everything, then we cannot hope for anything except what we already have – a treadmill of effort and life-destroying stress. (Margaret J. Wheatley, *Leadership and the New Science*, San Francisco, CA: Berrett-Koehler, 1992, p. 23.)

> My growing sensibility of a quantum universe has affected my organizational life in several ways. First, I try hard to discipline myself to remain aware of the whole and to resist my well-trained desire to analyze the parts to death. I look now for patterns of movement over time and focus on qualities like rhythm, flow, direction, and shape. Second, I know I am wasting time whenever I draw straight arrows between two variables in a cause and effect diagram, or position things as polarities, or create elaborate plans and time lines. Third, I no longer argue with anyone about what is real. Fourth, the time I formerly spent on detailed planning and analysis I now use to look at the structures that might facilitate relationships. I have come to expect that something useful occurs if I link up people, units, or tasks, even though I cannot determine precise outcomes. And last, I realize more and more that the universe will not cooperate with my desires for determinism. (*Ibid.*, p. 43.)

> Is there a magnetic force, a basin for activity, so attractive that it pulls all behavior toward it and creates coherence? My current belief is that we do have such attractors at work in organizations and that one of the most potent shapers of behavior in organizations, and in life, is meaning. Our main concern, writes Viktor Frankl in his presentation of logo therapy, 'is not to gain pleasure or to avoid pain but rather to see a meaning in . . . life.' (*Ibid.*, p. 134.)

> Discontinuous environmental change seems to require discontinuous organization change . . . In a world characterized by global competition, deregulation, sharp technological change, and political turmoil, discontinuous organization change seems to be a

determinant of organization adaptation. Those firms that can initiate and implement discontinuous organization change more rapidly
and/or prior to the competition have a competitive advantage.
While not all change will be successful, inertia or incremental
change in the face of altered competitive arenas is a recipe for failure. (David A. Nadler and Michael L. Tushman, "Beyond the
Charismatic Leader: Leadership and Organizational Change",
California Management Review, Winter 1990, p. 94.)

We are conceiving organizations and sets of organizations as networks, governed by fecund relationships among fully empowered
and informed front-line people. Such organizations without hierarchy do look chaotic by old standards. But on closer examination,
the richer order may be the only path to adapting instantaneously
amid today's tightly woven network of competitors, financiers, suppliers, distributors and customers. Our knee-jerk rejection of true
alternatives to comfortable hierarchies is much more than 'resistance to change.' It is primordial adherence to traditional models of
religion and science, the human touchstones that have guided civi-
lization for the last several thousand years. (Tom Peters, "Traditional Hierarchies Should Give Way to 'Chaos'", *San Jose Mercury
News*, January 5, 1989, p. 4F.)

". . . the more science and technology reshape the very essence
of business, the less useful the concept of management itself as a
science seems to be. On reflection, this paradox is not so surprising. The traditional scientific approach to management promised
to provide managers with the capacity to analyze, predict and
control the behavior of the complex organizations they led. But
the world most managers currently inhabit often appears to be
unpredictable, uncertain and even uncontrollable . . . In the face
of this more dynamic and volatile business world, the traditional
mechanisms of 'scientific management' seem not only less useful
but positively counterproductive. And science itself appears less
and less relevant to the practical concerns of managers. . . . while
traditional science focused on analysis, prediction, and control,
the new science emphasizes chaos and complexity. (David H.
Freedman, "Is Management Still A Science?", *Harvard Business
Review*, November/December 1992, p. 26.)

"Put simply, the nineteenth-century emphasis on predictability and control has given way to a late twentieth-century appreciation for the power of randomness and chance." (David H.

Freedman, "Is Management Still A Science?", *Harvard Business Review*, November/December 1992, p. 30.)

"Leaders must create an atmosphere where people understand that change is a continuous process, not an event." (Jack Welch, "A Master Class in Radical Change", *Fortune*, December 13, 1993, p. 83.)

"Our philosophy is that the key to achieving competitive advantage isn't reacting to chaos; it's producing that chaos. And the key to being a chaos producer is being an innovation leader . . . Our feeling is that this rapid, chaotic rate of change will continue forever and will continue to accelerate." (Edward R. McCracken, CEO, Silicon Graphics) (Steven E. Prokesch, "Mastering Chaos at the High-Tech Frontier: An Interview with Ed McCracken", *Harvard Business Review*, November/ December 1993, p. 136.)

Wishful Thinking

Prior to chaos theory many people were captivated by the phenomenon of anarchy in organizations. ". . . such organizations can be viewed for some purposes as collections of choices looking for problems, issues and feelings looking for decision situations in which they might be aired, solutions looking for issues to which they might be an answer, and decision makers looking for work." (Michael D. Cohen, James G. March and Johan P. Olsen, "A Garbage Can Model of Organizational Choice", *Administrative Science Quarterly*, (17), March 1972, p. 1.)

> The garbage can process is one in which problems, solutions, and participants move from one choice opportunity to another in such a way that the nature of the choice, the time it takes, and the problems it solves all depend on a relatively complicated intermeshing of elements . . . Although decision making is thought of as a process for solving problems, that is often not what happens. Problems are worked upon in the context of some choice but choices are made only when the shifting combinations of problems, solutions and decision makers happen to make action possible. (*Ibid.*, p. 16.)

Through discussing the rather messy way decisions get made in organizations the idea of managing in a chaotic environment is, by definition, symptomatic of human systems as well as a reflection of the complexities of our times. While chaos or confusion or complexity is a quality of life, it does not take a new science to realize that organizations need new technologies to bring people and ideas together – to help creative, communicative people build organizations that are productive and satisfying places to be. The struggles we engage in over decision making, participation or other processes of working together, are perhaps more a product of political realities and the character of the individuals involved than to any particular condition of the physical universe or its underlying structures.

"Neil Postman maintains that information has overwhelmed people and that technology has brought intensified chaos and noise, eroded people's trust of traditional social institutions, and undermined their sense of life's meanings." (Lew McCreary, "Postman's Progress", *CIO*, November 1, 1993, p. 74.)

Even amidst rapid change, and understanding the need to act, there are seven human dynamics of change that inhibit its smooth introduction:

> (1) People feel awkward, ill-at-ease, and self-conscious. (2) People initially focus on what they have to give up. (3) People feel alone, even if everyone else is going through the same change. (4) People can handle only so much change. (5) People are at different levels of readiness for change. (6) People are concerned that they don't have enough resources. (7) If the pressure is taken off, people revert to their old behavior. (Ken Blanchard, Seven Dynamics of Change", *Executive Excellence*, June 1992, p. 5)

> Chaos has become the century's third great revolution in the physical sciences . . . Like the first two revolutions, chaos cuts away the tenets of Newton's physics. As one physicist put it: "Relativity eliminated the Newtonian illusion of absolute space and time; quantum theory eliminated the Newtonian dream of a controllable measurement process; and chaos eliminates the Laplacian fantasy of deterministic predictability." Of the three the revolution in chaos applies to the universe we see and touch, to objects at human scale. (James Gleick, *Chaos: Making A New Science*, New York: Viking, 1987, p. 6.)

Unfortunately, as we revel in the scientific cachet, we foolishly presuppose that the theory can explain away human irresponsibility and ignorance. Invoking the science of chaos somehow excuses mere mortals from the audacious attempt to control their environment. Yet, as fascinating as the science of chaos is, its usefulness as a tool of management is far from clear; as instructive in the dynamics of human affairs, perhaps nil. But in an arena desperate for scientific legitimacy, chaos theory is embraced as a rationalization for past failure, current frustration, and future uncertainty even as managers contradict its lessons and try as desperately as ever to control, predict, and measure every aspect of their realms.

What acolytes of chaos theory have forgotten is that one of their primary tenets – the so-called butterfly effect – was a half-joking metaphorical reference to the impact of small initial changes on long-term outcomes. So, the butterfly in Tokyo flapping its wings today is said to cause or begin a chain of climactic events that results in a storm in New York next month. Where people had believed that small initial deviations and changes would result in small output deviations there came the realization that small changes at the beginning of a process would be grossly exaggerated over time. Every hiker understands this and realizes that one false step at the outset will deliver him or her to an entirely different destination. But the metaphor fails to account for compensatory behavior, the entire field of randomness, and in human systems, volition and the use of feedback.

Using science, rather than say, philosophy to repudiate the effects of science is a cultural game played out in an extraordinary scientific era. Rather than say you do not believe in authoritarianism at work because it is simply dehumanizing and leave it at that, we seek out scientific evidence to prove that authoritarianism at work is less effective than democratic alternatives. Thus, we have invoked the name of chaos theory to justify a call for more participative organizational systems.

The major difference between the physical world and the human system created in our organizations is the willfulness of the players, the variety of motives, the variety of options that can be utilized and the myriad consequences of those actions. Of course it is very chaotic but the science of chaos may be inappropriately applied to our management thinking. There are various resources and options that can be chosen purposefully in human endeavors. There are also various parts of the process which lend themselves more readily to control and prediction than others. It would be a mistake to jump to a universal assessment of the applicability of the science of chaos because it might actually undermine the power of human choice.

Science and religion have competed for the Western mind for a millennium but it has been only since the maturation of the industrial era that science has taken a leading role in defining our Western world view. The mechanical view of the universe was instrumental in creating reductionistic thinking and human dominance of the ecosystem. Later, quantum physics demonstrated the strength and importance of relationships in determining what we believe to be our reality. Today chaos theory suggests that underlying patterns (an implicate order) and the flow of events which might appear as chaotic in the short run, are influenced by natural forces whose logic is consistent as if created and governed by a supernatural force. Here is where spirituality merges again with science.

Regardless of the passing of different schools of thought and scientific paradigms and their influence on our world view, or at least the part about how the material world functions and our place in it, the established industrial model of being and its sense of purpose regarding the investment, husbanding and distribution of wealth have remained substantially untouched. At best, industrial systems and the role of money and wealth in our lives have defied the new awareness about connection, ecological systems, and the importance of relationships. The capitalist school has "beaten" those other schools of economics that stressed relationships: socialism and communism. This apparent paradox highlights the nature of contemporary human society which acts virtually independent of scientific findings. They either serve the money ethic or are ignored. The accumulation of money and power is all that counts. "Damn the relationships, full speed ahead."

Can human thought alone create the energy, the form, and the behavior that can manifest its intent? The parallel with quantum physics is the relationship between matter and energy. Can we expect that this is manifested at the human level where thought and behavior can be equated?

Can we expect that with inaction human affairs will self-organize? Can we look at the advent of "self-organizing" hurricanes and conclude that the forces within our human systems, if "left alone" will simply become, that is, unfold in a "natural and a beneficial pattern?

Perhaps without values, without aspirations, without a creative impulse, if we merely survived fulfilling our biological destiny these ideas would unfold in a fashion roughly similar to physical forces. But that is not the human state. We strive and create; we think about ourselves and events and respond thoughtfully or emotionally. We are driven to satisfy needs. There is a difference between human volition and physical determination and we possess qualities representative of both.

Perhaps more than anything else, the chaos theoreticians are pointing out how our fabricated organizations with their very limited purposes are expending enormous amounts of energy contrary to the best interests and natural behavior of the humans that comprise the system. Rather than pursuing money as an object we need to pursue an understanding of the shared experience and ways of unleashing the full energy inherent in organizations toward a mutual purpose.

To say that our science helps us understand our urge to participate because of an understanding of the organizing principles of the universe is ludicrous. We want to participate because it reflects our creative need for self-expression, our interest in control over relevant portions of our lives and a will to act for the good of the whole, but not because we mirror the behavior of sub-atomic particles. We need not justify our want – indeed our right to participate – with arcane science, or politics for that matter. Participation is an entitlement which has too often been denied us by the few who have too often abused their position of trust and their power in a system whose legitimacy is declining daily. When people are excluded from influencing their lives and cut off from a fair share of the ownership of the contemporary language of value – money – the system's very legitimacy is challenged.

"We will need to help the average employee develop greater participative competence, broader technical skills, and more understanding of the business. We will need to help managers learn how to accept change more gracefully, and to view input from employees as beneficial rather than threatening." (William Pasmore and Mary Fagans, "New Science, Old Values?", *Vision/Action*, Winter 1994, p. 3.)

Exemplars

Cray Research • ALCOA • GE • Ameritech • AlliedSignal • Tenneco

NEW PARADIGM BUSINESS: SPIRITUALITY IN ORGANIZATIONS

> I look at spirituality, at the way people live their lives. What is their motivation? Do they want things to be better? Do they want to be open and honest? . . . I don't think we're really teaching anything new. I think we're going back to basic, fundamental values – issues of trust, respect, dignity, commitment, integrity and accountability. The world is crying out for these things to become more important.
>
> – Michael Blondell in: Frank Rose,
> "A New Age for Business?",
> *Fortune*, October 8, 1990, p. 157.

What It is

The increasing interest in social values has given rise to the issue of management as a sacred act and work as a spiritual exercise. The meaning of organization itself is seen by some as establishing a spiritual context with several ramifications. First, an organization's and a manager's role in the community is seen as requiring the adherence to certain standards to earn the trust of neighbor and customer alike. Second, the treatment of people at work needs to be governed by ethical principles as well as a general adherence to decency and, in North America, Judeo-Christian principles. Tom Chappell, CEO of Tom's of Maine, a personal hygiene products company, sets one of the most notable examples. He has written about the concept of spirituality in business, from a practitioner's perspective, in his book, *The Soul of A Business: Managing For Profit and the Common Good*. In Japan, the concept of spirituality in organizations has been expressed in Zen and the Art of Management. In addition, Konosuke Matsushita's work, *Not for Bread Alone* in which he discusses higher level purposes for individuals and organizations has recently been re-released.

While spirituality suggests a religious experience, it is in the context of work and organizations, a renewed appreciation for the many facets of human life as they are expressed in the workplace or through performing your work.

Wisdom

So powerful is the bond between the company and many of its workers that observers, only half jokingly, have likened Southwest Airlines to some sort of religious cult. (CEO) Kelleher proclaims he is not the least offended by such comparisons, contending that his operation has always retained 'a patina of spirituality.' Says he: "I feel that you have to be with your employees through all their difficulties, that you have to be interested in them personally. They may be disappointed in their country. Even their family might not be working out the way they wish it would. But I want them to know that Southwest will always be there for them." (Kenneth Labich, "Is Herb Kelleher America's Best CEO?", *Fortune*, May 2, 1994, p. 50.)

If people are your greatest resource and creativity the key to success, then business results cannot be divorced from personal fulfillment. You can only get so much more productivity out of reorganization and automation. Where you really get productivity leaps is in the minds and hearts of people. (Frank Rose, "A New Age for Business?", *Fortune*, October 8, 1990, p. 157.)

James A. Autry, President of the Merideth Corporation, publishers of *Metropolitan Home, Better Homes and Gardens* and *Ladies Home Journal*, says "Good management is largely a matter of love. Or, if you are uncomfortable with that word, call it caring, because proper management involves caring for people, not manipulating them." (James Autry, "Love and Profit – The Art of Caring Leadership", *World Business Academy Perspectives*, Vol. 6, No. 1, 1992, p. 59.)

Wishful Thinking

It is precisely because of the stress of modern worklife that people are seeking to infuse their world with more spiritual activity. The sheer pressure of needing to be faster, sharper, more direct and unable to wonder, to think, to reflect, to enjoy your surroundings, to relate to others as people with a shared basis for enjoying each other's companionship belies the willingness of organizations to nurture this human need.

Exemplars

Merideth Publishing • Tom's of Maine • Republic of Tea

NEW PARADIGM BUSINESS: REINVENTING THE ORGANIZATION

> Our goal is to make the entire federal government both less expensive and more efficient, and to change the culture of our national bureaucracy away from complacency and entitlement toward initiative and empowerment. We intend to redesign, to reinvent, to reinvigorate the entire national government.
>
> – American President Bill Clinton
> announcing the National Performance Review,
> March 3, 1993.

What It is

Current workplace turmoil due to massive uncertainty while needing to act amidst an intensifying period of global competition has given rise to the notion of completely transforming "business as usual." Reinvention means starting with a blank sheet and literally re-examining the wisdom of doing things the way they have been done. It might turn out to be a "reengineering" project or a fundamental paradigm shift in the operating assumptions governing organizational behavior. Regardless of the particular approach one thing is apparent: entrepreneurial behavior is replacing bureaucratic behavior. In addition, the workplace environment and employee satisfaction are being revisited as important causal elements in customer service and the financial performance of the entity.

> Incremental change isn't enough for many companies today. They don't need to change what is; they need to create what isn't . . . When a company reinvents itself, it must alter the underlying assumptions and invisible premises on which its decisions and

actions are based . . . Reinvention entails creating a new possibility for the future, one that past experiences and current predictions would indicate is impossible. (Tracy Goss, Richard Pascale and Anthony Athos, "The Reinvention Roller Coaster: Risking the Present for a Powerful Future", *Harvard Business Review*, November/December 1993, p. 97.)

According to Tom Peters, "If you are not pursuing some damn dream and then reinventing yourself regularly, assiduously, you're going to fail. Period." (Owen Lipstein and James Mauro, "Tom Peters and the Healthy Corporation: An Interview", *Psychology Today*, March/April 1993, p. 56.)

Wisdom

The activities involved in reinventing an organization require persistence and flexibility, and include: (1) assembling a critical mass of stakeholders; (2) doing an organizational audit; (3) creating urgency, discussing the undiscussable; (4) harnessing contention; and (5) engineering organizational breakdowns. As an organization rides the roller coaster of reinvention it encounters peaks and troughs in morale, as initial euphoria is dampened by conflict and dogged task force work. Morale rises again as alignment among stakeholders occurs and then recedes in the long and demanding task of enrolling the cynical . . . (Tracy Goss, Richard Pascale and Anthony Athos, "The Reinvention Roller Coaster: Risking the Present for a Powerful Future", *Harvard Business Review*, November/December 1993, p. 97.)

Reinvention often results in the flattening of the hierarchy so organizations can be responsive and minimize the numbers of signoffs on decisions. In some cases computer technology makes it possible to have a virtually endless span of control. In the case of both Shearson American Express and Merrill Lynch "their 380 and 410 domestic brokerage offices connect directly with their parent's central information offices for routine needs, yet can bypass the electronic system for personal access to individual experts in headquarters." (James Brian Quinn and Penny C. Paquette, "Technology in Services: Creating Organizational Revolutions", *Sloan Management Review*, Winter 1990, p. 71.)

Federal Express, with 42,000 employees in more than 300 cities worldwide, has a maximum of only five organizational

layers between its non-management employees and its Chief
Operating Officer.

> There is no inherent reason that organizations cannot be made
> 'infinitely flat' – in other words, with innumerable outposts guided
> by one central 'rules based' or 'computer controlled inquiry' sys-
> tem. In designing service company systems, instead of thinking
> about traditional 'spans of control', our study suggests that the
> terms 'spans of effective cooperation', 'communication spans' or
> 'support spans' may have more meaning. (James Brian Quinn and
> Penny C. Paquette, "Technology in Services: Creating Organiza-
> tional Revolutions", *Sloan Management Review*, Winter 1990,
> p. 72.)

In government it is listening to customers (citizens) and responding quickly to their needs. It is also supporting entrepreneurial
activities focused on specific outcomes geared to a local, state or
national mission. It is results oriented, anticipatory government
where action is often taken with a competitive zeal even in a low
competition environment.

Wishful Thinking

". . . most federal workers are either unaware or openly skeptical
of total quality management and 'reinventing government' principles. The key to changing the US current system will be changing the risk intolerant culture of the bureaucracy." (Elizabeth H.
Curda, "Reinventing Government: Moving Beyond the
Buzzwords", *Public Manager*, Fall 1993, p. 33.)

Exemplars

Aetna • Supradur, Inc. (roofing materials) • Ford Motor • Kodak
• Häagen-Dazs • US Government (Selected Federal Agencies)

NEW PARADIGM BUSINESS: VISION/MISSION/VALUES

> The Vision statement holds the key to our future . . . Values will be
> the means to our success.

> – GTE Vision/Values Statement

What It is

Visions, Missions and Values are the basis for creating alignment between all employees and the purpose of the organization. Identifying the vision – what the organization wants to become – gives people the ability to act knowing how their actions will or will not help realize the vision. The mission is frequently the more general reason why the organization is in business and what it hopes to accomplish. It is shorter term and a more specific goal. The values are the organization's strongest beliefs about what is important to it and what behaviors are right and wrong. These guide specific personal actions as much as the vision because they identify specific constraints and duties accompanying each person's understanding of their role.

The vision is an imagined future state which guides a company's behavior. It is a state of being that the company attempts to grow into. The mission is the purpose of an organization. It is why the organization exists. Values are the qualities that shape beliefs and behaviors and serve as essential benchmarks for decision making by individuals in the organization.

Wisdom

W.L. Gore & Associates asks its associates to follow four guiding principles: (1) Try to be fair. (2) Use your freedom to grow. (3) Make your own commitments and keep them. (4) Consult with other associates prior to any action that may adversely affect the reputation or financial stability of the company. The four principles are often referred to as Fairness, Freedom, Commitment and Waterline. The Waterline terminology is drawn from a ship analogy. If someone pokes a hole in a boat above the waterline, the boat will be in relatively little danger. If someone, however, pokes a hole below the waterline, the boat is in immediate danger of sinking. (Frank Shipper, Charles C. Manz, "Employee Self-Management Without Formally Designated Teams: An Alternative Road to Empowerment", *Organizational Dynamics*, Winter 1992, p. 53.)

Marion Labs, now Marion Merrill Dow: "We have a responsibility for excellence and innovation. We do all that we do to the very best of our ability and with the strongest enthusiasm we can generate. It is the very nature of our business to do things that have never been done before and for which there are always reasons they cannot be done. Success for us requires the ability and the spirit to find a pathway through any obstacle, even when no pathway is visible at the start." (John P. Schuster, "Transforming Your Leadership Style", *Association Management*, January 1994, p. L 42.)

Wishful Thinking

A charismatic leader who often spearheads the creation of a vision may be doing a disservice if he or she creates the vision alone and through personal charisma conveys its meaning. The commitment will come as individuals connect with the creation of the vision either at its inception or as it is conveyed on a daily basis. A leader therefore really needs to be a catalyst of each individual's excitement and commitment. (James C. Collins and Jerry I. Porras, "Organizational Vision and Visionary Organizations", *California Management Review*, Fall 1991, pp. 30–52.)

Developing a new program at Microsoft, the Windows NT became the subject of a book, *Show Stopper*, in which the culture of Microsoft was displayed in all its glory and ferocity.

One manager rents a large screen TV to show the Super Bowl at the office as a way of luring engineers away from their homes. An employee's wife talks of organizing a Microsoft Widows Club with a picture of a black widow spider as its logo. A star whose marriage is falling apart jokes that Microsoft should pay for divorce lawyers. A programmer realizes that he missed a full year of his 3-year-old daughter's life and wonders whether that was worth a million dollars of Microsoft stock options. (Alan Deutschman, "The Soul of Microsoft's Machine", *Fortune*, November 14, 1994, p. 260.)

We do not have a mission statement. Most corporate mission statements are a bunch of nonsense – pleasant sounding, flowery words written by corporate executives. Most employees never read them or care about them, and the statements really do not bear any relationship to what the company is doing or how it is operated. (Kenneth F. Iverson, CEO Nucor Corporation; "Changing the Rules of the Game", *Planning Review*, September/October 1993, p. 9.)

Exemplars

Hewlett Packard is famous for "the H-P way" a philosophy

which encompasses a vision for the organization, a mission, and a set of values expected of all associates.

Levi Strauss also has a set of "aspirations"which encompasses its vision and values in terms of how it wants to "be" as an organization.

NEW PARADIGM BUSINESS: TRANSFORMATIONAL LEADERSHIP

> Great leaders have something in them which inspires a whole people and makes them do great things.

> – Jawaharlal Nehru

What It is

Transformational leadership is a process of stimulating a group to aspire to a new state of being. It is characterized by the creation of a vision and the ability to help an organization identify with and work toward that vision in such a way that individuals are highly engaged in the process and motivated to making the vision a reality.

Wisdom

Transformational leaders have demonstrated a clear sense of direction, emphasized organizational objectives and their followers' needs, displayed a strong sense of values and ethics, created high standards, and served as an example for others to follow. Such executives are viewed as effective by both peer and subordinates, and as possessing the courage to foster an environment of growth and development. (J. Bruce Tracy and Timothy R. Hinkin, "Transformational Leaders in the Hospitality Industry", *Cornell Hotel & Restaurant Administration Quarterly*, April 1994. p. 18.)

Transactional leadership is found wherever power is the rule. Transformational leadership, however, appeals to people's higher levels of motivation to contribute to a cause and add to the quality of life . . . The advent of total quality management, flattened hierarchies, and empowered staff are signs of transformational leadership at work. Major qualities of the transformational leader include: (1) holding a vision for the association that is intellectually rich, stimulating and true; (2) being honest and empathetic; (3) having a well developed character without ego power; (4) evincing a concern for the whole; and (5) being able to share power. Of all the qualities, perhaps the capacity to envision is probably the most important. (John P. Schuster, "Transforming Your Leadership Style", *Association Management*, January 1994, p. L39.)

"Transformational leaders have been characterized by four separate components: (1) idealized influence; (2) inspirational motivation; (3) intellectual stimulation; and (4) individualized consideration." (Bernard M. Bass and Bruce J. Avolio, "Transformational Leadership and Organizational Culture", *Public Administration Quarterly*, Spring 1993, p. 112.)

Leaders may wish to employ the following strategies for organization-wide learning and transformation: (1) Tap into the deepest held values. (2) Articulate a bold vision and communicate it repeatedly. (3) Invite others to participate in the realization of the vision. (4) Become comfortable with and adept at managing resistance. (5) Refrain from holding individuals accountable for the system. (Oscar G. Mink, "Creating New Organizational Paradigms for Change", *International Journal of Quality and Reliability Management*, Vol. 9, No. 3, 1992, p. 21.)

You find transactional leadership wherever power is the rule. Its tools are power brokering, withholding favors, and quid pro quo. Transactional leadership at its best is networking and at its worst, abusing position. It is always tied to position power, the status and influence that comes from one's rank in the hierarchy. Transformational leadership, on the other hand, appeals to people's higher levels of motivation to contribute to a cause and add to the quality of life on the planet . . . it can cause fundamental change, answer deeper issues, and create new paradigms . . . Empathy, love, caring, self-actualization are necessities for lasting leadership. (John P. Schuster, "Transforming Your Leadership Style", *Association Management*, January 1994, p. L39.)

The transformational leader has a concern for the whole, a well developed character, an interest in developing others, a willingness to share power, to accomplish common goals, willing to take a risk, to experiment, and to learn. The transformational leader also has a passion for the mission, can communicate effectively, celebrates the now, and persists in hard times. (*Ibid.*)

In a world undergoing a transformation in fundamental belief systems the transformational organization adapts these beliefs in an effort to refocus its own performance goals and assumptions of how people should be organized and relate to one another.

Wishful Thinking

Transformational leadership often utilizes charismatic powers and emotion which can be dangerous in organizations because they are temperamental and may become volatile, can be misdirected and are often short-lived. The excitement and emotional power of this form of leadership is inherently unstable, especially when employed irresponsibly or for personal ends.

> If the entrepreneurial heroes hold center stage in this drama, the rest of the vast work force plays a supporting role – supporting and unheralded. Average workers in this myth are drones – cogs in the Big Machines, so many interchangeable parts, unable to perform without direction from above . . . To the entrepreneurial hero belongs all the inspiration; the drones are governed by the rules and valued for their reliability and pliability . . . There is just one fatal problem with this dominant myth: it is obsolete. (Robert B. Reich, "Entrepreneurship Reconsidered: The Team as Hero", *Harvard Business Review*, May/June 1987, p. 77.)

The transformation of our world view has been announced. It is claimed to be sweeping the world – at least the industrial world and many individuals and managers espouse this new belief system. The trouble is evidencing the behavioral consequences of this so-called transformation. Where are the transformed organizations reflecting transformed individuals. The best examples are small, transient and fragile if they exist at all. The only stories are claims usually made by CEOs or the organization's PR machine in a less than candid, and often a self-serving, manner. Simply declaring the transformation does not make it so.

Commitment Needed to Make It Work

Being a transformational leader is more than a technique that perseverance alone can establish. It is a way of being. At its best, it suggests an individual with a very clear vision and the ability to convince others of its value. It is a style and a personality and a quality of character that is quite different from the contrasting transactional leader who is more a manager than leader; an administrator or functionary albeit a good one – even a motivational one. Thus, commitment is not enough. It must be accompanied with deliberate training, if it is not a natural part of your personality.

Exemplars

Roosevelt during the great depression serves as the prototype of an American example. Perhaps Mao in China, Ho Chi Minh in Vietnam, DeGaulle in France, Lee Kuan Yew in Singapore, and Churchill in the UK were also transformational leaders.

Matsushita at Matsushita Electronics, Welch at GE, Watson at IBM, Land at Polaroid, and Iacocca at Chrysler would seem to meet the criteria for corporate transformational leaders.

NEW PARADIGM BUSINESS: EMPOWERMENT

> The winners in the next few decades will be the companies with the most empowered workforces.
>
> – Michael Dell, CEO of Dell Computer Corp. quoted in Peter Burrows,
> "Power to the Workers",
> *Electronic Business*, October 7, 1991, p. 97.

What It is

"To be empowered is to have choice and control." (Peter Block, "Empowering Employees", *Training and Development Journal*, April 1987, p. 34.) Empowerment encourages each person to fully contribute to the organization's success.

Empowerment became a popular idea with the publication of Peter Block's *The Empowered Manager* in 1987. The idea is to give authority along with responsibility so individuals can act on behalf of the organization. Simply put, once agreement is reached on what people will do – the objectives they need to achieve – empowered individuals are encouraged and supported to pursue their objectives in the best way they see fit.

The classical management paradigm revolves around managers planning, organizing, staffing, controlling, and directing. Master/Servant; Brains/Brawn; Owner/Employee; Management/Labor – all dichotomies originating under Hammurabi with the separation of responsibility from labor. Control, order, and predictability are the three main pillars of the classical management paradigm.

"Literally, empowering is giving those to be empowered more ability to do the business at hand . . . Empowering is not another word for delegating, but a permanent transfer of both responsibility and authority." (Charles E. Whiting, Jr. and Neal E. Gilbert, "Reaching Hidden Stakeholders: TQM and Empowerment for Professionals", *Journal for Quality and Participation*, June 1993, p. 61.)

"As I see it, empowerment is a four-legged stool resting on: (1) authority and responsibility; (2) knowledge and skill; (3) adequate and timely information; and (4) feelings of confidence and self-esteem." (Phil Alexander, "Empowerment . . . Slogan or Operating Principle?", *Journal for Quality and Participation*, October/November 1992, p. 26.)

> The four general dimensions of empowerment are (1) Meaning – a fit between a given activity and one's beliefs, attitudes, and behaviors. Meaning is the value of an activity's goal or purpose, judged in relation to the individual's own ideals and standards. Empowered individual's belief in, and care about, what they do. (2) Competence or self-efficacy – the belief in one's capability to perform a role. (3) Self-determination – a sense of choice in initiating and regulating one's own actions. (4) Impact – an individual's belief that he or she can influence organizational outcomes. (Gretchen M. Spreitzer, "Individual Empowerment in the Workplace: Construct Definition, Measurement and Validation", *Proceedings of the Association of Employment Practices and Principles Conference*, October 1993, p. 210.)

Wisdom

Recent leadership studies argue that the practice of empowerment – or instilling a sense of power – is at the root of organizational effectiveness, especially during times of transition and transformation. In addition, studies of power and control within organizations indicate that the more productive forms of organizational power increase with superiors' sharing of power and responsibility with subordinates. (Jay Conger, "Leadership: The Art of Empowering Others", *The Academy of Management Executive*, Vol. 3, No. 1, 1989, p. 17.)

Bandura identified four means of providing empowering information to others: (1) through positive emotional support during experiences associated with stress and anxiety; (2) through words of encouragement and positive persuasion; (3) by observing others' effectiveness – in other words, having models of success with whom people identified; and (4) by actually experiencing the mastering of a task with success (the most effective source). (*Ibid.*)

People must be empowered to solve their own problems. It is efficient, it is motivational, it is quick. And, it is truly the only thing that is logical, rational, and effective.

Management practices at W.L. Gore & Associates give a new dimension to employee empowerment. Gore's example illustrates an approach that promises many of the advantages and benefits of formally established and empowered employee work teams, but without formally designated teams. The entire work operation becomes essentially one large empowered team in which everyone is individually self-managing and can interact directly with everyone else in the system. The primary features that characterize Gore can be summarized as a series of organizational themes such as: (1) A culture and norms supporting employee empowerment and success. (2) A lattice organization structure. (3) Many leaders but no bosses or managers. (4) Successful employees – called associates – who work without structure and management. (5) Unstructured research and development for increased creativity and innovation. (Frank Shipper and Charles C. Manz, "Employee Self-Management Without Formally Designated Teams: An Alternative Road to Empowerment", *Organizational Dynamics*, Winter 1992, p. 48.)

"A recent study found one thing in common among US firms that maintained their competitive edge – virtually all had implemented substantial labor-management innovations aimed at empowering employees." (Barry Bluestone and Irving Bluestone, "Workers (and Managers) of the World Unite", *Technology Review*, November/ December 1992, p. 30.)

While empowering people is a worthy end in itself in a democratic culture, organizations should focus on the productive basis for empowering individuals at work. It is primarily a method of involving everyone in the fulfillment of the organization's mission. In each case it has been shown that successful implementation leads to reduced costs, more and better innovations, higher productivity, higher customer satisfaction and more satisfied employees.

Empowerment has directly contributed to the success of recent Chrysler cars. All cars developed under their empowered team structure have come in under budget and cost-per-car target. Product development time was cut almost in half and cost to market was among the industry's lowest. Employees have worked much harder with much more pride. Success or failure is theirs. (Marshall Loeb, "Empowerment That Pays Off", *Fortune*, March 20, 1995, p. 145.)

> At Electro-Galvanizing: ". . . employees do not just run plant operations. They do their own scheduling, rotate jobs on their own, establish production targets, set pay scales that are linked to sales, fire co-workers and do the hiring. The all-salaried workforce has a base pay that increases as workers learn new skills. Workers, not management, decide when an employee has mastered a skill." (Michael Verespej, "Worker-Managers", *Industry Week*, May 16, 1994, p. 30.)

Team Zebra at Kodak empowers workers in the black and white film division. They successfully turned the division around. The lessons they learned about how to create an empowerment program include: (1) Make a full commitment to the empowerment effort. (2) Recognize the power of positive reinforcement. (3) Adapt rather than import or force it. (4) Recognize that people must empower themselves. (5) Maintain an awareness of the tenuous nature of trust. (Stephen J. Frangos and Steven J. Bennett, "Turnaround at Kodak Park", *Business Quarterly*, Spring 1994, p. 30.)

> The paradigm of leader responsibility for other people's performance, given today's circumstances, guarantees organizational failure. Under the new paradigm the leader's job is to make people responsible for their performance . . . At every level in the organi-

zation leaders must transfer ownership of work to those who execute the work, and create an environment for ownership in which each person wants to be responsible for his or her performance. Leaders must also coach the development of individual capability and competence and learn faster by learning themselves . . . Under the new paradigm leaders lead and employees manage. (James A. Belasco and Ralph C. Stayer, "Why Empowerment Doesn't Empower: The Bankruptcy of Current Paradigms", *Business Horizons*, March/April 1994, p. 29.)

Before empowering people be sure they have the skills, experience, tools, and motives to utilize their knowledge appropriately.

L.L. Bean changed managers into doers and coaches in order to create an environment conducive to empowerment. A large part of the process was employee development. The company boosted profits, increased customer satisfaction, reduced backlogs, and increased safety. They won Personnel Journal's Optima Award in managing change. (Dawn Anfuso, "At L.L. Bean Quality Starts With People", *Personnel Journal*, January 1994, p. 60.)

Four ways to reverse trends that disempower people are: (1) To recognize what empowers people. (2) To discover root causes of disempowerment. (3) To align before empowering. (4) To make empowerment part of a long-term structural change. (William J. Schwarz, "Principles of Empowerment", *Executive Excellence*, March 1993, p. 19.)

"As a manager, Sam Walton was applying such concepts as a flat organization, empowerment, and gain sharing long before anyone gave them those names. In the fifties he was sharing information and profits with all employees." (Bill Saporito, "What Sam Walton Taught America", *Fortune*, May 4, 1992, p. 104.)

Senior vice-president Craig Frier of ServiceMaster said, 'Our technologies enable employees to run things right. But we can't do anything or get to any of our goals for the facility until we can get rank and file maintenance, housekeeping, or dietary employees to understand and believe in themselves, their futures and their worth.' (James Brian Quinn and Penny C. Paquette, "Technology in Services: Creating Organizational Revolutions", *Sloan Management Review*, Winter 1990, p. 76.)

NEW PARADIGM BUSINESS 277

When your whole business environment changes overnight, as if hit by a giant, climate-altering meteor, you change with it or go the way of the dinosaurs . . . Don Schneider of Schneider-National flattened and democratized the organization, calling all employees 'associates' and removing status symbols like reserved parking places . . . He encouraged everyone from drivers on up to speak his mind to anyone in the company about how to improve operations. He gave his 8,500 drivers a fifth paycheck every month based solely on performance and poured on the latest technology. (Myron Magnet, "Meet The New Revolutionaries", *Fortune*, February 24, 1992, p. 96.)

To keep up in the race, managers must ... look to their underlings for guidance – and spend their time creating an environment in which that expertise is shared and implemented. "It isn't enough to just be a good employer anymore," says Joanne McCree, personnel manager at IBM-Rochester. "You have to find ways to help people make as much of themselves as possible." (Peter Burrows, "Power to the Workers", Electronic *Business*, October 7, 1991, p. 97.)

The info-age is ushering in new models of organizing. The high-tech firms of Silicon Valley seem to be implementing many, if not all, of these changes found by *Fortune* magazine: (1) Organizing work around tasks or processes while accepting constant reorganization as a way of life. A task-oriented company is more like a web of teams and projects than a clearly defined vertical hierarchy. (2) E-mail and other electronic forms of communication are promoted. It's faster and can be more honest through anonymity when a free flow of ideas is needed. It can overcome time/space limitations to other forms of communication – such as only using in-person meetings. (It can also bring out the worst, mean-spiritedness.) (3) The recruiting process becomes vital and line managers must be conducting the selection. In building relationships many hours are needed to get a real understanding of one another and how, and if, a fit will be achieved. (4) Break the company into small teams of 5–9 people. (5) Cultivate the most demanding customer as a way of challenging your company to faster innovation. (6) Do not make critical decisions until you must. With things changing so rapidly early decisions can set you back. (7) Glorify the people who create the product – who make your company happen. (8) Practice "coopetition" by cooperating with rivals when it comes to some things important to both like uniformity in specifications and then compete vigorously around core competencies and uniquenesses. (9) Help staff become world renowned by encouraging research, innovation, professional involvement, experimentation. Most companies that take an active role in their profession and industry seem to do better than those that discourage outside communication and contact. (10) Constantly innovate. (11) "Cannibalize" your own businesses before someone else does. (12) Spread information widely through the ranks. (13) Foster a sense of urgency and hold frequent "state of the business" briefings. (14) Grant sabbaticals to help people regenerate enthusiasm, recover from stress and avoid burnout. (15) Compensate people according to contribution not status and age. (Alan Deutschman, "The Managing Wisdom of High-Tech Superstars", *Fortune*, October 17, 1994, p. 197.)

> Applied to business, the old paradigm held that numbers are all-important, that professional managers can handle any enterprise, that control can and should be held at the top. The new paradigm puts people – customers and employees – at the center of the universe and replaces the rigid hierarchies of the industrial age with a network structure that emphasizes interconnectedness. (Frank Rose, "A New Age for Business?", *Fortune*, October 8, 1990, p. 157.)

Wishful Thinking

"In one recent survey, 77 percent of all office workers said that freedom to decide how to do their work is very important to them. Only 37 percent of their bosses guessed that. Only half of all bosses thought their employees could make a significant contribution to the company." (Ira E. Smolowitz, "A Dozen Enduring Myths About Management", *Business Horizons*, May/June 1994, p. 40.)

> Managers said that higher ups often overrode their input into the goals that they were expected to achieve . . . Managers suggested that this top down military model is becoming more frequent (contrary to much of the popular literature) because of competitive pressures and because goal setting is being used as a hammer instead of a motivational tool. Once goals were set, another frustration emerged. Managers seldom had a chance to discuss the means

to accomplish the goals – process and strategy issues. (Clinton O. Longenecker and Dennis A. Gioia, "Ten Myths of Managing Managers, *Sloan Management Review*, Fall 1991, p. 81.)

Hard times are sending some bosses back to the Stone Age. Beware of yo-yo empowerment, cost cutting mania, and the new McCarthyism . . . At many organizations, the retreat from power sharing, open internal communications, and general humaneness has been massive enough to thoroughly worry the experts . . . A few symptoms of management regression are: (1) The brass grab back whatever clout they had begun to share . . . Yo-yo empowerment doesn't just tick people off, it undermines them as well, poisoning the wellsprings of self-confidence and initiative. (2) The so-called leaders of the company begin to believe that cost-cutting is a corporate strategy . . . As one veteran manager put it: "You can't save your way out of trouble; you've got to sell your way out." (3) Top management imposes a sort of corporate McCarthyism, actively suppressing any criticism or dissent ... People clam up for fear of losing their jobs. (4) Rambo comes back into fashion. Ask the president of one of the country's ten biggest headhunting firms what kind of chief executive will be sought after in the nineties, and after a moment of thought he replies, "The tough-ass CEO." (Walter Kiechel, III, "When Management Regresses", *Fortune*, March 9, 1992, p. 157.)

"The vast majority of real organizations, especially those of moderate and large size, are mechanistic and, to a considerable extent, reflect the political realities of the organization." (Stephen P. Robbins, *Essentials of Organizational Behavior*, Fourth Edition, Englewood Cliffs, NJ: Prentice Hall, 1994, p. 218.)

"For every empowered employee, there is at least another cowering in his office, putting in longer hours to keep up with a job that used to keep two people busy. For every highly skilled worker moving up the ladder, there is another, marginalized, struggling to make ends meet." (Keith H. Hammonds, "The New World of Work", *Business Week*, October 17, 1994, p. 85.)

A 1990 study at Carnegie-Mellon University suggests that unions may do more to improve productivity than employee involvement programs. Participatory management has shown some well-documented positive results, but critics claim that many senior managers adopt only those aspects of employee empowerment that suit their own personalities. Participatory management is the most difficult style of management; it is difficult for employees to relate to, and it requires that many people function with the same philosophy . . . Most US companies still have the key decisions made by very few people at the top. (Donna Brown, "Why Participative Management Won't Work Here", *Management Review*, June 1992, p. 42.)

Empowerment is a misused term when it simply means delegation; when the assignments come from and are evaluated by a boss without giving real discretion to the employee(s) assigned the work. True empowerment is letting go of control over the means of getting the task done while having established a common goal for employees to strive for.

"People are continually being told they're empowered when they're not. And so employees are deeply demoralized because what they are being told does not match the way they are really being managed." (D. Quinn Mills, "The Truth About Empowerment", *Training & Development*, August 1992, p. 32.)

To instantly "empower" people is not sensible. It could unleash untold damage by releasing pent-up anger, an assortment of personal concerns and idiosyncratic expressions of personal needs in conflict with the group's. Empowerment alone can thus be a dangerous thing. Prepare people, train them, inform them of the purposes toward which they are being empowered. See that they understand what it is all about before empowering them. Be sure there is alignment between the organization's needs and what they understand of their new powers and equip them with knowledge, skills, and tools before setting them loose in the organizational system.

Enthusiastic managers may forget that many people do not want to be empowered and are simply not interested in earning it. And some people who are eager to be empowered do not have the required skills to succeed. Therefore, training and practice should be provided to those being empowered.

"The idea of empowerment – pushing things down – has lost much of its appeal . . . (1) Empowerment was oversold. (2) The political realities were ignored. (3) Workplace values changed radically. (4) Workloads increased dramatically." (Marilyn Moats Kennedy, "Empowered or Overpowered?", *Across the Board*, April 1994, p. 11.)

Be careful of making empowerment an excuse for abdicating

responsibility. Without accountability empowerment is abdication and wishful thinking. "Abdicators fail because they let go but do not take control. Meddlers fail because they grab control but cannot let go. Coaches know the critical difference between intervention and interference." (Wayne E. Baker, "The Paradox of Empowerment", *Chief Executive*, April 1994, p. 62.)

Also, be on the lookout for learned helplessness due to stunted, defeated self-esteem. Employees must not only have skills, knowledge, and abilities but also be in a positive culture where effectiveness and learning are rewarded and risk-taking is the norm. Where people are not empowered they learn to avoid responsibility.

> One basic problem with empowerment goes right to the root of the word – power. Some organizations have found that empowered people start wielding authority with the same kind of disregard for cooperation and teamwork that the empowerment movement is intended to eradicate. (Les Landes, "The Myth and Misdirection of Employee Empowerment", *Training*, March 1994, p. 116.)

What about the devious and those that seek power for its own sake only to misuse it? "Managers and other stakeholders are right to be cautious about the claims that are made for the new organization. The command-and-control system often lives on, concealed beneath the trappings of the facilitate-and-empower-philosophy." (Mahmoud Ezzamel, Simon Lilley, Hugh Wilmott, "Be Wary of New Waves", *Management Today*, October 1993, p. 99.)

"We increasingly demand that our workers take on responsibility and risk, yet their pay is falling . . ." Says MIT's professor Osterman, "You can't expect workers to keep contributing their ideas when they don't get rewarded for them." (Keith H. Hammonds, "The New World of Work", *Business Week*, October 17, 1994, p. 87.)

> Juanita Lewis is proud that she once worked 36 hours straight for Delta Air Lines after a crash – for free. Her enthusiasm for work began waning she maintains, after her boss gave her a hard time about medical and family problems. 'My attitude did change,' she says. 'I did what I had to but nothing extra.' Delta, she says, eventually fired her for refusing to relocate at her own expense. The airline declines to comment. (Bob Davis and Dana Milbank,

"Employee Ennui: If the US Work Ethic is Fading, 'Laziness' May Not Be The Reason", *Wall Street Journal*, February 7, 1992, p. 1.)

University of Southern California Professor Warren Bennis's studies "show that seven of ten people in organizations don't speak up if they think their point of view will vary with the conventional wisdom or their boss's POV [point of view] – even if they believe their boss is going to make an error." (Marshall Loeb, "Where Leaders Come From", *Fortune*, September 19, 1994, p. 241.)

> Certain circumstances . . . appear to lower feelings of self-efficacy. In these cases, subordinates typically perceive themselves as lacking control over their immediate situation (e.g., a major reorganization threatens to displace responsibility and involves limited or no subordinate participation), or lacking the required capability, resources, or discretion needed to accomplish a task (e.g., the development of new and difficult-to-learn skills for the introduction of a new technological process). (Jay Conger, "Leadership: The Art of Empowering Others", *The Academy of Management Executive*, Vol. 3, No. 1, 1989, p. 17.)

"Many Americans would prefer to think that Lee Iacocca singlehandedly saved Chrysler from bankruptcy than to accept the real story: a large team of people with diverse backgrounds and interests joined together to rescue the ailing company. (Robert B. Reich, "Entrepreneurship Reconsidered: The Team as Hero", *Harvard Business Review*, May/June 1987, p. 77.)

> Are OD (organization development) practices freeing middle management or are they redistributing the workload so that a newly 'empowered' work force is overburdened, underpaid, and unable to lead a balanced life; a life that includes fulfilling personal relationships and the development of our next generations? . . . Is the fact of fewer remaining leaders, and the erosion of a middle management-sustained middle class a recipe for egalitarianism, or for increased concentration of power and elitism? (Chuck Schaefer and Gregor Dixon, "Shadows and Soul", *Vision/Action*, June 1992, p. 1.)

Commitment Needed to Make It Work

Empowerment makes enormous sense in a downsizing world.

Since there will be less supervision, people will need the skills and authority to act on their own. By removing supervisors and by establishing a clear vision and shared goals, each person has the guidance necessary to make decisions and move quickly in a competitive world. But to make it happen a control orientation regarding subordinates has to give way to a coaching orientation. More than that, the seductions of power must be resisted and in a culture that rewards individualism and personal achievement over almost everything else, giving up control, and empowering others will be difficult, indeed. That is not to say it is impossible. The new paradigm is a virtual total renovation of the conventional wisdom regarding the distribution of power, control and the acknowledged stakeholders in a workplace. The new paradigm, because it is a multi-faceted, holistic revision of organizations as we have known them will support empowerment and redefine all aspects of the way we do business as long as it is part of a systemic change effort. The empowerment of everyone in reaching the new paradigm is just one, albeit, important step.

Figure 18.2 will help you grasp the significance of the emerging paradigm as many elements of the model are contrasted with the industrial era paradigm – the conventional wisdom.

Exemplars

Arco claims that:

> Environmental compliance in the refining industry in the 1990s will require every employee to participate in developing solutions and to be committed to meeting compliance goals . . . The company claims the philosophy led to collective grassroots innovations, pollution prevention, and policies and procedures that meet multiple environmental goals. ARCO's program shows that when refinery personnel are given the necessary tools and information, they make environmental awareness part of their daily jobs. (Anne K. Rhodes, "Employee Participation Key To Meeting Environmental Goals", *Oil and Gas Journal*, May 30, 1994, p. 60.)

Others include: L-S Electro-Galvanizing Co. • John Deere • W. L. Gore & Associates • Hewlett Packard • Ameritech • Pacific Forest Industries • Wal-Mart • Nucor Steel • Landmark Graphics • ESPN • Eaton

NEW PARADIGM BUSINESS: HEALTHY COMPANIES

> Contrary to popular myth, people produce more meaningful results
> in a stress-free, healthy climate, than in a high pressure one.
>
> – Robert C. Kausen, "Leveraging Leadership",
> *Executive Excellence*, April 1992, p. 20.

What It is

"The concept of organizational health rests on a single principle:
A company's health, productivity, and survival depend on its
ability to foster the health, success and development of its people." ("In Practice: Healthy Companies", *Training and Development*, March 1994, p. 9.)

Wisdom

> In any two-person relationship, the person who has the least power
> will hurt more and we don't appreciate the extent of the hurt. This
> is because the typical boss just has no idea what a powerful effect
> he has on the emotional health of his employees . . . I hope that five
> years from now we'll talk about employee abuse and neglect in the
> same way we've learned over the last ten years to talk about the
> abuse and neglect of children and women. (Mardy Grothe, co-
> author of *Problem Bosses: Who They Are and How to Deal With
> Them*, quoted in Walter Kiechel, III, "Dealing With the Problem
> Boss", *Fortune*, August 12, 1991, p. 98.)

Healthy companies are built around concern for thirteen dimensions as outlined by Robert Rosen in his book, *Healthy Companies:*
(1) Open communications. (2) Employee involvement.
(3) Learning and renewal. (4) Valuing diversity (and censure discrimination and prejudice). (5) Institutional fairness by promoting and protecting privacy, equity, respect, and dissent. In return
individuals observe policies and practices of the organization and
share responsibility for improving the quality of work relations.
(6) Equitable rewards and recognition. (7) Common economic
security that finds each person sharing in the economic pain and
gain. (8) People-centered technology to help eliminate bad jobs
and promote safety. (9) Health-enhancing work environments.
(10) Meaningful work that fosters a sense of purpose and jobs

that have variety, integrity, and significance. (11) Family/work/life balance. (12) Community responsibility. (13) Environmental responsibility. (*The Healthy Companies Story*, Washington, D.C.: Healthy Companies, 1992.)

There is more: The corporate health checklist was published by the Association for Quality and Participation. It includes: (1) connection to customers; (2) creativity; (3) goal setting; (4) coordination of work across functional departments; (5) personal initiative; (6) personnel development; (7) a programmatic approach to solving problems and conflicts; (8) a concern with quality; (9) sufficient recognition and incentives for employees; (10) attention to safety and health; (11) hiring and promotion policies that are consistent with needs and goals of the organization and respectful of people; (12) effective and communicative supervision; (13) fulfilling work and motivation; (14) teamwork; and (15) strategic vision. ("Corporate Health Checklist", *Team/Net*, April 1994, p. 8.)

Wishful Thinking

You cannot have a really healthy company in a sick system, and the global problems, of which all of us are increasingly aware, are symptoms of a sick system . . . Healthy people will not, in the long run, be content to 'give their all' for companies that merely 'make healthy profits and have healthy returns on their investments' without assuming creative responsibility for the well-being of the whole. (Willis Harman, "A Look at The Healthy Company", *World Business Academy Perspectives*, Summer 1991, p. 10.)

Commitment Needed to Make It Work

It is a way of life that expresses the belief that there is more to being in business than just profit. In fact, in order to consistently make a profit a company should be healthy.

Exemplars

In good times many of the Fortune 500 companies lead the way in being early adopters of enlightened management and workplace practices. Then, in tough times, some slide back to an austere existence. Many Silicon Valley companies such as Apple, Sun, Intel, Amdahl, and 3Com aspire to maintaining a healthy orientation though they too have been known for regressive actions in tough times. While trying to build a healthy company is certainly better than not trying, withdrawal of concern for organizational health in downturns only demonstrates to employees that management is an unreliable ally.

NEW PARADIGM BUSINESS: WORKPLACE COMMUNITY

> We live in a culture of brokenness and fragmentation. Images of individualism and autonomy are far more compelling to us than visions of unity and the fabric of relatedness seems dangerously threadbare and frayed . . . We have all but lost the vision of the public (as) our oneness, our unity, our interdependence upon one another.
>
> – Parker Palmer, in Boyte, H.C., *Community Is Possible*,
> New York: Harper & Row, 1984, p. 10.

> Those few American corporations that manage to convey a genuine sense of community and belonging to their employees are thriving as a consequence.
>
> – Tom Peters

What It is

It has now become a cliché to talk about the importance of people. Over the last decade Tom Peters has sold millions of books that have told the stories of companies that put this belief to work. W.L Gore, Hewlett-Packard, Levi Strauss, and Herman Miller were among his favorites. We know people are important – they generate the ideas and products that make a company what it is. How they do it successfully, in almost every case, is by stimulating creativity in a safe environment – one in which views can be exchanged freely and there is respect for one another.

Barbara is typical of people working for these companies. "Why do I like it here? That's simple," she said, "I feel I make a difference and people know I count. I care about my colleagues and they care about me. There is a real family feeling here."

Building a sense of community is above all else conveying the feeling that we are all in this together and we will thrive or perish together because of what we do or do not do together. This is as true in the corporate world as it is in any endeavor – farming community, commune, volunteer organization, army, or household.

Community is caring. Caring about your work, your colleagues, the standing of the organization in the marketplace and its success. It is also about knowing the organization will consider you in each of its decisions and that you have a stake in the outcome of those decisions. It is about knowing you will consider the organization in each decision about your life that will affect work and recognize that the organization has a stake in the outcome of those decisions. All will gain or suffer accordingly. It is feeling a sense of belonging and wanting to contribute. It is about taking your responsibilities seriously and making an effort to improve your ability to contribute through learning new skills. It is about thinking and being fully present in your experience of the organization. It is a context, an environment wherein participants sense that they belong, are an integral part of the organization (as if a citizen of the workplace) with both a right to be there, and a desire to be there along with a felt need to contribute. (Adapted from John Nirenberg's *The Living Organization: Transforming Teams Into Workplace Communities*, Burr Ridge, IL: Irwin, 1993.)

"The workplace is rapidly becoming a new neighborhood, and American businesspeople are helping make it happen." (James Autry, "Love and Profit – The Art of Caring Leadership", *World Business Academy Perspectives*, Vol. 6, No. 1, 1992, p. 59.)

Wisdom

In our case partnership works. And the closer you get to making all your employees feel as though they are partners, the better performance you get out of the business. Look, the essence of a family business is that people have a vested interest in its success, that they feel an ownership and a passion. And non-family businesses can create that same ownership, absolutely . . . We manage the company with a planning committee of ten people; everyone on it owns some stock options, and we regularly give ownership in terms of responsibility . . . The real family-business edge is about attitude not bloodlines. (Allen Razdow and David Blohm, "Why Every Business Can Be A Family Business", *Inc.*, March 1992, p. 80.)

Workplace communities do things differently. What they do have in common is a mindset, a way of thinking, a set of principles that turns the employee mentality upside down. Written in a mission statement the approach might read like this: This is a company of owners, of partners, of businesspeople. We are in business together. Our economic futures – which is to say, our jobs and our financial security – depend not on management's generosity ('them') or on the strength of a union ('us') but on our collective success in the marketplace. We will share in the rewards just as – by definition – we share in the risks. (John Case, "A Company of Businesspeople", *Inc.*, April 1993, p. 79.)

In some new-style organizations, democratic values are the guiding principle. Chaparral Steel, a mini-mill in Texas, boasts of being a classless organization. This is more than just camaraderie in the lunchroom and first-come, first-served parking. Education and training are poured on generously and employees have great freedom to take initiative. (Patricia A. Galagan, "Beyond Hierarchy: The Search for High Performance", *Training & Development*, August 1992, p. 21.)

An intentional community is a group of persons associated together (voluntarily) for the purpose of establishing a whole way of life. As such, it shall display to some degree, each of the following characteristics: . . . economic interdependence, social, cultural, educational, and spiritual inter-exchange of uplift and development. (Benjamin Zablocki, *The Joyful Community*, Baltimore, MD: Penguin, 1973, p. 19.)

Naturally these elements are altered to more suit the corporate setting as demonstrated by the mindful creation of shared traditions, heroes, supportive myths, symbols, artifacts, stories, etc. If they add ego reduction for the good of the group perhaps the environment for collaboration and community would then be complete. That is a reduction in interpersonal competition per se but not a disavowal of personal recognition for individual contribution.

Wishful Thinking

As with team building, reengineering, and other changes that affect an organization's culture, community building must not assume that the alteration of existing roles can take place without considerable re-adjustment and role redefinition. Resistance will be formidable especially since people are asked to surrender certain prerogatives and powers. Even among the willing, the sense of still being held personally accountable for the work of the group may deter delegation or a restructuring until at least everyone has accepted the devolution of responsibility and acts in the interests of the whole. (See Figure 18.2.)

You cannot be expected to give up power and responsibility before the group or community is willing to accept it. Before this can be done alignment must be achieved between the organizational mission and the willingness and commitment of each individual to accept the new configuration of duties and powers.

Commitment Needed to Make It Work

Typically, this requires the recognition of another way of being and a new set of operating instructions for most organizations. See Figure 9.1 for the contrasting descriptors of the two major paradigms characteristic of the industrial and postindustrial organization. One emphasis is fading and another is emerging. Unfortunately, in building workplace community or adopting the new paradigm, generally, people often find themselves "with one foot on the boat and one foot on the dock" as the turbulence unsettles the way they have been doing business and neither the old system is dead or the new system born.

Exemplars

MathSoft, Cambridge, Massachusetts software firm • Chaparral Steel • Wilkhahn Contract Furniture

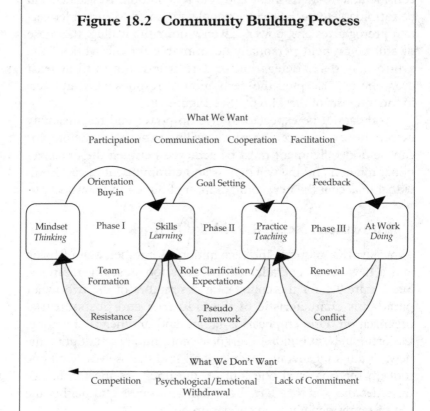

Figure 18.2   Community Building Process

The process of building a workplace community requires attention to three phases. In the first phase the organization examines its intention and examines the comparison of intentions with its existing mindset and practices. Is the change to workplace community sensible? Aligned with its values? Is there a willingness to commit to the process?

In the second phase the struggle to identify goals and roles and to learn and apply new skills takes place. Practicing new skills and aligning individual action with goals take place here.

Phase three is application, refinement, celebration, and renewal. Dealing with conflicts and setbacks occurs here as the cycle of change continues through implementation.

THE NEW PARADIGM EMERGING

Figure 18.3 contrasts the distinctions between the old command and control, hierarchical and bureaucratic model of organizing with the new paradigm of cooperative, collaborative, organic, network structures typical of organizations requiring high quality, customer responsiveness, innovativeness and intelligence routinely applied to daily business problems.

As you review the list, consider conflicts and difficulties your organization is experiencing. Along which dimensions do you believe the struggle is focused?

Describe a situation, problem or conflict where the basis of the difficulty is due to differences in orientation toward these polarities.

Review the categories and describe a current issue facing you or your organization along one of the dichotomies mentioned in Figure 18.3.

_____

_____

_____

_____

_____

_____

_____

_____

_____

_____

_____

_____

Figure 18.3

Major Emphases Industrial-era Paradigm	Major Emphases Postindustrial-era Paradigm
Acceptance	Learning
Acquiring	Experiencing
Action orientation	Mixed action/planning/ feedback correction
Adaptive learning (coping)	Generative learning (creating)
Adversaries	Partners
Alienated	Committed
Anthropocentrism	Ecocentrism
Assets are things	Assets are people/ideas
Autocracy	Informed consent
Blame	Responsibilities/Opportunities
Boss-centered	Customer-centered
Bottom line thinking	Process/goal/person thinking
Bureaucracy/hierarchy	Solacracy/solararchy
Centralization	Decentralization
Centripetal tendencies	Centrifugal tendencies
Certainty	Probabilities
Change management with a specific endpoint	Facilitating a continuous change process with occasional disconti- nuities and transformations
Class centered	Lifestyle centered
Compartmentalization	Integration
Competitive	Cooperative
Compliance	Consensus
Concrete	Abstract
Controllable	Uncontrollable
Conflict avoidance	Conflict confrontation
COP (Control-Order- Prescription)	ACE (Acknowledge- Create-Empower)
Domination	Cooperation
Control-oriented	Consensus-driven
Involvement-inducing	Vision-led
Command	Commitment
Concrete	Abstract
Counseling	Coaching/Mentoring

Figure 18.3 (*Continued*)

Major Emphases Industrial-era Paradigm	Major Emphases Postindustrial-era Paradigm
Dependency at work	Autonomy at work
Deterministic, reductionistic thinking	Holistic, synergistic thinking
Dispensability	Community membership
Domination/Submission framework	Partner/Peer framework
Economic person	Social person
Ego control orientation basis of power	Competence, knowledge and respect basis of power
Ego building	Community building
Exclusion	Inclusion
External control	Self control
External feedback	Internal feedback
Extrapolates data to see future	Constructs "what if?" scenarios
Extrinsic motivation (incentives)	Intrinsic motivation dominant
Fixed/Shared/Definite Meaning	Symbolic/Random/ Constructed meaning
Focus on "hard" science and data	Includes indeterminacy, intuition, "soft" sciences
Formal/hierarchical authority	Self-team direction
Fragmentation	Wholeness
Hero worship	Love of ideas
Higher standard of living	Better quality of life
Human costs	Human capital
Identity defined by status	Identity is with the community
Impersonal/denial of feelings	Personal/expression of feelings
Individual/organization centered	Organization as community/ part of society
Information/data	Knowledge
Inhibitions	Self-expression
Instant gratification	Immediate and delayed gratification
Interpersonal game playing	Authenticity
Job centered	Community/profession centered
Job specialization	Job enrichment

Figure 18.3 (*Continued*)

Major Emphases Industrial-era Paradigm	Major Emphases Postindustrial-era Paradigm
Labor serves capital	Capital serves human need
Leadership	Integrity
Left brain emphasis	Rational/intuitive balance
Lifeboat ethic	Spaceship earth ethic
Linear reasoning, reversible models exclusively used	Non-linear reasoning; irreversible models, evolutionary thinking also used
Live to work	Work in balance
Macho modeling	Androgyny
Management development	Organization/personal development
Manipulation	Collaboration
Material	Ideational
Material progress sole measure of value	Material and spiritual in harmony/balance
Mechanistic organizations	Living/Organic organizations
Monoculturalism	Multi-culturalism
Newton	Einstein
Now orientation	Today with links to future orientation
Nuclear family	Alternative Family
Obedience to boss	Respect to associates
Objectivity claimed	Subjectivity recognized
Order	Chaos
Organizational imperative	Individual Imperative
Output/Thing	Meaning/Message
Ownership of resources	Custody of resources
Parochialism	Holistic system's view
Paternalism	Community/Voluntarism
People as expendable resource/liability	People as renewable resource/asset
People as means to organization's ends	People as ends in themselves/ partners
People master nature	People as a part of nature
Performance evaluation as control	Evaluation for growth/learning

Figure 18.3 (*Continued*)

Major Emphases Industrial-era Paradigm	Major Emphases Postindustrial-era Paradigm
Permanence	Transience
Pessimistic philosophy of life	Optimistic philosophy of life
Planned obsolescence	Conservation
Policeman	Planner/Facilitator/Coach
Politics of deceit and secrecy	Openness and authenticity
Power over others	Empowerment of others
Private enterprise	Community enterprise
Problems as dangers	Problems as opportunities
Profit centered	Value centered
Property rights	Personal rights
Provincialism	Cosmopolitanism
Quantity mentality	Quality, aesthetic mentality
Reactive	Proactive
Return on investment	Return to community
Risk averse	Entrepreneurial
Rational	Also intuitive and holistic
Reductionistic	Holistic/Systemic
Routine work	Creative work/diversity of work
Secrecy/need to know	Openness
Segmentation	Integration
Sensate	Being
Self-centered behavior	Organization-centered behavior
Self-denial ethic	Self-fulfillment ethic in context
Self interest	Personhood/Community
Shareholder/manager focus	Stakeholder equity
Short-term fragmented thinking	Long-term holistic thinking
Single standard of success: ($)	Individual definition of success
Single knowable truth	Acceptance of paradox and ambiguity
Slicing the pie	Enlarging the pie/not eating pie
Slow evolving social life	Instant intimacy
Social Darwinism	Emphasis on connectedness
Standardized procedures	Integrated supervisory and work role
Static boundaries	Permeable boundaries

Figure 18.3 (*Continued*)

Major Emphases Industrial-era Paradigm	Major Emphases Postindustrial-era Paradigm
Sufficiency	Excellence
Suspicion	Trust
Tangible	Intangible
Theory "X"	Theory "Y"
Thing oriented	Idea oriented
Thinking about what is	Thinking about what could be
Thinking and doing separated	Thinking and doing integrated
Total planning	Spontaneity/intuition allowed
Traditional gender roles	Blurred gender roles
Trickle down theory as means to growth	Innovation, creativity as basis to growth
Turbulence/Planned change	Chaos/Unfolding systems
Universal social norms	Pluralistic social norms
Unlimited growth	Tempered sustainable growth
Vertical relations	Collegial relations
Visible	Invisible
We/They	Us
Win/Lose	Win/win
Work as drudgery	Work as fun/meaningful
Worker as automaton	Worker as dynamic colleague

Compiled and adapted in part from: Tannenbaum and Davis, "Values, Man and Organizations", *Industrial Management Review*, Winter 1969; Nirenberg, "On the Frontier of American Business: Eupsychian Management", *Malaysian Institute of Management Newsletter*, February 1978, and "Technological Change, Societal Transformation and the Future of Management", *1986 International Conference on Innovation and Management*, Carlsbad, Czechoslovakia, October 1986; Satin, *New Age Politics*, New York: Delta, 1979; Ferguson, *The Aquarian Conspiracy*, Los Angeles: Tarcher, 1980; Lippitt, *Organizational Renewal*, 2nd Ed., Englewood Cliffs, NJ: Prentice Hall, 1982; Yankelovich, *New Rules*, New York: Bantam, 1982; Plummer, *The Futurist*, January/February 1989; Renesch, quoted in Harman and Hormann, *Creative Work*, Indianapolis, IN: Knowledge Systems, Inc., 1991; Dolenga, "Productivity: Problems, Paradigms and Progress", *SAM Advanced Management Journal*, Autumn 1985, p. 29; Evered, and Selman, "Coaching and the Art of Management", *Organizational Dynamics*, Fall 1989; Henderson, *Paradigms In Progress: Life Beyond Economics*, Indianapolis, IN: Knowledge Systems, Inc., 1991; Schramm, "An Experimental Model for Socially and Environmentally Responsible Management Education", *6th Annual International Conference on Socio-Economics*, July 1994, p. 11.

Figure 18.4 Toward a New Paradigm: Expanding Personal and Organizational Capacity

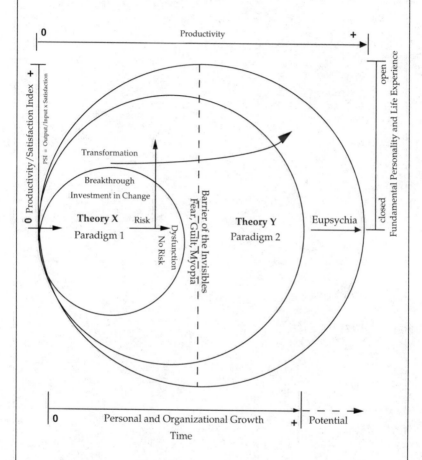

The contrasting paradigms are often thought of as bi-polar. In actuality the contrasting paradigms show a movement from a belief in certainty and uniformity (a modernist perspective) to the belief in variety and a more complex set of potentialities and possibilities. The Theory X personality tends toward a closed, narrow experience of the possibilities while a Theory Y personality is open to a wider choice of legitimate realities. Likewise, Paradigm 2 is a more holistic, responsive mindset more able to deal with uncertainty, diversity, and complexity.

Part III

AN ANNOTATED COMPENDIUM OF MORE THAN 100 TOOLS AND TECHNIQUES

If

You

Don't

Know

What

You

Are

Building

No

Tool

Will

Help

What's Useful, What's Not

More than one hundred tools and techniques have been defined. These annotated entries describe the concepts that have, over the last few years, swept through the management literature like a wind through wheat in Kansas. This will give you fingertip access to the most frequently talked about people-management tools and techniques in the management literature. See for yourself.

When you read through the following section, however, you will find something else – something more important, more instructive than the definitions. If you browse through these pages carefully you will see certain patterns emerge. These patterns are the important truths that we must ultimately grapple with building powerful and productive workplace relationships. It is about integrity, character, and communications.

References are almost always mentioned so you can follow-up on items of personal interest. They also demonstrate the sheer diversity of voices in the literature. What you will discover are the three factors comprising the "genetic code" determining the success of all people-management situations: your use of power (either for achieving clearly understood organizational goals as opposed to serving your personal ends), your ability to communicate fully, honestly and fearlessly in a timely manner; and, that policies, procedures and structures are either supportive of the organization's purposes or destructive (being simply control devices). Each of the following tools ultimately impacts one or more of these factors. Power, communications and the structures of relationships. Simple.

Figure 18.5 A Compendium of Current Tools and Techniques

360-degree Evaluations
Adhocracy/Temporary Organization
After-action Reviews
Alternative Dispute Resolution
Attila the Hun
Benchmarking
Best Practice
Boundarylessness
Breakthrough Action Teams
Centralization
Chaos Theory and the New Science
Competitive Advantage
Conglomeration
Contingent Work Force
Corporate Culture
Crisis Management
Cross-functional Teams
Customer Delight
Cycle Time
Deming System
Dialogue Group
Diversity
Double Bottom Line
Downsizing/Demassing
Economic Value Added
Employability
Employment Contracts
Empowerment
Enlightened Leadership
Entrepreneurship
Environmental/Green Marketing
Excellence
Fire Walking with the Giant Within
Future Search
Gain Sharing/ESOPs
Groupware
Healthy Companies
High Performance Organizations

Figure 18.5 (*Continued*)

Horizontal Organization
Impression Management (Kiss Up/Kick Down)
Intelligent Organization
Intrapreneurship
ISO 9000
Japanese Management
Job Enlargement/Job Enrichment
Just-in-Time/Just-in-Case
Lateral Thinking/Out-of-the-Box Thinking
Laws and Principles: Murphy/Parkinson/Peter
Lean Production/Lean and Mean
Learning Organization
Management by Objectives
Management by Walking Around
Management/Leadership Coaching/Mentoring
Managerial Grid
Mass Customization
Matrix Management
Micro-managing
Myers-Briggs
Networking (Personal Strategy and Structure/Information flow)
New Paradigm Business
One Minute Manager
Open Book Management
Organizational Transformation
Outplacement/Purgatory
Outsourcing
Outward Bound
Participative Management
Pay for Performance
Peer Appraisals/Review
Peer Mediation/Peer Intervention Teams
Principle-centered Leadership
Quality
Quality Circles
Quality of Worklife
Quick Response/Rapid Deployment Teams
Reengineering
Reinventing the Corporation

Figure 18.5 (*Continued*)

Reinventing Government
Restructuring
Results-driven Quality
Right Brain Thinking
Rightsizing
Scientific Management
Self-development Group
Self-managing Work Teams
Servant Leadership
Seven Habits
Situational Leadership
Skunkworks
Social Responsibility
Spirituality in Organizations
Stakeholder Issues
Strategic Alliances
Stretch Goals
Sun Tzu
Sustainability
Synergy
Systems Thinking
TA
T-Groups
Theory X/Y
Theory Z
Third Wave/Fourth Wave Organization
Trickle Down Technology
Transformational Leadership
Virtual Organization
Visions/Missions/Values
Wellness
Workout
Workplace Community
Zero-based Budgeting

Figure 18.6

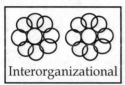

Interorganizational

Organizational

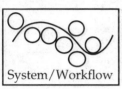

System/Workflow

Intergroup

Group/Team

Interpersonal

Intrapersonal

These icons indicate the prevailing usage for each particular tool or technique.

Some tools can be used as interventions at more than one level, however.

One crucial point to remember is that as interventions are applied at higher levels the pre-requisite degree of readiness becomes more complex. Thus, a culture change at the organizational level will probably require interventions at the intrapersonal, interpersonal, team, and intergroup levels. The implications must be examined.

360-DEGREE EVALUATIONS

360-degree evaluation uses the input from subordinates, colleagues, customers, and bosses to create an overall picture of your performance. It is used for training and development purposes as well as for personal feedback. It should not be used for promotional or pay determinations. See the earlier entry under General Electric in Part II for more details.

ADHOCRACY/TEMPORARY ORGANIZATION

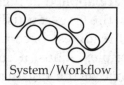

Adhocracy is the title of a recent book by Robert Waterman, New York: Norton, 1992, co-author of *In Search of Excellence*. The term was originally popularized by Alvin Toffler in his 1970 bestseller, *Future Shock*. He said: "This is the organization of the future. I call it ad-hocracy . . . Man will find himself liberated, a stranger in a new free form world of kinetic organizations. In this alien landscape, his position will be constantly changing, fluid and varied. And his organizational ties, like his ties with things, places and people, will turn over at a frenetic and ever-accelerating rate." (Alvin Toffler, *Future Shock*, New York: Random House, 1970, p. 108.)

Twenty years later he was describing the same phenomena: The pulsating unit is one that changes in size and organization from time to time; it could also pulse back and forth between centralization and decentralization as circumstances change. A good example of the pulsating unit is the United States Census Bureau. The two-faced unit, on the other hand, may remain the same in size, but shifts from hierarchical to non-hierarchical as need demands . . . spit and polish on the parade ground, informal in the trenches. (A.J. Vogel, "Breaking With Bureaucracy: Alvin Toffler Describes the Organization Man of the Future", *Across the Board*, January/February 1991, p. 18.)

The idea of adhocracy is manifested in network project-based and matrix organizations and in task forces which are all chartered to achieve specific objectives. Upon their attainment, members of the teams disband and either join another team or are assigned interim duties such as research or training.

AFTER-ACTION REVIEWS

Group/Team

The purpose of an after-action review is to conduct a debriefing of an event to understand what was successful and what failed. The goal is to improve individual and system performance. In the Army's case, it is a way of examining the structure and processes that contribute to creating an "agile, versatile and well-prepared army."

When maneuvers or engagements are over an after-action review takes place. It is a learning device which matches performance against goals. (Margaret Wheatley, "Can The US Army Become a Learning Organization?", *Journal for Quality and Participation*, March 1994, p. 50.)

The army has moved from a meat grinder approach to warfare . . . to one where commanders emphasize speed, surprise and deception, driven by initiative at the lowest levels. This is the military equivalent of decentralization, of pushing decision making down to the operational level . . . The new U.S. thinking is based on research that has found that most major battles have been turned not by a general's orders but by low ranking officers taking action based on a commander's plan. (Dyan Machan, "We're Not Authoritarian Goons", *Forbes*, October 24, 1994, p. 246.)

Consider after-action reviews elaborate and disciplined de-briefings. To be effective they require dialogue, empathy, and listening skills combined with the frank disclosure of exactly what happened. This requires a safe and cooperative environment so everyone can trust in the process.

ALTERNATIVE DISPUTE RESOLUTION

Interpersonal

Alternative dispute resolution (or ADR) is any method to get parties in conflict to consider handling their situation outside of the court system. More generally, it is any effort to resolve differences using non-traditional and, in most cases, informal avenues of conflict resolution. These avenues frequently serve as a starting point to avoid the expense, official ramifications, frequently long-time frame, and adversarial win/lose nature of the formal conflict resolution processes. If the alternative route is unsatisfactory the parties to the conflict can always avail themselves of the formal channels later.

For ADR to work participants need to be willing to commit to a discussion process until the solution is uncovered; preferably with an attitude that will allow finding a win/win solution.

In order for ADR to be useful, parties must recognize a dispute – a controversy and must voluntarily join the process and agree to the rules. Mutual agreement on a third party mediator, facilitator, or counselor, if necessary, must also be a condition of entering the process.

The process includes: (1) introduction; (2) problem determination; (3) summarization; (4) issue identification; (5) generation and evaluation of alternatives; (6) selection of proper alternatives; and (7) conclusion. (Andre Long, "Resolving Disputes While Preserving Relationships", *National Contract Management Journal*, Vol. 25, No. 2, 1992, p. 43.)

Hewlett Packard even has a "swat" team to intervene when three complaints about a manager are received. They go in and interview everyone around to see what is happening and to recommend next steps. The point here is to intervene at the first sign of an issue and to do so in a constructive, not punitive, manner.

ATTILA THE HUN

Interpersonal

Attila (c. 450) was known as the Scourge of God. He along with his brother, whom he eventually murdered, invaded the Balkan peninsula and Italy. He demanded tribute from those he merely threatened as well as those he defeated. He has symbolized brutality and gangsterism for centuries but came to be an inspiration for American managers with the publication of *Leadership Secrets of Attila the Hun* by Wes Roberts. More novelty than wisdom, the book was catapulted to the best-seller lists in the late 1980s when Ross Perot gave a copy to each member of the General Motors' Board of Directors. This novelty became a fad as would-be acolytes to successful business people, such as Perot, rushed to find out exactly how the Scourge of God treated his men.

BENCHMARKING

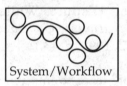

System/Workflow

"Benchmarking is an external focus on internal activities, functions or operations in order to achieve continuous improvement ... There are four types: (1) internal; (2) competitive; (3) industry; and (4) best in class benchmarking." (C. J. McNair and Kathleen H.J. Leibfried, *Benchmarking: A Tool for Continuous Improvement*, 1994.)

According to Robert Camp, one of the early proponents of benchmarking, "it is finding and implementing best practices." Usually it is done by examining specific processes or problems in your organization by comparing the best practice in a similar situation from the perspective of a different industry. Thus, Motorola studied Domino's Pizza and Fedex to learn about reducing their cycle time in delivering cellular telephones. (Alexandra Biesada, "Benchmarking", *FW,* September 17, 1991, p. 28.)

Xerox, an originator of the concept defined it as ". . . a continuous process of measuring products, services and practices against our toughest competition or those companies recognized as world leaders." (Mustafa B. Pulat, "Benchmarking is More Than Organized Tourism", *Industrial Engineering*, March 1994, p. 22.)

There are basically eight steps: (1) select a project champion who creates a sense of urgency and provides leadership; (2) assess current condition of work process/performance; (3) establish goals for your unit; (4) determine the gap between where you are and where you want to be; (5) study alternate methods and best practices; (6) determine a suitable model to begin change process; (7) innovate, customize and design a change program for your own needs; (8) assess the change process.

"The value of benchmarking does not lie in what can be copied, but rather in how much the experience energizes the group to reconsider its own goals." (Theodor Richman and Charles Koontz, "How Benchmarking Can Improve Process Reengineering", *Planning Review*, November/December 1993, p. 26.)

BEST PRACTICE

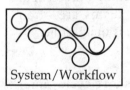

System/Workflow

Best practices are simply the techniques and processes that are recognized as best in their class and usually measured against a world-class standard. Benchmarking is usually the technique used to uncover best practices. (See benchmarking.)

BOUNDARYLESSNESS

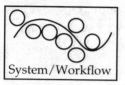

System/Workflow

Imagine being in a race through a maze with a competitor who was tall enough to see over the hedge! Boundarylessness is the recognition that rules, regulations, endless oversight, the frequently artificial and arbitrary departmental barriers, excessive hierarchical levels and geography put you at a competitive disadvantage. Boundarylessness is an attempt to remove every obstacle and delay in the process of creating a product or service and meeting customer needs. For further information, see the discussion of boundarylessness in Part II.

BREAKTHROUGH ACTION TEAMS (BATS)

Group/Team

Also known by a variety of other colorful acronyms such as CATS (corrective action teams) and VATS (value added teams), BATS are ad hoc, interdepartmental teams that are brought together to solve a specific problem. Once they finish they dissolve or wait for another problem in order to be reactivated. Quality teams are often involved in this kind of activity. This is quite similar to ad hoc teams.

In essence, this is TQM with a short cycle time. Results are seen almost immediately. This is a great strategy when each of the immediate improvements fit in to a larger change effort so that significant improvements can be seen in their cumulative effect.

Sometimes called Quality Improvement Teams (QITs) and Corrective Action Teams (CATs), these teams might have five to nine people spend a defined (or continuous) period of time on specific problem-solving/troubleshooting activities.

Performance Action Teams (PATs) are interdepartmental squads of personnel ready to act fast when an emergency arises such as a breakdown in a vital function but this is reactive while BATs are primarily proactive.

One caution: the short-term emphasis of BATS does not allow for more ambitious system-wide changes that might require a longer cycle time. This makes these efforts trivial at worst and merely incremental at best if used for more substantial changes. Not all needed large-scale change can be implemented in short bursts which promise immediate results.

CENTRALIZATION

Organizational

Centralization is out of favor today because the personal computer and telecommunications resources have actually made controlled decentralization possible. Some people still look at centralization as a way of maintaining control by requiring that most important decisions be made at the top of the organization or division. Mainframe computers made centralization possible. A more eclectic approach to organizing finds that some activities (standard purchasing practices, perhaps) are more appropriately centralized while others (such as defining the local mix of products in an outlet of a national drug store chain) are best decentralized.

CHAOS THEORY AND THE NEW SCIENCE

Organizational

"To some physicists chaos is a science of process rather than a state, of becoming rather than being." (James Gleick, *Chaos: Making A New Science*, New York: Viking, 1987, p. 5.) The new science is quantum physics and the study of sub-atomic phenomena. Many new discoveries regarding the nature of matter and energy and their relationship have overturned the Newtonian/Cartesian world. Recent attention has been focused on chaos theory and its application to human organizations and this inquiry is leading to a new definition of relationships in human systems.

Using insights from chaos theory as metaphors for organizational behavior in a complex era, leadership is conceptualized as more of a facilitative than control function and individual leaders help natural forces unfold in the organization. For a more complete discussion see the references to the new science in Part II.

COMPETITIVE ADVANTAGE

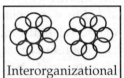

Interorganizational

This term is used to describe virtually any idea that a company uses to add value to its core competencies and its perceived standing amidst competitors. It is the identification and exploitation of some unique feature of its processes, service or product in a way that distinguishes it from all others.

The concept was popularized by Michael Porter, a Harvard Professor when his book, *Competitive Advantage* (New York: Free Press, 1985) hit the business books best-seller list. Basically it directs companies to examine how they add value in a unique fashion and to exploit that advantage.

A competitive advantage is derived from an extraordinarily effective execution of a function in the value chain such as in the area of input logistics, operations, output logistics, marketing, and sales and service.

Support activities are typically considered staff functions which enable the line to function efficiently. General administration, human resource management, research and development, information systems and procurement are examples.

Excelling in any of these areas has the potential of providing a real competitive advantage due to efficiencies, low cost or a strong compelling relationship with either an internal or external connection to the value chain – the process that results in the delivery of products and services to the marketplace.

Porter identified five basic forces which tend to shape the dynamics of competition and determine who adds the most value in order to win in the market: (1) the bargaining power of customers indicated by their ability to dictate or accept the terms of the relationship; (2) bargaining power of suppliers; (3) potential new entrants; (4) potential substitutes for your product or service and, perhaps most ominously; (5) the extent of the rivalry between players in the same market. (Michael Porter, *Competitive Advantage*, New York: Free Press, 1985.)

A refinement of the concept of competitive advantage is the recent popularity of the idea of core competence. Core competencies are the collective learning in the organization, especially how to coordinate diverse production skills and integrate multiple streams of technologies . . . "If core competence is about harmonizing streams of technology, it is also about the organization of work and the delivery of value . . . The skills that together constitute core competence must coalesce around individuals whose efforts are not so narrowly focused that they cannot recognize the opportunities for blending their functional expertise with those of others in new and interesting ways." (C. K. Prahalad and Gary Hamel, "The Core Competence of the Corporation", *Harvard Business Review*, May/June 1990, p. 79.)

"A rival might acquire some of the technologies that comprise the core competence, but it will find it more difficult to duplicate the more or less comprehensive pattern of internal coordination and learning." (C. K. Prahalad and Gary Hamel, "The Core Competence of the Corporation", *Harvard Business Review*, May/June 1990, p. 79.)

The sad reality is that real sustainable competitive advantages are few and far between. Often, like banks without ATMs or airlines without reservation systems, the best a firm can do is strive to eliminate a competitive disadvantage . . . On the positive side a firm can come to grips with the mortality of a particular competitive advantage and continue to innovate to improve and/or supplant a given advantage. (Bernard C. Reimann, "Sustaining the Competitive Advantage", *Planning Review*, March/April 1989, p. 30.)

"We find it ironic that top management devotes so much attention to the capital budgeting process yet typically has no comparable mechanism for allocating the human skills that embody core competencies." (C. K. Prahalad and Gary Hamel, "The Core Competence of the Corporation", *Harvard Business Review*, May/June 1990, p. 79.)

CONGLOMERATION

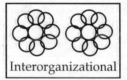
Interorganizational

Conglomeration is the acquisition of businesses whether or not they are related to the primary purposes of the organization. Major conglomeration spread through the US twice in the last thirty years, first in the mid-1960s and more recently in the late 1980s. Acquisitions and mergers characterized both periods though in the later period there was a more obvious strategic intent. All mergers and acquisitions seem to be plagued with an impenetrable thicket of behavioral, political, and morale issues that undermine the deals. But in some industries size is an important determinant of success and mergers become necessary. The consolidation of the defense industry after the Cold War is an example of how the market can no longer sustain a large number of competitors.

This technique was the hallmark of Harold Geneen's tenure at ITT. He acquired everything from hotels and rental car companies to bakeries and insurance companies. After fifty eight consecutive quarters of 10 percent-plus profit gains, ITT earnings declined. That was only the beginning of problems for the corporation; there followed sick divisions, divestitures, large write-offs, massive firings, quarrels with governments in Europe and congressional exploration of the disaster in Chile, where ITT was accused of having conspired with the CIA to create economic chaos and revolution. (Michael E. McGill, *American Business and the Quick Fix*, New York: Henry Holt, 1988, p. 99.) The rise and fall of Harold Geneen and ITT paralleled the rise and fall of diversified conglomeration. Today's acquisitions appear more related to product or industry groupings.

CONTINGENT WORK FORCE

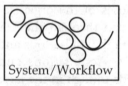
System/Workflow

A temp fills an unforeseen absence such as a receptionist being sick or a data entry clerk not showing up one day. A contingent worker is more of a planned part-timer or temporary worker with a longer employment horizon but definitely less than a year. The job assignment may or may not be renewable.

The US contingent work force comprising part-time workers, temporary employees, and independent contractors hired to work on specific projects in place of full-time permanent workers, has become the fastest growing segment of the labor market . . . These 'virtual' employees and independent contractors now total some 35 million people – or one out of every four civilian workers. (Larry Reynolds, "Washington Confronts Part-Time America", *Management Review*, February 1994, p. 27.) For a more thorough description see the entry in Part II.

CORPORATE CULTURE

Organizational

Corporate culture is the social manifestation of the organization's learning experience. It is the particular pattern of norms, beliefs, assumptions, relationships, shared meaning and symbols that distinguish the organization's members from others. In its entirety it is a way of being and a reflection of the productive capacity of the organization's human system.

Rensis Likert may have been the first to identify management systems (*New Patterns of Management*, New York: McGraw-Hill, 1961). However, he confined his focus on distinctly managerial variables in an organizational context. With the publication of Deal and Kennedy's *Corporate Cultures: The Rites and Rituals of Corporate Life* (Terrence Deal and Allan A. Kennedy, Menlo Park, CA: Addison Wesley, 1982) attention was drawn to aspects of organizational life that were previously ignored as important causal variables. They looked at rites, rituals, values and heroes, for example, as keys to understanding not only what is important to members of an organization but the kinds of influences that drive their current behavior. This led to an examination of the impact of culture on change efforts and suggested the importance of understanding the underlying cultural terrain before making any effort to change an organization. See the ladder of organizational behavior in Part I for a further discussion of this concept. For another look at how to change corporate cultures with some examples from the brewing industry to petrochemicals, see Charles Hampden-Turner, *Creating Corporate Culture: From Discord to Harmony*, Menlo Park, CA: Addison Wesley, 1990.

CRISIS MANAGEMENT

Group/Team

Crisis management has two meanings. The most common is how an organization responds to a sudden emergency. There may be contingency plans ready for any manager to institute a response such as when product contamination occurs or a fire hits a distribution center. A quick response team is sometimes established in each department for such eventualities. There may also be an overall communications center to help the employees, customers, and public know what is happening and what to expect in the future. That would be managed by a public relations/communications officer who may direct a central organizational strategy to keep everyone informed.

The second use of the term crisis management is as a learning device where managers are put through deliberately created "crises" to test their responses. This is effective for pilots using a simulator or firefighters at training centers but is questionable as a real-time practice in most organizations.

CROSS-FUNCTIONAL TEAMS

Group/Team

Cross-functional teams are teams composed of individuals from different departments or from within a department that represents a variety of functional specialties. They are usually brought together due to a problem that is interdepartmental or interdisciplinary and often as a task force to solve product development issues or to address unique customer needs. See the more complete discussion in Part II for details of the wisdom and wishful thinking of this technique.

CUSTOMER DELIGHT

Interpersonal

Customer delight is a term gaining wide acceptance from its first popular usage by AT&T. It is the notion of serving the customer in a way that literally results in an emotional response of great pleasure with the provider. The concept is captured in the clichés, "deliver more than you promise" and "go the extra mile."

The goal of customer delight in addition to making each transaction satisfy the need at the very least is to exceed a customer's expectation. Pure customization, delivered flawlessly and immediately to wherever it is required is the ultimate goal. (See Stan Davis and Bill Davidson, *2020 Vision*, New York: Simon and Schuster, 1991.)

The key, however, is to remember that service is an attitude, a culture, not a set of policies but a way of being.

For AT&T's Universal Card, "customer delight, continual improvement, teamwork and the ability to establish and use customer listening posts have spearheaded one of the most successful credit card introductions ever." (Howard Schlossberg, "GM and AT&T Cards Rise Above Competition", *Marketing News*, July 5, 1993, p. 2.)

AT&T Universal Card Services may have been the inventor of the phrase Customer Delight as a way of exaggerating the importance of customer service and mobilizing a management effort to meet and exceed customer expectations.

The concept of customer satisfaction is changing to incorporate the factor of emotion. An emerging belief is that total customer satisfaction is not possible without emotional fulfillment . . . Creating customer delight means meeting basic needs and then going beyond them; it means building into products new qualities like personality, friendliness, fun and surprise. (Howard Schlossberg, "Dawning of the Era of Emotion", *Marketing News*, February 15, 1993, p. 1.)

Customer service is widely regarded as an important way for an organization to distinguish itself from competitors. In one study customers speaking about wanting better service meant the following kinds of transactions: (1) where their opinions are respected; (2) where they are assisted by people to whom they can relate on an equal level; and (3) where sincere concern and kindness are evident . . . The four main ingredients of a customer delight program include being: (1) perxsonal; (2) spontaneous; (3) non-threatening; and (4) beyond the norm. (David Hall and Simon Haslam, "How to Achieve – And Measure – Customer Delight", *Business Marketing Digest*, Fourth Quarter, 1992, p. 17.)

To the customer, the most important person in the company is very often the one at the point of contact. What happens in the usually brief one to three minutes of that contact will demonstrate – or destroy – for the customer all the value the company so expensively has sought to create through its product, quality, distribution, and advertising investments. In some situations this consideration is so dominant that it has led to the concept of 'inverting the organization' to make all systems and support staff in the company 'work for' the front line person to deliver the company's full capabilities at the moment of customer contact. (James Brian Quinn and Penny C. Paquette, "Technology in Services: Creating Organizational Revolutions", *Sloan Management Review*, Winter 1990, p. 67.)

"Respondents in our study often asserted this theme: 'In services, execution is everything. If you can't deliver what customers want, when they want it, with the personal touch they like, all your strategic thinking and investments won't amount to much." (*Ibid.*, p. 75.)

For formulating your own strategy to guarantee customer service, here are a few suggestions: (1) Make it simple and easy to understand. (2) Commit to it for the long term. (3) Make sure employees know how to use their new authority. (4) Remind employees to take action to remedy a situation before a customer has to ask. (5) Make progress visible. Use graphs, displays and illustrations to show how effective the policy has been and employees have been in using it. (6) Give employees money, praise and limelight for good thinking and positive action. (Timothy W. Firnstahl, "My Employees Are My Service Guarantee", *Harvard Business Review,* July/August 1989, p. 28.)

CYCLE TIME

System/Workflow

Cycle time is the period of time it takes to complete a unit of service or produce a product. It is also considered the period of time from the beginning of any event to its conclusion or to the speed with which a change, an innovation or an adaptation can take place. A fast cycle time is associated with increasing efficiency and providing improved customer service. For some organizations it is the basis for a competitive advantage. The speed with which a customer can be served is important in the fast-food, rental car, printing and even consulting businesses. It is all about reducing waiting time, set-up time and decision-making time. The more time that is saved the faster customers can be attended to and the less waste remains in the system.

Deming System

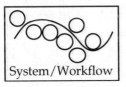

System/Workflow

W. Edwards Deming was one of the foremost quality gurus known for his success in helping rebuild Japan after World War II. According to Deming, the responsibility for quality is with the top people. Quality originates in the board-room. Because the source of innovation is freedom, an environment needs to be created to give people a chance to use their diverse capabilities, family life, education and hopes to accomplish their aims. He suggests eliminating performance appraisals because they cause humiliation and ruin learning, innovation and joy on the job. (Tim Stevens, "Dr. Deming: Management Today Does Not Know What Its Job Is", *Industry Week*, January 17, 1994, p. 20.)

The Deming idea of quality management uses as its foundation his concept of profound knowledge. It has four components: (1) The theory of variation which suggests that inherent in all matter and processes is the tendency to vary due at least to entropy and imperfection, if nothing else. This alerts individuals to check processes and systems before blaming individuals. There is always random variation. (2) A theory of knowledge, which states that without theory to interpret it, experience teaches us nothing. To apply the scientific method helps individuals learn systems and dispel myth, hunch and unreliable conclusions. (3) A theory of psychology. Individuals strive for self-esteem and want to take joy in their work; they always strive to do their best; teamwork is important and individuals are willing to cooperate but the system must provide an environment of security and freedom to contribute. Finally, (4) A theory of systems that instructs individuals to optimize the system not the sub-systems. Each part is designed to achieve a goal for the whole. Observe the system to discern its flaws.

Deming's system is characterized by fourteen points for the transformation of management:

(1)   Create constancy of purpose toward improvement of product and service, with the aim to become competitive, to stay in business, and to provide jobs.

(2)   Adopt the new philosophy. We are in a new economic age. Western management must awaken to the challenge, must learn their responsibilities, and take on leadership for change.

(3)   Quality. Eliminate the need for inspection on a mass basis by building quality into the product in the first place.

(4)   End the practice of awarding business on the basis of price tag. Instead, minimize total cost. Move toward a single supplier for any one item, on a long-term relationship of loyalty and trust.

(5)   Improve constantly and forever the system of production and service, to improve quality and productivity, and thus constantly decrease cost.

(6)   Institute training on the job.

(7)   Institute leadership. The aim of supervision should be to help people and machines and gadgets to do a better job. Supervision of management is in need of overhaul, as well as supervision of production workers.

(8)   Drive out fear, so that everyone may work effectively for the company.

(9)   Break down barriers between departments. People in research, design, sales, and production must work as a team, to foresee problems in use that may be encountered with the product or service.

(10)   Eliminate slogans, exhortations, and targets for the workforce asking for zero defects and new levels of productivity. Such exhortations only create adversarial relationships, as the bulk of the causes of low quality and low productivity belong to the system and thus lie beyond the power of the workforce.

(11a)   Eliminate work standards (quotas) on the factory floor. Substitute leadership.

(11b)   Eliminate management by objective. Eliminate management by numbers, numerical goals. Substitute leadership.

(12a)   Remove barriers that rob the hourly worker of his right to pride of workmanship. The responsibility of supervisors must be changed from sheer numbers to quality.

(12b)   Remove barriers that rob people in management and in engineering of their right to pride of workmanship. This means, inter alia, abolishment of the annual or merit rating and by management by objective.

(13)   Institute a vigorous program of education and self-management.

(14)   Put everybody in the company to work to accomplish the transformation. The transformation is everybody's job. (W. Edwards Deming, *Out of the Crisis*, Cambridge, MA: MIT Center for Advanced Engineering Study, 1992.)

The Seven Deadly Diseases:
(1) Lack of constancy of purpose.
(2) Emphasis on short-term profits.
(3) Evaluation by performance, merit rating, or annual review of performance. Evaluation nurtures rivalry and destroys teamwork.
(4) Management mobility. Job-hoppers never understand the companies they work for.
(5) Running a company on visible figures alone.
(6) Excessive medical costs for employee health care.
(7) Excessive warranty costs, fueled by lawyers' contingency fees.

Obstacles to Quality Transformation:
(1) Hoping for instant results
(2) Searching for ready made quality
(3) Making excuses for avoiding quality issues
(Mary Walton, *The Deming Management Method*, New York: G.P. Putnam's Sons, 1990.)

DIALOGUE GROUP

Group/Team

A dialogue group uses guidelines suggested by David Bohm who popularized "dialogue" as a way of developing shared meaning. The principle task among dialogue groups is to search for and examine your underlying assumptions – mental models – that may be driving one's belief system. See pages 42–45 for a discussion of the rules of dialogue.

DIVERSITY

Interpersonal

America is a construction of mind, not of race or inherited class or ancestral territory. It is a creed born of immigration, of the jostling of scores of tribes that become American to the extent to which they can negotiate accommodations with one another . . . America is a collective act of the imagination whose making never ends, and once that sense of collectivity and mutual respect is broken, the possibilities of American-ness begin to unravel. (Robert Hughes, "The Fraying of America", *Time*, February 3, 1992, p. 44.)

Diversity has come to mean to accept varied personal characteristics in the labor force. Women, racial minorities, the physically and mentally impaired, people over 40, homosexuals or bisexuals, and people with religious and language differences should not be denied access to, nor fair treatment and promotions within, the workplace.

Stereotypes not only divide people; they create narrow and restrictive mindsets. It is not just about race or gender or age, stereotypes can apply to almost any imaginable category; occupational categories and the amount of your financial resources, for example, can lead to stereotyping. The engineer or programmer who is a nerd; the statistician or accountant who is a dull number-cruncher or the poor person who is seen as a loser, all suffer from gross generalizations and inaccurate descriptions based on the flimsiest of data. The generalizations lead to behaviors by people believing in them and often to discrimination in the workplace on factors other than your ability to do the job.

There are three components of diversity management: (1) Managing diversity focuses on the diverse quality of employees' worklife needs, such as child care, family leave, and flexible holiday schedules. (2) Valuing differences centers around interpersonal qualities, such as race, gender and language. (3) Equal employment opportunities-affirmative action directs attention to laws that guide recruitment and promotion. Managing diversity looks at the diverse needs of employees not the cultural diversity of employees. Managing diversity also requires putting policies and procedures in place that empower managers to meet the diverse needs of employees.(Lisa Jenner, "Diversity Management: What Does It Mean?", *HR Focus*, January 1994, p. 11.) See Part II for a more thorough treatment of this concept.

DOUBLE BOTTOM LINE

Organizational

The double bottom line is a term suggesting that organizations account for social as well as financial performance. The second bottom line might report on the quality of worklife, the turnover of employees, the benefits offered, the relations with the larger community and the environmental impact of the organization's products, services, resource utilization and waste.

DOWNSIZING/DEMASSING

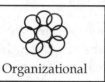

Organizational

The name given to any reduction-in-force but originally coined to mean a deliberate restructuring into a smaller, "leaner and meaner" organization. Any sizable retrenchment, divestiture, or redesign followed by a layoff is considered a "downsizing". Instead of symbolizing an intentional redesign to increase effectiveness, the term has become a euphemism for any mass layoff.

Nicely put, downsizing is really a continuous process of increasing or decreasing the labor force according to a careful assessment of the staffing requirements needed to accomplish essential tasks to achieve the organization's mission.

This often accompanies a reengineering effort or after the introduction of a higher level technology that displaces people. Rightsizing is finding the number of people reasonably required to successfully meet objectives. It sometimes seems that the right number is determined through a process of laying off people until those that remain cry foul. Usually a downsizing is not just about removing slack, it is about understanding how requirements have changed due to new technology.

We used to read predictions that by the year 2000 everyone would work 30-hour weeks, and the rest would be leisure. But as we approach 2000 it seems more likely that half of us will be working 60-hour weeks and the rest of us will be unemployed . . . Today's organization is rapidly being transformed from a structure built out of jobs into a field of work needing to be done. (William Bridges, "The End of the Job", *Fortune,* September 19, 1994, p. 62.)

"This year, I had to downsize my area by 25%. Nothing has changed in terms of the workload. It's very draining emotionally. I find myself not wanting to go to work, because I'm going to have to push people to do more, and I look at their eyes and they're sinking into the backs of their heads. [People] numbing. But they are not going to complain, because they don't want to be the next 25%," said a middle manager at a large high tech company undergoing reengineering. (Keith H. Hammonds, "The New World of Work", *Business Week*, October 17, 1994, p. 84.)

If wild swings in the need for labor should characterize a company, a tiered approach to employment should be considered. Establishing full- and part-time tiers regardless of place in the organization is one useful way of indicating that current realities do not allow for a company to extend full-time employment to all. It is an honest and practical way of dealing with the unforeseeable in a turbulent environment and the known swings in demand for specialized or hourly labor.

In this tough new marketplace, more and more of the employed will face permanent uncertainty about their security. The unemployed will find fewer new jobs similar to the ones they have lost. And relocating will be hard for the growing number of aging baby-boomers who are settled into homes, neighborhoods, and school districts . . . Some will be consigned to the 'contingent work force' where job security and a steady paycheck will be problematic. (Louis S.

Richman, "America's Tough New Job Market", *Fortune,* February 24, 1992, p. 53.)

"Downsizing is hardly a quick fix. It is not a strategy, and it is not a panacea for poor management. Healthy companies that slash payrolls instead of devising new game plans for growth are sending a demoralizing message to employees. Massive layoffs should be avoided when possible through shorter workweeks, wage and hiring freezes, and cutbacks in executive perks. But the idea that downsizing can't sometimes be an effective way for bloated, uncompetitive companies to cut costs is pure nonsense. General Electric went from 420,000 employees in 1981 to 220,000 today, yet the company has tripled its net profits and more than doubled its revenues." (John A. Byrne, "The Pain of Downsizing", *Business Week*, May 9, 1994, p. 61.)

Among fad followers, downsizing and rightsizing have both been achieved blindly through across-the-board cuts without any linkage to the systems and processes needed to achieve specific business objectives in the vain hope of cutting costs to make the bottom line look better or to discover slack in the system. These efforts are irresponsible because of their senselessness. Frequently people need to be re-hired because the cuts were not executed without cause and because the spirit of the organization is broken resulting in a drop in productivity and a drop in job-mindfulness.

But the new world of work is hardly wonderful for everyone – especially those who suffer the trauma of losing a job in a downsizing, only to have it happen again and again . . . This kind of life creates a tremendous emotional strain on families . . . The trauma can't be underestimated. 'In the first round of downsizings in the mid-1980s, there was a below-the-surface optimism in the survivors,' says Rosabeth Kanter, 'They knew there was fat and waste in their corporations. Not now. Layoffs are becoming routine. It's demoralizing for people who feel it's just a matter of time, no matter how well they perform.' (Bruce Nussbaum, "I'm Worried About My Job", *Business Week*, October 7, 1991, p. 94.)

ECONOMIC VALUE ADDED

Organizational

Economic value added (EVA) is a way of establishing a compensation system; usually for the chief executive. It measures after tax operating profits taking into account the cost of capital in order to determine the value added by a chief executive. To determine the EVA of any operation, the company simply subtracts from the net operating profit after taxes the value of the capital employed to produce that profit. Value is increased by earning a return greater than shareowners or lenders require; EVA is diminished when the return is less. (Daniel J. McConville, "All About EVA", *Industry Week*, April 18, 1994, p. 55.) EVA is becoming a common expression referring to the input each person brings to the workflow process. Your "adding value" through measurable performance indicators is increasingly becoming a necessity for all positions.

"EVA measures the wealth a company creates each year. It is defined as net income from operations, less the cost of capital needed to produce that income . . .

Generating big, positive EVA year after year is the key to enriching investors." (Shawn Tully, "America's Best Wealth Creators", *Fortune,* November 28, 1994, p. 143.)

"The idea behind EVA is that management will be rewarded when it wisely invests a company's capital in projects, new products, acquisitions and other activities that earn a return in excess of the cost of the invested capital." (John Fauber, "EVA-Economic Value Added", *Milwaukee Journal,* October 31, 1993.) The point is to maximize stockholder value.

"Despite its popularity, EVA does have its critics. Consultant Alfred Rappaport believes that EVA is a flawed concept, at least from the shareholders view . . . EVA is a short term measure based on sunken cost and can report value increases while the business is investing below the cost of capital, or value destruction while the company is actually investing above the cost of capital." (Daniel J. McConville, "All About EVA", *Industry Week,* April 18, 1994, p. 55.)

"The problem with EVA is that as a business concept, it is not holistic enough to deal with important issues such as employee morale and a company's long-term vision." (John Fauber, "EVA-Economic Value Added", *Milwaukee Journal,* October 31, 1993.)

For chief executives it may focus an inordinate amount of attention on too narrow a spectrum of performance indicators such as stock price or short-term return on assets. When used exclusively as an indicator of success it focuses entirely on shareholders short-term interest and ignores other legitimate measures of an organization's objectives. This is the kind of stimulus to the debate about American organizations that has been raging at least since Nobel Prize winner Milton Friedman declared "the sole purpose of business is to make money."

For lower level employees the EVA as well as other performance based pay programs and incentive schemes and merit rating plans, the results are clearly muddled and quite frequently counterproductive. Internecine competition and an inordinate amount of administrative overhead and time frequently subvert the process and divert attention from achieving goals to outscoring your peers or looking good to the evaluators.

EMPLOYABILITY

Intrapersonal

Clearly with the diminished bond between employer and employee what has become salient to almost everyone is the need for a skill-set that will enable a smooth transition to a new employer. From the company's point of view, employability is simply preparing individuals to acquire or polish skills that will keep them prepared to meet the demands of the company or for eventual outplacement. It is helping each person develop, maintain, and enhance their marketable skills. From the individual's perspective it is acquiring the skills, experience and education that will make keeping a job or finding another job easier when necessary. "What matters now is having the competitive skills required to find work when we need it, wherever we can find it." (Robert H. Jr. Waterman, Judith A. Waterman and

Betsy A. Collard, "Toward A Career Resilient Workforce", *Harvard Business Review*, July/August 1994, p. 87.)

Employability is knowing you have skills the market needs or the ability to make a living based on your application of skills you possess. It has as much to do with creating personal confidence and resourcefulness as it does about creating any specific competence or skill base. It is about finding a sense of purpose, affirming your commitment to achieving progress in realizing your mission and garnering the energy to continue, especially in adversity. These qualities being utilized among a work force within an organization seem to offer the potential of keeping the productive capacity alive as well as the innovative capacity of the workforce. Creating this work force requires an organization to provide the reciprocals – the environment that nurtures, supports, and rewards this behavior. Otherwise it is flooring the gas pedal while stepping on the brakes.

As employment security fades from the scene individuals need to become more mindful of their personal preparation, talents, skills and how to market them and do so aggressively as the need arises.

"If corporations won't guarantee your employment, they should guarantee your employability." (Rosabeth Kanter, Harvard Professor and author of *When Giants Learn to Dance*, quoted in *Business Week*, October 7, 1991, p. 96.)

"You are your own business. Listen to it again: You are your own business, and no one else is responsible for your development. You can't count on your employer

to watch out for you, or a mentor to bring you along."
(Kenneth Labich, "Take Control of Your Career",
Fortune, November 18, 1991, p. 87.)

Tax codes, health care and retirement systems, and
credit agencies actually penalize career changers and
people laid off. The state of perpetual insecurity does
not benefit anyone. Though, at first glance, this new
transient ethic does relieve the employer of any obligations, legal, moral or otherwise, to their employees,
short-term profit gains are derived at tremendous personal cost.

Employability, when stemming from job insecurity, is
a defensive strategy that actually begins an outplacement process. It is as if the company says it does not
have confidence in the future and cannot be depended
on. Thus, people must seek to develop new skills and
interests as a way of resting some control over their
employment future. In the end it may not benefit the
company at all.

EMPLOYMENT CONTRACTS

Interpersonal

"The old cradle-to-grave psychological contract – 'If I work
hard, the company will take care
of me' – is absolutely gone."
(William Morin, Chairman of Drake Beam Morin, a
New York-based outplacement firm in Anne B. Fisher,
"The Downside of Downsizing", *Fortune,* May 23,
1988, p. 42.)

"In the good old days the company elders may have
taken into consideration your long years of service,

your loyalty through the organization's good and bad times, your steadiness and dependability, even your financial obligations. No more." (Kenneth Labich, "Take Control of Your Career", *Fortune*, November 18, 1991, p. 96.)

"This paternalistic idea of the corporate culture has gone away . . . Companies have to be the best in the world every day. If you don't need someone on payroll, you don't have them. If you need them sometimes, you rent them. If you need them all the time, you buy them . . . Corporations can no longer be truly loyal, and employees cannot be truly loyal." (H. Tom Buelter, CEO, On Assignment, Inc. quoted in Tim W. Ferguson, "Temp Tycoon Steers Jobseekers Off the Straight and Narrow", *The Wall Street Journal*, October 4, 1994, p. A27.)

There is a movement from implicit long-term employment to an implicit contractor relationship with a short-term feel to it. The principles or dynamics underlying the formulation of a realistic charter include the following: (1) The charter must be based on the creation of wealth and then on its distribution. (2) Loyalty must be replaced with a mutual commitment to the creation of wealth. (3) The charter must take into account the legitimate needs of all stakeholders. (4) The company must offer opportunities for the development of skills and employees must seize these opportunities. (5) All stakeholders must realize that economic downturns have always demanded sacrifice. (6) A charter that emphasizes entitlement over self-responsibility is naive. (7) The new charter, tailored to the circumstances of this company in this industry, should be published. (Gerard Egan, "Hard Times – Contracts", *Management Today*, January 1994, p. 48.)

At the very least be mindful. Juries are finding oral contracts in supervisors' spoken assurances and implied contracts in personnel policies, benefit plans and past practices . . . A basic employment contract should establish: (1) the primary duties of the job, with a proviso that those duties may be changed; (2) terms of compensation, with the condition that earnings may be changed with reasonable notice; and (3) benefits to be provided with the stipulation that the existing plan is subject to change. (William Gaus, "Using Employment Contracts", *Small Business Reports*, June 1992, p. 20.)

"A new covenant under which the employer and employee share responsibility for maintaining – even enhancing – the individual's employability inside and outside the company" is evolving. Under the new covenant, employers give individuals the opportunity to develop greatly enhanced employability in exchange for better productivity and some degree of commitment to company purpose, and community for as long as the employee works there. It is the employee's responsibility to manage his or her own career. It is the company's responsibility to provide employees with the tools, the open environment, and the opportunities for assessing and developing their skills. (Robert H. Jr. Waterman, Judith A. Waterman and Betsy A. Collard, "Toward A Career Resilient Workforce", *Harvard Business Review*, July/August 1994, p. 87.)

While downsizing and the new attitude of "everyone for themselves in the workplace" seems to be redefining the psychological contract between employer and employee there are very definite signs that instituting some form of an employee bill of rights is in the air. Computer Professionals for Social Responsibility

(CPSR) and the American Civil Liberties Union (ACLU) have been working out a statement of principles. While this may give the appearance of recommended guidelines, the courts in some states have looked upon professional codes of conduct and ethical statements as a legitimate basis for employee action or inaction as the case might be.

The CPRS/ACLU working paper has included the following areas:
• Privacy of voice, paper, and electronic mail
• Impairment-testing versus drug testing
• Non-intrusion into employees' private lives
• Privacy of personal data on employees, customers, and others
• Electronic monitoring of employees' performance
• Protection of physical and electronic bulletin boards as open forums
• Protection of whistleblowers
• Due process in employee disciplinary cases
• Non-production of 'systems or products whose use would be intrinsically unethical' ("Computers in the Workplace Project", *Working Notes*, CPSR/Palo Alto, May 1992.)

What was a shocking new economic twist in the 1980s, the merger, acquisition, and divestiture strategies sometimes accompanied by the "downsize, dismantle and debt" strategy (brought home in the movie *Wall Street*) became a more palatable strategy in the 1990s of reengineering which inevitably resulted in massive layoffs. Somehow, over the years it became almost virtuous to talk about taking responsibility for your career and not expecting job security as if employees were no better than welfare cheats. By the late 1980s "The corporation's commitment to its employees has fallen at every level to the lowest point in 50 years." Today, it must be lower still. "The concept of free-agent managers has nasty implications for company loyalty and corporate cultures . . . The economic redefinition asserts that the sole obligation of top management at large publicly held firms is to continually increase the company's share price." (Paul Hirsch, "The Management Purges", *Business Month*, November 1988, p. 39.)

Yet the idea of the demise of the so-called benevolent paternalistic employment agreement to a "look out for number one" philosophy is not seen for the destructive influence that it is. It serves only a few people's interest and destroys the capacity for corporations to build a lasting creative culture. An organization of mercenaries can never produce the passion of commitment that people with a real connection to the organization maintain. The organization is more than a place to labor – especially in a knowledge economy. With the insecurity and anxiety created by this newly imposed "contract" everyone will lose. Until, of course, competitors realize the power of developing a new sense of place and purpose and invite talented individuals to join a secure environment where they share the risks together, not as mere commodities.

Regardless of what is said employers are risking their future by treating employees so casually. Their attitude of throw-away employees serves no one except to alert talented people that they would be wasting their time in service to such employers.

The new contract is fine in theory but it is still written by and for employers. "I am told to take responsibility for my career and to improve my skills," says one worker, "but when I request time to take an advanced course in my field I'm told I can't be spared, I'm needed on the project. But it's still my responsibility. Aren't contracts supposed to be among equals?"

EMPOWERMENT

Interpersonal

Empowerment became a popular idea with the publication of Peter Block's, *The Empowered Manager*, in 1987. The idea is to give authority along with responsibility so individuals can act on their own yet on behalf of the organization. Simply put, once agreement is reached on what people will do – the objectives they need to achieve – empowered individuals are encouraged and supported to pursue their objectives in the best way they see fit. See Part II for a thorough discussion of this concept.

ENLIGHTENED LEADERSHIP

Interpersonal

Buzz words seem to follow book titles. *Enlightened Leadership* by Oakley and Krug argued for a problem solving rather than blame oriented style of leadership. Getting the job done is the most important objective. Approaching it from a roll-up-the-sleeves, can-do orientation brings out everyone's best, most productive and creative qualities as opposed to traditional leadership which is oriented around ego, blame, and power which is often responsible for slowing and stifling problem solving.

What is needed is enlightened leadership – leaders who not only have the vision but who have the ability to get the members of the organization to accept ownership for that vision as their own, thus developing the commitment to carry it through to completion . . . Enlightened leadership is not so much about things to do as it is a place leaders come from with whatever they do. It actually is a state of being. (Ed Oakley and Doug Krug, *Enlightened Leadership*, New York: Fireside, 1991.)

Instituting employee involvement, participative management and self-managing work teams are frequently the impetus for a redefinition of leadership. Autonomous conditions evolving along with these newly empowered employees require self-leadership.

"Self-leadership is the missing link in managerial effectiveness. Self-leadership involves redesigning one's world to bring out one's best qualities and one's fullest potential." (Charles C. Manz, "Self-Leadership . . . The Heart of Empowerment", *Journal for Quality and Participation*, July/August 1992, p. 80.)

The enlightened leader is a positive force and first chooses to act from a position of the glass being half full, not half empty. In this way she or he constantly conveys the vision and purpose toward which the organization or group is working and clearly shows the link between each person's actions and the objectives. Each person is recognized for what they do well, given opportunities to learn and develop to acquire new skills and exercise more of their potential. People are expected to assume responsibility for their work.

"How do they do it? Ask them and they'll talk to you

about human values: empathy, trust, mutual respect – and courage." They will talk about creating a partnership and creating constancy, congruity, reliability and integrity. (Warren Bennis, "How to be the Leader They'll Follow", *Working Woman*, March 1990, p. 75.)

The leader should be a good teacher and communicator, a problem solver, have stamina, manage time well, be technically competent, not condone incompetence, take care of their people, provide a vision, subordinate their egos and ambitions to the goals of the group, know how to run meetings, be a motivator, be visible and approachable, have a sense of humor, be decisive but patiently decisive, introspective, reliable, open-minded, have high standards of dignity and exude integrity. (Perry M. Smith, "Twenty Guidelines for Leadership", *Nation's Business*, September 1989, p. 60.)

This form of leadership may be dangerous when it becomes overly dependent on the personal power of a single individual and its effectiveness rises and falls with that individual's disposition and tenure. It is usually quite powerful but short-lived. There are other dangers:

- Unrealistic expectations may be accompanied by demands for unrewarded self-sacrifice
- Dependency and counter dependency may be fostered by the presence of a strong personal influence and singular vision that may not account for much, if any, individual variance
- A reluctance of subordinates to disagree with the leader
- The need for continuing magic-proofing of the leader's worthiness

- Feelings of betrayal may be accentuated if failure or changes take place
- Lack of development for the up and comers
- The issues around which the charismatic leader develops may be transient or narrow and mitigate broader or more durable influence. (David, A. Nadler and Michael L. Tushman, "Beyond the Charismatic Leader: Leadership and Organizational Change", *California Management Review*, Winter 1990, p. 77.)

ENTREPRENEURSHIP

Intrapersonal

Entrepreneurship is the application of initiative, resourcefulness and creativity with a sense of psychological, and possibly financial ownership attached to your efforts in the workplace. The call for entrepreneur-like behavior reflects the need for resourceful, creative individuals taking responsibility for their work, their impact on the company and on their own performance.

ENVIRONMENTAL/GREEN MARKETING

Organizational

Attention to the environmentally sensitive consumer is only part of the reason for operating in an environmentally responsible way. Companies find that in reducing waste they reduce costs. That by recycling and reducing the flow-through of all materials in the product make-use-dispose cycle, benefits can accrue financially and a competitive advantage can be won in the marketplace. This consciousness keeps a company ahead of regulations which, as they become more severe, require retrofitting – quite a costly proposition.

With environmental issues more visible now than ever attention to marketing environmentally safe products is a strategy some companies are finding profitable as well as socially responsible. Church & Dwight Company, maker of Arm & Hammer baking soda products . . . was No. 5 in laundry detergents sold in food stores in 1990 when the company began to reach out to stakeholders and opinion leaders to promote its reputation as an environmentally responsible company. Sales of its powdered detergent began moving up rapidly and, within 18 months, the product had become the No. 2 brand in the United States. (Howard Muson, "Will The Environment Sell Soap?", *Forecast*, September/October 1994, p. 42.)

Green marketing is a way of appealing to consumers with environmentally friendly products, to the public as a non-polluter and to socially conscience investors with an appropriately socially responsible agenda. As a part of this marketing effort a company usually includes an environmental impact statement in its strategic plans and answers to both the Board of Directors as well as consumers, the general public, on environmentally relevant criteria.

In addition, "Green design considers the total life cycle of a product, taking into consideration not only the extraction of raw materials used in the production process, but also the ways in which products are packaged, transported and disposed of." (Kathleen

Dechant and Barbara Altman, "Environmental Leadership: From Compliance to Competitive Advantage", *Academy of Management Executive*, 1994, Vol. 8, No. 3, p. 7.)

Dow Chemical, a company whose name was once synonymous with napalm, Agent Orange, and fearsome opposition to what former chairman Paul Oreffice called 'nitpicking, ridiculous regulations,' is now among America's top ten environmental champion . . . Dow managers' salaries and bonuses are pegged to, among other things, how well environmental goals are met. (Faye Rice, "Who Scores Best on the Environment", *Fortune*, July 26, 1993, p. 114.) Its WRAP (Waste Reduction Always Pays) program has reduced waste going to landfills and has saved $310,000 a year in fees. Another program saved $420,000 in more efficient latex production.

Because of regulation, consumer demand, attention to environmental responsibility by everyone and newly discovered economies due to an environmental consciousness, the future will find more and more companies considering the environmental impact in new product and process developments and in their basic management thinking about quality.

EXCELLENCE

Organizational

A phenomenon sparked by the book *In Search of Excellence* (Tom Peters and Robert Waterman, New York: Random House, 1982). It is all about focusing on the customer, sticking to core competencies, communicating, managing by walking around, being creative, decentralizing some functions, and getting people involved.

Peters and Waterman identified eight factors that contributed to excellence but only if the spirit underlying the factors was vigorously maintained. Having a customer orientation, for example, is not enough. A company must be vigilant in keeping customers satisfied and anticipate their needs. Even that is not enough. Employees must be rewarded for contributing to customer satisfaction and be encouraged and supported in independent decision making in how best they can personally contribute to this goal. Excellence then becomes responsiveness, integrity and service. See Part II for a more complete treatment of this idea.

FIRE WALKING WITH THE GIANT WITHIN

Intrapersonal

Anthony Robbins is the new leader in the motivational arena attracting thousands of followers to his various seminars entitled *Unlimited Power* and *Awakening the Giant Within* – subjects of books he has written. Of course, as is true of all motivational speakers, but particularly so for Robbins, who has personally lived his principles, the dream attracts large numbers of followers. But the required individual responsibility and discipline deters many, and often eludes others. It is indeed inspirational to hear Robbins' story and the many others he tells of people overcoming enormous barriers in their lives to achieve great success.

For Anthony Robbins who leads packed seminars and who has become a mini-conglomerate of videotapes, books, and lectures, the strongest force in the universe is indeed a disciplined mind. Advisor to the successful and hopeful alike he has displayed the power of his convictions of mind over matter in frequent firewalking demonstrations where he and acolytes walk through a bed of simmering coals as testament to their mental concentration and belief in the power of mind over matter.

Firewalking, as Robbins says, "If you can make yourself walk through fire, what can't you do?" (Doug Stanton, "Aren't You Glad You're Tony Robbins?", *Esquire*, April 1994, p. 101.)

The motivational literature has been a staple for every salesman since Napoleon Hill's *Think and Grow Rich*. To read these tomes and their contemporary equivalents such as Zig Zigler's *Top Performance* is to literally swell with hope – even expectation that you, too, can enter the ranks of the idle rich. All it takes is a determination, some discipline, and a few specific goals. And of course a lot of practice in exercising your newfound conviction. The self-help industry and motivational gurus have been around since the traveling salesmen pitched tents to pitch products.

Most of the motivational literature glorify financial success almost to the complete exclusion of everything else. But for those that want it there is much to be learned. For example, we learn from these gurus of success that J. Peter Grace bathed at night to save commuter time and wore two watches and that Thomas Edison took almost 1,000 tries before he invented a lightbulb that worked. There are lessons in this literature, to be sure. Discipline, positive attitude, productive habits, hard work, persistence, commitment, conviction, a pleasant personality, long hours, vision, integrity, creativity, a willingness to learn, tight budgeting, networking, and openness to feedback are but a few of the truisms we are told to follow. And each quality **is** a virtue. Luck and timing are often missing from the lists, but as Horatio Alger stories informed the ambitious at the turn of the century, indeed "luck and pluck" were key.

Sustaining long-term periods of high motivation are, however, difficult. Frank Pacetta district sales manager for Xerox in Cleveland, Ohio, writes in his book *Don't Fire them, Fire Them Up* about his one year turnaround of what was about the worst performing sales district in the system. He said "As a leader, you must constantly change your definition of 'winning.' Keep moving the goalposts." (Frank Pacetta, "Don't Fire Them, Fire Them Up", *Success,* May 1994, p. 16A.) Yet, the emotional toll may have been too much as the stress on marriages, personal lives, and one another began to take its toll.

Building treadmills is the shortest of motivational devices and continuously changing the goalposts, as he puts it, eventually turns against you. While on the surface these methods suggest that they can be truly reinvigorating to a team, success is never defined – it is always out of reach. David Dorsey, writing of the same sales district as an observer, not the manager, gives a much different account and talks about the burnout and disillusionment that comes with constant pressure to out-perform themselves and sacrifice other aspects of their lives in the service of new sales targets. It so pervades their lives that salespeople begin to talk to

their spouses about "raising the level of their game."
(David Dorsey, *The Force*, New York: Random House,
reviewed in *Business Week*, May 16, 1994, p. 18.)

The need for motivational tools seems universal.
"People say, God, you mean to tell me you've got a
guy making a million and a half dollars and you got
to motivate him? I say absolutely." Tommy Lasorda,
Manager, L.A. Dodgers (Brian Dumaine, "Business
Secrets of Tommy Lasorda", *Fortune*, July 3, 1989,
p. 131.)

FUTURE SEARCH

Organizational

Future search conferences provide a complexity of stakeholders an opportunity to deal with
a common set of interests. The
purpose of the conference is to invite all interested
parties into a visioning process in order to create a
positive plan of action based on shared common
ground.

Though the antecedents to this technique can be
traced to early social systems theory before World War
II, the contemporary usage has been promoted by
Marvin Weisbord and others. According to Weisbord,
"Bringing the 'whole system' into the room makes
feasible . . . [the] release of creative energy leading to
projects none of us can do alone. People simultaneously discover mutual values, innovative ideas, commitment and support." (Marvin R. Weisbord and
Sandra Janoff, *Future Search: An Action Guide to
Finding Common Ground in Organizations and*

Communities, San Francisco, CA: Berrett-Koehler, 1995, p. 3.)

Future search has three generic uses: (1) to help stakeholders create a common vision; (2) to help stakeholders uncover shared intentions and take responsibility for their own plans; and (3) help participants implement a shared vision that already exists.

We do five simple tasks: (1) Review the past; (2) Explore the present; (3) Create ideal future scenarios; (4) Identify common ground; and (5) Make Action Plans. (*Ibid.*, p. 5.)

The difference between this and other organization development techniques is its emphasis on building from common ground instead of problems.

GAIN SHARING/EMPLOYEE STOCK OWNERSHIP PROGRAMS (ESOPs)

Organizational

Gain sharing is a way of conveying a sense of financial ownership to employees in order to elicit their best work. It does so by sharing profits with them according to any one of a limitless variety of formulas.

I have heard a number of organization development consultants say that the key to making an employee involvement program work is to give people a 'sense of ownership.' It's a good phrase. It can even be a good concept. But imagine if I invited these consultants to dinner. I let them smell the aromas. I encouraged them to soak up the ambiance. I had them study the menu. I even let them help pay for the meal. In short I give them a sense of dinner. But I got to eat it all because it was mine. A sense of ownership is a good thing, but it can leave employees hungry for more. After all, if they contribute ideas and information, why should they not reap some of the rewards? Perhaps gain sharing or profit sharing can do the trick, but if the concept of ownership is so important, why not offer people the real thing? (Rosen Corey, Executive Director of the National Association of Employee Ownership.)

ESOPs are Employee Stock Ownership Programs that come in many forms. Almost all are designed to transfer stock to employees for one or two reasons: (1) to more equitably distribute the financial rewards of the organization to everyone; and (2) to enable entrepreneurs to sell their companies to their employees upon retirement enabling them to enjoy higher prices for their companies and tax advantages for selling to their employees.

Gain sharing and ESOPs are also a philosophy of management which combines profit-sharing and employee involvement programs. Often the program combines a base pay and a differential determined by both the overall performance of the company and the performance of discrete subunits but with emphasis on the overall performance of the organization so it does not pit one group against another.

Gain sharing is sometimes a prelude to creating a full-scale ESOP that effectively alters the governance of the organization so that employees are owners in both the policy-making/decision-making sense as well as a financial sense. It is a way of rewarding employees for increases in performance and the company's financial success and recognizing employee involvement in the production process.

The relationship between productivity and compensation linked to performance has been consistently positive. A review of 27 studies found that the use of profit sharing was generally associated with 3.5% to 5% higher productivity in firms. (*High Performance Work Practices and Firm Performance*, Washington, D.C.: US Department of Labor, 1993, p. i.)

The American Management Association estimates that approximately 2,000 companies are now using some form of gain sharing . . . Several basic elements are required to make gain sharing a success, including (1) expert design and implementation; (2) involvement of everyone; (3) management commitment; (4) middle management cooperation; and (5) financial rewards. (Woodruff Imberman, "Gaining Performance, Sharing Productivity", *Manufacturing Systems*, April 1993, p. 54.)

Gain sharing does not always mean ownership in the sense of stock but it usually conveys a partial reward of ownership because as the company gains, so do the workers. Being economic, if not a legal fact, gain sharing does help people see the relationship between their effort and their compensation. As the company profits (or does not) so too does each worker. Pride, concern, and commitment follow when the link is meaningful, obvious, and rewarding. It also means that information is important. People need to know the financials of the entire company and how their performance and their unit's performance are contributing to the success of the company. Each employee becomes interested in their performance and asks: Are goals being met? What can each person and unit do to focus more sharply on the indicators of success?

In 1983, Jack Stack and 118 others bought out an International Harvester plant in Springfield, Missouri. It was that or look for another job. A 10-cent share of stock then was worth $18.30. As a result, hourly workers who had been with Springfield Remanufacturing from the beginning had holdings in the employee stock ownership plan worth as much as $35,000 per person – almost the price of a home in Springfield . . . What lies at the heart of [success] is a very simple proposition – that the best, most efficient, most profitable way to operate a business is to give everybody in the company a voice in saying how the company is run and a stake in the financial outcome, good or bad. (Jack Stack, "The Great Game of Business: Or, How I Learned to Stop Worrying and Teach People How to Make Money", *Inc.*, June 1992, p. 53.)

Another organization exemplifies the common destiny shared by employees in the pain and the gain: "We have not laid off or furloughed a single employee for lack of work in more than 20 years . . . Instead, we have a simple program called, 'Share the Pain.' During difficult economic periods (which are cyclical in the steel industry), we will work a plant five days a week instead of six. Hourly workers and foreman . . . see their pay reduced by 20–25%. At the next layer of management, the department heads . . . will see a 35–40% pay drop . . . At the final layer of management . . . officers' pay will drop as much as 65–70%." (Kenneth F. Iverson, CEO Nucor Corporation,

"Changing the Rules of the Game", *Planning Review*, September/October 1993, p. 9.)

The gain- and pain-sharing programs should be more than tokens and should be equitable. The ratio of CEO salary to lowest employee's salary is dispiriting to most employees. In 1993, "the average CEO of a major company made 149 times the average factory worker's pay of $25,317. . . ." (John A. Byrne and Lori Bongiorno, "That Eye Popping Executive Pay: Is Anybody Worth This Much?", *Business Week*, April 25, 1994, p. 52.) In 1980 CEO pay was only 42 times the pay of factory workers. (*Business Week*, May 4, 1992, p. 143.)

In contrast to: Incentive plans may produce adverse results, are difficult to sell to employees, and may be costly to maintain over the long run. . . The gain-sharing employee incentive plan has been proven highly successful within a wide variety of markets. A winning gain-sharing program has several key ingredients, including a deep commitment from management, simplicity, employee involvement and communication. (Thomas C. McGrath, "Tapping the Groove In Human Productivity", *Industrial Engineering*, May 1994, p. 16.)

There are many hard questions to answer before undertaking a gain-sharing program. Is management committed? Can this really motivate individual performance? Are the payouts closely linked to personal performance so individuals can know their contribution to the bottom line? Can the results of effort be distinguished from market and economic performance? Could it create divisiveness? Will the costs of its administration be worth it? Might not it be better used as a function of reward or penalty for the company's performance to stimulate a sense of ownership and overall responsibility?

GROUPWARE

Organizational

Given the inevitability of the telecommunications and knowledge revolution and its influence on the workplace, new methods of communicating and decision making are needed. This becomes apparent as computerization of functions, telecommuting, and interpersonal long-distance networking become commonplace. Groupware is a term representing any computer application that facilitates interpersonal communication, decision making, and scheduling or event coordination.

These programs allow two or more people either at one site or distant from each other to communicate, share information and jointly work on the same. The world wide web is enabling organizations to link employees everywhere for the purpose of a real-time communications and for information flow.

The use for communications and even the high-tech capabilities of sending and receiving all types of data still, however, does not overcome the fundamental inhibitors and facilitators of useful, meaningful, fearless communications. The technology does not replace the need to learn how to communicate, to trust those you communicate with and to be trustworthy to others. Though companies often spend small (and large) fortunes to create these systems they frequently find they have neglected the underlying basis for the success of their communications.

Some companies using even the relatively primitive e-mail concept to enhance communications find they do not like some of its potential. For example, the ability to reach everyone and anyone in the organization with anonymous messages, the ability for discussion groups to cross organizational lines and the forum for dissent that often is invited in such an open atmosphere is unsettling to many organizations. Companies have been known to establish policies constraining such use and imposing traditional channels of communication over the system.

There are advantages, however, in the speed and access features which make the tool a virtual necessity today. Speed and access, however do not address important issues of content type or quality of communications.

HEALTHY COMPANIES

Organizational

Healthy companies are those that meet various criteria for success, in addition to profitability. The criteria includes: a low-stress environment, a safe and physically healthy workplace, empowered employees, available avenues for dispute resolution, reasonable and responsible pay and benefits, and policies and procedures sensitive to balancing work and family interests.

"The concept of organizational health rests on a single principle: A company's health, productivity, and survival depend on its ability to foster the health, success and development of its people." ("In Practice: Healthy Companies", *Training and Development*, March 1994, p. 9.) See Part II for a fuller discussion of this concept.

HIGH PERFORMANCE ORGANIZATIONS

Organizational

High performance organizations deliberately design work and processes according to social science findings about motivation, job satisfaction, creativity and systems thinking. They recognize the importance of intrapersonal, interpersonal, intragroup and intergroup dynamics and manage them within the context of the organization as a human system.

A high performing organization is one that is productive in a high morale culture. Not all financially successful companies can be considered high performing. In using the term a major distinction is being made about the way people are managed and how they are involved in the achievement of organizational goals. There is a common vision, a free flow of information and knowledge sharing, an eye on the long-term and a personal sense of responsibility that is demonstrated through widespread adoption of self-managed work teams. (Robert Reich, "Leadership and the High Performance Organization", *Journal for Quality and Participation*, March 1994, p. 6.)

"A high performance organization sustains superior output, quality, and member satisfaction." (Marc Bassin, "Teamwork at General Foods: New And Improved", *Personnel Journal*, May 1988, p. 62.)

High performance work practices are "designed to provide employees with skills, incentives, information, and decision-making responsibility that improve business performance and facilitate innovation." (*High Performance Work Practices and Firm Performance*, Washington, D.C.: US Department of Labor, 1993, p. i.)

. . . high performance organizations are beginning to recognize that flat structures have inherent advantages over the traditional multi-level bureaucracies. The acronym FLAT is used to describe an organization that (1) reflects in clear, unambiguous terms the business Focus; (2) ensures that the number of Levels are congruent with effective decision making; (3) shows Alignment between the strategy, core competencies; business systems and information management; and (4) emphasizes the reality that Time is a strategic imperative. The key to organization design lies not in any single dimension but in the interrelationship of all factors. (John O. Burdett, "A Template for Organizational Design", *Business Quarterly*, Summer 1992, p. 35.)

A survey of 700 firms from all major industries found that companies utilizing a greater number of innovative human resource practices had higher annual shareholder return from 1986–91 and higher gross return on capital . . . A study focusing on the Forbes 500 found that firms with more progressive management style, organizational structure, and reward systems had higher rates of growth in profits, sales, and earnings per share over the five year period from 1978–83 . . . A detailed study of over 6,000 work groups in 34 firms concluded that an emphasis on workplace cooperation and the involvement of employees in decision making were both positively correlated with future profitability. (*High Performance Work Practices and Firm Performance*, Washington, D.C.: US Department of Labor, 1993, p. i.)

Characteristics of high-performance, high-commitment work systems: (1) autonomous units responsible for whole tasks or processes; (2) skilled employees; (3) a small number of management layers; (4) team structures; (5) management tasks performed by employees; (6) a strong customer focus and a strong commitment to quality; (7) flexible production systems with short cycle times; and (8) team processes for continuous improvement. (Michael Donovan, "Characteristics of High-Performance, High-Commitment Work Systems", *Training & Development*, August 1992, p. 23.)

It may come as a surprise to some people but, "It's not the gifted individuals who make peak performance possible as much as the dynamics of belief, collaboration and support." (Marc Bassin, "Teamwork at General Foods: New and Improved", *Personnel Journal*, May 1988, p. 62.)

Watch for the signs of a deteriorating commitment to high performance: increasing interpersonal conflicts, decreasing sense of purpose, elusive achievements, members being increasingly diverted from team business, and membership increasing without the consent of the members. Perhaps the sure giveaway that there is trouble occurs when the term "high performance" is being used to replace "productive" or "motivated" and becomes meaningless – just another buzzword.

HORIZONTAL ORGANIZATION

Organizational

The computerization of organizations coupled with the downsizings eliminating much of middle management has resulted in a flatter organization. The horizontal organization is a design that links work processes to one another with the intention of streamlining all tasks so that decisions are made at the lowest possible level, preferably within self-managed teams that focus on specific tasks. Rather than a burdensome hierarchy slowing down the production processes because of excessive information requirements, controls and supervisory activity, all tasks are integrated at the lowest point possible in the organization.

This structure is the natural result of integrating information technology and self-management in a process driven design using cross-functional teams.

IMPRESSION MANAGEMENT (KISS UP/KICK DOWN)

Interpersonal

Companies understand the importance of reputation and goodwill. Fortunes rise and fall with impressions customers and the public hold of them. Same with people. Impression management is creating a deliberate impression in the minds of those you work for and with. It is nothing new but social science has recently proven what everyone knew all along – that good impressions pay off in favorable assignments, promotions, performance appraisals, bonuses, and job longevity.

Doing favors for your boss, getting the coffee, for example, may have been apple polishing to observers but is now considered real politick. Giving public compliments to bosses and colleagues, being polite even under difficult circumstances and excelling at less desirable tasks can all win the favor of others and result in interpersonal benefits to yourself at work. Some are so strategically good at impression management they can shield their poor results and unfavorable management skills for long periods of time because they have so captivated their bosses and peers. The positive side of this behavior is what is commonly called acting "professional" withholding your emotions and authentic feelings and thoughts and being deferential to your boss and others in a position to further your career.

A leader's role includes managing information and morale which may involve "impression management" but the wiser course of action is to develop an authentic persona that needs no protection. Authenticity and integrity spring from a congruence between actions, words, and impressions.

Impression management leads to artificiality, form over substance and duplicity as a way of being. When the charade is discovered to be a front, the consequences are often disastrous with ostracism, reassignment, demotion and expulsion being possible outcomes. While you may be successful with managing the impressions of the occasional contact or your distant boss, it is very hard to keep the truth of your motives and relationships under your control. And certainly not for very long.

Thus, be careful what is considered "professional" behavior and what behavior, such as self-expression, is considered taboo. The distancing of people from themselves will always result in an artificial environment – one less and less creative; less and less inviting of commitment.

Intelligent Organization

Organizational

The intelligent organization is a post-bureaucratic organization that creates an environment in which people are engaged in the design, creation, and control over their own work but it is especially an environment that engages each person at a fundamentally respectful and responsible level.

The intelligent organization . . . will be structured from many smaller interacting enterprises, more like a free nation than a totalitarian state. Intelligent organizations will be pluralistic to the core, preferring conflict between competing points of view . . . to painful and costly discoveries that management control at a distance does not have all the answers.

Citizens of the organization will have rights – free speech, the right to associate with others across boundaries and ranks. The power to make fundamental work decisions, such as what to do and with whom to do it, will continue to be divested by the hierarchy and gradually distributed to smaller more flexible self-managing work groups who are responsible for their own work processes and accountable for their results. (Gifford and Elizabeth Pinchot, *The End of Bureaucracy and the Rise of the Intelligent Organization*, San Francisco, CA: Berrett-Koehler, 1993, p. 61.)

According to the Pinchots, an intelligent organization requires seven necessary conditions in order to exist: (1) widespread truth and rights – fully informed individuals with the right to seek out and confer with anyone in the organization; (2) freedom of enterprise – the ability to make decisions about your work; (3) liberated teams – organizing work through cross-functional team design; (4) equality and diversity among people; (5) voluntary learning networks established throughout the course of people and teams solving their problems; (6) democratic self-rule provides each a voice in how the whole system works; and (7) limited corporate government – whereby rules, policies and procedures are designed to facilitate the functioning of the teams and take care of organization-wide issues e.g., logistics, capital investments, regulatory compliance.

As with other tools and techniques this one depends on a sound footing in democratic values and the belief in a person-centered approach to organizing.

Another definition of the term was offered by James Brian Quinn who says that "reconceptualizing manufacturing and service corporations alike as 'intellectual enterprises' – seeking to dominate the critical 'service value' creation in their fields – is the key to long-term strategic success in most of today's rapidly changing global marketplaces." (James Brian Quinn, *Intelligent Enterprise*, New York: Free Press, 1992, p. 41.)

INTRAPRENEURSHIP

Intrapersonal

This term was coined by Gifford Pinchot to demonstrate the power of entrepreneurial behavior when harnessed inside large organizations. Intrapreneurship is a combination of a set of behaviors and a way of being which employees use to positively impact their organization. It can be fostered by the organization making available resources for employees to use in developing their ideas.

ISO 9000

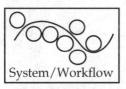

System/Workflow

This is an international quality movement originating in Geneva by the International Standards Organization (ISO) which promulgated standard 9000 (and others), to develop uniform guidelines for implementing a quality management system appropriate for each company. An ISO 9000 certification means that the quality system, not necessarily its output, meets the standard. Over sixty countries have adopted the standard and it is becoming a symbol of the presence of a baseline quality management system in an organization.

These standards were created in 1987 (and revised in 1994) as part of Europe's unification drive to convince the world of a high quality assurance standard as well as to unify the system previously subject to many diverse practices.

The standards suggest that a company has fully documented its quality procedures and abides by them consistently. Meeting the standards leads to entry into European markets. Even the process of meeting compliance requirements can help an organization reap cost savings.

For American Saw of East Longmeadow, Massachusetts, ISO 9000 meant better in-house communications, fewer accidents, fewer defects and more satisfied customers. (Amy Zuckerman, "ISO 9000: Free Trade Boon, Barrier or Boondoggle", *Journal for Quality and Participation*, January/February 1994, p. 89.)

Large companies such as DuPont, General Electric, and Eastman Kodak are among supporters of the standards and urge their suppliers to follow suit. To them, ISO 9000 is like the generally accepted accounting principles (GAAP) established by the accounting profession. It conveys a sense of security that not only have certain standards been met but that at least a minimum acceptable reliability has been established. In tangible terms, DuPont has been able to reduce test procedures at one plant site by one-third while on-time delivery increased from 70% to 90%. (Donald W. Marquardt, "ISO 9000: A Universal

Standard of Quality", *Management Review*, January 1992, p. 50.)

Experience has shown that companies that have implemented ISO 9000 programs as part of their TQM effort experience two primary benefits: (1) Internal wastage and rework is reduced, costs are brought down, and customers' needs are better satisfied. (2) As a supplier, gaining ISO 9000 and displaying the national quality mark associated with the standard is becoming more widely accepted; it creates a climate of confidence between customer and supplier, helping to safeguard existing business and assist in developing new markets. (Graham Cartwright, "Lessons Learned About ISO 9000", *Journal for Quality and Participation*, September 1992, p. 44.)

There is another side to this. While ISO 9000 sounds like an admirable standard – particularly to consumers, the standard may actually be below existing company or industry practice thus affording some of the lower quality producers, ironically, to enjoy a sense of achievement they have not really earned.

Smaller companies may not be willing to pay the sums required to follow through on this specific process even though they are able to produce high quality goods. Certification to one of the ISO 9000 standards does not necessarily guarantee a quality product, per se, only a consistent level of output . . . The National Tooling & Machining Association is asking its 3,000 members to 'conform' with ISO 9000 rather than pursue actual certification" because it is costly to earn. (Susan Avery, "What's Wrong With ISO 9000?", *Purchasing*, March 3, 1994, p. 49.)

Perhaps the greatest harm currently being done to the business community by the ISO 9000 fad is its detrimental impact on the progress of the American quality revolution . . . The information, procedures and material on which ISO 9000 certification requirements focus total to about 10 percent of what the Baldrige encompass. Perhaps the most telling gap between the two is the Baldrige's insistence on customer-impacting results, and plans and methodology for continuous improvement versus ISO 9000's emphasis on current procedures and their documentation. (Patrick L. Townsend and Joan E. Gebhardt, "Do ISO Instead of Applying Baldrige Criteria . . . Not!", *Journal for Quality and Participation*, January/February 1994, p. 94.)

JAPANESE MANAGEMENT

Organizational

The Japanese system of management is still the focus of much attention in the world because of their success in the global economy. Japanese management is a basket of techniques that countries have attempted to import for various, specific purposes. Overall, however, as a system, Japanese management in the Japanese cultural context is self-reinforcing and effective because of its synchronicity with Japanese culture.

The aspects of Japanese management which seem to be of most interest to Americans (and others) have been: quality circles which led to total quality management and the utilization of the Deming System (see definition above); bottom-up decision making (the *ringi* system) which encourages suggestions, ideas and initiative from first line employees (especially relevant in customer intensive processes); corporate strategic alliances; *keiretsu* (groups of companies) acting more as a conglomerate than an alliance; just-in-time inventory/delivery (JIT) which saves tremendous inventory and storage costs; the *kaizen* system which is attention to continuous improvement (related to the quality movement); flattening the hierarchy which allows for speedier innovation and decision making; and, lean production which emphasizes in addition to JIT a system of process engineering that continually reduces and streamlines inputs and processing. See Part II for a more thorough discussion of the Japanese management system.

JOB ENLARGEMENT/JOB ENRICHMENT

System/Workflow

Job enlargement is giving people more to do. It was a mistaken belief that enlarging a job would be motivational. Its only apparent advantage is diversifying tasks but in itself adding work does not motivate except when it is to counteract the effects of boredom or from being idle.

Real motivation stems from improving the inherent characteristics of the job through enrichment. This process alters the job to include challenge, feedback, control by the job holder, and an opportunity to succeed at the task.

According to Frederick Herzberg who originated this concept (*The Motivation to Work*, New York: John Wiley,

1959) one strategy to make a job motivational includes: (1) removing job controls while retaining employee accountability for their own work; (2) provide employees with a complete unit of work; (3) give employees direct feedback on job performance; (4) challenge employees with more difficult tasks; and (5) help employees build up their expertise and competence in necessary tasks.

JUST-IN-TIME/JUST-IN-CASE

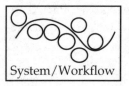

System/Workflow

Just-in-Time is a method of supplying inventory, parts or data at precisely the time it is needed. It is one of the aspects of Japanese management that has gained popularity because it shifts warehousing/inventory maintenance to suppliers and thereby allows for space savings as well as monetary savings. In order for it to work properly the supply chain cannot be broken and there must be a flawless communication system in place to insure that needs are identified in a timely fashion.

By way of contrast the just-in-case system is a way of stockpiling because of the fear that either supply will be interrupted or it will contain a large percentage of defects. Just-in-case has a more political application as well. It is the accumulation of a written record of events as if to build a case against an individual or a defense for yourself where practices and policies create undisclosed conflict. This is standard operating procedure in workplaces with a poor communications climate and low trust.

LATERAL THINKING

Intrapersonal

Lateral thinking is a concept invented and popularized by Edward de Bono (*Lateral Thinking: Creativity Step by Step*, New York: Harper Colophon Books, 1970). It is an applied creative thinking tool. He was perhaps the first to bring corporate attention to "outside-the-box" thinking in the 1960s. "Outside-the-box" thinking is a term used to describe the problem-solving process that requires creative, sometimes unorthodox approaches to finding solutions in less than obvious places. As opposed to linear thinking which more closely resembles the scientific method and the step-by-step, single cause-effect approach to decision making, lateral thinking emphasizes imaginative, intuitive, and experimental approaches to problem solving that allows for great leaps in perspective and identifying useful alternative methods.

LAWS AND PRINCIPLES

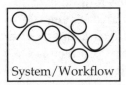

System/Workflow

Murphy's law is perhaps the oldest and most well-known law in business today. Simply put: If anything can go wrong it will. Thanks to Arthur Bloch who has written three volumes of Murphyisms (*Murphy's Law and Other Reasons Why Things Go Wrong*, Los Angeles: Price/Stern/Sloan, 1980) there are hundreds of derivatives; "Nothing is as easy as it looks," is one. "Everything takes longer than you think," is another.

Though humorous editorials on the times, they do offer some guidance to those too eager to take themselves or their work seriously. C. Northcote Parkinson is famous for several laws reflective of life at work. The first is, "Work expands to fill the time allotted to it." (*Parkinson's Law*, New York: Ballentine Books, 1957.) His second was, "Delay is the deadliest form of denial." (*The Law of Delay*, Boston: Houghton Mifflin, 1971.)

Laurence J. Peter invented what must have become the most repeated law which every subordinate seems to know: "In a hierarchy every employee tends to rise to his level of incompetence." (*The Peter Principle*, New York: Bantam Books, 1969.) While the mountains of evidence supporting these laws seems so conclusive remember Finagle's Third Law: "In any collection of data, the figure most obviously correct, beyond all need of checking, is the mistake."

LEAN PRODUCTION

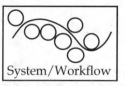
System/Workflow

Lean production is the concept of utilizing just-in-time inventory and a minimalist philosophy involving cutting costs and inputs wherever possible to produce a product as efficiently as possible. This concept of Japanese origin was popularized by Womack, Jones and Ross in their book, *The Machine That Changed the World* (New York: Rawson Associates, 1990) about the automotive industry. Using cross-functional, self-managing teams, a major advantage is created in cutting time from the production process.

LEARNING ORGANIZATION

Organizational

A learning organization is an adaptive enterprise that acquires and applies new knowledge. It encourages and supports employees' efforts to develop their individual capacities and share knowledge with one another. It is ultimately a cooperative, creative, and innovative workplace. See Part II for a more complete discussion of this concept.

MANAGEMENT BY OBJECTIVES

Interpersonal

Management by objectives (MBO) has a long history and is still a bedrock of basic management thinking. It is the creation of objectives for subordinates through a consultative process between a manager and his or her employees. The key to the process is determining observable, measurable targets that can be reviewed quarterly or yearly. It is an obvious way of creating alignment between a manager's expectations and a subordinate's efforts. Clarity is the essential outcome of the negotiation that occurs in establishing the subordinate's goals for the planning period. It is also a way for the manager to know how to best supervise, coach, lead the subordinate and what particular resources will need to be made available to each employee. However, the drawback of the MBO process is the lack of attention to hard-to-measure goals. For example, your role and contributions to teams and committees whose goals are beyond the individual's control. In addition, personal development efforts and training may not be recognized by an MBO system.

Though you could reasonably ask, "How can you manage without objectives?", the MBO model gives rise to specific flaws. For example, W. Edwards Deming found design flaws in the MBO process stemming from the performance evaluations required to implement the process: (1) MBO focuses exclusively on results (not on the processes). (2) It is typically quantified (losing attention to important non-quantifiable objectives, particularly those that do not begin to show up in the short run). (3) Concerned with a few projects rather than on-going responsibilities. (4) Encourages setting easy to attain objectives and thereby reduces innovation or risk taking. (Jim M. Graber, Roger E. Breisch and Walter E. Breisch, "Performance Appraisals and Deming: A Misunderstanding?", *Quality Progress*, June 1992, p. 59.)

Too much reliance on the process for individual evaluations and performance criteria mitigates against teamwork and cooperation. MBO systems that focus on group or team efforts can overcome some of these flaws but still places individuals and not the system, short- and not long-term goals and easily measured objectives ahead of the more subtle or innovative.

MANAGEMENT BY WALKING AROUND

Interpersonal

Management by walking around (MBWA) is the idea that a manager can best understand the needs and performance of subordinates by building personal supportive relationships with them at their workstation. It is a metaphor for getting out and seeing what needs to be done and what is happening in real-time. It is a way of staying in touch with employees, customers and suppliers. Peters and Austin were the first to popularize this concept in their book, *A Passion for Excellence* (New York: Random House, 1985).

What was called managing by walking around when first identified at Hewlett-Packard in the 1950s is now supplemented by what Andy Grove [CEO of Intel] dubs 'managing by reading around' in reference to E-mail and compuserve data bases that enable him to gather 'random insight.' (Alan Deutschman, "The Managing Wisdom of High-Tech Superstars", *Fortune,* October 17, 1994, p. 197.)

"For management by walking around to work, feelings of trust and familiarity between managers and employees must already exist." ("How to Successfully Practice MBWA", *Supervisory Management,* January 1994, p. 12.)

MANAGEMENT/LEADERSHIP COACHING/ MENTORING

Interpersonal

As teams become a larger part of workplace life and as the pressure to learn and experiment increases, leaders play more of a developmental role than ever before. Instead of being expected to know everything and to "boss" people, managers are becoming more team players and coaches. This requires encouraging and teaching more than giving orders. Accordingly, a manager's goals are developmental as well as control oriented. The purpose here is to help each team member, or subordinate, perform their best, and learn how to improve.

Coaching focuses on discovering actions that enable and empower people to contribute more fully, productively, and with less alienation than the control model [the traditional management model] entails. (Roger Evered and James C. Selman, "Coaching and the Art of Management", *Organizational Dynamics*, Fall 1989, p. 16.)

Mentoring has another meaning usually involving the furtherance of a protégé's career and giving guidance about the company and the nether regions out of reach of the mentee. In a career or corporate sense it is certainly focused on the utility of the individual in the workplace and the navigation of your career. More broadly it is the development of a personal relationship with an older individual who takes an interest in a younger person's development in its many aspects, not just organizationally.

It is an attractive basis for a relationship because "People have more respect for a coach than they do for any other authority figure." (Andrew DuBrin, Professor of Management, Rochester Institute of Technology.)

A true believer in the dawning of a participative management millennium would argue that coach is just a way station on the long march upward from boss as dictator. Eventual destination: the boss as facilitator or

– are you ready for this? – unleader . . . The unleader will take team development as his primary charge. He'll be an expert on adult learning, of course, understanding that different team members learn in different ways. But he will also know the ins, outs, ups, downs, and general convolutions of group dynamics – how teams form, reach agreement or fail to, act in concert or fall apart. (Walter Kiechel, III, "The Boss As Coach", *Fortune*, November 4, 1991, p. 201.)

"Coaching is that conversation which creates a new management culture, and is not a technique within the old culture. It occurs within a particular kind of relationship between the manager and the managed." (Roger Evered and James C. Selman, "Coaching and the Art of Management", *Organizational Dynamics*, Fall 1989, p. 16.)

A coach sees possibilities that you cannot. They may not be better performers but as observers are able to see opportunities and flaws that individuals may not. They help you see yourself afresh – and honestly either measured against an ideal or against your own potential.

Those who go to a coach generally are open to improvement, eager to learn from mistakes, and willing to try a new approach. People do not normally try to "look good" for a coach, or to convince him or her of how much they know, or what fine performers they already are. Contrast this with the way people commonly relate to a manager. Most often they hide or justify mistakes, attempt to "look good," and listen defensively rather than openly. (*Ibid.*)

According to Evered and Selman: Essential elements of coaching include:

1 Partnership, mutuality, relationship
2 Commitment to producing a result and enacting a vision
3 Compassion, generosity, non-judgmental acceptance, love
4 Speaking and listening for action
5 Responsiveness of the player to the coach's interpretation
6 Honoring the uniqueness of each player, relationship and situation
7 Practice and preparation
8 Willingness to coach and to be coached
9 Sensitivity to 'team' as well as to individuals
10 Willingness to go beyond what's already been achieved

Furthermore, they claim that "Creating an Organizational Culture Of and For Coaching" requires an organization to:

1 Educate people in the parameters of effective coaching
2 Commit to undertake a specific project with a specific timetable
3 Determine the 'players' in the project
4 Declare who will be the coach in each project relationship and what the person or persons being coached is committed to accomplishing
5 Be prepared for 'breakdowns' as the project progresses
6 Allow the day-to-day actions of the project to emerge from openings (new possibilities) that occur naturally in conversations with a coach

7 Validate and acknowledge accomplishments and breakdowns as opportunities to regenerate the originating commitment to the project

8 Complete everything as you go along

There are several qualities for successful mentors which include:

(1) Personal commitment. (2) Respect for individuals and for their abilities and their right to make their own choices in life. (3) Ability to listen and to accept different points of view. (4) Ability to empathize with another person's struggles. (5) Ability to see solutions and opportunities as well as barriers. (6) Flexibility and openness. (Internal Memorandum, DEC Corp., Maynard, MA.)

Additionally, put your mentee first; be a friend, not a buddy; build mutual respect; take time to get to know one another; be enthusiastic, positive and accepting; be interested; communicate attitudes and feelings – be real; share common experiences; clarify and interpret what the mentee says; do not be alarmed at remarks made by the mentee; do not make moralistic judgments; be sincere in praise; be flexible; do not ignore problems. (*Partners for Success: Volunteer Mentor Orientation and Training Manual*, The Enterprise Foundation.)

Mentoring has run into some criticism for actually narrowing the prospects of the individual being mentored. Being too closely associated with one individual may tie you too closely to the political fortunes of that individual. Worse, the individual may actually stifle the mentee if your own career is not moving.

Managerial Grid©

Intrapersonal

The managerial grid was a very popular management technique in the 1960s and 1970s. It was developed and copyrighted by Blake and Mouton. They helped managers assess their style which was postulated to be a blend of two fundamental dimensions – task-focus and person-focus. The ideal profile would be "high-high" – focused both on getting the task done and building supportive relationships with subordinates. While there is still validity to the Grid approach a new and vital dimension has emerged: the concern for and the facilitation of group or team effort.

Mass Customization

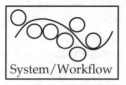

System/Workflow

Technology now enables manufacturers to have the efficiencies of mass production while customizing each product for particular customers or groups of customers. Computers and robots enable changing set-ups to meet specific customer requirements at virtually no extra cost for some products.

Mass customization is the ability to meet the specific demands and requirements of any one customer while utilizing the advantages of scale of mass production. Computer technology, robots, scheduling innovations, and the appearance of customization even while mass-produced all influence the ability to provide this customer level of customer service.

"A key to the future lies in using new technologies to deliver mass-produced goods and services to individuals on a tailorized basis and mass scale simultaneously." (Davis Stan M., *Future Perfect,* Reading MA: Addison Wesley, 1987.)

Mass customization strives to achieve the low cost production of high-variety, even individually customized goods and services. Five basic methods for mass customization are: (1) customizing services around existing standardized products or services; (2) mass producing customized services or products that customers can easily adapt to individual needs; (3) moving production to the customer to provide point-of-delivery customization; (4) providing a quick response; and (5) modularizing components to customize end products and services. (B. Joseph Pine, II, "Mass Customizing Products and Services", *Planning Review,* July/August 1993, p. 6.)

MATRIX MANAGEMENT

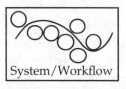

System/Workflow

This is sometimes known as project management where, within a functional organization, cross-functional teams are created to fulfill specific requirements that change with each customer. For example, an aircraft company might have teams developing different aircraft and draw members from various functions. This design often results in conflict between the demands of the functional leaders and the demands of the project leaders. Having two bosses and two sets of objectives results in stress as well as conflicting goals. One solution has been to subordinate the functional role to the project role by creating an ad hoc organization which reformulates itself for each project. Computer and network technology supports this happening with increasing efficiency. Note the movie industry which aggregates several companies to produce one film. The studio, marketing and distribution, and the production companies partner for one film at a time.

MICRO MANAGING

Intrapersonal

If organizations are machines, control makes sense. If organizations are process structures, then seeking to impose control through permanent structure is suicide. If we believe that acting responsibly means exerting control by having our hands into everything, then we cannot hope for anything except what we already have – a treadmill of effort and life-destroying stress. (Margaret J. Wheatley, *Leadership and the New Science*, San Francisco, CA: Berrett-Koehler, 1992, p. 23.) The reason this is classified as an intrapersonal issue is because micro-managing is a reflection of your personality more than a requirement of the situation. In an era filled with self-managing structures and talk of empowerment, micro-managing is a particularly dysfunctional personality trait with career limiting implications.

MYERS-BRIGGS

Intrapersonal

Myers-Briggs, a mother-daughter team of psychologists, developed the MBTI (Myers-Briggs Type Indicator) based on the work of the famed Carl Jung. Jung wrote *Psychological Types*, among many other works, and the MBTI is an assessment instrument that places people in one of sixteen personality profiles based on Jung's original twelve types. The point of understanding these types is to help individuals explain why they and others behave as they do. On the surface, it is a methodology that has helped people work with others and to see how conflicting or complementary styles can be managed to everyone's advantage. On the job it gives people a framework for working with differences and for exploring points of conflict between colleagues and manager-subordinate pairs. The MBTI has been around since the 1940s and has been a very popular starting point for discussing interpersonal issues.

It has been criticized for several reasons most notably for the categorization of individuals that has been misused. As with all instruments, there is a tendency to declare a person a particular type and to make erroneous gross generalizations about your talents, skills and motives. In that regard it served as a limiting tool rather than as a basis for further wholistic understanding of yourself and others.

There are many type indicators and many assessment instruments to establish a personality profile. A recent addition to the literature is the enneagram with nine profiles. Then, too there are the twelve signs of the zodiac with corresponding profiles of each person according to time of birth.

NETWORKING

Interpersonal

Networking (Personal/Structural) is a two-fold phenomenon. First, it is a characteristic of contacting people you need to remain informed of in your work and professional environment. It is important to build the relationships that enable people to get along with others, to know what is happening and to prepare for career changes and new projects. The other aspect of networking is derived from the language of computers and information technology. Networking is the connection of terminals whether within a single location or far flung sites. It is also a symbol for a new organizational structure that replaces rigid bureaucratic lines and replaces them with lines of communication and responsibility closely related to the workflow process and not simply to the flow of power in an organization.

NEW PARADIGM BUSINESS

Organizational

The "new paradigm" emphasizes a new set of management assumptions that are emerging in tandem with new industries along the high-tech frontier. It is a humanistic, customer, employee and community-centered orientation to designing and managing organizations and their output. It recognizes that organizations are an integral part of the societal and ecological fabric requiring attention to external concerns previously ignored as beyond the scope of the business' responsibility.

The new paradigm should be built on five principles: (1) The organization should be treated as a moral person with responsibilities toward individuals, and equal attention must be given to individuals' responsibilities toward the organization. (2) Such an organization must be viewed in the fullest sense as a community, in which each individual is accorded dignity and value. (3) An individual can contribute knowledge, skill, and creativity only when both a covenant and a contract exist between the members of the community. (4) Persons are treated as ends within themselves and as real assets. (5) In the structure of a business community, an individual can function creatively, providing peers with the full benefit of personal talent, knowledge and skill. (Michael Quigley, "Ethical Downsizing", *Executive Excellence*, March, 1992, p. 18.) See Part II for a more complete discussion of this concept.

THE ONE MINUTE MANAGER

Interpersonal

The one minute manager is a concept developed by Ken Blanchard in his book by the same name. It stresses the importance of managers giving "one minute" clarifications of objectives, "one minute" praisings for good work and "one minute" reprimands for mistakes. The system is clearly based on the operant conditioning techniques developed by behavioral psychologists to mold responses to planned stimuli.

Three secrets can help managers perform better and can significantly increase productivity and morale. The first secret is setting one-minute goals. Managers should be clear on what their goals are so that they will know what good behavior looks like. It is best to write out three to five goals on a sheet of paper, identifying for each what the present level of performance is and what level is desired. The second secret is one-minute praisings. The key to developing people is to concentrate on catching them doing something right instead of something wrong. Praisings should be immediate and specific and should tell people how their performance helps the organization. The third secret is one-minute reprimands. People must be held accountable, but the first alternative for poor performance should be redirection, which means going back to goal setting, trying to find out what went wrong, and getting them back on track. Reaffirmation is the most important part of a reprimand. (Kenneth Blanchard, "Three Secrets of the One-Minute Manager", *CPA Journal*, April 1992, p. 76.)

"The most important thing in training somebody to become a winner is to catch them doing something right." (Kenneth Blanchard and Spencer Johnson, *The One Minute Manager*, LaJolla, CA: Blanchard-Johnson Publishers, 1981.)

You could argue that while there is undisputed truth in the value of immediate feedback, the model of human relations underlying the concept of the one-minute manager is disturbing to many. It suggests a highly manipulative relationship where the manager always knows best and on whom subordinates are dependent for their learning, self-esteem, and performance feedback.

This reached fad status as soon as the book hit the best-seller lists. It appeared to be a panacea that worked because of its foundation in operant conditioning (reinforcement theory). Unfortunately people began to resist the patently inauthentic manner in which many managers used the ideas as merely a tool for their own control over subordinates. Even when the ideas are used sincerely there is a shallowness to the communicative process that in the long run undermines its own potential. Rome was not built in a day and people are not motivated in a minute.

OPEN BOOK MANAGEMENT

Organizational

A small band of business people believing in right livelihood and the new paradigm formed what was called the "Briarpatch" Network in the San Francisco Bay area and advocated open book management. They believed in opening their books to employees and customers alike. Today, spurred by the tremendous success of Springfield Remanufacturing Company and its story (*The Great Game of Business*, New York: Doubleday/ Currency, 1994) as told by Jack Stack the company's CEO, open book management is a practice that makes everyone a worker/manager/owner. Sharing information and business knowledge helps people see the financial consequences of their action. It is this economic feedback that helps people focus on how their behavior directly influences the success or failure of the organization.

ORGANIZATIONAL TRANSFORMATION

Organizational

Organizational transformation is a body of knowledge centered around large-scale systems change with the intention of helping organizations adapt to the emerging "new paradigm." The transformation encompasses structure, processes, and managerial assumptions and in most cases requires radical rather than incremental change.

The Chrysler Corp. plant at New Castle, IN. once targeted to close, has gone from running a deficit of $5 million a year to a savings of $1.5 million a year by employing six elements: (1) a consciousness of the need for change; (2) developing a vision for change; (3) opening decision making to all employees; (4) providing information to employees; (5) unleashing the brainpower of employees by creating a learning environment; and (6) the development of a clear, integrated change process." (Peter M. Tobia, "Chrysler Harnesses Brainpower", *Industry Week*, September 21, 1992, p. 16.)

This is one form of transformation. It suggests that a fundamental new way of thinking and behaving have occurred; that a substantial change has taken place to redirect corporate life from simply a concern for profit to a concern for the profit-making apparatus – particularly the employees within the organization. While there is often indulgence during good times and an espoused concern for employee well-being the continued pressures on the organization's ability to compete and to cut costs in doing so creates pressures that defeat the transformation. Unfortunately, in the conventional mindset people are means to an end. They are hired for specific purposes to serve the organization, not to be served by it. This fundamental philosophical underpinning drives the relationship. To transform this it is necessary to transform our notions about what an organization is and to which ends it pursues.

OUTPLACEMENT/PURGATORY

Intrapersonal

Outplacement is a process of helping fired individuals locate a new job. It sounds like a valuable service and does afford the laid-off access to help in moving on. Unfortunately it is too often a purgatory, a netherland between hope and despair that soothes the conscience of employers while blaming the victims for their plight.

It is a way station and can be useful in locating a new job but too often it serves merely to encourage individuals to quickly locate another job and be done with it – whether or not it is the right fit for the individual.

OUTSOURCING

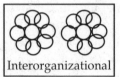

Interorganizational

Whatever is not a core process or competitive advantage in a company is a likely candidate for sub-contracting or outsourcing. In doing so a company will enjoy the efficiencies of a supplier's core process. A hospital probably does not operate its food service as well as, or as cost effectively as, a food service provider. A giant electrical parts manufacturer probably does not operate its office supply and printing/photocopying center as well as an outside office supply/printer. Thus, paring the organization down to its core processes and eliminating the extraneous, results in greater efficiencies, lower overheads and more flexibility.

In effect cost centers become profit centers when each unit of an organization must sell itself or justify its existence by competing favorably with external vendors. Some units such as an information processing unit or training department may be spun off to compete freely elsewhere as well as within the company as it gains its independence. All but core competencies could be subject to outsourcing and all existing internal services could be subject to dissolution, sale or intact separation with short-term support.

Taking advantage of others' functional specialization and your own need to remain flexible since skills can be brought to bear only when they are needed. In effect it is a just-in-time human resource system.

Outsourcing can be a great way to reduce costs, especially when other specialists can provide as good or better service than doing it yourself. EDS the $8 billion sales data processing company has grown by doing for businesses either what they could not do for themselves or could not do as efficiently.

Walden Paddlers has designed, produced, and marketed a technically sophisticated kayak fashioned from recycled plastic, one that significantly undercuts its competition on price and outmaneuvers in its performance. It is what's known as a virtual corporation, a company that outsources just about everything in the pursuit of eternal flexibility, low overhead, and the leading edge. (Edward O. Wells, "Virtual Realities", *Inc.*, August 1993, p. 50.)

In order to outsource effectively, know exactly what level of performance is minimally acceptable, the goals you wish to achieve by doing so, and link future plans and training efforts between your company and suppliers so that change to meet future contingencies occurs simultaneously among suppliers and your company.

Top ten reasons companies outsource: (1) Improve company focus. (2) Gain access to world-class capabilities. (3) Accelerate the benefits of reengineering. (4) Share risks. (5) Free non-capital resources. (6) Make capital funds available. (7) Reduce operating costs. (8) Looking for cash infusion. (9) Resources not available internally. (10) Function difficult to manage. (The Outsourcing Institute, New York, December 1994.)

Be careful, apparent short-term efficiencies could become liabilities when access to these services is interrupted or quality control deteriorates.

Outward Bound

Group/Team

Outward Bound is the name of an organization that provides wilderness experiences for management teams. The purpose is to help teams develop leadership and team-building skills. The name is now often applied to any physical (usually outdoor) team-building activity whether organized by Outward Bound or not. Ropes courses are a physically challenging set of outdoor experiences divided into high (advanced) and low (basic) activities where people participate as both individuals and members of a group.

"Part of the idea is to confound, surprise, shock and scare managers into breaching preconceived limits and thinking about new ways of doing things." (Colorado Outward Bound School.)

The processing of your confrontation of personal challenges as well as the required interpersonal relationships during the event provides the core of the individual's learning. The experience can take from one day to weeks of an extended adventure. Perceived personal risks vary though most events are in a protected environment where physical harm is unlikely.

"The programs are often a mixture of seminars, Scout camp, serious self-reflection and good-natured jokes about sore muscles." (Associated Press, "Execs Learn Teamwork In The Wild", *New Haven Register*, September 25, 1988.)

By using a physical analogy to the cerebral challenges back at work, you are able to assess issues and create solutions in a very different and stimulating way. The team bonding and trust building is an important feature of the experience.

It is about building camaraderie and teamwork, leadership and communicative abilities. It is also about developing compassion, humility, vision and a willingness to manage by consensus, not edict. Conquering fears and taking risks, learning to ask for help and self-reflection are all skills that can be addressed in the experience.

Personal confidence and a sense of mastery over formerly out of bounds activities can result in the transfer of additional confidence back on the job plus a sense that because they know their fellow employees a bit better a more spontaneous and closer relationship can develop.

The down side: whether the bonding, feelings of trust and exercises in self-disclosure survive back on the job is determined almost solely by the organization's willingness to create supportive structures that reinforce the new behaviors. Typical hierarchies, and performance evaluation processes actually divide people.

Guides do not often have the processing skills to help participants make the most of the experience and often the experience is not directly designed to help relate people's learning to workplace realities.

The physical challenges may be threatening to some and may close out the disabled from participating. The parallel with work challenges is not always apparent.

For some, rappelling down a 150-foot ledge may actually require less courage than speaking the truth to his or her superiors.

The physical struggle in the wilderness is a struggle between you and yourself. The struggle in the workplace is compounded by the struggle with others and the ambiguity resulting from different perceptions, needs, and wants. Thus, the transferability and the outcomes you might hope to experience back on the job, are questionable.

The trust falls and other techniques to build teamwork use one guiding principle – supervised safety to freely explore your potential. Back on the job all of the fears and insecurities return because of precisely the absence of a psychologically trusting and safe environment that is created during the outside experience.

PARTICIPATIVE MANAGEMENT

Group/Team

A management philosophy as well as a variety of techniques, stressing the importance and utility of having individual workers involved in decisions affecting their workplace and their work.

An increasing number of people want to take part in the decision-making process at work as in all areas of their lives. Because of circumstances, the workplace is the last environment that is democratizing and building methods for participation either through stock ownership or membership on employee focus groups/councils/forums or in less direct ways such as through routine surveys and feedback sessions. In either case, the participation trend appears to be spreading to organizations of all kinds and the workplaces of tomorrow will be more naturally participative – perhaps in a community-like fashion. Individuals may indeed be more than just employees or stakeholders, they may become active citizens of the organization with fully vested rights upon hire.

One method: hold focus groups with employees to learn the culture and readiness of the group to engage in a participative management program. A steering committee should guide this effort being composed of an organizational cross section of the company. Ascertain the motivation and commitment level of the employees and determine which issues will be tackled first and by whom. If a separate issue is present to create self-managing teams or to reengineer work processes additional skills may need to be taught to each employee who becomes involved in the process. Pay systems and rewards should reflect each person's support or understanding of the process and their being active contributors.

At Quad/Graphics close personal relationships are characteristic of a typical working environment. "Employees are considered partners in the quest for their livelihoods. They have achieved commitment from the workforce by focusing on effective peer group relations and meeting the needs of the customers." (John Simmons, "Is This Workplace Heaven? No, It's Quad/Graphics", *Journal for Quality and Participation*, July/August 1992, p. 6.)

At American Airlines "Quality depends on employees who have respect for each other and pride in their company – and who have a real commitment to excellence. It is possible to achieve that commitment only in a participative environment." (Robert L. Crandall, CEO American Airlines.)

For organizations to succeed at participative management it must fit in naturally with the issues, questions and challenges being faced by the workforce. One of the goals is to create jobs that are intrinsically motivating but where that is not possible, a participative environment encourages each person to innovate where possible and to contribute in the broader area of their responsibilities.

"Participation is a responsibility, not just a right bequeathed by management." (Corey Rosen, "Making Ownership Real Through Participation and Vice-Versa", *Vision/Action*, September 1992, p. 13.)

"A review of 29 studies found that employee participation was associated with positive effects on productivity in 14 studies and negative effects in only 2 studies – while the remaining 13 studies had ambiguous results." (*High Performance Work Practices and Firm Performance*, Washington, D.C.: US Department of Labor, 1993, p. i.)

Caution: Participative management can become confused with an endless gripe session. While organizations need to be responsible and allow individuals a role to play in determining their own lives at work and successful practices, each worker must engage in the participative process responsibly. It is too easy to focus solely on personal needs and wants and lose sight of the good of the organization toward which everyone strives. Thus, good organizational citizenship practices must be taught and participative management needs to be defined so that everyone understands the role they are expected to play and how best the system can work for themselves and the company.

It is possible the participative mechanism may have to delineate a time and place for discussing different categories of interests and issues. For example, the weekly staff meeting may be focused on quality issues while the monthly forum can discuss working conditions and personal matters. The possibilities are endless but do need to be thought out so that the participative process does not destroy the productive mission of the organization.

Some so-called participative schemes are elaborate charades. They give the appearance of involvement but end up destroying more. For example, the frequently held meetings where people are expected to participate that are really forums for the manager or convener to simply tell an audience what he or she expects and because of a high level of mistrust or cynicism among participants, requests for input are met with only supportive or trivial contributions.

Since participation is an ethic as well as a technique, an atmosphere of trust is required and participants' contributions need to be meaningfully put to use. Otherwise the sessions are merely wasting everyone's time and serve as a rubber stamp for decisions already made by others.

Prior to becoming Secretary of Labor, Robert Reich reminded us that "Underneath the veneer of participatory management, it is business as usual – and business as usual represents a threat to America's long term capacity to compete." (Robert B. Reich, "Entrepreneurship Reconsidered: The Team as Hero", *Harvard Business Review*, May/June 1987, p. 77.)

PAY FOR PERFORMANCE

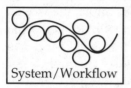

System/Workflow

A pay plan that ties a person's compensation to their actual contribution. It is sometimes judged according to a percentage of plan. This means your pay is determined by the degree an individual has met performance targets established at the beginning of a review period. Sometimes skill-based pay is added whereby the possession of proven skills contribute to enhancing your compensation. The assumption here is that having skills means using them and this criteria may be relevant when it is hard to determine the degree to which a person's contributions contributed to plan such as when a person is a member of a team.

Not only does performance related pay (PRP) not achieve any tangible efficiency, it may fail even to relate to performance.

More traditional styles of using money as an incentive or reward involve bonus pay. Not necessarily tied to profit or stock performance this incentive is given to promote attention to specific operational goals such as waste reduction, safety or skill enhancements that enable employees to contribute in more areas. A new survey by consultants Hewitt Associates shows that nearly two-thirds of midsize and large companies have some form of incentive pay for non-executives.

(Howard Gleckman, et al., "Bonus Pay: Buzzword or Bonanza?", *Business Week*, November 14, 1994, p. 62.)

"Performance pay can't replace good management. Throwing cash at a frustrated or bored worker solves nothing. But as part of an overall management system that aims to bring out the best in its workers, incentive pay can be more than the latest fad." (*Ibid.*)

PEER APPRAISALS/REVIEW

Interpersonal

This is the utilization of peers in the individual development process. On the job coaching along with self-development is increasingly required to cope with complexity and rapid change. Learning from each other (peer coaching) is seen as an essential component of team-building.

When peers rate each other the developmental possibilities are great. They are best when no record is kept but each person feels comfortable in conveying their honest perceptions regarding the individual's performance. Skills for assessing, describing and communicating your personal performance appraisal of a peer (or anyone) need to be taught. But used on an on-going basis as a way of communicating and helping one another would add a built-in developmental component to the working relationships. Theoretically all would benefit from this insight.

The coach employs a variety of skills to help clients/peers fulfill their self-generated agendas:

(1) Clarify wants and needs. (2) Seek permission. (3) Ask powerful and directed questions. (4) Listen to identify their values. (5) Determine if actions are aligned with values. (6) Question underlying assumptions. (7) Make powerful requests, clarify perceptions. (8) Identify blind spots. (9) Lead client/peer to self-reflection. (10) Reframe perceptions. (11) Brainstorm solutions, next steps. (12) Provide acknowledgement; cheerleader. (13) Trust in yourself – speak from intuition. (14) Tell the truth. (15) Intrude when appropriate. (16) Point to the learning. (17) Facilitate ongoing personal planning. (Diane Westin, "Coaching Skills", *The Learning Community Newsletter*, July 1994, p. 3.)

Peer review of grievances to the point of having informal juries to hear and then rule upon employee concerns about mistreatment or other issues now takes place in at least 334 companies including at least one GE plant and Taco Bell restaurants have made binding rulings about reprimands, demotions, and firings. (Kim Clark, "Peer Review Replacing Union Grievance Rules", *Denver Post*, September 19, 1994)

There are several drawbacks that must first be overcome. For example: "Though research shows peers often have the best information about co-workers' performances, they may not give it freely. Some may attack a peer they dislike. Others pull punches to spare a co-worker's feelings or career." (Sue Shellenbarger, "Reviews From Peers Instruct – And Sting", *The Wall Street Journal*, October 4, 1994, p. B1.)

In addition getting employees to be honest and then able to deal with the fall out is a challenge that is worth taking but costly in terms of training and processing time. Most importantly, perhaps, criticism from peers can raise strong emotions in the workplace that are hard to handle.

PEER MEDIATION/PEER INTERVENTION TEAMS

Interpersonal

Peer mediation is an extension of peer coaching. It is the empowerment of individuals to settle disputes among themselves or by requesting help from specially trained individuals in the organization. These individuals most often hold down regular jobs and are used as mediators as the need arises. They can be from any level in the organization. Peer intervention teams (PITs) step in to solve interpersonal or other problems using mediation techniques but in an informal way where individuals still take the responsibility for resolving their own problems.

"It is estimated that 25% of managerial energy is devoted to interpersonal conflict, which thwarts a sense of community teamwork and dedication to the organization's mission." (Nancy Branham Songer, "Mediation As A Management Tool", *Business and Economic Review*, October–December 1993, p. 17.)

"Problem solving is the point – not victory, not vindication, not vengeance." (Ralph Finizio and John Kirkwood, "A Quality Approach to Dispute Resolution", *Journal for Quality and Participation*, June 1993, p. 52.)

Many companies are now requiring at least an initial

pass at mediation, or other non-legal but voluntarily binding alternative dispute resolution process to avoid court-based dispute resolution.

Anyone can successfully mediate by applying several key concepts, including: (1) Focus on the future – trying to assign blame for what has happened in the past is counterproductive. (2) Focus on the facts of the situation, not principles. (3) Conduct the mediation session so that each side can present its viewpoint without interruption. (4) Meet with the parties individually if necessary. (5) Focus on the relationship – lead both parties to the conclusion that their ongoing working relationship is more important than any particular incident. (6) Put the agreement in writing. (Roland B. Cousins and Linda E. Benitz, "Every Supervisor Needs Mediation Skills", *Supervision*, May 1994, p. 3.)

In mediation: both sides have to be willing to accept responsibility for solving their problem and to work at the solution until it is resolved. Then of course they must keep their commitment to upholding their side of the bargain. There are several options in taking a grievance to mediation. First, if no solution is possible it may be dropped from mediation and either left for the complainant to take up through formal channels or drop a resolution altogether. A second approach would be to have binding arbitration. That, however is usually an option of last resort since it removes responsibility from the disputants. Peer mediation is to enable people to solve their own problems and to do so with minimal outside intervention. However, a third party – a peer – is usually invited to facilitate the process and the only record kept is the agreement arrived at by the parties.

Mediation encourages disputants to think of how they can each get what they need instead of demanding all of what they want. Having to live and work side-by-side encourages compromise when they work out their own solutions. It is also somewhat preventative of escalating disputes when they know they have only themselves to depend on for the resolution of conflicts.

Steps:
Prepare for mediation: agree to the process, set aside time without distractions for discussion. Listen to each other and repeat what the other is saying to reach agreement on what is at stake and why. Think of solutions and discuss what you are willing to do to reach an agreement. Put the agreement in writing and maintain clear expectations of each person's responsibility and when/how it will be fulfilled. Acknowledge each other's contribution.

Remember, however, that mediation is inappropriate for issues that involve organizational components such as policies, structures, and rules that may lead to conflict. Since the organization may need to adjust one of these components it is unsuited to a mediation process. In this case a more formal review and official action may be required.

Mediation is also inappropriate for serious breaches of conduct or illegal or unethical behavior that should be handled with appropriate disciplinary sanctions.

Principle-centered Leadership

Interpersonal

Centering on principles provides sufficient security to not be threatened by change, comparisons, or criticisms; guidance to discover our mission, define our roles, and write our scripts and goals; wisdom to learn from our mistakes and seek continuous improvement; and power to communicate and cooperate, even under conditions of stress and fatigue. (Steven Covey, *Principle-Centered Leadership*, New York: Summit Books, 1991, p. 22.)

"Attributes such as integrity, humility, fidelity, temperance, courage, justice and the Golden Rule are the concepts that underlie Covey's Seven Habits as well as his management philosophy – principled-centered leadership." (Beverly Geber, "Q&A With Steven Covey", *Training*, December 1992, p. 37.)

But, "According to Covey, organizations fail to empower their employees for several reasons. One reason is that people have had so little intrinsic satisfaction in their work that they have adapted their work and lifestyle to find satisfaction mostly off the job. They simply do not want to be empowered. Another reason is that many supervisors and managers have a 'scarcity mentality.' This means that their sense of personal worth always has to come from a contest with the rest of humanity." (*Ibid.*)

Quality

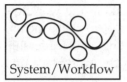

System/Workflow

Quality is the emphasis on the creation and attainment of performance targets reflective of an increasingly high standard. Quality goals signify the continuous search for improvement as well as a standard of performance. Quality is sometimes thought of as a means of continuously improving processes to narrow variation, eliminate defects and spur constant innovation. See Part II for a more complete discussion of this concept.

Quality Circles

Group/Team

An aspect of Japanese management is the idea to gather employees either on a workteam, proximate to one another in the work process or as part of a cross-functional intervention in order to explore ideas to improve their work and the relationships among the individuals in the work flow process (see: Japanese management).

It is a process of getting groups of workers together to raise and solve problems they share in common. Their focus is usually on problems directly related to work flow, cost-cutting, production efficiency or interpersonal relationships that have direct bearing on their work performance. They were first used in the US at Lockheed in 1974. The concept was imported from Japan where they were developed in the 1960s.

Getting people to concentrate on mutual problems and develop skills required to deal with them were steps to worker involvement that delivered on their promise of reducing costs and making the workflow process more efficient. People developed skills such as in problem solving, communications, and leadership that were applicable elsewhere in the workplace and even in their personal lives.

It really motivated a lot of people who wanted a creative outlet and to apply problem-solving skills. The acknowledgement by management also enabled some people to get noticed for their own career advancement. Morale and motivation frequently increased with the formation of circles because the promise to get involved in a meaningful way was welcomed.

Respect and dignity were enhanced as individuals were offered and accepted greater responsibility not only for their individual work but for the success of their companies.

Because circles typically were limited to making proposals to management, the tight boundaries of their involvement and the contingent nature of their work often resulted in a lack of commitment and real interest. Many of the circles were voluntary and that time seemed wasted to some people who found their hard work and good ideas vetoed or shelved indefinitely.

Benefits did not really accrue to the participants who felt exploited. While they wanted to do their jobs they began to resent that management would pick their brains but not be adequately rewarded while management frequently took the credit and the bonuses.

With narrowly defined boundaries early successes were possible with the picking of the "low hanging fruit." Later improvements were harder to achieve because they frequently hit sub-system limits. Additional improvements would need to come from a system's analysis and an enlarged arena for change which circles rarely, if ever, were assigned. Additionally, when the easy issues and problems were solved motivation declined as tasks got beyond their capabilities and/or involved long range quasi-managerial decisions which were never part of their charge.

QUALITY OF WORKLIFE

Organizational

Quality of worklife (QWL), like healthy companies, is a way of viewing the suitability of the workplace environment from the employees point of view. Wages and conditions of work, health and safety considerations, pensions, benefits, and opportunities for personal development and advancement, employee rights and grievance handling, and other agreements between management and labor comprise most of the components of the quality of worklife. While productivity and effectiveness are usually enhanced by attention to building a high quality of worklife there is resistance to these issues as too costly to implement.

Professor Richard E. Walton, identified eight major components of the quality of worklife which include: (1) Adequate and fair compensation. (2) Safe and healthy working conditions. (3) Immediate opportunity to use and develop human capacities. (4) Opportunity for continued growth and security. (5) Social integration in the work organization. (6) Constitutionalism in the work organization. (7) Work and the total life space. (8) The social relevance of worklife." (Richard E. Walton, "Quality of Working Life: What Is It?", *Sloan Management Review*, Fall 1993, p. 11.)

"The real thrust of quality-of-worklife programs – improving organizational life and behavior and the fundamental health of the organization – should result in a higher level of organizational performance and a better work environment." (David A. Nadler and Edward E. Lawler, "Quality of Work Life: Perspectives and Directions", *Organizational Dynamics*, Winter 1983, p. 20.)

This is still a serious issue – even in the postindustrial age. "By some estimates, more than 10,000 workers die each year from on-the-job injuries – about 30 every day. Perhaps 70,000 more are permanently disabled." (Richard Lacayo, "Death on the Shop Floor", *Time*, September 16, 1991, p. 28.)

QWL is not just about treating people well and creating safe and secure working environments with proper tools. It is also about creating an environment, a community, in which people can develop and become, in a sense, better people living according to higher order needs and principles.

The QWL effort will only last as long as there are gains in productivity and efficiency as measured both in resource utilization and cycle time.

Quick Response/Rapid Deployment Teams

Group/Team

Quick response was developed for the Crafted With Pride in the USA Council in 1984 to speed manufacturing and order processing in the apparel industry. "Quick response is a business strategy that links retailers, manufacturers and their suppliers to speed the flow of information and merchandise through the production and merchandising pipeline." ("Quick Response: What It Really Is", *Apparel Industry Magazine*, March 1994, p. QR4.)

"In its efforts to achieve world-class status, Foxboro concentrates on quality, rapid response and cost. Total employee involvement and intensive training programs are ingrained at Foxboro. It has been named as one of the US's best plants for 1992." (Brian M. Cook, "America's Best Plants: Foxboro", *Industry Week*, October 19, 1992, p. 45.)

Black and Decker took elements from several popular new approaches – synchronous manufacturing, agile manufacturing, and just-in-time – and added some of its own twists to pursue a strategy with two main goals: flexibility and quick response . . . They reduced the company's 8–10 week manufacturing time to just a few days . . . In the event of equipment breakdown or material shortage, the system would be able to generate new schedules for every operation in the system within five minutes. (Joseph Cosco, "Black and Deckering at Black and Decker", *Journal of Business Strategy*, January/February 1994, p. 59.)

In another application the idea of quick response is simply to act as fast as possible. In employee complaints, as in customer complaints, it is important to solve issues before they are major confrontations and goodwill is lost. For example, Marriott's Guarantee of Fair Treatment includes: (1) mediation; (2) a toll-free hotline; and (3) peer review. (Ron Wilensky and Karen M. Jones, "Quick Response: Key To Resolving Complaints", *HR Magazine*, March 1994, p. 42.)

Quick response is also a needed factor in a crisis. Johnson & Johnson demonstrated the prototypical response during the Tylenol scare in the early 1980s. Pepsi managed its syringe scare in the early 1990s in a similarly straightforward and immediate fashion. Source Perrier was not as fortunate and when communications broke down between different corporate components the crisis grew and its reputation suffered. Some companies have adopted the quick response time to crisis management contingency planning.

The idea of quick response is an effort to anticipate and, in real time, be able to respond to an emerging demand or a changing situation in such a way that the organization best positions itself against the competition, a standard or a situational demand. Even the White House has a political quick response team to be able to meet the opposition's moves. When Perot or Bob Dole takes a policy initiative, the quick response team is ready to counter and begin the "positioning" process.

These are generally strategic external (industry-based) approaches to facing environmental threats such as that from foreign competition, but the concept is more generally used to mean any organized ad hoc or cross-functional team that attacks a special internal problem requiring coordination between departments or teams.

REENGINEERING

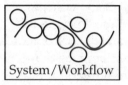

System/Workflow

The mother of all contemporary fads, reengineering is defined by Michael Hammer and James Champy as "using the power of modern information technology to radically redesign business processes in order to achieve dramatic improvements in their performance." (Michael Hammer and James Champy, *Reengineering the Corporation: A Manifesto for Business Revolution*, New York: Harper Business, 1993.)

Reengineering to many people is a euphemism for downsizing. Though frequently downsizing follows, reengineering is about redesigning the organization around core processes rather than functional and vertical hierarchies. The trend toward a flatter, horizontal, team-based process-centered design is clear. Simply put, "managing across" is more important to get the work out than "managing up and down." It is more efficient to design the organization's inputs as they "flow" to the customer. See Part II for a more complete discussion of this concept.

Reinventing the Corporation

Organizational

The idea to reinvent the corporation was proposed by John Naisbitt and Patricia Aburdene in their book of the same name as a way of responding to several of the "megatrends" identified by Naisbitt and others, namely: global competition, demand for quality, greater appreciation for diversity in the workforce, and employee empowerment.

Current workplace turmoil due to massive uncertainty while needing to act amidst an intensifying period of global competition has given rise to the notion of completely transforming business as usual. Reinvention means starting with a blank sheet and literally re-examine the wisdom of doing things they way they have been done. It might turn out to be a "reengineering" project or a fundamental paradigm shift in the operating assumptions governing organizational behavior. Regardless of the particular approach one thing is apparent: entrepreneurial behavior is replacing bureaucratic behavior. In addition, the workplace environment and employee satisfaction are being viewed as important as a concern for profits – mainly because it is finally true that people's motivation and commitment are directly related to the attention a company gives a customer and with the financial performance of the company. See Part II for a fuller discussion of this concept.

REINVENTING GOVERNMENT

Organizational

An initiative by Vice-president Al Gore in 1993 to streamline the US government along the lines of private industry and to seek out ways of applying continuous improvement to the civil service. (See previous entry, Reinventing the Corporation.)

RESTRUCTURING

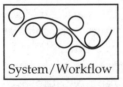

System/Workflow

A restructuring is any attempt to redesign an organization or shuffle the reporting obligations of individuals in an organization. This may occur for political as well as business purposes and is done to meet new strategic initiatives, after mergers and acquisitions, and often follow the installation of a new CEO. When accompanied by massive layoffs it is often called reengineering or downsizing.

"Giant pyramid structures reached their peak in the early 1980s. A typical company was Bethlehem Steel, with 14 layers of management, 3,400 wage incentive schemes, and 400 industrial engineers timing jobs and setting rates of work." (Patricia A. Galagan, "Beyond Hierarchy: The Search for High Performance", *Training & Development*, August 1992, p. 21.)

Moving away from "functional silos," "chimneys," "stovepipes," "towers," "foxholes." But, "You can only get so much more productivity out of reorganization and automation. Where you really get productivity leaps is in the minds and hearts of people." James Baughman, GE's former head of management development. (Frank Rose, "A New Age for Business?", *Fortune*, October 8, 1990, p. 157.) (See downsizing and reengineering.)

RESULTS-DRIVEN QUALITY

System/Workflow

Results-driven quality is TQM that is energized with a short cycle improvement process right out of the starting blocks. It is not a return to 'quick fix' or 'short term gains at any costs' mentality. Rather RDQ embraces TQM's long-term vision, values and prescriptions while helping managers make immediate, tangible improvements. (Ken Myers and Ron Ashkenas, "Results-Driven Quality . . . Now", *Management Review*, March 1993, p. 40.)

Many businesses report their TQM programs have not yielded any real improvements. These poor results may be attributed in part to the 'quality bandwagon' effect created by the critical demand to match the quality of competitors as well as to a growing 'technocracy' of quality professionals. The effect of the technocrat's 'continuous process improvement' is to build performance expectations while burdening TQM with too much front end activity and too little focus on urgent outcomes. Results-driven quality is a short cycle TQM program that seeks to capture the natural motivation people experience when they are directly involved in short time-frame projects which attract attention by achieving results which measurably contribute to the organization's purpose. (Ken Myers and Ron Ashkenas, "Results-Driven Quality", *Executive Excellence*, May 1993, p. 17.) (See also: Breakthrough Action Teams, Quick Response/Rapid Deployment Teams, and Cross-Functional Teams.)

RIGHT BRAIN THINKING

Intrapersonal

As opposed to utilizing the left hemisphere of the brain with its logical, methodical, and rational thinking capacities – the symbolic representation of a scientific approach to business and decision making – right brain thinking utilizes mental capacities in the right hemisphere of the brain which can also contribute to improving business processes. Intuition, creativity, spontaneity, playfulness, and imagination are representative of right brain thinking. Decision making has typically ignored these attributes in favor of the left brain skills. Our culture has demonstrated its propensity to teach and reward the left brain talents and ignore right brain qualities. Thus, attention is drawn to the usefulness of "new" human qualities that can help organizations improve their performance.

RIGHTSIZING

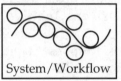

System/Workflow

A short-lived euphemism for downsizing. Though arguments can be made for the reorganization of a business and the resulting loss of people, what it is called changed to soften the perception of its actual human impact. Rightsizing is suggestive of a rational, perhaps obvious, restructuring as a response to changed business conditions. It assumes that there is in fact a "right" number of people for an organization at any particular time. The term is used infrequently today, replaced by reengineering, another term suggestive of a rational, sensible obviously necessary loss of jobs and people. (See Downsizing, Reengineering, and Employment Contracts.)

SCIENTIFIC MANAGEMENT

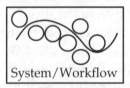

System/Workflow

The precursor to reengineering it was the first application of the scientific method to management. Proposed by Frederick Taylor at the turn of the twentieth century, it remained the driving philosophy of management thinking for fifty years. To this day "management science" suggests that there is a single right way of doing things and that it can be discovered through rational decision-making techniques. (F.W. Taylor, *The Principles of Scientific Management*, New York: Harper & Row, 1911.)

SELF-DEVELOPMENT GROUP

Intrapersonal

Self-development is the recognition that individuals can control much of their destiny, can improve their performance, can plan for their own education, and expand their skill set and can do all of this when aided by a willing group of peers. Thus, the self-development group is a self-selected group of people who help one another develop and stick to a personal development plan. They may or may not share the same agenda for personal growth. (Paul Temporal, "Self-Development Groups In Industry – What Actually Happens", *Management Education and Development* Vol. 13, Pt. 1, 1982, pp. 3–9.) (See also: Barbara Sher and Annie Gottlieb, *Teamworks,* New York: Warner, 1989.)

SELF-MANAGING WORK TEAMS

Group/Team

One of the most powerful new developments in work design, self-managing teams are empowered groups of people able to determine how to do their own work, set objectives, solve their own problems, make their own decisions, and respond to necessary demands in their environment according to means they see fit to use. Often cross-functional by nature, a self-managing team takes upon itself duties normally reserved for supervisors and foremen. Thus, they have been crucial in reducing the number of layers in the hierarchy and speeding up the responsiveness of the organization. Scheduling, personnel selection, training, and evaluation of team members, conflict resolution and distributing rewards are not unusual additional functions of self-managing teams. See Part II for a more complete discussion of this concept.

SERVANT LEADERSHIP

Interpersonal

The Robert K. Greenleif Center in Indianapolis is largely responsible for the spread of this concept which claims that leadership, by definition, is the service to others and that the true measure of a leader is how well he or she empowers, encourages, and serves subordinates and the society at large. (Robert Greenleif, *Servant Leadership*, Indianapolis, IN: Robert K. Greenleif Center, 1991.) Making your subordinates successful is indeed a reflection of your own success in meeting goals. Servant leadership is the idea that it is the leader's job to facilitate the work of the group. Max DePree, CEO of Herman Miller, talks about a covenant between a manager and employees, a sacred obligation that bonds the two.

"The role of manager has changed from giving orders, seeing they are followed, and holding people accountable if they are not. Today's managers are concerned primarily with how to shape more supportive work environments and how to find ways to help each employee to be more productive . . . According to the National Study of the Changing Workforce, the top three variables considered most important in deciding to take a job were open communication, effect on personal and family life, and the nature of work. (Ken Blanchard, "Changing Role of Executives", *Executive Excellence*, April 1994, p. 7.)

Servant leadership emphasizes service to others, personal development, and shared decision making – characteristics which can be found in today's empowerment, total quality, and participative management concepts . . . Some experts state that servant leadership allows managers to turn to the collective wisdom of the group to glean knowledge. (Chris Lee and Ron Zemke, "The Search for Spirit in the Workplace", *Training*, June 1993, p. 21.)

"What the servant-leader does more effectively than any other style of leader is bring out the leader in everyone. The servant is an enabler." (Megan Smolenyak and Amit Majumdar, "What is Leadership?", *Journal for Quality and Participation*, July/August 1992, p. 28.)

An important leadership role is to build competent teams, clarify required behaviors, build in measurement, and administer rewards and punishments so that individuals perceive that behavior consistent with the change is central for them in achieving their own goals. We will call this type of leadership instrumental leadership since it focuses on the management of teams, structures, and managerial processes to create individual instrumentalities (a means for acquiring valued outcomes). (David A. Nadler and Michael L. Tushman, "Beyond the Charismatic Leader: Leadership and Organizational Change", *California Management Review*, Winter 1990, p. 85.)

Servant leaders serve the servers, inspiring and enabling them to achieve. Such leaders fundamentally believe in the capacity of people to achieve, viewing their own role as setting a direction and a standard of excellence and giving people the tools and the freedom to perform." (Leonard L. Berry, A. Parasuraman and Valarie A. Zeithami, "Improving Service Quality in America: Lessons Learned", *Academy of Management Executive*, 1994, Vol. 8, No. 2, p. 42.)

SEVEN HABITS

Intrapersonal

In The Seven Habits of Highly Effective People, Steven Covey identified seven qualities which, if followed religiously, enhance your effectiveness in life as an employee/leader, a partner in a relationship, and as parent/citizen and community member. Time management, personal discipline, and sensitivity to the eternal virtues lead to success. Motivational like Anthony Robbins, but from a more spiritual point of view, Covey stresses taking personal responsibility. He believes that success can be realized by everyone who follows the seven habits.

The seven habits are: (1) Be proactive. Have a personal vision. (2) Begin with the end in mind. Take leadership in your own life. (3) Put first things first. Manage your own priorities. (4) Think win/win. Take interpersonal leadership. (5) Seek first to understand, then to be understood. Communicate empathetically. (6) Synergize. Understand creative cooperation. (7) Sharpen the saw: understand the principles of self-renewal.

Character is ultimately more important than competence. Courage and consideration are the key building blocks of emotional maturity, and that emotional maturity is foundational to all relationships . . . It is the ability to express feelings and convictions with courage, balanced with consideration for the feelings and convictions of others. Organizations need to stop managing people by performance appraisals where a supervisor is judging someone else's character and competence. ("Character First", *Executive Excellence*, May 1994, pp. 3–5.)

Develop a personal mission statement focusing on the values and principles upon which being and doing are based. Relationships and a focus on outcomes supersede a focus on to do lists and efficiency. (John Davies, "Personal Effectiveness: The Time of Your Life", *Managers Magazine*, April 1993, p. 27.)

SITUATIONAL LEADERSHIP

Interpersonal

Situational leadership is the understanding that because people and circumstances differ, a leader needs to develop the capacity to alter his or her style to be effective. Basically, it is the modulation of involvement with subordinates according to their level of skill, knowledge, and maturity. Thus, if an individual is mature and skillful he or she needs little leadership and if the individual is not skillful, knowledgeable or mature enough to follow through without direction, the leader needs to devote more attention to that person. (See: Paul Hersey and Ken Blanchard, *Management of Organiza-*

tional Behavior, 6th Edition, Englewood Cliffs, NJ: Prentice-Hall, 1994.)

SKUNKWORKS

Group/Team

The informal name of the Lockheed team that developed the idea for the stealth bomber and a term now meaning any pseudo-clandestine – actually officially recognized – ad hoc team designed to utilize breakthrough thinking, overcome bureaucratic resistance to innovation, and apply imaginative approaches to immediate challenges facing the organization. This concept is frequently utilized for new product development.

"With skunkworks, it's not just that the organization is ad hoc, it's that it is officially relieved of most of the bureaucratic responsibilities that the other divisions have to deal with. It's an IBM or a Motorola saying to a bunch of its people, 'Go off and do it. We won't bother you with reporting every week . . .'" (A.J. Vogel, "Breaking With Bureaucracy: Alvin Toffler Describes the Organization Man of the Future", *Across the Board*, January/February 1991, p. 18.)

SOCIAL RESPONSIBILITY

Organizational

The idea is that public organizations are a franchise granted by society and therefore have a responsibility to act in a way that both fosters the advancement of social policy and is respectful of the environment. In addition there is the belief that as a primary influence in our lives, these entities should take an active part in promoting the social good. This philosophy is in contradistinction to those who believe that institutions and business in particular are merely the expression of individuals' will and an exercise in the right to freely use their personal property in any manner he or she or it (the corporation) so chooses. Certainly one thing is agreed to by adherents to both beliefs – obedience to the law is a necessity. Thus the political battle centers on the role and extent of regulation. See Part II for a more complete discussion of this concept.

SPIRITUALITY AT WORK

Intrapersonal

With increasing interest in social values a corresponding interest has grown around the issue of management as a sacred act and work as a spiritual exercise. The meaning of organization itself is seen by some as a spiritual exercise with several ramifications. First, an organization's and a manager's role in the community is seen as requiring the adherence to certain standards to earn the trust of neighbor and customer alike. Second, the treatment of people at work needs to be governed by ethical principles as well as a general adherence to decency and, in North America, Judeo-Christian principles. Tom Chappell, CEO of Tom's of Maine, a personal hygiene products company, sets one of the most notable examples. He has written about the concept of spirituality in business, from a practitioner's perspective, in his book.

(*The Soul of A Business: Managing For Profit and the Common Good*, New York: Doubleday/Currency, 1993.)

I look at spirituality, at the way people live their life. What is their motivation? Do they want things to be better? Do they want to be open and honest? But I don't think we're really teaching anything new. I think we're going back to basic, fundamental values – issues of trust, respect, dignity, commitment, integrity and accountability. The world is crying out for these things to become more important. (Michael Blondell in Frank Rose, "A New Age for Business?", *Fortune*, October 8, 1990, p. 157.) See Part II for a more complete discussion of this concept.

STAKEHOLDER ISSUES

Organizational

Many parties have an interest in the profitability and performance of an organization. Obviously employees and shareholders are concerned but so are government bodies, for example, not just for the tax contributions but because of employment stability and adherence to regulations. The community is also concerned as are suppliers, unions, creditors, and even competitors! Given that so many people have an interest in the success of an organization, it is understandable that the emphasis of their various interests would often be at odds with each other. This broad panoply of interests vies for influence in the governance and decision-making apparatus of each organization. How these interests are handled results in the support an organization receives from various constituencies. To ignore any constituency could have serious consequences.

STRATEGIC ALLIANCES

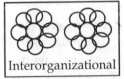

Interorganizational

Strategic alliances are created when organizations join forces, as partners, to accomplish a particular goal that each will benefit from but which could not be as effectively achieved alone. The IBM/Apple alliance to create new system software is an example of each bringing unique talents to bear on a common problem neither could accomplish as effectively alone. And, in this case, while they cooperate in one endeavor they still remain fierce competitors in others.

Strategic alliances occur because companies realize that they lack the competencies or resources to compete alone in the global markets . . . A well defined process for creating successful strategic alliances treats strategy development, partner assessment, contract negotiations and implementation as separate steps. (Abram I. Bluestein, "A Four Step Process for Creating Alliances", *Directors and Boards*, Winter 1994, p. 25.)

Mayo and Deere developed a strategic alliance along several dimensions. Mayo will continue to supply Deere with consulting services for the development of additional primary care clinics and Deere will utilize Mayo administrators to manage the daily operation of these clinics. Mayo will be the preferred, but not exclusive, provider of tertiary care services to Deere patients. ("John Deere and Mayo Establish Strategic Alliances Between Payers and Providers", *Health Care Strategic Management*, May 1994, p. 10.)

Variations include: Partnerships, joint ventures, licensing agreements.

A recent Conference Board report on strategic alliances observes that it is often competitors that enter into alliances, and that these companies tend to be suspicious, finding a number of means whereby either they or their partners might violate the agreement without it being immediately detected. (Michael F. Wolff, "Building Trust in Alliances", *Research-Technology Management*, May/June 1994, p. 12.)

STRETCH GOALS

Intrapersonal

This techniques – to set goals way beyond what a person can accomplish is used by many managers to precipitate massive change or fundamental rethinking of the challenges. Where stretch goals are sufficiently beyond the normal capacity of the system to handle routinely, it forces a reconsideration and new thinking.

Honda used this technique when it needed a new car for the American market. Assembling a young engineering and design team it gave only two constraints: be fundamentally different and be inexpensive. The result was the Civic.

Frequently setting a stretch goal is simply a professionally sounding term that spells overwork for those being "stretched." "To meet stretch targets, people use the only resource that's not constrained, which is their personal time. I think that's immoral," says Steven Kerr, Chief Learning Officer at GE. "People are under tremendous stress . . . to achieve these stretch targets." (Strat Sherman, "Stretch Goals: The Dark Side of Asking for Miracles", *Fortune*, November 13, 1995, p. 231.)

Not everyone should be given stretch goals – especially if they are already taxed to the limit or are consistently setting their own high standards of performance. People should not be blamed for not reaching the goals and time limits need some flexibility because, typically the stretch goals are wishful thinking. When they become vital, then they are no longer stretch goals. When the goals are hit, reward the people who achieved it. At GE they split any savings by around 50–50. Remember, this gain-sharing payout is a reward for special achievement; and, that is what a stretch goal is. Finally, remember that stretch goals for one person invariably influences other people, so expectations must be moderated likewise and/or support must be provided by others first.

SUN TZU

Interpersonal

Sun Tzu, a warrior from ancient China wrote *The Art of War*, a strategic handbook for undertaking battle which has been very influential among corporate strategists. His advice on when and how to confront an adversary is considered powerful. This work along with *The Book of Five Rings*, and *Bushido: The Code of the Samurai* from Japan have become the cornerstones of a literature for the corporate planner and strategist drawing upon ancient military arts. (See: Attila the Hun.)

SUSTAINABILITY

Organizational

Sustainability is a techno-eco-economics that strives to ensure that organizations act in a way that does not deplete the environment. Thus, with the requirement that organizations' actions result in sustainability, society is assured that material utilization, processing and waste will not harm the environment or human/animal life. The concern centers around your perceived responsibility to future generations.

By reducing the quantity or quality of resources faster than they can be renewed, depletion occurs. The phenomenon is often referred to as the consumption of the resource's 'capital': the capital generates income that can be tapped for human consumption. A sustainable economy can therefore be defined as one that leaves the capital intact and undamaged so that future generations can enjoy undiminished income. (Thomas F. Homer-Dixon, Jeffrey H. Boutwell and George W. Rathjens, "Environmental Change and Violent Conflict", *Scientific American*, February 1993, p. 38.)

The concept of sustainable development, however, calls for moving business decisions simultaneously toward a healthy environment and a healthy economy.

Such a mindset requires a fundamental rethinking of traditional notions of disposability, risk, responsibility, and the right to pollute beginning at the top of the organization and moving right through it. (Kathleen Dechant and Barbara Altman, "Environmental Leadership: From Compliance to Competitive Advantage", *Academy of Management Executive*, 1994, Vol. 8, No. 3, p. 7.)

It may be impossible to develop a sustainable approach to economic management because of virtually uninhibited and uncontrolled reproduction. Population growth alone leads to threatening shortages of resources. Even arable land is diminished from the simple need to house the expanding population which, itself diminishes its ability to feed itself. The continued skewed distribution of access to and benefit from resources is an added reason that inadequate husbandry may lead to conflict and destruction. See Part II for a fuller discussion of this topic.

SYNERGY

Group/Team

Synergy is the creation of an outcome only possible through a combination of independent elements. The human being is more than the sum of his or her parts. In the same way, when people work together they can create more than any one person working alone and often unimaginably so.

SYSTEMS THINKING

Organizational

The recognition that all activity takes place within an arena of action and that for every activity within that arena there are multiple causes and effects which are themselves often undetectable and unpredictable is systems thinking at work. In more common terms it is the recognition of a connection between and among all things. To think in a systems fashion is to identify, explore, and understand, the connections between things. In organizational terms, the organization is the whole system and the functions and/or work processes represent sub-systems. See Part II for a more complete discussion of this concept.

TRANSACTIONAL ANALYSIS

Interpersonal

Transactional analysis is a methodology of examining the communications patterns between people to discern whether or not they are complementary (appropriate) or crossed (discordant leading to conflict) and to understand why. Invented and popularized by Eric Berne in *Games People Play: The Psychology of Human Relationships* (New York: Grove Press, 1964) he pointed to three prevailing styles of communicating: as a parent, a child or an adult – representing the ego states of the individual at the time a stimulus was received and a response formulated.

T-GROUPS

Interpersonal

Training groups established for the purpose of understanding and improving interpersonal relationships are called T-groups. In the late 1960s they were the rage. The idea was to expose and confront personal mental models of the world and to help individual participants become more sensitive to others. The variations of the original training groups became known as sensitivity training or encounter groups. The T-group in its original form, however, is still utilized as a practical way of exploring interpersonal issues and group learning.

"The T-group can provide a valuable setting to gain needed skills . . . The T-group can help managers at all levels of the organization learn about their enacted worlds in a way that is based on their own experience." (William Van Buskirk and Dennis McGrath, "The Culture Focused T-Group: Laboratory Learning From the Interpretive Perspective", *Public Administration Quarterly*, Fall 1993, p. 316.)

In an effort to make brainstorming and other forms of idea sessions more effective a modified T-group design is possible. For Sibson & Company, four rules prevail: (1) be honest; (2) take risks; (3) share 'airtime'; and (4) listen to one another. (George Bailey and Richard A. Moran, "A Window of Opportunity", *Sibson & Company Newsletter*, May 1992, p. 15.)

When an organization either denies the validity of emotions in the workplace or seeks to permit only certain kinds of emotions, two things happen. The first is that managers cut themselves off from their own emotional lives. Even more important they cut off the ideas, solutions, and new perspectives that other people can contribute. (Jeanie Daniel Duck, "Managing Change: The Art of Balancing", *Harvard Business Review*, November/December 1993, p. 110.)

The willingness of people to express themselves to the point of interpersonal vulnerability varies. The level of discomfort can make routine and all encompassing attempts to involve everyone at this level can be downright painful for some. In T-groups, you are allowed to visit pity city but are not allowed to live there.

Theory X/Y

Intrapersonal

Theory X and Theory Y are archetypes of authoritarian and democratic mindsets. They were first postulated by Douglas McGregor in, "The Human Side of Enterprise", *Management Review*, November 1957. These dramatic differences in outlook drive distinctly different organizational and managerial philosophies. See Chapter 8 for a more complete discussion of this concept.

Theory Z

Organizational

Theory Z is a synthesis of American and Japanese management styles and was the subject of a book written by William

Ouchi in the early 1980s. It identified and merged the best of both systems in a way that would be compatible within the American cultural context. Hewlett Packard was said to exemplify the theory. (See: William G. Ouchi, *Theory Z*, New York: Avon, 1981.) As he says in his acknowledgements, "This book, therefore, is about trust, subtlety and intimacy," explaining that organizations are social systems and need to connect each person.

THIRD WAVE/FOURTH WAVE ORGANIZATION

Organizational

The wave metaphor to describe change was popularized by Alvin Toffler in his book, *The Third Wave* (New York: Morrow, 1980) describing the advent of a new era. The first wave was the agricultural era. The second was the industrial era. Today we are seeing something new. Though we are not certain exactly what it is we are calling it the information age, the computer age, the postindustrial age, and the post-modern age. The fourth wave organization represents a devolution of power to individuals yet in a network-style organization characterized by a consciousness of caring for the planet.

TRICKLE DOWN TECHNOLOGY

Organizational

For more than a century, the conventional economic wisdom has been that new technologies boost productivity, lower the

costs of production, and increase the supply of cheap goods, which, in turn, stimulates purchasing power, expands markets, and generates more jobs . . . Its logic is now leading to unprecedented levels of technological unemployment, a precipitous decline in consumer purchasing power, and the specter of a worldwide depression of incalculable magnitude and duration . . . While technology enthusiasts, economists and business leaders rarely use the term trickle-down to describe technology's impact on markets and employment, their economic assumptions are tantamount to an implicit acceptance of the idea. (Jeremy Rifkin, *The End of Work*, New York: Tarcher/Putnam, 1995, p. 15.)

This has given rise to a serious questioning of the effect of continued automation and the computerization of work on society as well as individuals whose jobs and skills are displaced. The very nature of work will shift and, on the hopeful side, socially useful work (e.g., services, care, public works) will be rewarded and recognized more than the mere creation of material wealth (consumables).

TRANSFORMATIONAL LEADERSHIP

Interpersonal

Transformational leadership is a process of stimulating a group to aspire to a new state of being. It is characterized by the creation of a vision and the ability to help an organization identify with and work toward that vision in such a way that individuals are highly engaged in the process and motivated to making the vision a reality. See Part II for a more complete discussion of this concept.

VIRTUAL ORGANIZATION

Organizational

A virtual organization is, "a temporary network of organizations assembled to exploit a specific opportunity. No hierarchy, no central office, no organization chart." (Mark Landler, "It's Not Only Rock and Roll", *Business Week*, October 10, 1994.)

Using integrated computer and communications technologies, corporations will increasingly be defined by collaborative networks linking hundreds, thousands, even tens of thousands of people together. These collaborative networks make it possible to draw upon vital resources as needed, regardless of where they are physically and regardless of who 'owns' them – supplier or customer. Several factors are driving businesses toward virtual enterprising. For example, global competition puts corporations under tremendous pressure to cut the time it takes to deliver product from the workbench to the showroom . . . Traditional offices will shrink to mere landing sites, where mobile workers dock for an hour or so at a communal electronic desk. (Samuel E. Bleecker, "The Virtual Organization", *The Futurist*, March/April 1994, p. 9.)

Thomas W. Hubbs, vice-president and chief of staff at VeriFone, Inc. sets up his 'virtual office' wherever it makes sense on any given day – even in a hotel bathroom, if that's the only place a phone jack for his laptop computer can be found . . . While VeriFone's nominal headquarters is located in Redwood City, CA, its peripatetic executives view their primary meeting place as the company's computer network . . . CEO Hatim A. Tyabji spends 80% of his time on the road, the senior vice-president for operations is located in suburban Los Angeles. Its human resources director is based in Dallas. And the chief information officer lives and works in Santa Fe, New Mexico. To maintain some human contact, they meet face-to-face every six weeks. (Russell Mitchell, "Virtual Worker: Anyplace I Hang My Modem is Home", *Business Week*, October 17, 1994, p. 96.)

VISION/MISSION/VALUES

Organizational

Visions, Missions, and Values are the basis for creating alignment between all employees and the purpose of the organization. Identifying the vision – what the organization wants to become – gives people the ability to act knowing how their actions will or will not help realize the vision. The mission is frequently the more general reason why the organization is in business and what it hopes to accomplish. It is shorter term and a more specific goal. The values are the organization's strongest beliefs about what is important to it and what behaviors are right and wrong. These guide specific personal actions as much as the vision because they identify specific constraints and duties accompanying each person's understanding of their role.

If you want to use a mission statement make sure they are helpful by applying "the three-C audit which checks content, congruence, and credibility . . .

Mission statements that pass the 'content' check use words that convey real meanings to the people inside the organization, delivering a central message or set of messages . . ." Congruence is the mission statement's expression of what is really taking place in the organization. It is a consistency between its mindset, policies and strategies. Credibility is the fit between the words of the mission statement and day-to-day actions of members of the organization. They must be in synch or the statement is a farce. (Ellen C. Shapiro, *Fad Surfing in the Boardroom*, Reading, MA: Addison Wesley, 1995, pp. 15–23.) See Part II for a more complete discussion of this concept.

WELLNESS

Organizational

This is a deliberate attempt to help foster personal well-being in the workplace through attention to proper personal habits of eating, exercise, and stress management. This effort must be in an appropriate environment and under correct ergonomic conditions.

WORKOUT

Interpersonal

This is a method requiring that managers be responsive to employees. It calls for frank public discussions of issues characterized by managers answering employees' questions with direct answers, or a promise to get the answers within a fixed period of time. This technique was first popularized by its use in General Electric.

Workout is a method of making managers responsive to employees. The workout program originally designed by General Electric has four goals: (1) Building trust. (2) Empowering employees. (3) Eliminating unnecessary work, and (4) creating a new paradigm which includes ideas such as boundarylessness, integrated diversity, searching out and improving upon 'best practices', and global leadership in their markets. (Noel M. Tichy and Stratford Sherman, "Walking the Talk At GE", *Training and Development,* June 1993, p. 26.) See Part II for a more complete discussion of this concept.

WORKPLACE COMMUNITY

Organizational

The conceptualization of organizations as communities brings organizations back to the basics, yet creates many exciting possibilities. First, there is an emphasis on building solid interpersonal peer relationships. In workplace community this is essential. Commitment to relationships is the norm. Second, the boundaries between management and labor collapse and divisiveness ebbs; everyone is considered a valuable, integral part of the organization. Fearless communication exists. Organizations as communities convey a sense of partnership and purpose and reward everyone, in part, according to the organizations success (or failure) in the marketplace. In addition there is a sense of place and psychological, if not actual ownership exists on the part of each person. See Part II for a more complete discussion of this concept.

ZERO-BASED BUDGETING

Organizational

Here the purpose is the development of budgets from zero instead of currently funded levels. This method of budgeting asks managers to justify expenses based on program requirements according to various levels of service or specified performance targets. It better explains the utilization of funds than budgets based on historical data or political contingencies. It is a way to see budgetary requirements according to program effects and to understand the consequences of funding levels. It immediately shows the impact on current and future staffing levels and enables individuals and organizations to understanding the ramifications of their decisions on employment.

Name Index

Organization names in bold.

SUBJECT INDEX

Page numbers in bold print refer to main entries.

ABOUT JOHN NIRENBERG

JOHN NIRENBERG, PhD., is the Executive Director/Department Chair for Doctoral Studies at the University of Phoenix and a partner in the Center for Workplace Community.

The University of Phoenix's Doctor of Management degree program specializing in organizational leadership is the first program of its kind designed for working adult students. It specifically provides mid-career, mid-life professionals *a time to think, to create, and to contribute* to the development of responsible leadership for the 21st century.

The Center for Workplace Community helps individuals, in an organizational context, think deeply about their workplace environment in order to meet the challenges of the 21st century.

John is the author of *The Living Organization: Transforming Teams Into Workplace Communities*, published jointly by Irwin Professional Books and Pfeiffer and Co. (1993). John, along with Peter Senge, M. Scott Peck, John Gardner, Marvin Weisbord and Amitai Etzioni, was a featured contributor to K. Gozdz (Ed.), *Community-Building: Renewing Spirit and Learning in Business* (New Leaders Press, 1995).

John's consulting clients have included: National Semiconductor, Southern New England Telephone, NCR, Hyatt, Esso, the Civil Service College of Singapore, National Mutual Life Insurance (Australia), and the US Office of Education.

He is a stimulating and thought-provoking speaker.

e-mail: Center-for-Workplace-Community@worldnet.att.net